Maynard's Revenge

Maynard's Revenge

*The Collapse of Free
Market Macroeconomics*

Lance Taylor

Harvard University Press
Cambridge, Massachusetts
London, England
2010

Copyright © 2010 by the President and Fellows of Harvard College
All rights reserved
Printed in the United States of America

Library of Congress Cataloging-in-Publication Data

Taylor, Lance, 1940–
Maynard's revenge : the collapse of free market macroeconomics / Lance Taylor.
p.   cm.
Includes bibliographical references and index.
ISBN 978-0-674-05046-4 (alk. paper)
1. Keynesian economics.   2. Macroeconomics.   3. Financial crises.
4. Global Financial Crisis, 2008–2009.   I. Title.
HB99.7.T37 2010
339—dc22   2010012970

Contents

Preface — *vii*

1. Macroeconomics — *1*
2. Macroeconomic Thought during the Long Nineteenth Century — *28*
3. Gold Standard, Reparations, Mania, Crash, and Depression — *86*
4. Maynard Ascendant — *114*
5. Keynesian Growth, Cycles, and Crisis — *173*
6. The Counterrevolution — *221*
7. Finance — *255*
8. The International Dimension — *304*
9. Keynesianism and the Crisis — *337*

References — *359*

Index — *369*

Preface

Maynard Keynes's revenge is simple. He was correct about how to do macroeconomics. Initial reformation and then revolution against his ideas beginning in the 1940s were misleading and often wrong. The ways he proposed to analyze macro problems are the only ones of any use in understanding the global crisis of 2007–2009. Being right about such fundamental points ought to be recompense enough for the way his version of macroeconomics has been treated since the 1970s.

This book is about these points. I wrote it with two main groups of readers in mind. One is made up of people who are willing to put their feet up on the table, nose to the grindstone, and so on and *think* about how Keynes and his closest followers (most from the University of Cambridge, some from elsewhere in the UK and the United States) did macroeconomics. Their approach differs notably from that of modern mainstream "new Keynesians," for example, the people who formulated economic policy under President Barack Obama during 2009. I believe that it is important to bring a proper Keynesian alternative into public view.

The emphasis on "think" above is on purpose. As far as I can tell, the arguments in the book are correct, but some are closely worded—dense, if you prefer. Some involve high school algebra, equations written out in words or, even worse, in symbols (with Greek letters at that!). But serious mathematical manipulations and proofs are absent. It just seemed easier to insert the equations rather than waste space talking around them. Many are in fact accounting relationships like ones built into bookkeeping spreadsheets. Without too much exaggeration it is fair to say that most of the mathematics could have been set out in Apple Numbers or Microsoft Excel. There are also numerous tables and figures. They were designed with two purposes in mind. One is to provide a visual complement to material in the text. The other is to present data about macroeconomic performance in the United States (mainly) since World War II.

The second group of potential readers comprises students who desire to be inoculated against what they are taught in mainstream classes in economics (the dominant genre in the United States and most other industrialized economies). I'm not saying that introductory and intermediate economics courses are complete nonsense, but they do impart ideas about macroeconomics that are not very sensible or are even wrong. One thing they omit is perspective on how contemporary economic thought draws on its own history and on the way economists have tried to deal with events like the Great Crash and the subsequent Great Depression in the last century and the recent crash on the real and financial sides of the economy. Many passages in the book are aimed at filling these historical gaps.

Discussions of factors leading into the 2007–2009 catastrophe appear throughout. A summary appears in Chapter 9, with a few references to earlier passages as well as diagrams and tables. The page-flipping was adopted to avoid repetition. The gist of the argument boils down to nine factors that contributed to the crisis followed by a discussion of future possibilities. Keynes put great emphasis on "fundamental uncertainty"; that is, there is much about the future that we cannot now conceive of, let alone "know." Former secretary of defense Donald Rumsfeld's "unknown unknowns" will play a crucial role.

Keynes's own ideas are spelled out initially in Chapter 1 and more completely in Chapter 4. Chapters 2 and 3 provide historical background for the economics of Keynes and his successors. Chapter 2 goes over nineteenth- and early-twentieth-century history of economic thought with emphasis on the macro aspects. It begins with analysis of the "real economy"—outputs and uses of goods and services and their prices—by two waves of thinkers, the classical economists from Adam Smith to Karl Marx and then their neoclassical successors (direct ancestors of the contemporary mainstream). The latter part of the chapter is devoted to monetary economics as it has been construed by economists and policy actors for around three hundred years. Several old ideas appearing in the chapter feed directly into modern discussion. They are singled out in passages about "flash forwards."

Chapter 3 covers parts of nineteenth- and early-twentieth-century economic history that influence current thought. Two examples are the gold standard as it functioned in the late nineteenth and early twentieth centuries, and experience before and after 1930 with the Great Crash, Great Depression, and New Deal.

After the in-depth discussion of Keynes in Chapter 4, Chapter 5 takes up the ideas of Keynes's close successors and uses them to illustrate developments in the United States, with extensive use of diagrammatic data presentation. It becomes clear that there was a major shift in macroeconomic behavior after around 1980 that ultimately fed into the crisis. As emphasized in Chapter 9, the change was part of a broader transformation of political economy from the interventionism of the New Deal and the parallel European completion of the welfare state to a much more "liberal" (in the European sense of the word) orientation. Whether and how this worldview will change in the wake of the recent crisis are the most significant future known unknowns.

Chapter 6 recounts how the economics profession responded to Keynes, from the initial reformation around 1950 of his core ideas into mainstream Keynesianism (the sort practiced by the teachers of Obama's advisers), on to a monetarist palace coup led by Milton Friedman, and then to Keynes's complete repudiation around 1970 by "new classical" economists such as Robert Lucas Jr. who today dominate the academic side of the discipline. Friedman himself was a throwback to the turn-of-the-twentieth-century Swedish economist Knut Wicksell, while new classical economics is a restatement of extreme nineteenth-century neoclassical ideas decked out in mathematics borrowed from 1960s rocket science. A familiar neoclassical ploy is to serve up old economic ideas in new bottles imported from pure mathematics or the physical sciences. One reason why a few formulas appear in the book is to illustrate the details.

An important example of this maneuver is "finance theory," described in Chapter 7. It appeared in the 1950s and served as an intellectual elixir for deregulation and the proliferation of exotic financial instruments that led into the boom and crash. Much of it is based on mathematics designed to analyze physical phenomena ranging from planetary motion to pollen grains bouncing around in water under a microscope (a phenomenon discovered by a Scottish botanist early in the nineteenth century with a mathematical description first set out by Einstein early in the twentieth). The formulas are elegant but misleading for reasons proposed by the American Keynesians Hyman Minsky and Charles Kindleberger.

Chapter 8 presents highlights from open economy macroeconomics, a topic expansive enough to deserve a book of its own. There are many theories which are often misstated in popular discussion. One goal of the chapter is to describe them correctly. Another is to emphasize that there are very few "degrees of freedom" in global interactions among economies open to international trade and financial flows. In other words, balance-of-payments positions and levels of exchange rates are closely linked. You set one, and then there is little you can do to control the other. Chinese-American international transactions are strongly influenced by this relationship, for example. This observation feeds naturally into Chapter 9.

No book by a professor can possibly be written without unstinting support from his or her colleagues. This one is no exception. The seeds were planted almost fifty years ago when I first read the *General Theory* in a Caltech macro class taught by Alan Sweezy.

Mike Aronson at Harvard University Press was remarkably helpful and tranquil throughout the project, which began in fall 2008. Duncan Foley, Deepak Nayyar, and Servaas Storm read the whole manuscript as it was being written. They helped shape the book, along with picking up numerous errors. Amitava Dutt, Geoff Harcourt, Codrina Rada, and Armon Rezai also read all or most of the chapters and had many useful suggestions. I am grateful to Rudi von Arnim, Rob Davies, Laura de Carvalho, John Eatwell, Korkut Erturk, Peter Flaschel, Wynne Godley, Kazimierz Laski, Jeff Madrick, Will Milberg, Ben Mitra-Khan, José Antonio Ocampo, Jørn Rattsø, Anwar Shaikh, and Helen Shapiro for comments and ideas.

Laura de Carvalho and Armon Rezai provided superb research assistance. They were supported by the Schwartz Center for Economic Policy Analysis at the New School with the backing of Teresa Ghilarducci, the Center's director. The material on finance draws on discussions with John Eatwell, Bill Janeway, and Tarik Mouakil when I visited at the Centre for Financial Analysis and Policy at the University of Cambridge during spring 2008.

My wife, Yvonne, our kids, their spouses and kids, and all the critters at Black Locust Farm as usual made the whole effort possible. Sincere thanks to them all!

Maynard's Revenge

— 1 —
Macroeconomics

"I believe myself to be writing a book on economic theory which will largely revolutionize, not I suppose at once but in the course of the next ten years—the way the world thinks about economic problems. I don't merely hope what I say, in my own mind I'm quite sure." So wrote John Maynard Keynes to George Bernard Shaw in January 1935 (14:492–493), the year before the publication of his *General Theory of Employment, Interest, and Money*. Although the word *macroeconomics* had been coined a couple of years before by the Norwegian economist Ragnar Frisch, Keynes was writing the foundational text. His self-congratulatory mood was characteristic, and correct up to a point, but he had no way to foresee what would happen to his creation over the more distant future.

He was right about the next few decades, but by the 1960s his revolution in theory was well on the way to being overwhelmed by the kinds of thinking he believed he would demolish forever. Now, after another five decades, the ideas that he and his followers invented have been shown by the 2007–2009 crisis to be sound.

Why Keynesian macroeconomics was displaced and why it has returned in force is a fascinating tale, a complicated blend of how economists think, the private and public economic behavior that their thinking affects, how the economy itself responds and also shifts for other reasons, and back to the economists again. This circle suggests a system demonstrating "reflexivity" as proposed by the financier-philosopher George Soros. He argues that economic actors have an imperfect understanding of the world they confront and have limited ability to change it on the basis of the knowledge they possess. According to his definitions, they engage in simultaneous "cognitive" and "manipulative" activities with interactions that at times have large and unforeseen consequences.

Soros's opinion, as noted in his 2009 book, was that former Federal Reserve chairman Alan Greenspan had great manipulative skills but a less than perfect cognitive understanding of the risks built into the U.S. financial system as it developed after the 1980s. That combination led Greenspan and his successor, Ben Bernanke, to pursue policies and public pronouncements that helped create and probably worsened the 2007–2009 crash.

Tracing circles of causation through these astonishing events is well worth the effort, especially because many actors were involved. For example, from the early 1980s through the mid-2000s, the U.S. income distribution shifted strongly from wages toward profits, while wage income itself became more concentrated toward the top. With many people suffering from stagnant or falling incomes, households tried to maintain living standards by increasing the share of consumption in their disposable income by around 12%. They did so by reducing saving and running up mortgage and credit card debt. Their debt-to-income ratio more than doubled.

Within the U.S. financial sector, the huge increase in household debt wasmade possible by financial deregulation as advocated by Greenspan, Bernanke, and a host of other notable economists (many of whom became key players in the Obama administration in early 2009). A doubling of the "real" (corrected for inflation) price of housing served as collateral for mortgage loans. Low interest rates engineered by Greenspan helped stimulate both the explosion of debt and bubbles in equity and housing prices.

The mortgages were "securitized," or packaged together in the form of financial "derivatives" (described in more detail below and in Chapter 4) by the originating banks and sold to other investors. Supposedly the risk of mortgage defaults was thereby diversified and spread to many asset holders. Prices of derivatives to be marketed were calculated according to models based on the assumption that "risk" is a quantifiable concept like the temperature of the air or the voltage driving an electrical current. In practice, supposedly quantified risks were so transformed by securitization and associated inventions of the financial engineers that they became impossible to trace. The disconnect between models and reality came clear when housing prices crashed in 2007.

Finally, the U.S. economy as a whole became a large net borrower from the rest of the world. There was not enough saving being generated internally to finance the increase in debt. So the whole scenario would have been impossible had not a few countries—China, Japan, Germany, and the oil exporters—pumped out substantial flows of saving.

In sum, cognitive misperceptions and inappropriate actions at many levels and in many countries acted together to create the crisis. Understanding the causes and consequences and trying to devise economic policy changes adequate to deal with them is a work in progress.

A good place to begin the task is with Maynard himself, no doubt the economist of the twentieth century best able to bring theory to bear on observed economic events with the aim of doing something about them. I should add that in Poland, Michal Kalecki (rough pronunciation: ka-LET-ski) came up with similar ideas about the real side of the economy at roughly the same time. He emigrated to England in 1936, became the leading left Keynesian, and will figure prominently in later chapters.

The Framework of the *General Theory*

Keynes explicitly and emphatically rejected the notion that risk is quantifiable. Instead he thought that economic decisions are subject to "fundamental uncertainty," meaning that it is impossible to describe the future in terms of probabilities or odds for and against various events occurring. Moreover, the macro system itself always generates unforeseen endogenous responses.

Subject to these limitations, the *General Theory* and Keynesian economics more generally seek to describe how the economy as a whole hangs together, with attention to three crucial issues: the determination of the level of economic activity by effective demand, the macroeconomic significance of money and finance, and the roles of collective social actors and the distribution of income and wealth among them. These and other ideas are outlined in this chapter, with much more detail to follow in Chapter 4 on Keynes's thought and Chapter 5 on the contributions of his closest successors.

Aggregate Demand

What forces set the levels of employment and output? Keynes's answer in the *General Theory* is unequivocal. The main determinant of economic activity is *aggregate demand,* the sum of households' spending on private consumption and residential capital formation (or *investment* in the form of new physical capital in housing, in economists' usage of that overextended term), spending on nonresidential investment by business, exports to buyers in foreign countries, and public consumption and investment by government at all levels. Analysis of aggregate or, in practice, *effective* demand relies on Keynes's *postulate* that an economy's domestic product or output always equals its domestic income. Income—wages, profits, rents, and interest—is in turn generated by ongoing production activity.

An important part of the *General Theory*'s legacy is the system of national income and product accounts (or the NIPA compiled by the Commerce Department, which include gross domestic product or GDP and related indicators). They were pioneered by Keynes and younger colleagues around 1940 and are explicitly put together to satisfy the income = output postulate. The standard measure of output is GDP. If one treats imports as an additional source of supply, then the sum of imports and GDP must equal aggregate demand as defined above. Applied macroeconomics necessarily operates in this Keynesian framework, which is acceptable if the NIPA estimates broadly reflect what is going on in the real economy, out there. At least in rich countries where statisticians can gather and combine the requisite data into the numbers, they seem to do so.

Keynes's economic model rests on the idea that some components of output—in particular business investment, government spending, and exports—are relatively insensitive to current income. Households' consumption, by contrast, *is* tied to income. So is the part of their income they *don't* consume (or pay out as taxes, interest, and so on) and thereby save. Keynes argued that consumption, saving, and income *adjust* so that income will equal output, including its more or less autonomous investment, government spending, and export components.

In the simplest stripped-down version of this theory (with household investment, government, and transactions with the rest of the world suppressed), output is made up only of consumption and business investment, while income is used for consumption and saving. Hence the income = output equation implies that saving = investment, with the level of economic activity emerging from this relationship. The bottom line is that if households as a group try to save more than the current level of capital formation, then their reduced overall consumption will lead income generated by production to fall, until total saving comes back into equality with investment.

This *paradox of thrift* embodies a *fallacy of composition,* a phenomenon that shows up frequently in Keynesian macroeconomics. A small set of actors can successfully save more or less without perturbing the system. But if, for example, many or most households optimistically choose to consume more and save less in an upswing, then output will grow faster until various limiting factors, discussed in later chapters, start to restrict its rise. In a downswing, trying to save more at the macro level will just make the situation worse. Such *pro-cyclical* or *positive feedback* behavior is one reason why macro systems are intrinsically cyclical and possibly unstable—ideas developed by Keynes's immediate followers as discussed in Chapter 5.

The paradox does not sit well with modern mainstream economists. They prefer to believe that additional saving is automatically directed toward capital formation so that the level of output cannot decline. They trace this notion to Adam Smith's *invisible hand*, which is supposed to ensure that the economy operates to bring all participants to the highest possible level of well-being. The general well-being is obviously not being optimized if output is low and labor is unemployed!

Following this logic, the key change in mainstream economic thinking in the 1960s was to abandon effective demand. As discussed in Chapter 6, current events were interpreted as supporting this shift in opinion, but fundamentally it was driven by ideology. The mainstream postulated that domestic income is determined from the supply side by full employment of all inputs into production, especially labor. (Economists are quite fond of axioms and postulates that generate the outcomes they desire.) Fully employed households decide how much of their incomes to save or consume; in the simplest story, this implies that investment must adjust to meet available saving. The accumulation of new physical capital is driven by forces of *productivity and thrift*.

Keynes called this idea *Say's Law* after the early-nineteenth-century French classical economist Jean-Baptiste Say, who had said more or less the same thing, with some contemporary empirical justification as discussed in the next chapter. Keynes did his best to drive Say into oblivion. Three to four decades after the publication of the *General Theory,* in the eyes of the economics profession and the policymakers and journalists it influenced, he had failed. The events of 2007–2009 show that he was on target. The contribution of investment to aggregate demand collapsed when the financial crisis forced lending to business by banks and other institutions to plummet. Driven by fear, consumers' saving rates shot up. Because of the demand shock and the paradox of thrift, income and output contracted dramatically late in 2008 as the financial crisis spilled over to the *real economy*.

Money and Finance

How do money and finance influence aggregate demand? Note the references to "interest and money" in the full title of the *General Theory*. The rate of interest in Keynes's view has a big influence on household and business investment, and therefore aggregate demand. A high rate makes investment more expensive and slows down new capital formation, especially in residential housing. A low rate has the opposite effect.

In normal times the central bank—the *Federal Reserve* or *Fed* in the United States—can in principle control the short-term interest rate for socially beneficial ends. (The Fed did not do that in the 1990s and 2000s, as we shall see below.) When money markets seize up as they did in the latter part of 2008, the Fed loses much of that power, because banks do not dare to undertake new lending for fear that borrowers will default, whatever the rate of interest.

Market determination of the interest rate can also be interpreted as supporting Say's Law. Prior to the *General Theory*, it was widely accepted that the rate would adjust to clear a market for *loanable funds*. The supply of (loanable) saving was supposed to increase in response to a higher interest rate, while investment demand would be repressed. If, say, investment exceeded saving, then the interest rate would increase to drive them back toward equality. Perhaps quite rapidly, the rate would converge to a *natural* level, ensuring that the saving = investment equality would hold.

Loanable funds is a nonmonetary theory of the rate of interest, of the sort later criticized by Keynes. If output is assumed to be fixed because of Say's Law supported by adjustments in the interest rate, then the money supply cannot influence the volume of production. The only thing it can do is affect the price level. In the jargon, there is a *dichotomy* between macro prices and quantities. The idea that money drives prices is called the *quantity theory*, discussed further in Chapter 2. This doctrine was accepted by Keynes in his 1923 *Tract on Monetary Reform*, but over the next dozen years he decisively broke away—a characteristic career move, as we will see.

The quantity theory is the ultimate monetarist position, with echoes in contradictory policy pronouncements by two leading twentieth-century exponents: the Yale economist Irving Fisher's suggestion that monetary policy should be actively deployed to control prices, and Milton Friedman's argument from the University of Chicago against active policy because its effects on output are visible only with "long and variable lags," while money rules the price level best in the long run.

There are two immediate extensions of loanable funds reasoning.

First, the Swedish economist Knut Wicksell argued in the 1890s that if bankers were holding the rate below its natural level, then investment demand would exceed saving supply. Banks could then lend money to firms by injecting funds into their deposit accounts (see Chapter 4 for the details), which would permit them to fulfill their investment plans.

The usual assumption, which fell increasingly wide of the mark in the late twentieth century, more so in the United States than in Europe, is that loans and money are respectively the banks' principal assets and liability. An increase in loans thereby creates money automatically. If output is set from the supply side, then prices of goods and services have to rise to clear markets when the firms start to spend the newly available money. Actors already holding money as their main asset will see their real wealth decline. If they step up saving to offset their capital loss, the paradox of thrift will kick in, reducing consumption to offset the higher investment. Say's Law remains in force because of this *inflation tax* on monetary wealth.

As further expounded in Chapter 2, Wicksell's narrative was the first explicitly *monetarist* inflation model. With modern adornments tacked on, it became the centerpiece of Milton Friedman's attack on Keynesianism in the 1960s.

The second extension of the natural rate model comes into play if one includes government spending not financed by taxes (that is, government *net borrowing*) as another source of effective demand. As I explain more fully below, if this fiscal deficit increases, there can be upward pressure on interest rates or on inflation if the central bank does not allow rates to rise. Such arguments based on loanable funds provided the intellectual justification for relatively restrictive fiscal policy under the Clinton administration.

The macro theory in Keynes's *Treatise on Money* (1930)—the major steppingstone between the *Tract* and the *General Theory*—is Wicksellian. Keynes transformed himself from being merely a brilliant post-Wicksellian into the greatest economist of the twentieth century by writing the *General Theory*, in which he consciously broke from the *Treatise*, the natural rate, and Wicksell by postulating that the interest rate is determined by *liquidity preference* between money and bonds. That is, it is set in markets for available *stocks* of securities rather than *flows* of funds for desired saving and investment. The distinction between determination of the interest rate in a market for flows (loanable funds) or stocks (liquidity preference) is quite general, especially in recent times, when forms of financial claims have proliferated well beyond simple money and bonds.

In Keynes's model, a "moderate" return on bonds means that investors will stay partly liquid, holding some money in hopes that a more profitable opportunity will turn up. If the central bank creates additional money to buy bonds by crediting bondholders' bank accounts, the interest rate can decrease, stimulating investment demand. When it is effective, *monetary policy* is pursued along such lines. There was an active debate in the 1930s about whether "liquidity preference versus loanable funds" was the better theory. On the basis of abstract arguments, it was largely settled in Keynes's favor at the time, but it reverberates to this day.

Money, or more generally finance nowadays, creates further complications. Although he ran up big losses in 1920, described in Chapter 8, and had to be bailed out by family and friends, Maynard was a serious and largely successful speculator. (After all, he had his artist friends in the Bloomsbury group, the Cambridge Arts Theatre that he founded, and King's College, where he was the bursar, all to support.)

His adventures taught him to see the financial system as being intrinsically unstable, as players seek to take advantage of one another and at the same time search for *fundamental* knowledge which they can utilize in placing their bets. The market has recently blown up a blizzard of derivatives, or contracts contingent on future events. How derivatives fed into the 2007–2009 crisis when their purported fundamentals failed is elaborated in detail in Chapters 4 and 7.

Buying and selling insurance is the oldest example of trading a derivative contract. During the past few decades much more complicated arrangements—from simple swaps and options in the 1970s on up through murky and extremely risky *collateralized debt obligations* (collections of debt contracts packaged or *securitized* into a sort of bond) and *credit default swaps* (insurance contracts against the possibility of defaults on debt which were *not* backed by financial reserves) in the 2000s—were invented to pay high, seemingly secure returns to financial investors.

Faith in fundamentals was at the heart of this financial explosion. Yet fundamentals are at best a metaeconomic concept, impossible to define precisely. Here are some examples. For the traditional insurance industry, fundamentals such as the likelihood of house fires, car accidents, or dying at a certain age can be plausibly calculated from historical data. But what is the fundamental price of oil? As of 2009 something like $80 per barrel could keep producers and consumers reasonably content, but there is no obvious means by which the price will stay at or near that level. In financial markets, fundamentals boil down to *expectations* about key indicator variables: interest rates, price-to-earnings ratios, expected growth in *asset prices*, and so on. In practice, as Keynes and Soros emphasize, formulation of expectations is a socioeconomic process, with characteristics that can change surprisingly and dramatically from time to time.

Asset Prices

Asset prices are crucial to their reasoning. A capitalist economy has two distinct systems of prices, for *flows of goods and services* from production, for consumption, investment, and so on, and for *stocks of assets*. The latter can be either durable assets (houses or nonresidential productive capital) or financial assets (shares, bonds, claims on commodities, or foreign exchange). Asset prices are more volatile than prices of goods and services, and there is no reason to expect the relevant price indexes to move together. Figure 1.1 illustrates the distinction.

The diagram plots the *GDP deflator* (the macro price index best suited

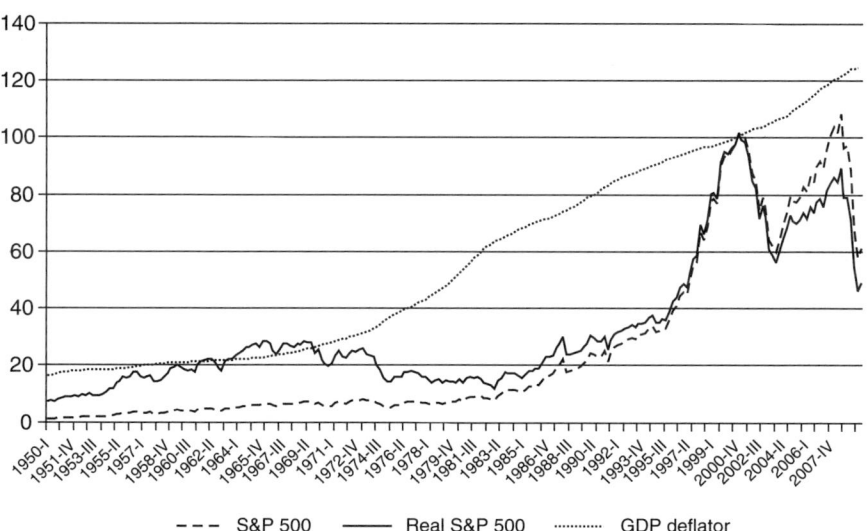

Figure 1.1 Indexes of nominal and real S&P 500 and GDP deflator rescaled (2000Q1 = 100)

to track overall inflation for goods and services) against the S&P 500 stock market index in nominal and deflated (or real) terms. All the indexes were rescaled to take the value 100 in the year 2000. Several patterns stand out.

Prices of goods and services maintained a rising trend, increasing more than sixfold between 1950 and the late 2000s. The implied long-run inflation rate is about 3% per year.

From the late 1960s through the early 1980s the nominal S&P grew slowly while the real index "moved sideways." Interrupted by the 1987 downward "correction," both the real and nominal indexes grew rapidly thereafter.

Between 2000 and 2008 the GDP price index grew faster than the nominal S&P 500, which dropped sharply and then recovered. The real S&P did not return to its level of 2000. After October 2007 the GDP deflator rose slowly and share prices went steadily downward with widespread adverse consequences. It remained to be seen whether a recovery in 2009 would be sustained.

To add another asset to the discussion, Figure 1.2 presents various indexes of housing prices. The Shiller 10 and 20 indexes (from the Yale economist Robert Shiller) refer to U.S. metropolitan areas. The HPI comes

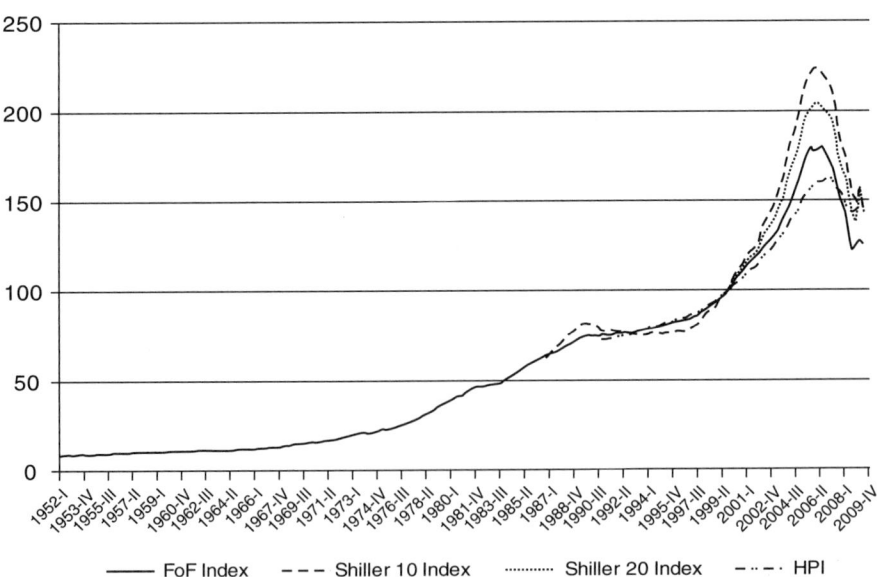

Figure 1.2 Various real indexes of U.S. housing prices (2000Q1 = 100)

from the U.S. Federal Housing Finance Agency. The FOF index (by far the longest series) was constructed by using asset price increases and was based on a value of 100 in 2000Q1. All tell a broadly similar story of a rise in housing prices after 1980 which accelerated strongly around the year 2000 (more so in the big metropolitan areas). At mid-decade prices started to crash. We have been living with the consequences.

The housing price acceleration also appears in Figure 1.3, which plots two indexes together with the GDP deflator. The main point is that price indexes for housing and for goods and services moved closely together until the late 1990s, when the former took off. This housing price bubble, which with benefit of hindsight stands out in the diagram, was at the root of the 2007–2009 crash.

The distinction between the two sets of prices is present in both the *Treatise* and the *General Theory*, but especially in the later book Keynes could have been more explicit about bringing it out. That task fell to his successors Hyman Minsky and James Tobin.

When financial markets are behaving well, most players can gain from their expectations held in common; Keynes's metaphor was a specific form of a *beauty contest*, discussed in Chapter 4. At times the consensus col-

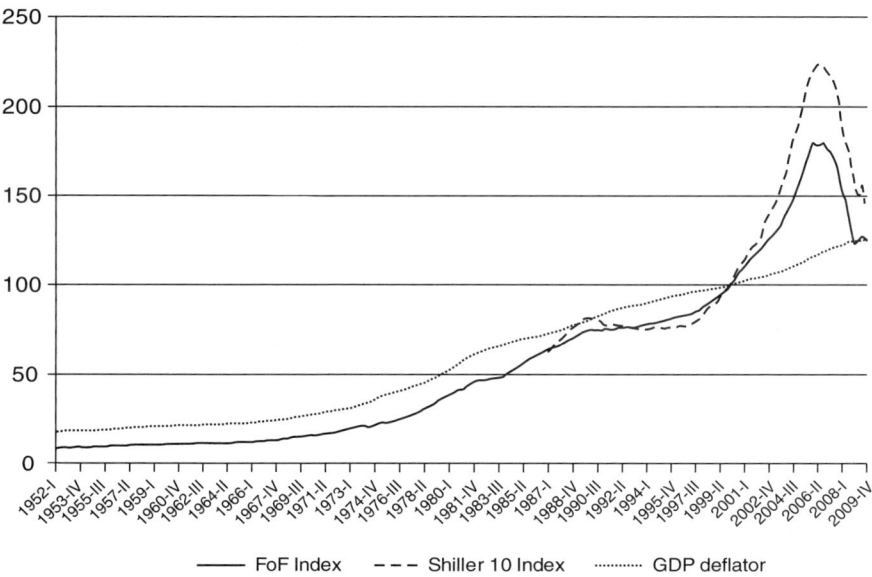

Figure 1.3 Housing price indexes and GDP deflator (2000Q1 = 100)

lapses, for reasons presented at several points below. There can follow a contagion of deep uncertainty and fear, with all players running toward liquidity in the form of very safe assets. Several consequences follow.

One is that the players cannot *all* dispose of assets suddenly perceived as being highly risky. The only outcome from such a fire sale must be plummeting asset prices and liquidation of wealth. Here we have an example of the fallacy of composition on the down side.

Players also flee from normal financial transactions into hoarding cash. They stop advancing credit, which means that the real side of the economy gets caught in a *liquidity trap.* Aggregate demand collapses, and we are back to the crashes of 1929 or 2008. The most recent example of a Keynesian trap (as of this writing) has already been noted. Late in 2008 banks stopped lending to one another and to other customers so that they could sit on their cash.

Capitalist financial crises have been occurring repeatedly for four centuries. Remarkably in light of this history, an idea called the *efficient market hypothesis* (or *EMH*) became the central financial dogma after the 1960s. It basically says that "no one can beat the market," or in stronger form that market transactions are a fair and intrinsically stable game among equally perceptive players. (How Warren Buffett and Soros fit into this story is never made clear.)

In applied situations, the EMH is usually interpreted to mean that competition among the players ensures that asset prices amble in a *random walk,* perhaps sliding up or down but generally rising along a predictable trend supported by overall economic growth. In the option pricing model that is the crown jewel of finance theory, the trend growth in asset prices is assumed to be equal to the real interest rate, contrary to the facts (see Chapter 7).

According to the EMH, the magnitude of deviations of an asset price from a fixed level or a trend can be reliably predicted on the basis of historical data. As discussed in Chapter 7, the mathematical formalism built into asset pricing models effectively does not permit abnormally large deviations to occur. If prices are going steadily upward subject to small, stable fluctuations, market players as a whole should have positive returns from *capital gains* on holding assets. (The "gain" is the increase in an asset price over a given period of time, usually calculated in growth rate form as the ratio of the change to the price level.) In turbulent periods with all manner of asset prices crashing through the floor, no model of financial markets could be further from the truth.

Social Classes and Distribution

Do social relationships influence macroeconomic performance? Keynes, like others in the long tradition of political economy dating to the classical economists around 1800, tended to think in terms of collective social actors. One justification is that the socioeconomic circumstances in which groups of people operate—be they sweepers in Mumbai or traders on Wall Street—impel them toward shared economic attitudes and patterns of behavior. Traditionally recognized "classes" such as wage earners and industrial and financial capitalists would be typical examples.

While Keynes in the *General Theory* did not pursue class analysis as explicitly as David Ricardo and Karl Marx, he was well aware of how redistribution of income or wealth can impact on effective demand. Examples from the 1920s and the *Tract on Monetary Reform* are discussed in Chapter 3. Chapter 4 takes up redistributive macroeconomic adjustment in the *Treatise on Money,* and Chapter 5 emphasizes how Keynes's Cambridge followers concentrated on income distribution. In the *General Theory,* a major theme is that cutting workers' *nominal* or *money wages* would *not* cure depression unemployment. (Keynes, a master polemicist, often set up rhetorical scarecrows that he could summarily dispatch. A position he called the "Treasury view" asserted that wage-cutting would be effective.)

As is set out in more detail in Chapter 4, his key argument was that if nominal wages were to decrease and thereby reduce costs of production, competition would force firms to cut prices more or less in proportion. If firms hold their pricing markups over cost roughly constant (as proposed by Kalecki), the result follows automatically. The *real wage* (nominal wage divided by a price index), and therefore aggregate demand, would be largely unaffected.

Note here that Keynes in the *General Theory* is advocating a *cost-based* or *structuralist* influence of wages on the price index. (Much of the argument is in fact phrased in terms of relatively stable value/wage ratios or *wage units.*) This approach is diametrically opposed to his assumption in the *Tract* that the money supply sets the level of commodity prices. This contrast is not a surprise. As will be seen, modern believers in output determination by effective demand usually favor structuralist inflation theories. Monetarists with their quantity theory usually accept Say's Law because it is easier to argue that changes in the money supply will affect only prices if the level of output doesn't move (the dichotomy mentioned above).

In financial markets Keynes chastised two more specific and probably overlapping groups of wealthy people: high savers and bear speculators. Because of the paradox of thrift, people who spend relatively small shares of their income on consumption hold down aggregate demand. Bear speculators tend to hoard liquid assets, thereby restricting finance for investment in new productive capital. Love of money pushes the macroeconomy toward stagnation.

For somewhat complicated but consistent reasons, Maynard thought that the importance of these disturbing actors would diminish over time. In the last chapter of the *General Theory* he rather cheerfully anticipated the "euthanasia of the rentier" in a future in which capital is not scarce and investment decisions have largely been taken over by the state. The rationale is discussed below and (with a considerable input from Keynes's younger philosopher friend Frank Ramsey) in Chapter 2.

As described in Chapters 6 and 7, beginning in the 1990s Keynes's financial class structure broke down. Wall Street and City of London bear speculators were replaced by high rollers, and high savers by low-saving households which ran up the debt that financial traders could exploit. With investment finance readily available at low interest rates, output levels were high. The boom years of the 1990s in the United States and the UK fit these predictions from Keynes's theory to a T.

The *General Theory* did *not* emphasize the dire economic consequences of general euphoria and rising debt such as persisted from the mid-1990s until the late 2000s, although they can readily be incorporated into a Keynesian worldview. After all, the book was written against the background of the Great Depression, not exactly a euphoric time.

For both finance and the real side, many of Keynes's and Kalecki's followers were and are deeply concerned with the implications of the distributions of income and wealth for macroeconomic performance and vice versa. Although he cannot be pigeonholed as a Keynesian—his range of ideas is far too broad—the great social scientist Albert Hirschman pointed out that distributive conflicts over income can get *displaced* into either inflation or debt accumulation.

The German hyperinflation discussed in Chapter 3 is an example of the former. Hirschman's illustrative debt scenario is the New York City crisis of the 1970s, in which an inability to finance rising, politically driven spending led to near default and a loss of fiscal autonomy. As I observed at the beginning of this chapter, poor and middle-class U.S. households kept up their consumption growth after around 1980 by increasing debt even as the income distribution was shifting strongly against them. ("Displacement" here is an idea borrowed from psychoanalysis: emotional conflicts get directed toward substitute targets. To lift another term from Freud, rising U.S. debt in the 2000s was *rationalized* as the emergence of an "ownership society" by George W. Bush. The problem is that mortgage borrowers did not really "own" their houses; they just used them as collateral to run up debt.)

Such distributive concerns will appear throughout this book.

Beyond the General Theory

Keynes is often accused of being overly preoccupied with the short run. One reason is that his most famous statement is often quoted out of context. The full version from the *Tract* is an argument that a crude form of the quantity theory can be valid only in the long run: "But this *long run* is a misleading guide to current affairs. *In the long run* we are all dead. Economists set themselves too easy, too useless a task, if in tempestuous seasons they can only tell us that when the storm is long past the ocean is flat again" (4:65). In a contemporary example, there are times such as 2008 when long-run worries about fiscal deficits should not rule out expansionary policy in the face of a collapse in aggregate demand.

It *is* fair to observe that Keynes had little to say about the accumulation of debt and the possibility of associated financial bubbles. In the 1920s and 1930s, however, he thought hard about industrial policy and an appropriate role for international transactions. In the 1940s he made a profound contribution to long-run international trade and financial stability post–World War II. He did not foresee how the growth of real output would become central to economic thinking, but the *General Theory* provided the blueprint for all subsequent growth models. Finally, the analysis of business cycles is central to macroeconomics, and Keynes had interesting things to say about them.

Deficits and Debt

Contemporary conservative economists often fault Keynes for not taking into account the implications of running up debt, a critique of immediate concern after the events of 2007–2009. One way to think about debt in macro terms emerges from the saving = investment relationship at the core of the *General Theory.* The point is that this equation holds only at the *aggregate* level. In financially normal times, an individual or collective actor—household, firm, government, nation-state—can usually spend more than it earns (or invest more than it saves) by the simple expedients of selling assets such as physical capital or securities, or increasing liabilities in the form of taking on loans or issuing new equity. But because spending on output equals income overall, for *all* actors these transactions must net out to zero. In slightly fancier terminology introduced above, an actor whose expenditure exceeds income is undertaking *net borrowing.* The sum of levels of net borrowing for all actors has to be equal to zero. In rich economies these transactions are tabulated in the *flows of funds (FOF)* accounts.

Another important accounting detail comes into play: *wealth* or *net worth* changes in response to saving *and* capital gains (or losses) due to rising (or falling) asset prices. Summing up an actor's flows of funds and capital gains or losses over time generates a *balance sheet* which states that the value of assets (including financial assets along with tangible capital, which is cumulated investment less depreciation) must equal the value of financial liabilities plus net worth. In FOF accounting the liabilities include debt *and* the market value of outstanding equity that the actor may have sold. (Standard business accounting adjusts the value of equity to make net worth equal to zero.)

At least two potential problems arise. One is that a net borrower may consistently spend more than he earns and so risk running up a volume of debt with associated interest and amortization obligations that cannot be met from current income. This is a classic road to individual ruin, extensively mapped by the American Keynesian Hyman Minsky.

Fiscal "deficit hawks" in countries around the world emphasize how very high levels of government debt relative to GDP can be ruinous, or at least very difficult to finance, if interest and amortization obligations rise to a high proportion (say, 10%) of tax revenue. Sometimes such dire predictions come to pass. With escalating debt in the United States from the bailouts after 2007–2009 and rising federal spending, resident fiscal hawks warn about a dire future. At the end of 2009 and into 2010 they were more immediately concerned about prospects of a sovereign default by Greece. Their arguments are discussed further in Chapter 6.

More relevant, perhaps, were the consistent warnings from the Keynesian Laocoön Wynne Godley that beginning in the 1990s, household debt levels in the United States were becoming unsustainably high (the lion's share of the obligations being in the form of mortgage loans). He derived his conclusions by tracking net borrowing flows from the FOF accounts for households, business, government, and the rest of the world. The key results are presented in Chapter 5.

The second problem with liability accumulation can be devastating at the macro level. It involves many individual actors who issue liabilities to buy assets which are generating capital gains from rising prices. A *cumulative process* (Wicksell's phrase) can occur, combining asset price inflation with equally rapid growth of new liabilities to finance more purchases of assets. The liabilities can take diverse forms, as described in later chapters. In the mid-2000s subprime mortgages and debt within the financial system played central roles; in the late 1920s the speculative asset price boom was supported by borrowing *on the margin* to buy corporate shares as well as by equity issued by investment trusts which were controlled by the major banks. Like *special purpose vehicles* in the latest boom, the trusts were *off–balance sheet* entities created by banks to shield their speculative activities from regulatory scrutiny.

Regardless of the source of liability finance, the consequences are much the same. Such a bubble is inherently unstable. It always leads to the "mania, panic, and crash" scenario that was made famous by the Keynesian economist Charles Kindleberger, with substantial input from Minsky. The run-up to the panic always lasts longer than the crash. But as in the Great Depression, low and downward-drifting asset prices can persist after the crash for many years. Calling the events of 2008 a "Minsky moment" became commonplace in the financial press, though a "Kindleberger moment" would have been a more apt description.

Very low interest rates orchestrated by the Fed after 2000 probably played a role in bidding up the housing price bubble. There are many theories of asset prices, but a common one is based on the idea that the return to holding a unit of an asset such as an apartment house is the ratio of its rent roll to its value. A typical arbitrage argument then asserts that competition in the housing market should ensure that returns so measured will equalize across all units. One more arbitrage step would then equate these returns to the cost of capital, or rate of interest. A final step sets

$$\text{Value of a unit} = \text{Rent from the unit} / \text{interest rate}.$$

That is, the value of the building should be its rent return *capitalized* by the interest rate.

Figure 1.4 presents time series data for the United States. The diagram

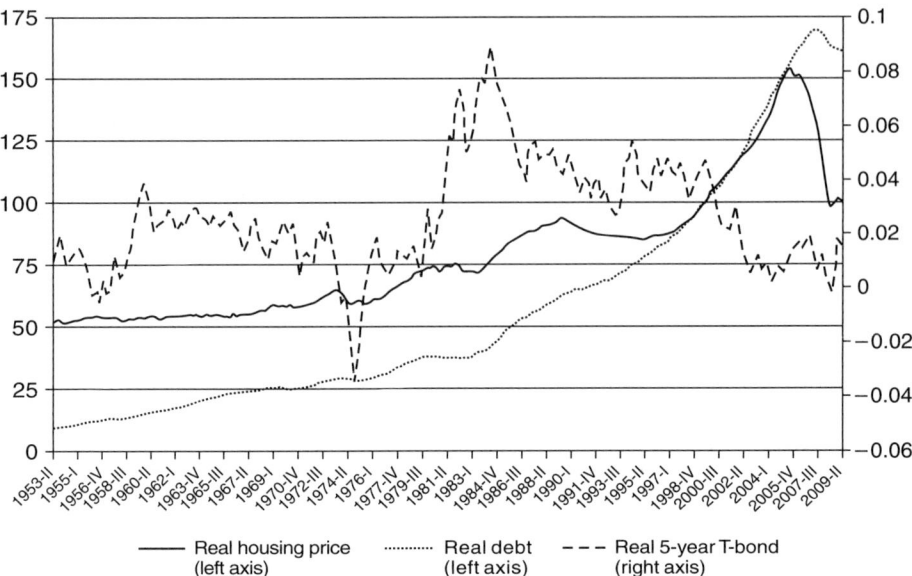

Figure 1.4 Real medium-term interest rate, housing prices, and real household debt

shows the real housing price, a real medium-run interest rate (the nominal rate minus the rate of inflation, as discussed further in Chapter 2), and real household debt.

The downward trend in the interest rate after the early 1980s began before the growth of housing prices accelerated. As discussed in Chapter 7, steadily falling rates can be interpreted as resulting from an explicit policy decision by the Fed led by governors Greenspan and Bernanke to support asset prices. Mere correlation does not imply causality, but the co-movement of the two time series is consistent with the asset pricing theory outlined above. Real household debt also began to grow faster, suggesting that a speculative process got under way in which rising debt was used to purchase housing in anticipation of capital gains from further price growth.

As recounted in Chapter 3, low rates also fed into the stock market boom of 1928–29. In both cases cheap money was probably a *necessary condition* for a mania, but other factors helped launch the rocket. After all, there have been many other periods in which low rates simply stimulated effective demand, as Keynes thought they should.

Figure 1.4 shows a downward break in the housing price index in the mid-2000s, probably because borrowers started to renege on mortgage debt service obligations when low initial *teaser rates* began to go up. The resulting foreclosures halted the price spiral. Note that real debt continued to rise after housing prices stopped growing. Such *overshooting* behavior is characteristic of many speculative processes.

To my knowledge, Keynes himself never put much emphasis on destabilizing debt dynamics at the national level. But it fits naturally into his intellectual framework.

The Failure of Laissez-Faire

Industrial policy figured in one of Keynes's concerns in the 1920s: how to cope with "structural unemployment" (as opposed to the sort of unemployment stemming from deficient aggregate demand) in England's declining coal and cotton industries. In a 1926 article titled "The End of *Laissez-faire*" he provided a litany of reasons why purely competitive market processes would not act to offset structural problems: "(1) when the efficient units of production are large relative to the units of consumption, (2) when overhead costs or joint costs are present, (3) when internal economies tend to the aggregation of production, (4) when the time required for adjustments is long, (5) when ignorance prevails over knowledge, and (6) when monopolies and combination interfere with equality in bargaining" (9:284–285).

To counter all these problems, he proposed the establishment of public and quasi-public corporations to regulate economic activities subject to economies of scale, ignorance about future prospects, monopolistic market structures, and so on. Later, in the *General Theory*, he argued for substantial state control or *socialization* of investment.

"Let goods be homespun"

Keynes's reserve about fully market-based policy also showed up in a piece written for the *Yale Review* in 1933 called "National Self-Sufficiency." Breaking from his earlier enthusiasm for free trade, he argued against *globalization* (in contemporary usage) in the form of free international mobility of goods and capital on the grounds that it put countries "at the mercy of world forces" such as foreign meddling and capital flight. Moreover, gains from the international division of labor of the sort emphasized by the English economist David Ricardo (see Chapter 2) appeared to be less than they had been in the nineteenth century.

Keynes proposed a gradual move toward greater economic isolation and national self-sufficiency: "[L]et goods be homespun whenever it is reasonably and conveniently possible, and, above all, let finance be primarily national.... It should not be a matter of tearing up roots but of slowly training a plant to grow in a different direction" (21:240–241).

Open Economy Accounting

In the 1940s Keynes carried similar caution at the macro level over to the global arena, where both trade and fiscal deficits and surpluses involving two or two hundred countries matter greatly. He made fundamental contributions. But before we get to them, it makes sense to sort out international economic accounting. Nothing very difficult, but unavoidably messy.

In the jargon, an economy is running a *current account* surplus if its income flows from abroad (from exports of goods and services and interest, profit, and wage remittances) exceed flows going to foreign countries (imports and outgoing financial transfers). Flow of funds logic points to two immediate conclusions. One is that the sum of surpluses worldwide is equal to zero. All countries' deficits and surpluses must offset one another. (This condition is not satisfied in available data, which show the world running a current account deficit of a few hundred billion dollars with itself—an illustration of the difficulties that arise in consolidating diverse national accounting systems.)

The other conclusion rests on the observation that if the exchange rate (see below) stays constant, then the increase in an economy's *net foreign assets* is equal to its surplus on current account, just as the increase in a domestic sector's net worth is equal to its saving when it has no capital gains or losses. *Net* foreign assets are gross assets minus gross liabilities. In more detail they take the form of *international reserves* held by the central bank and liabilities of the rest of the world such as bonds and shares held by the national private sector *minus* "home" country liabilities held abroad by private actors and central banks as reserves. (U.S. Treasury and other government-backed obligations make up around two-thirds of reserves held by non-U.S. central banks.)

Changes in these items sum to the surplus on *capital account* and offset the country's current account position. The other way 'round, if a country buys more than it sells, then it has to persuade the rest of the world to provide finance by acquiring the home liabilities to cover the resulting deficit. As discussed in Chapter 5, beginning in the early 1980s through 2008, both the government and private sectors in the United States undertook extensive net borrowing to finance a growing current account deficit.

The local central bank's holdings of international reserves are a key indicator of an economy's international situation. From the preceding paragraphs we see that the change in reserves is the current account surplus plus the increase in home country liabilities held abroad, minus the increase of the home private sector's holdings of foreign liabilities. Big reserves signal that the home country has a history of current account surpluses or that it has been receiving *capital inflows* (acquisition of national liabilities by foreign investors) exceeding its current account deficit, if there is one. In the 2000s China's swelling reserves reflected both sorts of transactions—high current account surpluses and massive capital inflows.

Finally, there are *exchange rates.* They are the most puzzling objects in macroeconomics, as discussed in Chapter 8. An exchange rate between two countries or regions (pounds versus dollars, euros versus yen, and so on) scales one country's entire price system in terms of the other's. Confusion reigns even with regard to the definition. The common practice is to express the rate in units of the home currency, say, the U.S. dollar, to a unit of the foreign currency, for example, a rate of $1.50 per euro. (As with driving on the left side of the road, Britain and a few other countries prefer to express the rate upside down, that is, in dollars per pound.) With the standard convention, a weaker, devalued, or depreciated rate has a *higher* value; a stronger or appreciated rate is *lower.* If, say, the dollar weakens with respect to the pound, then presumably America's current account with respect to Britain's will improve. Not always the case, of course, but useful as a rule of thumb.

Keynes and the International System

During the Great Depression (see Chapter 3) the world went through a collapse of all international transactions. Trade flows fell drastically, and capital movements dried up. There were competitive exchange rate devaluations and tariff escalations as open international economic warfare broke out. The countries that gained the most (the United States, Germany, Britain, Brazil) did so by being more aggressive in combining protectionism and devaluation with expansionary policies at home, thereby forcing unemployment on the rest of the world. In a phrase from Keynes's younger colleague Joan Robinson, beggar-my-neighbor policies succeeded for the more ruthless.

As the subsequent shooting war came to an end, a consensus emerged that a new international economic order was needed to allow the resumption of trade. On the basis of draft proposals put forward by Keynes and the American Harry Dexter White, an agreement was hammered out at a conference at the Bretton Woods ski resort in New Hampshire in July 1944. The system that emerged featured fixed exchange rates between all countries. Any country was permitted to restrict capital inflows or outflows as it saw fit. Such capital controls were nearly universal after the war but were gradually phased out, leading to the ultimate demise of the Bretton Woods system three decades later—a run long enough to allow White and Keynes to be reliably deceased.

At Bretton Woods, Keynes was highly concerned with unbalanced external positions, both deficit *and* surplus. He thought that ample financial support should be provided to deficit countries while they worked on improving their positions; surplus economies should be taxed or sanctioned. Both proposals were vetoed by the United States, which did not want to bankroll subsidies to deficit economies and saw no need for its postwar surplus to be penalized.

Another feature of the Bretton Woods system was the creation of the World Bank and the International Monetary Fund to subsidize and regulate, respectively, the international economic system. (Borrowing a line from Wordsworth about two peaks in England's lake district, Keynes called them the system's "lusty twins.") The Fund was effectively empowered by the system's lack of support for external deficits to force recessions on countries (at least poor and powerless ones) suffering from them. The goal was to cut their demand for imports and improve current accounts. This bias was only fully recognized with the Asian crisis more than five decades later. It still appears to persist as the Fund is beefed up to deal with the developing countries hit by the 2007–2009 crisis. Its public pronouncements had been sounding increasingly Keynesian in its old age, but that seemed to stop as it gained new money and power. The Bank initially was willing to pursue industrial policy, but veered sharply away from that orientation with the conservative counterrevolution of the 1970s.

Economic Growth

Economic growth involves the expansion of *real* output (that is, the level of output as estimated in current prices in the NIPA system deflated by an "appropriate" price index) over time. Growth is usually measured in terms of percentage changes of output per year. One can also consider economic growth per capita, meaning the growth rate of real output minus the growth rate of population. A related concept is labor productivity, that is, output per worker per year, or per hour of work. Positive economic growth per capita is always associated with a positive growth rate of labor productivity.

Keynes was well aware of the possibilities growth can create. In the late 1920s he wrote a piece called "Economic Possibilities for Our Grandchildren," in which he calculated that over a hundred years, levels of per capita income in the "civilized" part of the world would grow by between four and eight times. At such income levels, he thought, there would be much more leisure time, demand for consumption would be satiated, and capital would not be scarce (hence the vanishing rentier mentioned above). He was more or less correct about income growth, but his vision of a leisurely future did not work out. The turn-of-the-(twentieth)-century gadfly Thorstein Veblen, as will be seen, pointed to conspicuous consumption as a basic reason why—enhanced throughout the century, one might add, by a continuous stream of new products to consume. (Sooner or later even I will buy a smart phone.)

What Keynes also missed is that the economic growth process has an intrinsic logic of its own, which took a few decades to be worked out. Some of his immediate colleagues—notably the Cambridge polymath Frank Ramsey and the economists Roy Harrod, Joan Robinson, and Nicholas Kaldor—made substantial contributions. More mainstream economists such as Robert Solow from MIT also took up the task.

One key issue is how to conceptualize growth along lines already laid out in the *General Theory*. Is it driven largely by forces of demand or from the supply side à la Say's Law? What are the sources of productivity growth, economies of scale, and decreasing costs? Are they brought into play by robust demand for output, or increasing labor's capacity to produce by, say, more education? Such questions are at the forefront of current policy debate. Keynesian and mainstream models tend to give different answers, to a large extent because they respectively reject and accept Say's Law.

Business Cycles

All macroeconomic variables—prices and quantities, interest rates, asset prices, and the like—fluctuate over time. These movements are usually graced with the name "cycles," although they are far too irregular to fit the well-defined periodicity usually associated with that word. Irregular "waves" or even "rhythms" might be better descriptions.

In the *General Theory,* Keynes saw cycles as resulting from swings up and down in investment, saving, and liquidity preference. Their interactions are fairly easy to trace in the data, a task taken up in Chapters 4 and 5.

The *Treatise* focuses more on the financial side, in an analysis with a family resemblance to liquidity preference but with its own interesting twists. The story centers on how bulls and bears respond to changes in asset prices. Keynes concentrates on holding money and short selling as typical bear positions, and sketches a cycle between the extent of bearishness and asset prices. Intriguingly, a very similar dynamics played out between asset prices and leverage in financial markets after the 1990s. Again, the details will come in Chapter 4.

The Counterrevolution

Polemics about the *General Theory* broke out as soon as it was published. They will be discussed in detail in later chapters, but a preview will be useful.

The first criticism which proved to be long-lasting came from Keynes's Cambridge colleague A. C. Pigou. It was based on an "effect" reminiscent of the inflation tax in Wicksell's theory. The details can be safely postponed, but it provided the basis for a complete macro model in Franco Modigliani's Ph.D. thesis at the New School for Social Research (my own institution), which was published in 1944. His main conclusion was that unemployment happens because money wages are too *high* "relative to the quantity of money," directly contradicting one of the *General Theory*'s central arguments. As discussed in Chapter 6, Modigliani's "nominal rigidity" of the wage (presumably due to institutional factors) became a central tenet of the post–World War II mainstream "neoclassical synthesis" interpretation of the *General Theory*. The Pigou-Modigliani line was further elaborated in (then) popular "general equilibrium" terms by the American-Israeli economist Don Patinkin. Along with wage rigidity, he emphasized the dichotomy between prices and quantities in a Say's Law world.

The next attack came from the University of Chicago, led by Milton Friedman. It initially featured a "permanent income hypothesis" stating that consumption and saving are mostly independent of current income, displacing the principle of effective demand. Friedman and Edmund Phelps from Columbia University independently reclothed Wicksell's monetarist inflation model in Pigovian apparel to establish a "natural rate of unemployment" à la Say's Law. They allowed "slow" adjustment of output and employment toward the natural rate. Friedman's Chicago colleague Robert Lucas then argued in 1972, largely on a priori grounds, that convergence would be very rapid. The macro system would basically stay close to full employment. At that point, in the eyes of most of the economics profession, the *General Theory* was well and truly dead.

Before Maynard

Despite the fact that the *General Theory* is the *ur*-text of modern macroeconomics, Maynard did not invent the subject. Rather, he carried on a tradition of political economy in Great Britain that can be dated to the original publication in 1776 of Adam Smith's *Wealth of Nations*. Smith did not do that much macro, but his successors such as David Ricardo, Thomas Malthus, and Karl Marx—usually now grouped as the great "classical" economists—certainly did. Kalecki and (probably) Keynes were influenced by Marx in their thinking about economic disequilibrium and crisis.

For the economics profession as a whole, the classical or political economy school was largely supplanted beginning in the 1870s by "marginalist" or "neoclassical" scholars who concentrated on the "microeconomic" behavior of actors such as households and firms and (with notable exceptions such as Wicksell and later Irving Fisher at Yale) let macro fall by the wayside. They utilized a deductive and mathematical form of reasoning as opposed to the historical, inductive style shared by the classical economists and to a large extent Keynes. Most modern mainstream economists think of themselves as being neoclassical and pay scant attention to whimsical artifacts such as social classes and history.

It is important to connect Keynes's ideas with those of his predecessors, neoclassical and especially classical. At the same time, he drew upon British traditions of monetary analysis and Wicksell. Chapter 2 discusses all this background.

The next questions concern what Keynes had to say in detail in an early *Treatise on Probability*, the *Tract on Monetary Reform*, the *Treatise on Money*, and the *General Theory*. After that we have to go on to post-Keynesian developments—his revolution, how his close collaborators extended it, why it was pronounced dead, and why it has recovered. But first, back to 1776!

Notes

John Maynard Keynes was born on June 5, 1883, in Cambridge to a family high in the English academic hierarchy. He died on April 21, 1946, from an infective heart disorder he had contracted around 1930. He was called both Keynes and Maynard in his lifetime (apparently only his mother used John), so both names will be employed here.

Maynard led an eventful life. He was reared by his economist father, John Neville, to be a genius, and admirably succeeded. He stood out in the brilliant intellectual galaxy in Cambridge in the first decades of the twentieth century. In his *Autobiography* the *über*-philosopher Bertrand Russell said: "Keynes's intellect was the sharpest and clearest that I have ever known. When I argued with him I felt that I took my life in my hands, and I seldom emerged without feeling something of a fool" (Russell, 1967, 88).

Beyond Cambridge, he was a central figure in the Bloomsbury circle. He wrote the *General Theory* while in declining health in his fifties. He served Britain well during the war as an economic planner (inventing with colleagues the NIPA system along the way) and diplomat, while he simultaneously served the world in setting up the Bretton Woods international monetary system. After years of being (in contemporary usage) gay, he married London's prima ballerina Lydia Lopokova in 1925. They had no children.

The first biography was by Keynes's collaborator Roy Harrod, solid but overwritten and inclined to suppress his subject's homosexuality. The biography now most read is by Robert Skidelsky, occupying three volumes (1992–2001). It is a fascinating 1,800 pages. His 2009 update usefully relates Keynes's ideas to contemporary problems. The collected works, now partly out of print, were published in thirty volumes by the Royal Economic Society. Citations herein to Keynes refer to volume and page number of this collection.

The academic literature on Keynes is enormous. No attempt is made to pursue it in detail here. This book is about a particular interpretation (my own) of the work of Keynes and his successors and how it fits into policy-oriented macroeconomics. The presentation is backed up by scholarly contributions to be introduced in context. For those in touch with modern economics, deductive, somewhat mathematical, and distinctly non-neoclassical versions of many arguments herein appear in Taylor (2004).

Soros (2009) is his latest book on reflexivity and finance. Kalecki (1971) is a good selection of relevant papers. Amadeo (1989) gives a lucid review of the transition via the *Treatise* between Wicksell and the *General Theory*. The essay by Albert Hirschman (1981) summarizes his thinking about spillovers of distributive conflict into inflation and debt.

Kindleberger and Aliber (2005) is the final edition of the first author's classic. Minsky (1975) is perhaps the clearest version of his "financial instability" model. Crotty (1999) reviews Keynes's views on industrial policy in the 1920s.

— 2 —

Macroeconomic Thought during the Long Nineteenth Century

There are not many new ideas in economics. From the twentieth century among the few that matter is the principle of effective demand and associated relationships as stated by Keynes and Kalecki.

The ideas that do exist get recycled and restated by the academic industry, often over recent decades with mathematical decorations that may earn tenure for their designers but add little to the beauty of the thought. The best way to understand contemporary anti-Keynesian macroeconomics is to trace it to its origins. This chapter takes up the task. It is long, sometimes dense, and many variations on the basics are introduced. Almost all will be relevant in subsequent discussion. The presentation falls roughly into thirds—on classical and then neoclassical theories of the real side of the economy, followed by money, finance, inflation, and crises. A checklist is provided at the end.

The time frame follows from the distinguished contemporary economic historian Eric Hobsbawm's definition of the years between 1789 and 1914 —between the French Revolution and World War I—as the "long nineteenth century." He argues that this period was a distinct historical era. For our purposes Hobsbawm's long century computes, although we can pretend that it began with the *Wealth of Nations* in 1776. The social structures that support Keynesian macroeconomics developed gradually over that span of time. The fundamental change was the erosion of Say's Law, a cornerstone of classical economics early in the long century which, at least in the richer corners of the world, became irrelevant after its end.

Classical economists practicing political economy were dominant early in the century. Around 1870, in analysis of quantities and prices of goods they were succeeded by neoclassicals (a label coined by Veblen). The transition marked a shift from political economy involving collective social actors and a degree of self-interested behavior to theories based on pure micro-level optimization devoid of institutional and macroeconomic content.

The financial sphere was shaken by repeated crises (with serious ones roughly once a generation) and saw increasing sophistication in available instruments and transactions. Theory did not keep up, focusing principally on money and its connections with the price level. Notwithstanding its narrow focus, this analysis is of interest because much of it supports anti-Keynesian macroeconomics to this day.

International economic transactions toward the end of the century were dominated by a *gold standard*. After World War I it passed through protracted hemorrhage and death. It was finally succeeded by the Bretton Woods system. As will be seen in the next chapter, both the gold standard and finance had macroeconomic consequences early in the twentieth century which became part of the background for Keynes.

At a few points the discussion flashes forward to ideas popular in the twentieth century and into the twenty-first. These maneuvers save flashbacks in later chapters, and are noted explicitly in the text.

The Classical Perspective

As society and its economic relationships changed, Say's Law lost its grip in two dimensions. One was the emergence of Keynes's *coordination problem* between saving and investment emphasized in Chapter 1. Most economic activity around 1800 was rural. On an English manor being converted to a farm, for example, the activities associated with enclosing the commons constituted investment. The saving counterpart, or abstinence from consumption, took place on the farm as well. If workers were paid in kind, there would have been less grain in the landowner's storehouse. Had he not pursued the enclosure and just built up his stocks, that would have been investment in another form! Similar observations apply to manufactures, of which many enterprises were owned and operated by families. Plowing money back into the firm amounted to saving that was automatically translated into new capital formation.

Over time, decisions about saving and investment became socially separated. Certainly, retained earnings were reinvested in business (itself shifting from a family-dominated to a corporate structure of governance), but a visible share of the sector's *surplus* or profits was distributed as dividends, rent, and interest. Insofar as their investment exceeded retained earnings, firms had to tap outside sources of saving, with decisions about supply being made by rentiers' and even workers' households. The saving-investment coordination problem came to the fore, for example, in Wicksell's inflation analysis late in the nineteenth century.

The second manifestation of Say's Law could be called full *underemployment*. Western European death rates circa 1800 were very high by modern standards, with life expectancy at birth in the range of twenty-five to thirty years. But survivors did scrape by. To use the label applied in contemporary development economics, there was a large *subsistence sector* in which some income was generated and shared out through family, community, and other ties. Whether the level of output would change as people drifted in and out of subsistence has been hotly debated. The answer is probably that overall subsistence output would not change by very much, so that people in the sector were effectively underemployed. But in any case subsistence output was enough to support them at a very low income level per capita.

Full underemployment gradually evaporated as urbanization and industrialization proceeded and traditional social support mechanisms eroded. Wage-based employment contracts became the rule. It became possible to be functionally *un*employed, perhaps supported by a dole or remaining family ties, and modern macroeconomic adjustment mechanisms came into play.

The classical economists broadly accepted Say's Law. They recognized the existence of *trade cycles*, however. Malthus thought there might be *general gluts*, which Keynes in a biographical article (10:71–108) construed in terms of deficient aggregate demand. By mid-century Marx had a "floating" *reserve army*, made up of workers displaced in a "modern" sector who could not easily reenter subsistence. In the United States the obvious examples would be unemployed urban workers during the Great Depression who no longer could make it from Detroit or Chicago back to the farm. Many Asian urban workers faced a similar challenge after the crisis in 1998.

Nevertheless, prior to Marx, gluts and cycles were seen as transient fluctuations around the basic classical model. It also featured social differentiation. All classical authors thought broadly in terms of collective social actors, such as workers who received wages (quite possibly in kind), landowners who were paid rents (often in kind), and capitalists who took profits. There was a clear correspondence between "classes" defined in this fashion and the *functional income distribution,* which focuses on different forms of payments flows.

Adam's Contributions

The *Wealth of Nations* is chock-full of ideas, most of great interest and many mutually contradictory. Four are pertinent for Keynes and twenty-first century macroeconomics. The first is how a capitalist economy is supposed to operate to optimize the general good; this is the fable of the *invisible hand.* Although Smith does not point it out, the optimization can be upset by two forces. One is the presence of economies of scale and decreasing costs, which Smith (along with Keynes's colleague Nicholas Kaldor) sees as the driving forces behind economic progress. The other is imperfectly shared knowledge among economic actors, say, bank regulators and banks. Finally, there is a discussion of the *theory of value,* which underlies Keynes's identification of income with output a century and a half later.

One of Smith's goals in the *Wealth of Nations* was to combat *mercantilism.* Very broadly speaking, mercantilist writers saw economic relationships among nations as (in contemporary usage) a zero-sum game. If one nation were to gain, some other(s) must lose. The metric for many writers was the national store of gold, the principal medium of exchange for settling international transactions. Gold inflows could be stimulated by export promotion and import restriction, that is, by hands-on state intervention.

Smith emphasized that real national income, as later built into Keynes's NIPA system, is a far superior measure of a nation's well-being. He thought that the invisible hand operates to increase national income. We will see how that may or may not be the case. It also bears noting that Smith did not slay the mercantilist dragon. The doctrine that for an individual country, aggressive export promotion can generate rapid output growth and high employment remains alive and well in the twenty-first century (see Chapter 8).

The Invisible Hand

The idea behind the invisible hand is that the pursuit of private economic interest will lead to an overall social gain. For example: "It is not from the benevolence of the butcher, the brewer or the baker, that we expect our dinner, but from their regard to their own self interest. We address ourselves, not to their humanity but to their self-love, and never talk to them of our own necessities but of their advantages" (Smith 1776, 1994, 15).

This theme has been dear to conservative economic thinking ever since. It implicitly presupposes that Say's Law is enforced. If our aggressive comparison shopping among the butchers leads them to cut prices so enthusiastically that some are forced out of business, there will always be openings for brewers, bakers, or underemployed rural laborers. Neither structural nor demand-driven unemployment of labor or capital enters the discussion.

Before we take up the famous pin (or nail) factory, here is a modern example of economies of scale. An oil refinery is, to a large extent, a collection of tanks. If we think about a spherical tank for simplicity, its surface area goes up as the square of its radius; its volume increases as the cube. The cost of the tank is driven by the amount of steel needed to fabricate its surface; its capacity goes up in proportion to its volume. So the cost of the tank goes up (roughly) as the 2/3 power of capacity. There are decreasing costs associated with larger scale—assuming, of course, that the greater capacity really gets utilized!

Smith himself saw decreasing costs as being driven by *division of labor*. In his example, one person could make a pin from scratch, or else the task could be divided into many specialized operations along the lines of early-twentieth-century time-and-motion studies. He estimated that so organizing pin production could lead to more than a hundredfold increase in labor productivity. More generally, he thought that division of labor enhanced productivity by increasing workers' dexterity, reducing time lost in passing from one task to another, and permitting the use of machinery to undertake specialized tasks. Today machinery, including such facilities as the massive computer farms operated by Google, which utilize very high levels of energy per worker and take advantage of "natural" scaling phenomena of the sort discussed above, is the main factor underlying productivity growth.

Decreasing Costs

For our purposes, decreasing costs are of interest for two reasons. One is that they are incompatible with the invisible hand. Larger firms are a natural consequence of increasing returns, meaning that small pin factories are likely to consolidate into a monopoly, which will then drive up prices to enhance its own profits—scarcely an example of enhancing social well-being!

This contradiction is usually suppressed in neoclassical economics, which simply assumes that there are no processes of production with decreasing costs. When they do surface, as in "new" theories of industrial organization, international trade, and economic growth in the 1990s, they are typically transformed away, for example, by the assumption that consumers prefer "variety" (pins with pink versus blue heads, BMW versus Benz, Internet Explorer versus Firefox, and so on) and shop around so that several firms enjoying economies of scale can flourish.

This trick, which has led to a Nobel Prize or three, is amusing as far as it goes, but it completely ignores the fact that decreasing-cost industries are continually subject to boom-bust cycles driven by what Marx called *excess competition* between firms striving for maximum possible size. If several of them seek to increase their capacity levels at the same time, the total may well exceed demand for the product in question (think of fertilizers, petrochemicals, DRAM computer chips, or liquefied natural gas), leading to a price collapse and a vicious shakeout. There can also be adverse repercussions in the future. Low oil prices could well lead to a cutback in exploration and capacity building, setting the stage for a new price spike a few years later.

In practice, excess competition can be regulated by industrial policy. At the macro level (our second point of interest), decreasing costs are likely to be less destructive when demand for output grows rapidly, stimulated by expansionary policy. Indeed, rapid and sustained output growth is itself likely to stimulate labor productivity by the introduction of new technologies and appropriation of economies of scale. This positive feedback effect is a key component of demand-driven Keynesian theories of economic growth, as proposed by Kaldor among others. His mechanism, usually supported by the data, is that faster real GDP growth stimulates more rapid increases in labor productivity (see Chapter 5).

Flash Forward: Asymmetric Knowledge

The invisible hand notwithstanding, Smith had shrewd insights into situations in which market mechanisms can break down. In one frequently quoted example he argued *in favor* of usury laws putting ceilings on interest rates: "If the legal rate of interest . . . was fixed so high as eight or ten percent, the greater part of the money which was to be lent would be lent to prodigals and projectors, who alone would be willing to give this high interest. Sober people, who will give for the use of money no more than a part of what they are likely to make by use of it, would not venture into the competition" (Smith 1776, 1994, 388).

The call for financial regulation is quite clear. But the detail is beside the point for the 2007–2009 crisis. The "prodigals and projectors" who pushed subprime mortgage lending did so because they could take profits by *securitizing* or packaging the mortgages into collateralized debt obligations and selling those bonds into the market at high prices. The debt that the buyers assumed to buy the bonds was available at *low* rates of interest. In this instance, usury laws would not have protected sober borrowers. Along with higher rates, better-detailed regulation of the mortgage market might have done so.

Smith's issue with the prodigals and projectors is called *adverse selection* in the contemporary literature because "good" borrowers are driven out of the market. Together with a companion problem called *moral hazard* (if I insure my house for more than 100% of its value, then regardless of my morals, burning it down becomes a tempting thought), it was rediscovered and restated in mathematics by the mainstream in the 1970s. A few more Nobels were involved.

A great deal of fashionable macroeconomics relies on *asymmetric information* of the moral hazard and adverse selection sort (although *asymmetric knowledge* is a better label, which is adopted here). In recent literature they are amplified by *principal/agent* problems. The basic idea is that a "principal," such as someone owning shares in a bank, can set up financial sticks and carrots to ensure that an "agent," such as the bank's CEO, will maximize shareholder value. Relationships involving power and deception emerge on both sides. *New Keynesian* macro, which captivated the center-left of the mainstream in the 1980s, put a lot of effort into working out such games while in practice ignoring Maynard and effective demand. At the micro level, principal-agent analysis supports an emphasis on maximizing shareholder value as the sole purpose of business firms, to the detriment of all other stakeholders. Revulsion against this oversimplification became widespread in 2008–9.

Asymmetric knowledge, principals, and agents are not central to a Keynesian understanding of the economy, but they can shed light. Although it is clear that they did not fully understand the implications of securitization and credit default swaps, banks in 2009 which held *toxic assets* perhaps knew a bit more about their potential risks than outsiders attempting to insure or buy them out. That gave them a leg up in any potential bargaining situation. Similarly, if over time the authorities have repeatedly rescued financial institutions that have gotten themselves into trouble, incentives for more risky behavior in the future become stronger. This sort of moral hazard is central to models of financial instability proposed by Hyman Minsky, George Soros, and many others.

Flash Forward: Theory of Value

Finally, like all the classical economists, Adam Smith wrote extensively on the theory of value. The goal is to explain *why* a commodity or service has a "value" in the sense of a positive price and then further to say *how* relative prices of different goods get determined. Theories of the *functional* income distribution extend these lines of analysis to "payments to factors of production," including wages, profits, interest, rents, and taxes.

For macroeconomics the main interest lies in the determination of aggregate indexes of prices of goods, wages for different broad types of labor, and (in the open economy case) exchange rates between different national price systems. Smith had a couple of useful things to say.

One is that components of cost add up to give the total values of output. A complication arises because many goods are used as inputs into the production of others (flour into bread, steel into automobiles, and so on). Such *intermediate inputs* contribute to both demand and cost. They are built into *input-output tables* (or matrixes), as introduced by the Russian American economist Wassily Leontief in the 1930s.

After the costs of intermediate inputs are subtracted from the total value (price × quantity) of a product, what is left over is the *value added* that its production creates. In turn, value added breaks down into *factor payments* to labor, capital, land, and so on. Smith recognized that such payments "add up" to value added but said little about what determines their levels. Keynes built on Smith when he postulated that income (or value added) equals output (or total demand net of intermediates). Classical economics did not explore this macroeconomic linkage.

Like the other classical economists, Smith accepted a *labor theory of value*, recognizing that wage costs are often the largest component of value added. Keynes reasoned broadly along such lines when he argued that money wage cuts would not stimulate employment because they would bid down prices in proportion and leave the real wage largely unchanged. But despite acute observations about how labor markets function, neither Keynes nor Smith had completely convincing explanations about how the level of the *money* wage gets determined. Ricardo aided by Malthus provided the central classical theory about the *real* wage.

Ricardo's Analytics

Adam Smith was an academic. He served a stint as professor of moral philosophy at Glasgow, then became a tutor to a young aristocrat and toured the Continent with him (along the way picking up the economic ideas of the French physiocratic school, which preceded Leontief in inventing input-output analysis), and finally returned to Scotland to write the *Wealth of Nations*. Along with his friend David Hume, he was a central figure in the Scottish Enlightenment. Despite his ivory tower career, one of the most striking aspects of his great book is its deep grounding in the commercial life of the time.

The contrast with David Ricardo is striking. He was born into an enormous Sephardic Jewish family, eloped with a Quaker, and became a man of the world: businessman, financier, and member of Parliament. He wrote in an abstract and unapproachable fashion. Nevertheless, he made many crucial contributions to classical economics. Several are relevant to contemporary debate.

First comes a theory about determination of the real wage by socioeconomic forces, specifically the pattern of population dynamics made famous by Thomas Malthus. Next Ricardo emphasized that when Say's Law is in force, there has to be an inverse relationship between the real wage and the rate of profit. (A dozen decades later, Kaleckian economists pointed out that if aggregate demand is stimulated by real wage increases when Say's Law does *not* apply, an income redistribution favoring labor can also boost profits. Unfortunately, labor productivity increases not offset by expansionary macro policy will destroy jobs under such circumstances.)

The fixed real wage also supports the labor theory of value, which Ricardo clarified and Marx pursued. The labor theory underlies Ricardo's defense of free trade, a hardy perennial for mainstream economists, and enters into his "dismal science" model of economic growth. In his long run, capitalists are euthanized, and most people end up at a subsistence level of income.

This outcome is one example of a central idea about the long run in economics: one or more key indicators tend toward *natural* levels. The classical economists focused on a natural real wage. As will be seen, Wicksell and many successors such as Keynes's opponent (and friend) Friedrich von Hayek emphasized a natural rate of interest, and the contemporary mainstream has a natural rate of unemployment. As already mentioned in Chapter 1 and discussed below, Keynes along with Ricardo tended to think that the profit rate would tend toward zero in the long run. Such perceptions about the future can strongly influence economists' policy analysis in the here and now.

The Real Wage

Ricardo's theory of the real wage later came to be known as the *iron law of wages*. The gist is that the real subsistence wage is the cost of maintaining a livelihood, given the "habits and customs" of the population. There will be a tendency for the real wage to "gravitate" toward this natural level, perhaps because of the population dynamics emphasized by Malthus.

Their basic idea was that a higher real wage draws more workers into the labor force (possibly by increasing the birthrate), while at the same time it reduces the number dropping out (perhaps by death). The natural wage rate is the one at which numbers of new entrants and dropouts are equal. If the wage is above its natural level, the faster labor force growth that results will increase the supply of labor and push the wage back down. Marx later transposed this sort of dynamics to his reserve army of labor, and we have already seen an interpretation in terms of underemployment in the subsistence sector. Regardless of the specific justification, the key classical idea is that the real wage is determined by *social* forces, not simply by the demand for and supply of labor.

The iron law together with Say's Law have strong implications for income distribution and are relevant to Keynes and left Keynesians. Say's Law asserts that a certain quantity of output is available. The wage gravitates to its natural level, so that the total payment to the subsistence population is set. The remaining *surplus* output goes as rent to landowners and profit to capitalists who operate enterprises and provide working capital to do so. If we ignore land for the moment, then the *profit rate* or payment per unit of capital is determined.

Two Souls

One immediate implication is that an increase in the real wage must be met by a fall in the profit rate. This *wage-profit relationship* is ubiquitous in a Say's Law world in which labor and capital are the principal inputs into production of value added. It precludes fully independent theories of wages and profits because if output is constant, they are constrained to move against each other.

The German Keynesian Peter Flaschel calls this antagonism the *two souls problem,* after a pivotal soliloquy from Goethe's *Faust:* "Two souls, alas, are housed within my breast, / And each will wrestle for the mastery there." In one translation Faust goes on to say that one soul "hugs a world where sweet the senses rage," and the other has far loftier aspirations. Fleeing from Goethe's subtleties (there are many) for less poetic macroeconomic purposes, we note that the interest lies in distributive strife between the soul of labor and the soul of capital. As will be seen in Chapter 5, this contest was an important factor leading into the crisis of 2007–2009.

Flash Forward: Wage-Led and Profit-Led Demand

Class struggle over the income distribution may be less acute in a Kalecki-Keynes world. The reason is that in the macro model in which the principle of effective demand applies instead of Say's Law, the level of output and rate of growth may respond in either direction to income redistribution in favor of (say) labor. Some implications are sketched here. After algebraic notation has been set up, there is a more mathematical discussion in Chapter 5.

Suppose that wage earners consume most of their income. Then if wages rise (or taxes on labor income go down), the higher output due to their extra spending could very well bid up effective demand as well. Such a *wage-led* demand increase has long been central to the thinking of left Keynesians, beginning with Kalecki and his younger colleague Josef Steindl. It is sometimes called the *paradox of costs.*

But there is a downside when there is labor productivity growth. In England around 1810, skilled textile workers formed a *Luddite* movement (named after a possibly mythical Ned Ludd who destroyed machinery around 1780) to smash mechanized looms that were putting them out of jobs. Perhaps in response, Ricardo added a chapter "On Machinery" to his *Principles of Political Economy and Taxation,* in which he wondered whether "such an application of machinery . . . as should have the effect of saving labor" could be "injurious to the interests of the class of laborers." In contemporary terminology, will an increase in labor productivity be injurious to labor?

Ricardo's answer to his own question was convoluted, but one can show that the outcome could be injurious in a wage-led economy. Overall well-being will improve insofar as lower unit labor costs coming from the productivity jump get passed along into lower real commodity prices. Implications for employment are not so favorable. In a first round of effects, the loss of consumption demand by workers whose jobs are eliminated would lead to a further reduction in effective demand, further job losses, likely downward pressure on the real wage, and so on. Because of the real price reduction, most economists over the years have emphasized the beneficial effects of productivity growth, but they are not inevitable.

This injurious causal chain need not play out under other circumstances. Suppose that effective demand in a Keynesian world is *profit-led.* By reducing unit labor cost at a given money wage, productivity growth will increase profits. By itself the cost reduction may boost exports, and higher profits could stimulate investment demand. For both reasons, output and employment could rise. Evidence discussed in Chapter 5 suggests that demand in the contemporary U.S. economy is in fact profit-led. Interactions of demand shifts with productivity growth along Kaldorian lines affect the business cycle as proposed by Marx (see below). After the early 1980s there was a sharp shift in distribution against wages which ultimately spilled over into the crisis.

Finally, when Say's Law *does* apply, the displaced workers will find employment elsewhere and will benefit from a higher real wage due to lower prices.

Labor Theory of Value

The foregoing reasoning ventures into the contested terrain of the labor theory of value. Ricardo thought that the *natural price* of a commodity should depend on the labor *embodied* in its production, for example, the number of person-hours needed to make a ton of bread *plus* the person-hours needed to produce the flour to make the bread *plus* all the other inputs down the production chain, including the labor used to make fixed capital goods such as buildings and machines.

Ricardo hoped that the commodity's natural price would be determined by its embodied labor. But the calculation is fraught. The input-output matrix algebra needed to compute prices when there are intermediate inputs such as flour going into bread did not become widely known for more than a hundred years. (The first big application in economics outside the USSR was Leontief's input-output study in the 1930s for the United States.) Nor was it clear how to account for producers' markups as well as interest on the loans they had to take on to acquire intermediates (or working capital) and machines (or fixed capital). In later Marxist terminology, the key issues were:

> How to calculate *prices of production* in the sense just indicated. Dividing the money wage by a price index could then provide an estimate of the real wage.
> How to check if a commodity's price of production is related in any coherent way to its embodied labor (or *labor value*).
> How to check if profits computed in terms of prices of production are related to *surplus value* computed in terms of embodied labor.

These questions are still debated, despite well over a century's worth of anathemas lately bristling with matrixes being hurled among contentious scholars. What *is* interesting from a Keynesian point of view is that *cost-based* or *structuralist* inflation theories implicitly rely on the assumption that observed market prices track closely with prices of production based on observed money wages and labor costs, other contributors to cost such as the exchange rate, and producers' markups. From this angle Ricardo looks almost modern, despite the fact that he accepted Say's Law and thought that the general price level was determined by the quantity of money (so that the macro price index would have to determine the money wage rather than the other way around).

Free Trade

Contrary to Keynes (at least at times; recall the discussion in Chapter 1), Ricardo was a free trader. In a line of thought that was picked up by the textbooks, the labor theory of value helped him attack the Corn Laws, or import restrictions on grains ("corn"), mainly wheat. He constructed an example comparing the welfare of two countries ("England" and "Portugal," the latter in reality engaged in ongoing trade disputes with the UK over its role as a grain importer from the United States under the British blockade against Napoleon). The two countries in the model either did not trade *(autarky)* or else enjoyed free trade. They both would benefit initially by moving from autarky to trade.

The reason why is that *within* each country, the prices of two commodities ("wine" and "cloth") were set directly by their labor contents; that is, the prices of production were the same as labor values. Portugal was supposed to use less labor to produce both goods so that it had an *absolute* advantage. In *relative* terms, however, England had a *comparative* advantage in cloth. The ratio of its labor required to produce a unit of cloth to the labor required for a unit of wine was lower than Portugal's.

Enter Say's Law once again. It is the linchpin of the argument in support of the benefits from trade. If commerce suddenly becomes possible between the countries, *and if* their labor forces remain fully employed, then a little thought shows that Portugal will start exporting wine and importing cloth because it can gain from arbitrage. The opportunity cost of wine in terms of cloth is higher in England, so it would pay Portugal to sell wine and buy cloth. As discussed below, Ricardo was well aware of the long-term deleterious effects of specializing in an industry like wine production, which was subject to increasing costs or decreasing returns to scale, but chose not to emphasize it for his version of Portugal.

Just why Portugal doesn't use its absolute advantage to blow inefficient English producers out of business is not explained, nor does the example recount the historical fact that in response to English frigates parked in Lisbon harbor, Portugal renounced industrial development in the Methuen Treaty of 1703. Be that as it may, Ricardo's defense of free trade and subsequent neoclassical extensions became a powerful economic orthodoxy which is still very much with us. As discussed in Chapter 8, the doctrine is the rationale for trade liberalization as pursued by the World Trade Organization and other international institutions that attempt to regulate the global economy.

Economic Dynamics

Portugal's problem with decreasing returns is central to Ricardo's model of macroeconomic dynamics built around an explicit class structure: workers, capitalists, and landowners. It predicted that the economy would arrive at a *stationary state,* with most of the population living at subsistence at best. Economics became known as the "dismal science" because of Ricardo's and Malthus's analyses of the long run.

In a simple summary, one can imagine a country with many small plots of land. With an application of technically fixed levels of capital and labor, each plot can yield a quantity of corn. The plots can be ordered by their yields from the most to the least productive. Bringing a new plot into production produces a decreasing yield of corn.

Away from the stationary state, some plots won't be cultivated because there is not enough capital and labor available to employ all the land. Total corn production at any time is the sum of outputs from plots being used—ranging from a large quantity on the most productive land to much less on the least productive at the *extensive margin.*

Workers get paid a quantity of output set by the product of their number and the subsistence wage per person. The remainder (or surplus output) is divided between capitalists who undertake farming and landowners who rent land out. Ricardo argued that the outcome of their bargain could be predicted from "marginal" analysis of the sort later emphasized by the neoclassical economists. He made two points. First, the owner of the marginal plot could charge virtually no rent for its use, since many plots with nearly equal yields are available. And second, competition among capitalists would force one operating a non-marginal plot to earn a profit after paying rent equal to the profit on the (nearly) zero-rent marginal land. With profits so equalized across plots, capitalists' total income is determined. The remaining surplus product goes to landlords. The amounts range from very little rent for the owner of the marginal plot to a lot for the owner of the piece of land with the highest yield.

Workers and landlords spend all their incomes on corn and the products of an ancillary urban industrial and service sector. (Think of Squire Allworthy in Fielding's *Tom Jones* going shopping in London.) Capitalists save their income and invest (Say's Law applies!) in expanding production. Accumulation proceeds until the extensive margin is pushed to the point where the yield on the least productive plot is just equal to the subsistence wage. Profits are driven to zero, the capitalist class is euthanized, and landlords get all the surplus.

Ricardo's model is tightly reasoned and convincing on its own terms. It had a profound impact on the thinking of both Marx and Keynes, who in different ways took aboard the idea that the capitalist class is doomed to oblivion by the way macroeconomics works. (Keynes's version relied on work by Frank Ramsey; see below).

What Ricardo and Malthus failed to build into their own thinking is that as they wrote, England was going through an agricultural revolution based on enclosure of common land, mechanization, and a four-field crop rotation which added clover and turnips to the traditional grains and fallow. People ate better as a consequence, and population increased. Productivity growth has been the wellspring of rising per capita incomes in the now rich economies since before the time of the classical economists. Although he overstated the significance of the division of labor as a source of ongoing productivity growth, Smith was much closer to the truth than Malthus and Ricardo in this regard.

In his magisterial *History of Economic Analysis,* the Austrian American economist (and exact contemporary of Keynes) Joseph Schumpeter has high praise for Ricardo, but still accuses him of the "vice" of building strong, simple models to make a point rather than using large, complex ones, as in the neoclassical mathematical tradition that he admired. Keynes indulged in the Ricardian vice as well. It is striking how much greater their influence has been than that of the designers of big neoclassical machines.

Friar Lawrence did not do well by Romeo and Juliet, but perhaps for macroeconomics he was correct when he said, "Virtue itself turns to vice, being misapplied, / And vice, sometimes by action dignified."

"Pop" Malthus

Thomas Robert (the name he used during his lifetime) Malthus became Britain's first professor of political economy at the East India College. He will be famous for centuries because of his ideas about population growth sketched above. Allegedly his students called him "Pop," for population.

On the side of macroeconomics he is notable for not quite believing in Say's Law. He opposed repeal of the Corn Laws, for example, because he thought that reducing landlords' income by importing cheap grain would cut back their consumption demand, presumably reducing nonagricultural output.

On similar grounds, he thought that there was a real possibility that gluts or overproduction could occur. But there is no paradox of thrift in his reasoning, because he thought that higher saving would automatically be invested. If output goes up as a consequence, then how can the newly produced goods be sold? One way would be through falling prices and (in terminology favored by Marxists) a *profit squeeze*. But then as Ricardo pointed out, the real wage would rise according to the wage-profit relationship, which is scarcely consistent with Malthus's theory of population! Alternatively, the heavy-spending landlords could step in to save the day.

Cyclical Marx

This book concentrates on Maynard's ideas, not Karl's, although the latter will appear often enough. It makes sense here to sketch briefly what Marx thought about macroeconomics, as a general background for later discussion.

Like all other classical economists, Marx was well aware of institutional context. He emphasized that economies change in irreversible historical time in an overall framework such as "capitalism," "feudalism," or "oriental despotism." Any such mode of production can be characterized by specific social devices for appropriation of surplus product over subsistence consumption.

For the most part, Marx concentrated on the capitalist mode. Its expansion results from accumulation, as in Ricardo, but also from ongoing technical change. Producers adopt new technologies to edge out competitors or because rising real wages can wipe out surplus value, thereby wiping out laggard capitalists as well. Many decades later Schumpeter gave a specific form to such processes when he wrote about innovation-induced *creative destruction* of obsolete technologies and firms.

In contrast to Ricardo's corn-based economy as it monotonously marches toward the stationary state, Marx stressed a *cyclical* theory of growth. At the bottom of a cycle, the real wage is held down by a large reserve army of un- or underemployed workers, and capitalists can accumulate freely. As output expands, however, the reserve army is depleted and the real wage rises, forcing a profit squeeze. Capitalists search for new labor-saving technologies and also invest to build up the stock of capital and reduce employment via input substitution. Excessive funds tied up in machinery, sectoral imbalances, and lack of purchasing power on the part of capitalists to sustain investment (or on the part of workers to absorb the output that new investment produces) can all underlie a "crisis" or cyclical collapse.

In a bit more detail, the profit squeeze will reduce aggregate demand if output and growth are profit-led—one reason why Kalecki and Steindl (both with Marxist training) preferred a wage-led system. Marx's cycle *is* consistent with the pattern in the U.S. economy. Labor productivity growth accelerates along the lines proposed by Kaldor as the growth of output speeds up when it emerges from recession. Rising profits help boost demand until real wages start to go up in a tightening labor market. The profit share then begins to fall, slowing the growth of effective demand at the top of the cycle. Although he set up a model in terms of Say's Law with all profits being automatically invested, in the 1960s the Cambridge economist Richard Goodwin got the dynamics right. Later extensions brought in effective demand (see Chapter 5).

Excess competition in industries with decreasing costs could add to the pressure on profits. A *disproportionality crisis* might occur if (say) productive capacity in consumer goods sectors got out of line with the growth of real wages. General overcapacity from excess past investment could lead to a *realization crisis* or slump. There could also be complications on the financial side of the economy, but they tended to be downplayed in the Marxist tradition.

Interestingly enough, the Austrian school of neoclassical economists shared many of these concerns, both real and monetary. But first we have to look at where their central ideas lay.

Schools of Neoclassical Economists

Neoclassical economics emerged in the last third of the nineteenth century, independently in England, France, and Austria. In retrospect, one can see the new discipline as combining three elements.

The first is *marginalism,* or the idea that consumers solve problems in their heads as to whether to buy a bit more meat or bread. If the prices of both goods are given, they will equate the increase in well-being or *marginal utility* from buying an extra gram of each to its price. Similarly, producers shop for production inputs until they set the *marginal product* of each equal to its cost in the market.

In philosophy this sort of utility-maximizing, cost-minimizing behavior is sometimes called *instrumental rationality.* The idea goes back to the Greeks but is often traced to Hume's *Treatise on Human Nature* of 1740. Neoclassical economists accept it wholeheartedly, with the extension that inconsistent behavior by any actor is not permitted. Moreover, each actor responds only to prices as observed in the market. In this way, *methodological individualism* rules all behavior.

As will be seen in Chapter 4, Keynes could argue with brilliance along such lines. But his analyses of probability and financial markets were significant exceptions. He (along with Soros) emphasizes how financial *conventions* control behavior. The reasoning is close to that of the "later" or "anthropological" Ludwig Wittgenstein's theory of knowledge: cognition, action, and structure of knowledge mutually emerge in a *social* setting. The complication in financial economics is that at times, as in 2007–2009, all aspects of knowledge can be highly unstable!

Competition and arbitrage are a second set of neoclassical building blocks. There are supposed to be many butchers selling meat, so that by comparison shopping, consumers can find the cheapest. On the supply side, a farmer raising grain can switch sales toward cattle breeders or millers, depending on which potential buyers offer better prices. The breeders and millers get their price signals from the butchers and bakers, who need to buy their products, while their own selling prices in turn are determined by consumer choice. Thanks to arbitrage, a single price for the same good for all producers and consumers will be established. All excess profits and rents will be driven to zero when these processes work out.

The third component of marginalism is *accounting* for how markets interact. If demand in some market (say) exceeds supply, then the value of its *excess demand* is demand minus supply multiplied by the current price. Adding up across the economy gives *Walras's Law*, which states that the sum of the values of all excess demands (or, alternatively, *excess supplies*) must be equal to zero. If one market is not clearing, then one or more others must not be clearing as well. Keynes's equilibration of the values of income and output simply asserts that all such market imbalances go away. Neoclassical economics devotes a lot of effort under highly stylized assumptions to show that Keynes's postulate must be true.

The English version of neoclassicism concentrated on the first point and the French on the third. Both accepted that competition and arbitrage rule. The Austrians over several generations elaborated an economic philosophy emphasizing that an *entrepreneur* plays an essential role in supporting competition and arbitrage. They also worried about time lags and technical discontinuities in the structure of production.

In what follows, the history of each marginal variant is briefly sketched. But the real interest lies in how marginalism provided the *micro founda-*

tions for the macroeconomic counterrevolution against Keynes. For future reference, several nineteenth-century formulations are restated in the way that they are used by mainstream economists today.

Jevons and English Marginalism

To a large extent, marginalism in England was an attempt to generalize Ricardo's theory of rent to create an overall explanation of economic behavior. The emphasis was on the demand side and consumer choice, with cost structures and production more or less ignored. The institutional orientation of the classical economists receded, as "political economy" became "economics." William Stanley Jevons is universally acknowledged as the founder of English marginalism.

His main idea in microeconomics was that a rational consumer maximizes *utility* subject to a *budget constraint*, saying that the sum of the values (price × quantity) of purchases of goods is equal to his or her income. Utility goes up with increasing consumption of each good. For the maximization exercise to work, there has to be *diminishing marginal utility*, meaning that an additional gram purchased of any good brings less satisfaction than the gram acquired just before. If a consumer displays such moderation (no ecstasy or meth here), he will achieve the optimal level of satisfaction in the economic aspect of his life. Working out the amounts of goods he consumes is a standard problem in introductory microeconomics. Competition and arbitrage among consumers and their suppliers will ensure that each one faces the same set of prices, so the market balances out.

Flash Forward: The Permanent Income Hypothesis

The habitual physics and mathematics envy of economics begins with Jevons's simple consumer's problem in the differential calculus, something that (say) a Caltech or MIT freshman would have been able to solve in high school, or before. Jevons and his European co-inventors of utility maximization all had some familiarity with mathematics and/or the natural sciences. Their knowledge may not have extended to the *calculus of variations*, which deals with optimization over time (a topic our technological undergraduate would study as a freshman or sophomore). Outside physics, this branch of mathematics is nowadays reworked into *optimal control theory* and is at the heart of mainstream macroeconomics. The formalism was set up during the cold war (more by Soviet than by American mathematicians) to ease the task of guiding missiles. Economists then decided it would help them guide economies as well.

A typical problem involves a lifeguard who spots a person in trouble in front of her tower. She wants to go to the rescue as quickly as she can. Should she run straight toward the water and then go in, or save time by veering off to the side and covering more distance on land because she can run much faster than she can swim? The answer is obvious, but it takes a little effort to work out the quantitative details.

Now consider a simpler problem involving someone who can exactly foresee her lifetime income up to her known time of death, including all the fluctuations up and down. She can borrow and lend money at a zero interest rate. What path of consumption will maximize her lifetime utility? The answer is that her consumption at any time will be a constant equal to the total income she will receive divided by her length of life. (Costless borrowing and lending lets her attain this goal.) The reason is that any blip of consumption upward would have to be met by a blip downward at some other time to hold total lifetime consumption equal to income. But there is diminishing marginal utility of consumption. So the gain in satisfaction from the blip up would be less than the loss from the offsetting blip going down. She will never choose to move away from the constant consumption path.

This little exercise may seem farfetched, but it is in fact the rationale for Milton Friedman's *permanent income hypothesis,* which states that there is 100% *consumption smoothing* in the face of varying income. For most economists in the 1960s, it displaced Keynes's idea that consumption rises and falls with the level of income. They found Friedman's tale more convincing than rival theories discussed in Chapter 6 because it followed from the utility analysis that Jevons and others had pioneered a century before.

Insofar as capital gains are a form of income, the hypothesis was falsified in the United States after around 1980. As sketched in Chapter 1 and detailed in Chapter 5, households increased their consumption markedly, using debt to transform their "transitory" capital gains on equity and housing into higher spending. In 2007–2009 the consumption surge collapsed after falling asset prices made consumers' newly assumed debt burdens unsustainable.

Marshall and Keynes

Following Jevons, Alfred Marshall became the leading English economist and a professor at Cambridge, where he taught Keynes. He raised the mathematical sophistication of economics considerably but buried most of that work in appendixes and footnotes to his *Principles of Economics,* in which he tried to overlay equations with metaphors from evolutionary biology. In so doing he was trying to describe the laws of motion of an economic system which itself was changing over time. The person best equipped for the task would be a participant observer.

Although the influence waned over time, Keynes got much of his methodological approach from Marshall. Referring to Marshall in a letter many years later, he wrote:

> Economics is a way of thinking . . . in terms of models joined to the art of choosing models which are relevant to the contemporary world. It is compelled to be this, because, unlike the typical natural science, the material to which it is applied, is . . . not homogeneous through time. . . . Good economists are scarce because the gift of using "vigilant observation" to choose good models . . . appears to be a very rare one. . . . [E]conomics is essentially a moral science, not a natural science. (14:296–297)

One might add that whenever Marshall was confronted with a macro-level problem, he shied away from it. It took three decades for his star pupil to apply vigilant observation of macroeconomics to construct the *General Theory.*

Walras, Pareto, and General Equilibrium

Joseph Schumpeter thought that in contrast to Smith, Ricardo, and Marx, Léon Walras was "the greatest of all economists." The reason is that he tried, but did not succeed, in writing down a system of equations to show how the economy will function when the individual actions of *all* its participants are taken into account. In other words, he wanted to describe the workings of the invisible hand in all their minute detail. The motivation was to give Adam Smith's metaphor a solid mathematical grounding, and thus to show rigorously how competition leads to a high level of economic well-being. The attempt largely has failed.

Walras made a number of strong assumptions to support his research program, aptly summarized by the great mathematician Henri Poincaré in correspondence in 1901: "You, on your side, regard men as infinitely self-seeking and infinitely clairvoyant. The first hypothesis can be admitted as a first approximation, but the second hypothesis calls, perhaps, for some reservations" (Ingrao and Israel, 1990, 159). An assumption of complete knowledge of economic events, present and future, is characteristic of neoclassical thinking. Especially for financial markets it aroused the wrath of Keynes, for good reason.

The program led to mathematical proofs in the 1950s that a *general equilibrium* for a highly abstract economy exists with various attractive and not-so-attractive properties, sketched below. At the time, the theorems in topology utilized to establish the existence of equilibrium were only a few decades old, adding immensely to the proofs' mathematical appeal for mere economists.

Walras became a professor at the University of Lausanne in Switzerland, where his successors, especially the Italian economist and sociologist Vilfredo Pareto, made up a school. *Pareto optimality* or *economic efficiency* was a major idea they formulated: a general equilibrium will be efficient if claims on goods and services are allocated in such a way as to equalize prices for all agents.

In an efficient equilibrium an improvement in the welfare of one actor is impossible without a deterioration for another or others. Neoclassical economists hope to guide the economy toward a Pareto optimal income distribution, but since many distributions satisfying the efficiency condition are possible, the criterion does not define desirable alternatives very precisely. In one simple example, suppose that there are two agents and ten units each of two goods available. Then an allocation with the first agent having ten and the second zero units of both goods can be efficient, while a situation in which both agents have five units each can be efficient as well. No "welfare" criterion is given to judge between the pair. A *social welfare function* is sometimes invoked to provide a ranking, but where that comes from is never made clear.

Overall, the mathematical results are not heartening. If all consumers have diminishing marginal utilities, all production processes do *not* have economies of scale, and there is infinite clairvoyance à la Poincaré, then the existence proofs go through. The ones most cited were by Kenneth Arrow and Gérard Debreu. They are frequently invoked to underline the virtues of perfect competition, but as pointed out earlier, the invisible hand and decreasing costs are not compatible.

Flash Forward: Wealth Effects and Fat Tails

Further results show that if clairvoyance fails, then an equilibrium will not be Pareto efficient, and that mere rationality in the form of "well-behaved" utility functions puts no restrictions on the nature of equilibrium. In particular, many equilibria may exist. The reason is that price changes create *wealth effects* (or capital gains), which can feed back into one another to destabilize any particular equilibrium. The housing price bubble in the United States provides a practical illustration: the macro economy changed drastically between 2000 and 2007.

Pareto also pioneered the study of inequality and proposed a way to describe a distribution of income or wealth with *fat tails*, which permits a significant portion of the population to be very rich. (This work coincided with a shift in his politics from advocating free enterprise toward some sort of socialism or syndicalism and support of Mussolini.) As discussed in Chapter 7, observed distributions of asset prices and returns usually demonstrate fat tails, to the dismay of standard finance theory.

Flash Forward: Lowbrow Walras

If a general equilibrium is assumed to exist, then usually a *distortion* such as a tax or tariff will rule out full economic efficiency. (Asymmetric knowledge can have the same effect.) The implication is that removing the distortion will lead to a welfare gain. Using a technique first suggested by French engineer-economists in the 1830s who wanted to estimate the benefits of building bridges, a huge microeconomic industry has grown up, trying to quantify the welfare changes.

Figure 2.1 uses standard microeconomic supply-and-demand diagrams for one good to illustrate *deadweight loss* analysis for a fixed (or *lump sum*) sales tax, which is added to the price per unit of output that suppliers charge. The diagrams are a good illustration of how standard microeconomics operates. They are presented here mostly because their logic carries over to the *new classical* and (especially) *supply-side* macroeconomic models discussed in Chapters 4 and 6.

With no tax, the point at which the supply and demand curves intersect

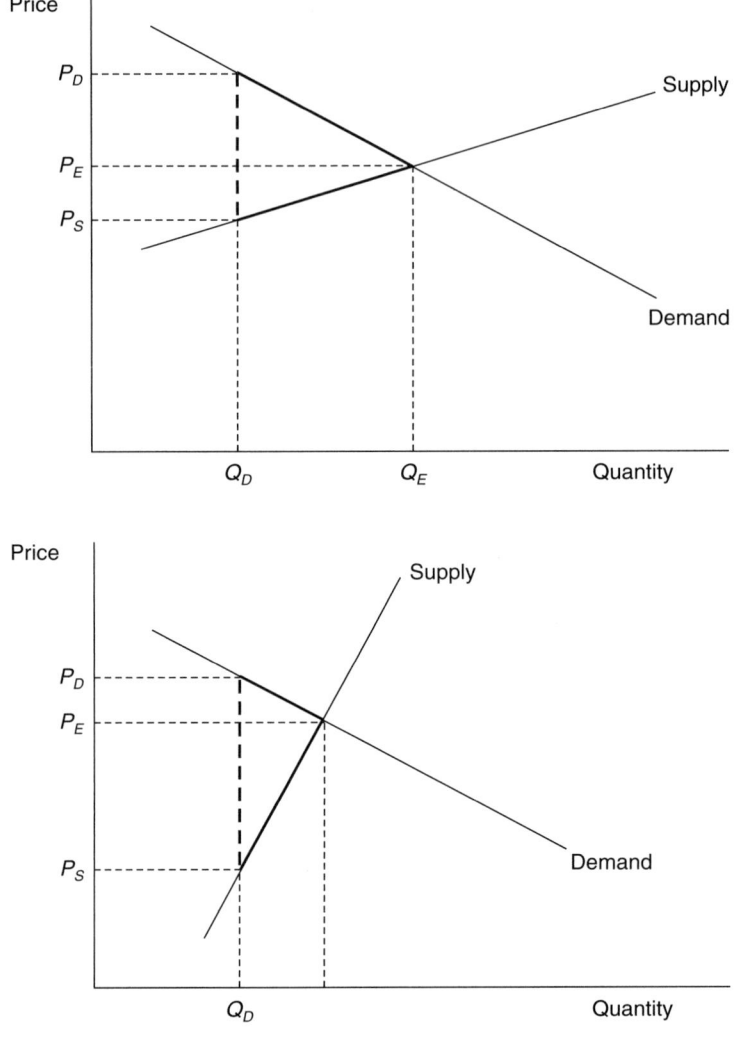

Figure 2.1 Little triangle estimates of welfare losses from a tax when supply responds strongly (upper diagram) and weakly (lower diagram) to a price change

determines the quantity of production and its price. When the tax is imposed, the price consumers pay rises from P_E ("equilibrium") to P_D ("distorted"). The corresponding output levels are Q_E and Q_D. The price that suppliers receive changes from P_E to P_S.

The *little triangles*—or, more elegantly, *triangulitos* in Spanish—marked by the heavy lines are supposed to measure the welfare loss of both *consumers' surplus* and *producers' surplus* caused by the tax. Removing the tax would allow consumers to purchase more (the upper section of the triangles) and producers to make more money (lower section).

Quick points: In applied microeconomics, the triangles are in fact little. With standard parameters describing the supply and demand curves, estimated gains from removing a very steep tax are usually in the range of a percent or two of output. In the upper diagram the supply curve has a shallow slope, meaning that a small price change induces a relatively large change in output. The supply curve in the lower diagram is *inelastic,* or shows a weak price response.

In the upper diagram, when the tax (heavily shaded dashed line) is imposed, the relatively large output decrease implies that the *triangulito* for welfare loss is also large. Total tax revenue (the area between the triangle and the vertical axis) is small. These results reverse in the lower diagram, with its weak response of supply to the price. Because they like to emphasize the welfare losses caused by taxes and other distortions, mainstream economists usually assume that supply (and demand) responds strongly to price changes.

At the macro level, Say's Law would dictate a relatively weak supply response. That idea underlies the famous Lucas macro supply function discussed in Chapter 6.

The Austrian School

Austrian economics emerged with Carl Menger, originally trained as a lawyer and less oriented toward mathematics than Jevons or Walras (though his son Karl became an eminent mathematician). Nevertheless, he shared their goal of replacing classical cost-based theories of value with price determination by marginal utility. He also founded a school of thought that still flourishes.

More than his English and French counterparts, Menger stressed methodological individualism in the sense that each person acts on her own volition and knows best which actions will be beneficial. Her choices are arrived at subjectively, in her own head. These ideas have resonated strongly with libertarians and conservatives who advocate (for example) low taxes because individuals are much better equipped than the government to handle their own money. Because utility is subjective, one cannot make interpersonal comparisons of well-being (as in the example of Pareto efficiency above). After all, a poor man may be happy while a rich man is paralyzed by angst. Therefore economic policy aimed at income redistribution is inadmissible—a message that continues to resonate on the Right.

As already noted, another idea central to Austrian thought is the presence of entrepreneurs who seek to take advantage of perceived opportunities in a world imperfectly and differently understood by economic actors. Successful entrepreneurs may make a fortune; their choices in business advance overall economic welfare. Unsuccessful competitors savor the fruits of bankruptcy. Clearly a process is involved, with implications developed by several generations of Austrians (see below).

Appropriately enough for bourgeois gentlemen and aristocrats from Mitteleuropa, the Austrians were strongly anti-Marxist. Menger's student Eugen von Böhm-Bawerk wrote extensively against Marx in the latter part of the century. The details are not of interest here, but other aspects of his economics are. He worked on the rate of interest, elaborating a "real" theory which complements loanable funds. Interest in this view is a price for transactions between the "present" and a perfectly foreseen "future." The interest rate is supposed to be positive for three reasons.

The first is "different circumstances of want and provision" in present and future, an example being different income levels that affect the marginal utility of consumption (in more modern jargon). Second comes "underestimation of the future," or pure time preference. Finally, we get technical differences between the present and future, for example, more or less "round-aboutness" of production activity in Austrian terms (greater or lesser "capital intensity" in current terminology). These three reasons all fit into contemporary optimal savings models, as discussed below. The market interest rate presumably adjusts to balance these forces, becoming the natural rate equilibrating demand and supply of loanable funds as emphasized by Wicksell (who studied in Vienna).

Böhm-Bawerk also was Schumpeter's thesis adviser. Schumpeter became a deep scholar of Marx from an anti-Marxist point of view but drifted away from mainstream Austrian analysis by emphasizing the role of the entrepreneur in promoting the technological innovations emphasized by Marx. Later in life he thought that corporations were the main vehicle for technical change. Either way, creative destruction of old technologies by newer ones was a natural consequence.

These ideas made Schumpeter a hero in Silicon Valley a few decades after his death in 1950. (He was born in 1883, also the year of Keynes's birth and Marx's death.) Curiously, at the same time that he was elaborating his ideas based on sociology and institutions (almost as an aside, he proposed an economic theory of democracy now widely accepted in political science), he idolized Walrasian general equilibrium but couldn't handle the mathematics. An erratically brilliant man, indeed.

Other notable Austrians include Hayek and Ludwig von Mises. They formulated a business cycle theory complementary to Marx's. As with Wicksell, the primary cause is an interest rate that is being held too low. The consequent credit expansion and stimulus-to-investment demand lead to the same sort of overexpansion of capital and potential imbalances that Marx emphasized.

There can also be an asset price boom, of the sort that led into the events of 1929 (both Mises and Hayek have been credited with predicting the Great Depression) and 2007–8. At some point a credit crunch ensues, leading to a contraction as excess capacity is worked out of the system. This reasoning led Hayek to oppose easing monetary policy to combat recessions, which created controversy with Keynes and his colleagues in the 1920s (see Chapter 4).

Finally, a word on the Austrian view of competition as a process, not a structural characteristic of the economy as postulated by the other neoclassical schools. Simply put, imperfect competition in all its forms—oligopolies, distorted wages, externalities, indivisibilities, asymmetric knowledge, and so on—is doomed to disappear in some not very lengthy run. It will be undone by entrepreneurial forces. Through entry of new firms into oligopolized markets, markups will be driven toward zero; unemployed workers will toil with high productivity at low pay to bid down real wages until every willing hand finds a job; and so on.

The Austrians never went so far as to say that economic externalities or production indivisibilities will be "internalized" through bargained market solutions until socially optimal marginal benefit = marginal cost equalities apply. They were too subtle to engage in teleology around Pareto-efficient resource allocation. But they certainly hinted that economies tended to go in that direction.

Many economists around the North Atlantic—Alan Greenspan, for example—took Austrian assertions to heart. After all, that is why they opposed regulation of financial institutions. Their own self-interest and competitive processes would ensure that they regulated themselves!

Neoclassicals: The Next Generation

Despite this significant impact of the Austrians on contemporary economic thought, it is fair to say that neither they nor the British Marshallians shaped the future of the profession. Rather, as would have pleased Schumpeter, it became overwhelmingly Walrasian. Three people developed ideas that have strongly influenced current views: Irving Fisher and John Bates Clark in the United States and Frank Ramsey in Cambridge.

Fisher, Physics, and Interest

Irving Fisher was active during a key juncture in neoclassical economics and strongly influenced Keynes. He studied at Yale with the great mathematical physicist Josiah Willard Gibbs, who along with many other contributions played a key role in inventing the matrix algebra needed to do the mathematics of input-output and prices of production. Together with a few others he formulated the Second Law of Thermodynamics, which loosely states that "entropy increases." Entropy is disorder, which in any isolated system rises: you can't put Humpty-Dumpty back together again.

Flash Forward: Increasing Entropy versus Reversibility

Gibbs was a master of an older form of mathematical physics that predated the invention of calculus by Isaac Newton and Gottfried Leibniz around 1680. For example, the lifeguard's problem mentioned above was solved—for a ray of light going through a lens, where it travels less rapidly than in a vacuum—by Pierre de Fermat in 1662. This physics of *conservative systems* completely ignores the Second Law. Fisher was a pivotal figure in building it into the neoclassical tradition.

Entropy-free physics reliably describes fundamental processes such as gravitation and quantum mechanics. A basic premise is reversibility, meaning that any dynamic process can be unwound. In practical situations, the postulate of reversibility breaks down. A ray of light presumably does not care which way it runs through a lens. But our poor lifeguard would find it difficult to reverse her motions from her point of rescue to get back to her tower in the same amount of time as it took her to arrive.

In financial markets with asset prices drifting upwards, reversibility implies that traders can rapidly and costlessly place and unwind bets around that trend, regardless of how the price is moving at any particular time. (*Dynamic hedging* is a label frequently applied.) From the Long Term Capital Management hedge fund in 1998 through Enron in 2001 and on to the myriad disasters in 2007–8, traders learned to their sorrow that they cannot always safely borrow to bet that (say) a falling asset price will reliably revert to trend. If there is a fire sale and flight to liquidity when the price does not behave as predicted, the debt remains when those bets cannot be reversed. When debt cannot be honored, bankruptcy awaits.

Regardless of his Newtonian, un-Gibbsian predilections, Fisher made acute observations about macroeconomics. His main contributions were to interest rate theory, from the 1890s to the 1930s, in a long sequence of books and papers. The important ideas included the definition of a real rate of interest and a related potential form of arbitrage between interest and profit rates, a theory of depressions based on commodity price deflation, the notion of an own-rate of interest which entered into Keynes's theory of investment demand, and a model of interest rate determination by loanable funds when there are many actors in the economy.

Flash Forward: Fisher Arbitrage

A *real interest rate* can be defined as the observed nominal rate minus a price inflation rate. If the real rate is defined with respect to inflation of prices of goods and services, then *Fisher arbitrage* says that it should tend to equality with the profit rate from productive activity. One can similarly define a real rate with respect to asset price inflation. In a boom that rate is clearly negative, inducing more asset accumulation. It is painfully positive when prices fall in a crash.

Figure 2.2 demonstrates that at the macro level the real interest rate (defined with respect to commodity price inflation) and the profit rate tend to vary in opposite directions; a high value of one is often observed along with a low value of the other. How this phenomenon fits into Keynesian business cycle theory is discussed in Chapter 4.

There are many ways to estimate a profit rate. The data used to construct the diagram were total profits net of interest and taxes from the NIPA

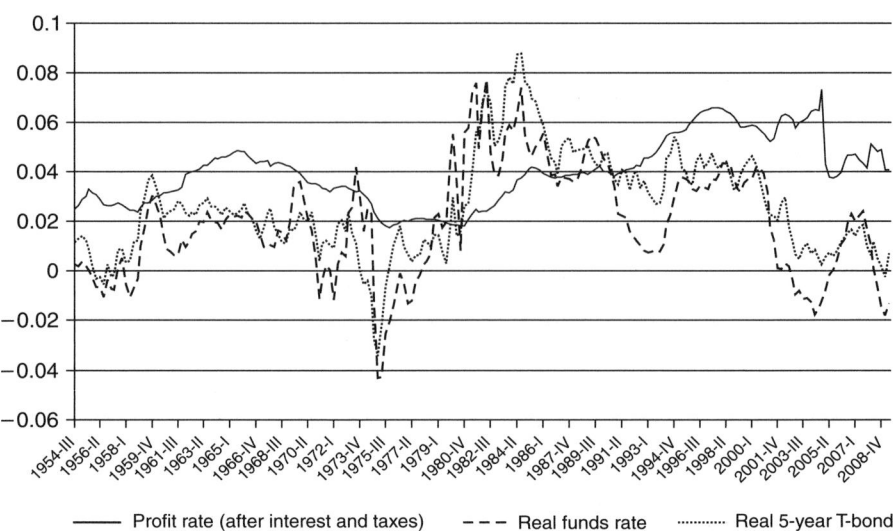

Figure 2.2 Profit rate and real short- and medium-term interest rates

numbers and business tangible capital net of inventories from the FOF accounts. The U.S. profit rate calculated in this way follows the same time pattern as other estimates. Levels are in the range of 10%. The rate trended downward from around 1960 until 1980 and then began to move back up as the income distribution steadily shifted against labor.

The real interest rate for prices of goods and services also varies markedly over time. Based on the GDP deflator, the real short-term Fed Funds rate and the five-year Treasury bond rate were negative during the inflationary 1970s, approached 10% after the Fed's aggressive monetary shock around 1980, drifted slowly downward, and then fluctuated between (roughly) −2% and +2% beginning in the late 1990s. They became negative when the Fed aggressively eased monetary policy in 2007–8.

The *General Theory* contains at least three theories about how investment is determined. One of them, called the *marginal efficiency of capital*, shows up in Chapter 11. It resembles Fisher arbitrage in saying that a firm will compare the marginal or extra return generated by a new investment to the (real) interest rate and go ahead with the project if it is higher. The argument is plausible but clearly of insufficient force to make the profit and interest rates move closely together.

Debt Deflation

Even if the nominal rate is low, the real rate can be strongly positive if there is price *deflation*. In the 1930s this fact led Fisher to propose a *debt deflation* explanation for depressions. With falling prices of goods, debtors' real payment burdens increase. They can be driven to the wall, leading to strong output contraction as they fail to meet their obligations. Attempts to dispose of assets to pay off debt can create another downward spiral as their prices also plummet, liquidating net worth. Along with many New Dealers, Fisher strongly advocated *reflation*. The tools could include monetary expansion, exchange rate devaluation to drive up the price of imported goods, and such direct interventions as the massive hog slaughter program in 1933–34. Japan's problems with generating sustained output growth since the 1990s in the face of stagnant or falling prices is the most salient contemporary example of the ill effects of deflation.

Flash Forward: Own-Rates of Interest

An *own-rate of interest* (or own-rate of return) is a concept introduced by Fisher in the 1890s. An asset will typically have a *spot* price now. One could also pay a (usually) lower *forward* price now for delivery one period (a quarter or a year) in the future. Finally, there will be an *expected* price now which economic actors believe will have to be paid to buy the asset next period. The difference between the expected and spot prices divided by the spot price is a measure of the asset's expected return or own-rate. In other words,

$$\text{Own-rate} = (\text{Expected price}) / (\text{Spot price}) - 1.$$

It will be positive when there is an expected capital gain.

In the early 1920s own-rates figured in a controversy between Piero Sraffa (a Cambridge economist close to Keynes) and Hayek. The focus was on Hayek's emphasis on "excessive" capital formation when the market rate of interest lies below the natural rate.

In opposition, Sraffa said that the short-term interest rate is at best a center of gravitation for the diverse own-rates of other assets. Out of full neoclassical equilibrium there are many observed own-rates. Even in equilibrium they will differ because they represent diverse trends in relative prices, as Fisher realized. With so many potential candidates it is not possible to ascertain what *the* natural rate might be: no observable natural rate, no theory of the trade cycle, and no justification for Hayek's preferred contractionary monetary stance (especially because he himself did not think it makes a lot of sense to compute averages of rates of return across different sectors).

Ironically, in proposing another analysis of liquidity preference and the investment decision in Chapter 17 of the *General Theory,* Keynes to an extent argued along Hayek's lines. The emphasis here is on investment, because the discussion of liquidity preference is muddled, to put it mildly. The basic ideas go as follows.

If firms or rentier investors are thinking about increasing their holdings of a tangible asset (say, a new piece of machinery or an apartment building in New York City), their cost of funds is the short-term interest rate. They will tend to purchase the asset when its own-rate exceeds the interest rate.

With a stable or sluggishly moving expected price of the asset, from the formula above, more purchases will tend to drive up the spot price until the asset's own-rate of interest falls to the level of the short-term rate. At that point investors will stop buying. In other words, there *are* market forces driving own-rates toward the short rate, although they may not complete the task in any brief period of time.

To get to a theory about new capital formation, suppose that the short-term interest rate drops, perhaps in response to expansionary monetary policy on the part of the central bank. The asset's own-rate suddenly exceeds the market rate, making it more attractive than short-term funds for firms or rentiers to hold. In a well-functioning market, a buying process will begin, driving the spot asset price up as just discussed. Typically, the forward price will also increase so that the *spot premium* stays stable. This co-movement of spot and forward prices is what triggers capital formation.

To see why, we also have to bring in the *cost price* of producing the asset. When the forward price rises relative to the cost price, entering into production for forward sale of the tangible asset becomes an appealing option for the enterprises that manufacture it. In other words, there will be an increase in production of new capital goods. This Sraffa-Keynes theory of forward-looking capital formation is deeper than the standard marginal efficiency of capital argument. As discussed in Chapter 5, it was further developed by the Keynesians Hyman Minsky and James Tobin.

Several observations are worth making. The first is that the decision-making process just described relies on the stability of both the expected and cost prices. Suppose that the forward price moves in proportion to the spot price (the spot premium is stable) *and* that the expected price moves in proportion to the forward price. Then the investment increase just described can never happen. An initial rise in the spot price will be matched proportionately by a higher expected price, and a reduction in the own-rate cannot occur. Similarly, if the cost price jumps up when the forward price does, no one can make a profit by producing more of the asset. Basically, the lower interest rate just spills over into price jumps, with no effect on the level of capital formation.

This latter observation shows that nominal cost anchors are an essential attribute of capitalist accumulation. Investment cannot take place unless costs (and in particular wage costs) are relatively stable. Similarly, the current economic situation cannot move unless changes in expectations are sluggish. To state it differently, we have just proved a *policy ineffectiveness* proposition: even if investment is very low, reducing the interest rate will not stimulate more capital formation when prices jump rapidly in response.

Contrariwise, if one believes that the current configuration is "optimal" in some sense, then rapidly adjusting or "rational" expectations become a powerful rhetorical weapon. We're in the best of all possible worlds, and speedy adjustment of expectations will keep us there. Chapter 6 describes how aggressively new classical economists have sold this line.

Loanable Funds: Crusoe and Friday, the United States and China

Finally, Fisher's theory of real interest rate determination provides a rationale for loanable funds. The argument resembles Ricardo's contrast between autarky and free trade for England and Portugal.

"Robinson Crusoe" (a favorite character for economists but no kin to Daniel Defoe's competent colonizer) lives alone and allocates resources between now and next period. He can either consume or invest now, and in the future consume the product produced by the investment. The investment (think of planting corn) will have a marginal own-rate of return. Crusoe also has a marginal *rate of time preference,* with a higher value insofar as he prefers consumption now instead of next period. Standard neoclassical reasoning suggests that he will invest up to the point where the two marginal rates are equal.

Next, suppose that the possibility of transactions with "Friday" opens up. Arbitrage possibilities arise, as with Ricardo's two countries. If Friday has a lower rate of time preference, he will lend corn now to Robinson, who will pay him back next period. Both gentlemen gain in well-being from the commerce, and a natural interest rate emerges to mediate their terms of trade. Such transactions need not be limited to just two players, so in effect Fisher proposed a market-wide determination of the natural rate with loans flowing back and forth among all parties.

In recent neoclassical open economy macroeconomics, it has become customary to identify Crusoe with the United States and Friday with China. The thrifty Chinese have a lower rate of time preference than spendthrift Americans, so they lend us money. From the accounting discussed in Chapter 1, loans from China flowing into the United States must be offset by a deficit or excess of imports over exports on current account. It is as simple as that, although whether mumbo-jumbo about time preference truly "explains" the United States' external gap is perhaps another question. Nor is it obvious that the U.S. current account is driven by capital movements exclusively. International current and capital transactions interact in complex fashion, although analysts often impose highly simplified causal schemes, as will be illustrated in Chapters 3, 6, and 8.

Flash Forward: Clark, Production, and Income Distribution

John Bates Clark started his professional life as a Christian socialist and evolved into a fierce defender of perfect competition. He argued that laws of economics, not conflict and compromise among collective actors, determine the distribution of income between capital and labor. Significantly, the biggest award given by the American Economics Association (to the leading economist under forty) is named after him. Because they are a foundation for mainstream analysis, it makes sense to rephrase Clark's ideas in contemporary terms.

To expand on the discussion in Chapter 1, *gross domestic product at market prices* is the sum of levels of value added across productive sectors (numbered in the tens, the way the data are usually presented). Value added comprises payments to labor, profits, rents, proprietors' incomes (from unincorporated enterprises), and indirect taxes. Ignoring the taxes (so we are now talking about *GDP at factor cost*), lumping rents into profits, and somehow assigning proprietors' incomes (around 10% of the total in the United States, much higher in developing countries) splits value added into payments to "labor" and "capital." As signaled in Chapter 1, dividing nominal value added by a price index based on labor and capital costs (a *GDP deflator*) gives real GDP.

Clark thought that it is possible to construct indexes of labor and capital inputs which can be plugged into an *aggregate production function* to generate real GDP. A production function at the factory level is supposed to be a set of rules for turning inputs (flour, water, energy, labor, and so on) into an output (bread). An aggregate function would somehow net out sales and purchases of intermediate inputs and catalog the rules for producing real GDP from aggregate capital and labor. Not an easy task, with results made even less likely to be realistic because people who play with aggregate production functions in their computer models always assume that they have mathematically "nice" properties as well.

Because we are *not* permitting economies of scale, each input into the aggregate will have a decreasing marginal product in the sense that adding a unit of either capital or labor to an existing production process will create less extra output than a unit added previously (just like the falling productivity of land brought into production at Ricardo's extensive margin). The GDP deflator will embody the two souls conflict mentioned above: if the real wage rises, the profit rate must go down.

On standard neoclassical logic applied across a number of sectors, all of the above turns out to be nonsense, as established in the "Cambridge controversies" in capital theory in the 1960s and 1970s between economists based at MIT led by Paul Samuelson and Robert Solow (who defended Clark) and at the University of Cambridge led by Joan Robinson and Nicholas Kaldor. The technicalities don't need to be rehearsed yet again, but the conclusion is that an aggregate measure of capital as well as aggregate production and cost functions cannot exist. Existing or not, to this day they continue to be used extensively in neoclassical models of macroeconomic growth.

Clark went a step further. As just noted, decreasing returns to labor mean that its marginal product declines when an additional unit is employed. The theory says that firms will hire labor up to the point where its marginal product equals its real cost or *product wage* (the nominal wage divided by the price of the firm's output). That is how the income distribution gets determined by the "laws of economics," including Say's story about full employment of all inputs.

In the *General Theory*, Keynes displayed the annoying habit of calling all economists prior to himself "classical." One of his rhetorical ploys was to accept what he labeled the *first classical postulate:* that to get higher employment, labor must accept a lower real wage. Presumably he adopted the postulate to lure in the orthodox, because he had not shown any such inclinations before (recall his arguments in "The End of *Laissez-faire*").

Empirically, the classical postulate turns out not to be true. It is not easy to define appropriate indicators of labor input and the real wage, but on most metrics the wage tends to increase when output rises, an observation that distresses neoclassical economists. When Keynes was confronted by the data in the late 1930s, he sidestepped his mistake and then suggested that people should go read Kalecki.

Just where these findings leave Clark and neoclassical growth models is not clear. They operate on false premises but retain the loyalty of the bulk of the economics profession. The central example is a model of economic growth deriving from the ideas of Frank Ramsey. It is the backbone of the modern macro view of the world.

Flash Forward: Ramsey on How to Plan Growth

A mathematical version of Irving Fisher's interest rate model discussed above can be extended to include many market participants over any (finite) number of time periods. The market for loanable funds in any period operates because the participants *differ* with regard to their time preferences and production possibilities. These differences create the possibility of *gains from trade* resulting from borrowing and lending among them.

Modern mainstream macroeconomists apparently feel that Fisher makes life too complicated and focus instead on a conveniently immortal single *representative agent* (made up of a growing population of identical individual sub-agents). This entity is a higher-tech version of the consumer featured in Friedman's permanent income hypothesis. Blessed with perfect foresight, it optimizes utility per capita from consumption (or output minus saving) over an infinite time horizon. Output at any time is set by an aggregate production function with inputs from labor provided by the growing population and capital. Thanks to Say's Law, investment automatically equals saving and accumulates into a growing capital stock over time. The template for this model was provided by Frank Ramsey in 1928.

As a philosopher and mathematician, Ramsey stood out even in Cambridge in the 1920s. He was thought to rival Wittgenstein as a philosopher, but had no chance to prove it because he died at age twenty-six. The tone of the writing in his paper on optimal saving suggests that he considered it to be no more than a clever fling of the calculus of variations at an economic problem of some interest. Had he lived a normally long life, in the 1970s Ramsey would presumably have been astounded to see his toy machine supplant the *General Theory* as the central model for macroeconomics. We can quickly go over a contemporary version.

In a bit more detail, the agent maximizes the *discounted* value of utility from consumption per capita over the aforementioned infinite span of time. The discounting is needed to hold maximized utility to a finite value, and to allow the optimization to work, the "pure" discount rate has to exceed the rate of population growth. (Otherwise, discounted utility over time will be infinite.) The discount rate's value is higher insofar as Böhm-Bawerk's second reason for a positive rate of interest ("underestimation of the future") is stronger. In Fisher's terminology, a high rate signals a high rate of time preference. Utility itself increases with consumption but at a decreasing rate. This formulation corresponds to Böhm-Bawerk's first reason ("different circumstances of want and provision").

When the model is solved, it shows that consumption per capita and the capital stock per capita rise over time toward a steady state at which *levels* of both variables grow at the rate of population growth. And that's it—a rather dreary march toward a stable situation less forbidding than Ricardo's stationary state. We'll see in Chapter 6 how new classical economists build productivity growth and cycles into the story and in Chapter 7 how they incorporate risk, but the basic structure of the model remains. Its message for the mainstream is that the economy has a strong tendency to stay close to an "optimal" growth path with full employment while obeying J. B. Clark's distributive rules. No room for financial crises, redistributive policies, and certainly Keynesian macroeconomics in this view of the world.

There is one key decision rule built into the scenario, which brings in Böhm-Bawerk's third reason: a declining profit rate or marginal product of capital as the capital stock increases (in contemporary jargon). It is usually called the *Keynes-Ramsey rule* from a suggestion by Keynes when Ramsey was writing his paper. It says that the growth rate of consumption per capita is proportional to the *difference* between the marginal product of capital (which will be higher when less capital has been installed) and the pure discount rate. The size of the factor of proportionality reflects the strength of Böhm-Bawerk's first reason. As will be seen in Chapter 7, it also stands for the immortal agent's degree of risk aversion in a world with a known probability distribution describing random shocks to the system.

The Keynes-Ramsey relationship describes the time path of per capita consumption before the economy reaches the steady state (assuming it gets there, as discussed a bit farther below). Because the marginal product of capital is falling as capital accumulation proceeds, per capita consumption growth steadily slows to zero at the steady state, described by the condition: Pure discount rate = marginal product of capital.

Discounting figures strongly in contemporary versions of the model, but in the original Ramsey ignored the pure discount rate by assuming that the marginal utility from additional consumption falls to zero at a finite consumption level he called *Bliss*. (He obviously did not foresee modern capitalism's endless ability to create new sorts of goods which consumers feel obligated to buy; see Veblen's ideas on this matter just below.) If the economy settles at a steady state with Bliss, the infinite horizon calculus of the variations problem can be solved even if the pure discount rate is zero. From the Keynes-Ramsey rule, the marginal product of capital then must also fall to zero.

Keynes may have had such a Ricardo-like scenario in mind in his paper "Economic Possibilities for Our Grandchildren" and in the *General Theory*, where he foresaw the euthanasia of the rentier in a zero-profit world. Keynes and Ramsey seem to have shared a *teleological* or *Whig historical* view of long-term economic progress in which the system progresses to an ultimately beneficent end. "Dynamic" mathematical economic growth models usually tend toward steady states in which all variables (or ratios thereof) assume constant values. Model designers often see the steady state as a good predictor of where the economy is going in the "long run." People who work with Ramsey models often fall into this trap. As discussed in Chapter 5, the United States at least has been diverging from any plausible steady state for the past three decades.

Finally, as explained in Chapter 6 after a couple of additional ideas about how economists' (or really physicists') models behave over time have been introduced, the Keynes-Ramsey rule is satisfied by an infinite set of growth trajectories for consumption and capital. Only one will in fact reach the steady state, with the others all diverging toward zero or infinite levels of capital. Such *saddlepoint* behavior shows up in all dynamic optimizing models. In classical physics the analysis describes lightning bolts coming down from the sky. But in economics the diverging paths have to be assumed away on the basis of a superoptimizing invisible hand with perfect foresight forever. Believe it if you want to!

The Anti-Neoclassicals

Neoclassical hegemony in the late nineteenth century was not complete. The Austrians battled with a German historical school, and later with communists, economic sociologists such as Karl Polanyi, and even some Walrasians in a "calculation debate" about whether central planning could be effective. Walrasians aside, the opponents agreed on the irrelevance of the Austrians' abstract economic reasoning based on subjective utility and rational actors. Similar thoughts were raised by an American "institutionalist" school. The leading early members are agreed to be Thorstein Veblen, John R. Commons, and Wesley Clair Mitchell. The latter two, at least, had an impact on Keynes.

Veblen was active around the turn of the twentieth century. He remains famous as a world-class iconoclast with a wickedly satirical writing style. He pilloried neoclassical theory, and his book *The Theory of the Leisure Class* (1899) introduced conspicuous consumption and status emulation as key driving forces behind economic growth. (Ramsey's Bliss would have been quite irrelevant.) The fact that households in the United States ran up debt to keep up living standards after the early 1980s verifies Veblen's insight.

His *Theory of Business Enterprise* (1904) features an analysis of business cycles not far from the ideas of Marx and the Austrians. Veblen was heavily influenced by Herbert Spencer and social Darwinism, and sought to ground economics on evolutionary processes. To a degree, this focus was adopted by later institutionalists.

Commons's contributions are not easy to summarize. He undertook massive empirical studies of labor relations and government policy formation. His theoretical work emphasized the need for rules or controls over conflicting private interests and the competitive process. Perhaps the closest contemporary analogy would be the mutual relationships among labor, business, and the state that constitute the "Nordic model." Keynes paid a great deal of attention to Commons in his industrial policy phase in the 1920s, when to an extent he pursued corporatist goals like those built into Sweden's "middle way" of the time.

Mitchell's influence was more direct, emerging from his lifelong effort to compile data for the analysis of business cycles. He helped found the National Bureau of Economic Research (NBER), which pioneered the empirical analysis of cycles in the United States. His mentors were Veblen and John Dewey, who helped shape his pragmatic conviction that neoclassical theory could not explain cycles.

His prolonged interaction with businesspeople and accountants with their double-entry bookkeeping pointed his interests toward national accounting with an emphasis on the income as opposed to the output side of the ledger. In the 1930s Simon Kuznets took the leading role at the NBER, concentrating on the use of national income as a measure of welfare. Keynes and colleagues (in the late 1930s Erwin Rothbarth at Cambridge and subsequently Richard Stone and James Meade at the UK Treasury) explicitly adopted income = output accounting conventions from the *General Theory* as discussed in Chapter 4. Keynes was in contact with Mitchell and Kuznets, probably knew about their data, and to an extent appropriated their concept of national income. But his double move of postulating the NIPA "identity" and sundering output from a Say's Law aggregate production function was part of his own intellectual journey from the *Treatise on Money* to the *General Theory*.

Money and (Some) Finance in the Nineteenth Century

Most economic thought about the financial system during the nineteenth century was devoted to sorting out the workings of money and banking and trying to figure out if there were linkages between money and the overall price level. Some effort went into describing how to deal with financial crises. Before we get into monetary theory, a good place to begin a discussion is with the balance sheets of the sort of macro financial system that ruled in the nineteenth century.

Financial Structure

Table 2.1 sets out balances for five types of agents or sectors: households, business firms, the government, commercial banks, and the central bank. The entries represent values of *stocks* of physical capital and financial claims.

As already observed in Chapter 1, the values can change in two ways.

Table 2.1 Financial system balance sheets for the nineteenth century

Households		Firms		Government		Commercial banks		Central bank	
Net worth	Capital	Loans	"Faith & credit"	Bonds	Loans	Money	Bonds	Bank reserves
Money					Bank reserves		International reserves	

One is through *flow* accumulation or decumulation over time of the stocks in response to capital formation and net lending or borrowing by different actors. The other mechanism applies to tangible capital and securities such as outstanding shares. (Only the first appears in Table 2.1, but we'll get to equity later.) They have explicit asset prices, so their values can jump "instantaneously" as a result of capital gains or losses. A movement in an asset's price changes its own-rate of interest, as discussed above.

Assets are on the left under each "T-account" heading in the table, liabilities on the right. The sums of entries on both sides must be equal. Households hold only "money" in the form of bank deposits, which constitutes their net worth. Firms hold capital, which they finance by borrowing from commercial banks. There is no significant bond market, so households and banks do not hold liabilities issued by the government. It borrows only from the central bank. The corresponding asset is the "full faith and credit" of the state.

Canceling terms shows that net worth of households is the sum of the value of capital, government bonds (or the state's faith and credit), and *international reserves* (a liability of the rest of the world in more complete systems of accounts; see Chapters 1, 4, and 8). *Primary wealth* as just defined will enter centrally into later discussions.

The money supply is the sole liability of the commercial banking system. Bank equity, though crucial in the 2007–2009 crisis, is omitted here for simplicity. The same goes for non-deposit forms of money such as currency and coins, although they were important in nineteenth-century practice. In simple financial systems, a typical monetary policy instrument is to require commercial banks to hold *bank reserves* (or "high-powered money") against deposits, usually in some fixed proportion (a *reserve requirement*) which is less than 1. Besides deposit reserves, the only other commercial bank asset is outstanding credit or loans to firms. Loans and money are linked via the reserve requirement. Boosting its level forces banks to contract both money and credit. A reduction will be expansionary unless banks choose not to lend and therefore hold *excess reserves*—not an unusual situation after a financial crisis.

Besides the bonds placed with it in one way or another by the government, the central bank's other asset is international reserves. (Holdings of gold and foreign currency by households and firms are assumed to be negligible.) Consolidating the balance sheets of the central and commercial banks shows that the money supply is the sum of loans to firms, credit to the government, and international reserves. As will be seen below, balances of this sort play a central role in monetarist macroeconomics.

Liquidity is often interpreted as a measure of the financial flexibility of an individual actor, group of actors, or the financial system as whole. At a first approximation to be refined in Chapter 4, it constitutes "wherewithal"—the resources readily available for purposes of capital formation or financial transactions. For the household sector in Table 2.1, liquidity takes the form of one *asset,* namely money. Nothing else is at hand.

Flash Forward: Monetarist Policy Analysis

The accounting framework just sketched puts strict limitations on policy options. To fast-forward to the twentieth century, it underlies "open economy monetarism" and the "twin deficit" theory of the balance of payments. To capture the details, assume that money demand is determined by the *equation of exchange:*

$$\text{Money} \times \text{Velocity} = \text{Price level} \times \text{Output}.$$

Velocity is just a factor of proportionality in this equation. The value of output (perhaps GDP) is measured as a *flow* of transactions per unit of time, so velocity measures how many times the money supply, a *stock,* turns over in that time period. Velocity becomes part of a theory of money demand if it is *postulated* as a first approximation to be constant. If output is set by Say's Law, and the price level comes from an inflation forecast or target, then money demand must follow.

Suppose that money demand, somewhat mysteriously, is always equal to the supply provided by the commercial banks. Suppose further that loans to business are set by the needs of production. Then the sum of the government bonds held by the banking system and international reserves must be equal to the money supply minus loans. If international reserves are targeted to increase as the current account or inflow of external finance improves, then government debt must fall via a larger fiscal surplus. For monetarists at least, a clear policy recommendation follows: a bigger fiscal surplus or lower deficit will *cause* the external deficit to decline.

Unfortunately for monetarism, two problems arise. These particular twins are not frequently observed in the data. For most countries (including the United States) in most time periods, roughly offsetting movements of the current account deficit and *private* net lending are the rule. And even when fiscal and foreign deficits appear to be correlated, causality from the latter to the former is often a more plausible narrative than the other way around. (Russia's fiscal deficit contracted smartly when the oil price started to rise in the early 2000s, for example.)

The equation of exchange also supports closed economy monetarist logic. With money supply equal to demand, velocity fixed, and Say's Law in force, the *quantity theory* asserts that the money supply drives the price level. This narrative supports the monetarist theory of inflation as set out by Wicksell and adopted by Friedman. Government becomes the villain behind inflation if a higher fiscal deficit must be *monetized* as an asset of the banking system because there is no private market for public bonds.

Because liquidity in most economies now comprises a spectrum of financial assets and liabilities far wider than just money, twin deficit and monetarist inflation models should be anachronistic. Inflation in Zimbabwe, which took off in the mid-2000s, can be interpreted along monetarist lines, but such events have not been common in the industrialized world. But who knows about the future? Financial systems always contract ("implode" might be a better word) after major crises, restoring a more pivotal role for mere money.

By practicing *quantitative easing* or, in older terminology, *open market purchases* of securities in an attempt to drive the whole spectrum of interest rates down, the central banks of industrialized countries engaged in massive monetary creation in 2008–9 (more details in Chapters 4 and 7). Old-fashioned monetarist inflation could possibly follow. It would harm the United States as the major international debtor nation far less than, say, its creditors China, OPEC, and Japan.

Financial Crises

Crises have been with us for four hundred years, even in financial systems as simple as the one outlined in Table 2.1. Each new sequence of mania, panic, and crash has its own unique features, but the overall patterns are depressingly similar.

One familiar scenario can follow if the government holds financial assets. They might be claims on hypothetical future revenue streams (the South Sea and Mississippi cases discussed below) or equity of state enterprises (a standard case in late-twentieth-century developing country events). Suppose that the assets are privatized in the form of shares and sold through a dealer to the public. If the dealer happens to have a captive commercial bank at his disposal, he can lend money to himself and his cronies to bid up the market price of the assets, leading to a capital gain or ongoing asset price inflation. Other actors may start borrowing from the captive bank and other banks to try to buy shares, setting off a boom that ends inevitably in a crash. The central bank has to permit the expansion of credit and money underlying this process to occur, but that has happened often enough in financial history. (Just consider the Fed in the 2000s!)

Premier examples were the Mississippi and South Sea crises early in the eighteenth century, in which John Law's Banque Générale in Paris and the Swordblade Bank in London issued the loans. With international complications, the Chilean crisis of 1982–83 followed the same pattern around public enterprises privatized by General Augusto Pinochet's Chicago Boy economic team to benefit their graduate school classmates in the private sector.

These examples illustrate a recurring theme (already noted in Chapter 1) in financial instability: capital gains are financed by liquidity in the form of *liabilities* assumed by financial actors to buy the appreciating assets. Manifold possibilities along these lines (including the 2007–2009 crisis, in which the assets featured securitized mortgage loans) are described below and in later chapters.

Money or Credit, Prices or Quantities?

How does money affect the macroeconomy? This question has been hotly debated among economists and more sensible people since before 1750. It can be posed from at least three angles.

First, does money largely control or just respond to developments elsewhere in the economy? Is it "active" (exogenous and determined prior to other variables) or "passive" (endogenous)?

Second, do changes in the money supply mostly affect the volume of activity or the price level? What are the channels through which money has its impacts on quantities and prices?

Third, should we concentrate on changes in "money" (banking system liabilities) or "credit" (banking system assets)?

The standard view is that there is a predetermined money supply which influences prices, as in the monetarist inflation theory discussed above. But in fact over the long sweep of economic thought, one can find eminent partisans of all eight analytical positions implicit in this three-way classification. Table 2.2 presents an outline. I will go through the entries to sketch informally the theoretical views underlying each cell, in roughly chronological order. Lessons for modern macro will be drawn.

Mercantilism and Open Economy Macro

Among the earliest participants in the table are two political parties—the "Hats" and the "Caps"—appearing in the active/quantities/credit and active/prices/credit slots. They flourished in a parliamentary democracy for a few decades between divine right despots in Sweden in the mid-eighteenth century. As their names suggest, the parties represented the big and small merchant bourgeoisie. These obscure historical groupings are of interest because the Hats and Caps were the first proponents of distinctively structuralist and monetarist positions in macro theory.

The Hats were policy activists, urging credit creation to spur the Baltic trade. The Caps countered with arguments that excessive spending could lead to inflation, payments deficits, and related ills. The Hats held power from 1738 until 1765 and pursued expansionary polices supported by subsidies from France. As often happens with such strategies, they pushed too hard, and the Caps' fears were realized. They took over the government and applied strongly contractionary IMF-style remedies. Again as often hap-

Table 2.2 Positions of different monetary analysts

	Main effects of money/credit			
	On prices		On quantities	
Causal status of money/credit	Via money	Via credit	Via money	Via credit
Passive	Hume	Thornton Wicksell Schumpeter	Malthus Banking school	Marx Kaldor Minsky Real business cycle school
Active	Ricardo Currency school Mill Fisher Monetarists	"Caps"	Keynes	"Hats" John Law

pens, this policy line led to a widespread slump, setting up a brief return to power by the Hats and then a coup d'état which reinstated the monarchy with Gustav III on the throne in 1772. Passing from economics to opera, he undertook a successful Hat-style invasion of Russia but was assassinated by aristocratic rivals in 1792, providing the plotline for Verdi's *Ballo in maschera*.

Despite their respective policy failures, the intellectual points raised by the politically warring Swedes carry down through the years. Both parties were mercantilists, hoping to generate a healthy trade surplus. A few decades before, John Law and the backers of the Swordblade Bank resembled the Hats but thought that credit creation could spur domestic enterprise directly rather than just through trade. Caps, Hats, and Law all thought that credit could be controlled by the relevant authorities.

Part of the intellectual reaction against mercantilism took the form of a theory which treated changes in the money supply and the trade surplus as endogenous flows. To keep the story simple, assume that the sole asset of the Table 2.1 banking system is international reserves held in the form of gold (or "specie"). In 1752 Adam Smith's philosopher friend David Hume set up a *specie-flow* model, which leads directly to contemporary open economy monetarism.

Hume's location in the passive/prices/money slot follows from his reliance on Say's Law and the quantity theory. The analysis is quite direct, another example of the Ricardian vice. Suppose that there is balanced trade so that specie is not flowing in or out of the country. If, like the Hats and John Law, policymakers attempt to stimulate the economy by monetary expansion (say, by letting the banking system's money/specie "reserve requirement" decrease), then the price level will rise. Home country exports become more expensive abroad and decline. The resulting trade deficit must be financed by specie flows out of the country. The money supply contracts, and prices fall. As a consequence, "our" exports sell better, the trade deficit declines back toward zero, and specie flows back in.

One implicit assumption is that the export response to falling prices will be strong enough to restore balanced trade. (In the jargon, a *Marshall-Lerner condition* must be satisfied. More on whatever that may mean in Chapter 8.) Another assumption is that the monetary authorities do not attempt to *sterilize* the initial loss of gold by further monetary expansion. In many cases they do just that, forestalling Hume's scenario at least for a time.

In this model, expansionary policy gets you nowhere. Although they reasoned on different grounds and far less cogently, the Caps would have approved of the conclusion. The same is true of the contemporary exponents of policy ineffectiveness described in Chapter 6.

Quantity Theory or No?

In addition to gluts, Malthus and Ricardo disagreed about money. We have already seen that the former argued along proto-Keynesian lines that food prices should be kept high by import restrictions so that landlords (notoriously low savers) would spend on luxuries to support industrial demand. A precursor of the structuralist English *banking school,* Malthus thought that the money supply and/or velocity adjusted endogenously in the equation of exchange to meet demand, or the *needs of trade.*

Ricardo, a superb monetary theorist, consistently accepted Say's Law. He naturally adopted monetarist analysis, most notably in 1810, when he attacked "excessive" British note issue to finance the war against Napoleon. His evidence included a premium on gold in terms of notes within Britain, and a fall of the exchange value of sterling in Hamburg and Amsterdam. His logic was based on the quantity theory and *purchasing power parity (PPP),* or the idea that prices of traded goods rapidly equalize across countries. In 1920 Keynes lost a great deal of money speculating on such price responsiveness (see Chapter 8). Both the quantity theory and PPP are standard components of all subsequent open economy monetarist models.

Ricardo's main policy recommendation was a Friedmanite rule called the *currency principle,* recommending that the outstanding money stock should be strictly tied to gold reserves. Money should not be created for frivolous pursuits such as combating tyranny, and its supply should be allowed to fluctuate only in response to movements of gold. In effect, Ricardo sought to steer monetary policy along the trail blazed by Hume.

The Currency School and Crisis

The currency school, which took the monetarist side in British financial debates well into the nineteenth century, was founded on Ricardo's principle. Its great victory was Prime Minister Robert Peel's Charter Act of 1844 for the Bank of England, which put a limit on its issue of notes against securities. Above the limit, notes had to be backed by gold. This triumph of principle over practice was short-lived, since there was a run against English banks in 1847. The Bank of England acted (correctly) as what the many-sided Walter Bagehot—the defining editor of the *Economist* magazine—in the 1870s christened a *lender of last resort.* It pumped resources into commercial banks in danger of collapse. To this end, the chancellor of the exchequer (Britain's title for its finance minister, who has unusually broad powers) wrote to the bank, saying that the Treasury would indemnify it for any losses, thereby sidestepping the law.

Lenders of last resort are an enduring response to financial panics. Witness the central banks in Washington, London, and Frankfurt attempting to put a floor under the crisis in 2007–2009! One difference in the recent situation is that "commercial" banks had become financial conglomerates in the 2000s, using their deposits as a base for borrowing to acquire increasingly obscure and risky assets. More on this adventure in later chapters.

As the currency school flourished, the liberal philosopher-economist John Stuart Mill (who, like Keynes, was reared by an ambitious father to be a genius and on the whole succeeded) was putting together his own synthesis. In the British tradition, it served as a bridge between Ricardo and Marshall. Mill had some sympathy for the banking school, and also observed that if saving is used to increase holdings of money rather than going directly into capital formation, then Keynesian coordination problems can arise. But he is placed in the active/prices/money slot because he codified the doctrine of loanable funds. He followed Henry Thornton, a contemporary of Ricardo, in thinking that the interest rate would adjust to erase any difference between aggregate saving and investment, thereby validating Say's Law.

After Mill, the quantity theory continued to flourish, featuring the equation of exchange, an exogenous money supply, and Say's Law. Besides writing about loanable funds and the real interest rate, Irving Fisher was a leading exponent of the theory in the first half of the twentieth century. Friedmanite monetarists then took up the task but added little intellectually to a doctrine that had already been in vogue for two hundred years.

Schumpeter and Forced Saving

The final entries in the passive/prices/credit niche of Table 2.2 are Thornton, Wicksell, and Schumpeter (in the case of Schumpeter, at least with regard to the short-run macro adjustment scenario in his doctoral thesis, published in the United States as *The Theory of Economic Development*). Schumpeter's vision transcends mere monetary analysis. It is interesting enough to justify a digression and also introduces *forced saving,* a macroeconomic adjustment process essential to Wicksell and the *Treatise* but repudiated by Keynes in the *General Theory.*

The starting point is rather like the mainstream's Say's Law–Walrasian models of steady growth, which Schumpeter calls *circular flow.* An economy in circular flow may be expanding, but it is not "developing" in his terminology. Development occurs only when an entrepreneur makes an innovation—a new technique, product, or way of organizing production—and shifts production functions or the rules of the game. He gains a monopoly profit until other people catch on and imitate, and the economy moves to a new configuration of circular flow.

The invention or insight underlying the innovation need not be the entrepreneur's. Schumpeter's "new man" simply seizes it, puts it in action, makes his money, and (more likely than not) passes into the aristocracy when he retires. Ultimately his innovation and fortune will be supplanted by others in the process of creative destruction that makes capitalist economies progress.

The key macroeconomic question about this process refers to both the financial and real sides of the economy: How does the entrepreneur obtain resources to innovate? As will be seen, an endogenous money supply and redistribution of real income flows are normally required to support his efforts. Both sorts of processes figure centrally for Wicksell and the early Keynes.

To get his project going, the entrepreneur must invest. According to Silicon Valley legend, Steve Wozniak and Steve Jobs had to rent space and buy inputs to put together the first Apple I and II computers. In Schumpeter's model, their outlays would constitute additional effective demand imposed on an economy already using its resources fully in circular flow. Jobs and Wozniak were financed by a partner, but more typically an innovator would have to obtain loans from the banks. New credit and thereby money are created in the process.

Thanks to Say's Law, the bank loans must be used to purchase goods in momentarily fixed supply. Their prices are driven up, so that real incomes (nominal incomes divided by a price index) of other economic actors decline. The most common examples are workers receiving temporarily fixed nominal wages or the cash flows of non-innovating firms. This process is usually called *forced saving* because workers' lower real incomes obligate them to consume less. Social actors receiving windfall income gains are implicitly assumed to have higher saving propensities, so that overall aggregate demand declines. Meanwhile, routine investment projects may be cut back.

In summary, the transition between states of circular flow is driven by new investment demand, and short-run macro adjustment takes place through income redistribution via forced saving with an endogenously varying money supply. From the principle of effective demand in the *General Theory*, higher output generated by the new investment would permit saving to rise. But Schumpeter believed in Say's Law and thus needed the forced saving mechanism to make his model work.

Schumpeter's beloved Walrasian "marginal this equals marginal that" resource allocation rules that reign in circular flow are necessarily ruptured by the price changes underlying redistribution (a point that Kaldor later emphasized). In a longer run, there can be a cyclical depression due to *autodeflation* as bank loans are repaid; workers can regain real income via falling prices if the innovation cuts costs by raising productivity.

The Banking School and Endogenous Money

Wicksell's macro adjustment story is similar, but before we go there, it makes sense to cover the remaining entries in Table 2.2. The passive/quantities/money banking school was the main rival of the currency school in nineteenth-century British debate. The group is famous (or notorious, depending on one's perspective) for espousing the doctrine of *real bills*. Around the turn of the nineteenth century, the British banking system devoted most of its efforts to accepting, at a discount, paper issued by merchants in pursuit of trade. Following Adam Smith, the banking school's doctrine stated that the banks should discount all solid, nonspeculative commercial paper, that is, true or real debts backed by goods in inventory or transit. How in practice a banker should identify paper tied firmly to the needs of trade was not spelled out, but Smith (if not some of his followers) was well aware of the dangers of a credit collapse if traders were unable to honor bills they had issued which were not backed by material goods.

Thomas Tooke was a well-known member of the banking school with two controversial ideas. One was that higher interest rates drive up prices by increasing the cost of working capital, a notion that resonates to this day. The other countered Smith with a *law of reflux,* through which excessive lending would drive up activity and/or prices and lead the private sector to pay off loans and buy gold: there would be an automatic contraction of the money supply in response to overly aggressive attempts to expand it! Hume's policy irrelevance reappears in structuralist guise, albeit without his specie flow considerations.

Real bills ideas have downside implications as well. If credit needs are *not* satisfied by banks, then new, non-bank financial instruments are likely to be invented to meet the needs of trade. Hyman Minsky in the twentieth century put a lot of emphasis on this sort of financial innovation. Reflux notions show up in the 1959 report on the British monetary system by the Radcliffe Committee and in attacks on Friedman and monetarism by Kaldor. The latter is worth quoting: "If . . . more money comes into existence than the public, at the given or expected level of incomes or expenditures, wishes to hold, the excess will be automatically extinguished—either through debt repayment or its conversion into interest-bearing assets" (Kaldor, 1982, 22). One notes a certain affinity in structuralist positions across 150 years.

Endogenous Money?

The final entries in the table are the real business cycle school and Marx, perhaps demonstrating that economic perceptions can unite strange political bedfellows. The former group is an offshoot of new classical economics, at the mainstream's Walrasian verge extreme. Its members argue that business cycles in advanced economies are due to strong substitution responses (labor versus leisure choices, and so on) to supply-side shocks to the macro system. For example, they say that the Great Depression was caused by a mysterious collapse in productivity growth after 1929.

They deem money unimportant and subject to "reverse causality." They are joined by Kaldor and most post-Keynesian economists in their view that typical central bank responsiveness to the needs of trade plus the presence of inside money render monetary aggregates endogenous: their leads and lags with output depend on institutions and contingencies beyond the analytical reach of standard econometric probes.

Marx, as always, is more complex. The existence of money was central to his view of capitalism, incarnated in the famous $M-C-M'$ sequence, in which exploitation arises as money M is thrown into circulation of commodities C (incorporating labor power and the means of production), which yields a money return M': surplus value is $M'-M$. Access to M gives capitalists a leg up in the economy, making their extraction of surplus possible. At a more applied level of abstraction, Marx roughly adhered to banking school ideas, arguing that money supply varies to satisfy the equation of exchange. This view is consistent with the endogeneity of *inside money,* for example, financial obligations created and destroyed by transactions among firms.

Wicksell's Synthesis: The Inflation Tax

Wicksell's macro adjustment narrative predated Schumpeter's and set the tone for macroeconomics until the *General Theory.* Much of the analysis had been anticipated by Thornton almost one hundred years before, but Wicksell put it on a firm footing. I have already noted that the Keynes of the *Treatise on Money* was a stalwart post-Wicksellian along with Schumpeter (and in the *Tract on Monetary Reform* he backed the quantity theory). Only his revised views in the *General Theory* place him in the active/ quantities/money cell.

Wicksell extended loanable funds theory by proposing that inflation is a *cumulative process* based on the discrepancy between new credit demanded by investors and new deposit supply from desired saving by households (corresponding to a zero rate of inflation) at a rate of interest fixed by the banks.

Suppose that the banks set the interest rate too low. Then an excess of new credits over new deposits leads to money creation. Through the equation of exchange at presumed full employment, the consequence is rising prices. Inflation is driven by endogenous monetary emission, responding to "excess" credit creation.

The key analytical question is how saving and investment are brought together to secure macroeconomic equilibrium *ex post.* Forced saving can provide part of the adjustment, if wages are incompletely indexed to price increases. The rest comes from the *inflation tax* mentioned in Chapter 1. The idea is that an increase in the price level reduces households' *real balances,* or their holdings of money divided by an appropriate macro price index. People are then supposed to increase their saving to restore the real value of their money stock. Like forced saving on the real side of the economy, the "tax" on money leads to a reduction in aggregate demand. It is easy to see that the tax base erodes if velocity increases when inflation speeds up (the monetarists' second approximation to the determination of velocity).

Wicksell thought that after a time, bankers would raise the interest rate to its natural level to bring the cumulative inflation to a halt. (This response was forgotten for decades and then reinvented by mainstream economists as a "Taylor rule" late in the twentieth century.) The key point from Wicksell for our purposes is that through the inflation tax and forced saving, a rising price level liquidates *ex ante* excess aggregate demand. This model is the clearest monetarist alternative to structuralist inflation theories.

Although they both reduce aggregate demand, it bears note that the inflation tax and forced saving operate through different channels. The former reduces real wealth while the latter redistributes real income from low to high savers. In both cases "saving" occurs because consumption falls, with output set by Say's Law. Keynes's Cambridge colleague Dennis Robertson called the inflation tax "induced lacking" (people could choose to consume less) and forced saving "automatic lacking" (they had no choice), if that makes anything clearer.

Wicksellian adjustment mechanisms are not highlighted in the post–World War II mainstream literature, but they are active behind the scenes. Consider the standard textbook aggregate demand/aggregate supply (*AS/AD*) model discussed in Chapter 4. Forced saving is implicit in the model's acceptance of a decreasing real wage as output rises along the AS curve. On the AD side, the inflation tax underlies a drop in demand when the macro price level goes up.

In poor economies, forced saving and the inflation tax routinely show up after inflation stabilizations when consumption jumps and in external crises when supply is constrained by scarce foreign exchange and inflation jumps to hold consumption down. In economies with developed financial markets, money makes up a much smaller proportion of total wealth than in the nineteenth century, while other components such as real estate, equity, and mutual funds may have valuations which go up more or less in line with prices of goods and services (except in the 2007–2009 crash, of course). With credit cards and home equity loans, richer households, which account for the bulk of consumption spending, are less cash-constrained. But they are also more burdened with debt, so that a fall in housing prices, for example, can hit their balance sheets hard. The distributive impacts of price changes that Wicksell and Keynes emphasized are still very much with us.

Wicksell's work is also a steppingstone to the *General Theory*. He assumes that the inflation rate is a decreasing function of the interest rate. As noted above, bankers increase interest if inflation speeds up. One (defective) interpretation of Keynes is that he assumed that a higher interest rate cuts back on effective demand, while a higher level of output may push up the rate because of increasing *transactions demand* for money. Short-term equilibrium levels of the interest rate and output may emerge, similar to Wicksell's mutual adjustment of the interest rate and inflation.

That's not the whole story, of course, but Keynes's move away from the natural rate and Say's Law was an essential contributor to his own new synthesis.

Lessons for Maynard and Friends

Economics in the nineteenth century had much to offer Keynes and his colleagues, but it needed massive reconstruction to serve their purposes. Here are the main points.

Say's Law was (and is) an essential building block in many macroeconomic theories. Its repudiation in the *General Theory* was at the heart of Maynard's revolution. Equally important were his reformulation of the theory of value to set income equal to output and his rejection of the invisible hand's sure guidance of the economy toward full employment with an optimized level of national income. The two souls problem and potential distributive conflict were implicit in the *General Theory* and explicit in the work of later followers of Keynes and (especially) Kalecki.

Wicksell's model of inflation with its forced saving and inflation tax macro adjustment mechanisms obviously had a strong influence on the *General Theory*. So did cost-based structural inflation ideas.

The same is true for several features of Fisher's interest rate theories, especially own-rates of interest.

Keynes adopted the orientation of the classical economists in thinking about collective economic actors. The American institutionalists provided insights on how to fit them into a consistent national accounting framework. They also influenced his ideas about industrial policy.

He was sympathetic to Malthus and the banking school, although in the *General Theory* he adopted a predetermined money supply from the currency school, to be used as a policy instrument.

Ricardo's "dismal science" long-run macro model had echoes in Keynes's views as elaborated by Ramsey. The Ramsey model's steady state reflected prevailing Cambridge opinion about socioeconomic aspects of the long run.

Keynesians after World War II had to wage long battles against the quantity theory of money and its equation of exchange. There was also continuing tension between loanable funds and liquidity preference theories of the interest rate.

Applied macroeconomics has always been bedeviled by recurrent financial crises; the early twenty-first century is no exception.

Smith's emphasis on economies of scale and labor productivity growth resonates with the economic growth models proposed by Kaldor and Robinson.

Finally, as a rhetorical device in the *General Theory*, Keynes picked up John Bates Clark's theories about income distribution, but his heart was not in it.

Notes

Eric Hobsbawm's trilogy (1962, 1975, 1987) covers the long nineteenth century in a masterly way, with his 1994 book bringing the narrative up to date. Karl Polanyi (1944) provides complementary historical background on socioeconomic changes.

The best introductory books about nineteenth-century and later economic thought are by two of my New School colleagues, the late Robert Heilbroner (1999) and Duncan Foley (2006). Blaug (1997) is a slightly distended compendium. The classic scholarly history is Schumpeter's (1954). Dobb (1973) is also very good. John Cassidy (2009), who writes on economics for the *New Yorker* magazine, supplies a helpful summary of mainstream microeconomics and its zoo of "market failures."

Adam Smith is a great read. For nonscholars, Ricardo, Malthus, and Marx are somewhat less so. The standard edition of the *Wealth of Nations* is edited by Edwin Cannan (Smith, 1994). Foley (1986) is an excellent introduction to Marx. Goodwin (1967) set up a Marxist model of cyclical growth which has subsequently been reformulated along Kaleckian and left Keynesian lines. Leontief (1986) summarizes the input-output model, and Flaschel (2009) introduces the two souls problem. You can see the distinction between wage- and profit-led demand in Kalecki and Steindl's own writings, but it took a long time to be set out explicitly, independently by Bob Rowthorn (1982) and Amitava Dutt (1984).

Philip Mirowski (1989) and Joseph McCauley (2004) stress the influence of the physics of conservative systems on neoclassical economic theory. Mirowski also points to the contribution of the institutionalists to Keynes's use of the concept of national income. Bruna Ingrao and Giorgio Israel (1990) describe the correspondence between Walras and Poincaré, and summarize general equilibrium. Ramsey (1928) pioneered the optimal growth model incorporating the Keynes-Ramsey rule. In the context of foreign trade, Taylor and Arnim (2006) go on at length about the imperfections of welfare analysis based on *triangulitos*.

The writings of the early marginalists are not of much contemporary interest. John Bates Clark's *Distribution of Wealth* (1908, 2008) gives a good view of where the turn-of-the-century generation was coming from, methodologically and ideologically. Friedman (1957) presents his consumption function. Irving Fisher (1930, 1967) provides a final summing-up of his views about interest rates. His 1933 article on debt deflation is well worth reading.

Kindleberger (1985) pointed out the historical significance of the Caps and Hats. Schumpeter (1934) is the English-language version of his thesis from 1906. Creative destruction and the economic theory of voting make their bows in his "popular" *Capitalism, Socialism, and Democracy* (1947).

D. H. (Dennis) Robertson was Keynes's student and became his main intellectual foil during his Wicksellian period. Their relationship deteriorated as Keynes shifted toward output adjustment in the *General Theory*. Robertson (1933) presents his "lacking" terminology.

— 3 —

Gold Standard, Reparations, Mania, Crash, and Depression

The goal of this chapter is to use quite old historical episodes to shed light on contemporary policy conundrums. Complications both within a single economy (mostly in the United States) and internationally enter the discussion.

Macroeconomic analysis reacts to shifts in how economies operate. (One hopes that the events of 2007–2009 will provoke a major rethinking!) As Keynes demonstrated, economists do have a learning curve, but especially for an open economy context it can be depressingly shallow. Decades-old events involving international payments flows, financial manias and crashes, and depression still provide lessons for analysis, diagnosis, and prescription for the 2007–2009 crisis.

At the global level the "high" *gold standard* was the organizing principle prior to World War I. As will be seen, its rules helped shape patterns of class conflict, trending prices, and the ways in which financial crises played out. Analysts at the time largely accepted the fiction that the gold standard system operated on the basis of Hume's price-specie flow mechanism outlined in Chapter 2. In practice it did serve as an international equilibrating machine but operated through channels distinct from internal price adjustments in response to gold flowing in and out of a national economy. Changes in interest rates, levels of economic activity, cross-border capital movements, and international terms of trade all played adjustment roles. They could do so because exchange rates were linked to gold and remained stable for decades, removing the destabilizing effects of changing expectations about their levels.

By the time the *General Theory* was published in 1936, the gold standard had expired. Keynes gave the funeral oration by establishing that changes in national incomes were the principal macro adjustment mechanism. Moreover, shifts in the balance of payments did not reside in a Say's Law system of their own but were intimately connected with internal imbalances between incomes and expenditures. Interventions aimed at moving the imbalances necessarily spilled over into external deficits and surpluses.

These conclusions are as relevant today as they were seventy or eighty years ago. Contemporary proposals to restructure the international financial architecture in many ways focus on how to establish a stable system for global macro adjustment. Re-creating the high gold standard (which was *not* so stable and equitable after all) is out of the question, but the myth of its virtues lives on.

With the gold standard as the background, this chapter reviews the histories of debt deflation and the gilded age in the United States in the latter part of the nineteenth century, financial panics, the actual workings of the international economy (with war reparations as significant perturbing events), the German hyperinflation, the Great Crash, the Great Depression (which resulted to a large extent from international macro imbalances), and the New Deal. All influenced macroeconomic thought and practice in significant fashion.

Depression and Gilded Age

It makes sense to begin with a quick summary of the high points of late-nineteenth-century economic history. The 1870s and 1880s did not provide a hopeful beginning for the decades that followed. People in the 1930s searching for historical precedents for their own Great Depression went back to that period. Although there was substantial output growth, contemporary observers saw it as a time of economic malaise. The worst symptom was not mass unemployment but rather steadily falling prices, or deflation. As a consequence, real wages in fact rose. In economies that remained broadly agrarian Say's Law applied so that in line with the two souls relationship from Chapter 2, profits were squeezed. As Irving Fisher later observed, debtors were hit hard by high real interest rates. (Low profits and high real interest showed that Fisher arbitrage did not apply.)

Except in Britain, still the "workshop of the world," which was winding down its agriculture, 40% or 50% of employed males in the now industrialized countries were farmers or farm workers. Declining food prices led to peasant revolts in Europe and an upsurge of agrarian populism in the

American Middle West. The United States did not fully adhere to the gold standard, using instead a form of *bimetallism* in which the value of the dollar was tied to both gold and silver. That permitted populism to animate William Jennings Bryan's famous speech of 1896 to the Democratic national convention in favor of a *silver standard* (details below): "We will answer their demand for a gold standard by saying to them: You shall not press down upon the brow of labor this crown of thorns, you shall not crucify mankind upon a cross of gold."

The United States was still a capital importer, so that at the time Bryan was backing a lost cause—silver to fuel inflation and save the farmers against gold as supported by bankers and big business, which wanted to ensure that money would continue to flow in from London—but that did not detract from his oratorical powers. The "Cross of Gold" speech was a major milestone in the transition of the Democrats from a party of losers advocating limited government toward being the party of easy money and tacit opposition to financial and industrial capital, a transformation that after four decades came to fruition with the New Deal.

For reasons that are not well understood, deflation gave way to economic optimism just as Bryan was making his speech. The period from the mid-1890s until the outbreak of the First World War came to be known as the Gilded Age (the title of an earlier satirical novel by Mark Twain), or more poetically as the *belle époque*. With the end of deflation, real wages fell, while profit incomes along with asset prices tended to rise.

There was substantial technological innovation: the telephone, movies, the phonograph, airplanes, and most notably automobiles. (The first Model T rolled off the assembly line in 1907.) Schumpeter saw long-term cycles as being driven by innovation, and for this period he appears to have been correct. Business was restructured in line with the new technologies, as trusts and cartels thrived.

As usual, financial crises continued to strike. Charles Kindleberger and Robert Aliber's summary table lists eight big ones in Europe and the United States between 1873 and 1907 (2005, 294–303). The panic that began on Monday, October 21, 1907, in New York City was the most severe in the United States and led ultimately to the creation of the Federal Reserve system. The financial collapse took place during a deep output recession. It was triggered by an attempt by Montana mining magnates to corner the copper market by borrowing from New York banks and trusts to buy shares in the United Copper company. They planned to force up prices and bankrupt short sellers but couldn't borrow enough to make their scheme succeed. Runs on the banks they were dealing with ensued, and the stock market crashed.

A *private* lender-of-last resort intervention was orchestrated by J. Pierpont Morgan, the leading banker of the era, who had already raised Wall Street money to bail out the U.S. Treasury in the silver-induced panic of 1893 (see below). Morgan almost literally knocked the relevant heads together in a series of meetings in his library. He brought in New York bankers, John D. Rockefeller, and United States Steel to advance money to the afflicted banks and trusts, which could then (barely) meet requests for withdrawals. Morgan urged the city's preachers to calm the faithful the following Sunday, meanwhile sending emissaries to President Theodore Roosevelt, who had returned from a hunting trip in Louisiana. On Monday he was persuaded to swallow his antitrust reservations about the participation of U.S. Steel, and the panic ended.

Morgan's outsized role set off debates about the plutocracy and the formation of a national reserve bank. After melodramatic episodes including aggressive questioning of Morgan in front of the House Committee on Banking and Currency and a secret meeting of the leading bankers on an island off the coast of Georgia in 1910 (the participants didn't refer to one another by name for fear that the servants would leak), Congress finally passed the Federal Reserve Act in late 1913. It set up a dozen "regional" banks to be concerned with local economic fluctuations and a board of governors in Washington, D.C. Morgan's deputy Benjamin Strong, whom we will meet again, became the first president of the New York Fed and the dominant figure in the system.

The Gold Standard in Practice

As a medium for transactions, precious metals and paper currency started to be tied together early in the nineteenth century in England when bank notes backed by gold superseded bills of exchange. The Bank of England was granted an effective monopoly on the issue of notes in the Charter Act of 1844. In principle, notes could always be traded in for gold.

Defining a unit of circulating currency in terms of a certain amount of gold was the essence of the gold standard. With their currencies tied to gold, countries following the practice had fixed exchange rates with one another. Bimetallism was a complicating factor because it allowed a unit of currency to be tied to some amount of gold *or* silver. The system broke down in Europe after France was forced to pay heavy reparations to Germany mostly in gold after the Franco-Prussian War of 1871. Germany created a new gold standard for its currency, running an inflation in the process. It thereby unloaded tons of silver onto the market. Fearing the spread of inflation (remember the quantity theory of money from Chapter 2!), neighboring countries quickly switched to a pure gold standard as well. One reason why the system functioned in practice was an upsurge in gold production during the latter part of the nineteenth century.

The United States went through a similar episode a bit later when there was a spike in the supply of new silver. It fed into the panic of 1893, with speculation in railroad shares also playing a role. Advocates of "free silver" were pushing for a massive issue of silver coinage to offset price deflation. The Sherman Silver Act of 1890 was a compromise which obligated the Treasury to purchase silver with notes backed by either silver or gold. The scheme backfired as investors sensibly traded in silver-backed Treasury notes for solid metal gold dollars, draining the government's gold supply. Morgan rode to the rescue, the Sherman Act was repealed, and the economy finally turned around in 1896, the year when Bryan made his last-ditch defense of free silver.

While the United States did not officially join until 1900, the high gold standard was effectively in force after the 1870s. One widely accepted rationale, invoked to this day, was that it was anti-inflationary because it tied money supplies to a stable quantity of gold. As noted above, Hume's price-specie flow model suggested that in addition a gold standard should be self-stabilizing, but in fact the system did not work that way. One reason is that central banks could at least partially sterilize movements in gold reserves, increasing domestic credit when reserves started to drop. Capital movements and interest rate changes really played the stabilizing role.

The details are illustrated in Table 3.1 (following Hyman Minsky), which gives a schematic summary of payments flows under the high gold standard. The fulcrum was the Bank of England. As illustrated in the table, Britain had a strong surplus $+A$ on interest and dividend income from investments abroad, which offset a deficit $-B$ on trade in goods and services. The overall current account $+C$ was usually positive. London was the new issues center for the world economy, so that the outflow of funds $-L$ for new long-term investments abroad was a strongly negative item in the overall balance of payments, usually exceeding the current account surplus in magnitude.

Table 3.1 Schematic balance-of-payments flows under the gold standard

	Britain	Rest of world
1. Interest and dividends	$+A$	$-A$
2. Trade and services	$-B$	$+B$
1 + 2	$+C$	$-C$
3. Long-term investments	$-L$	$+L$
1 + 2 + 3	$C - L < 0$	$L - C > 0$
4. Short-term capital, gold	$+G$	$-G$
1 + 2 + 3 + 4	0	0

$+$ = surplus, $-$ = deficit

The balancing items $+G$ were movements of gold and British short-term borrowing. The London money market paid better interest rates than sterile gold, so that specie flowed out only when foreign actors perceived their sterling balances as being too great. (Keynes later saw specie loss as a signal of speculation against the pound. As outlined in Chapter 8, the same thing happened to the dollar in the 1960s.) The Bank of England operated with minimal reserves in comparison to trade flows and debt. Hence when gold started to leave, it would raise short-term interest rates. Long-term rates were also pushed up, making borrowing on the part of other countries more expensive and reducing Britain's long-term investment flows. The sum $C - L$ of the first three tiers in the table became positive, or at least less negative. The balance of payments was mainly brought into line not by changes in imports and exports but rather by movements in the flow L of long-term investment funds.

Less radical analysts have offered additional twists. The Yale economist Robert Triffin (who will appear again in Chapter 8) argued that high British interest rates forced peripheral countries exporting raw materials to reduce inventories and sell into the market. Cheaper British imports (an improvement in Britain's *terms of trade*) reduced the deficit $-B$ in Table 3.1's second tier at the cost of crises in the nonindustrialized world.

In Keynesian fashion, Kindleberger further argued that British long-term lending was *counter-cyclical,* falling when the level of economic activity in the UK was high and rising in slumps. The model is broadly consistent with Minsky's, insofar as an increase in activity would reduce the current surplus $+C,$ inducing a speculative loss of gold and an increase in the interest rate on long-term loans.

In a British recession, the rest of the world's exports to the UK would fall and their terms of trade decline. Rising long-term investment from London, however, would increase capital inflows for the rest of the world, offsetting their deterioration on current account. As will be seen in Chapter 8, such stabilizing behavior does not always occur. Late in the twentieth century the *pro-cyclicality* of U.S. capital movements had a strongly destabilizing effect on the global macro system.

Reparations, Recycling, and Inflation

Movements of international financial capital *not* driven by market forces can also be of fundamental importance. War reparations are an important example.

Recycling Reparations: France Pays Germany

In some ways the imposition of massive reparations after World War I on Germany was payback for payments extracted *from* France after the 1870–71 Franco-Prussian War. How such an international *transfer* can be *effected* is of analytical interest. Open economy macroeconomics pays a lot of attention to the issue, as discussed in Chapter 8.

Table 3.2 presents a schematic of the issues involved. At the table's level of aggregation the accounting restriction that all rows and columns must sum to zero strictly limits the *degrees of freedom* within which the included flow variables can adjust. Such limitations arise frequently in macroeconomic analysis. The incompatibility of Say's Law and the principle of effective demand is only the most prominent example. It is illuminating to work through a simplified version of the widely discussed open economy *transfer problem* here.

France has to transfer an amount T of gold to Prussia. If it has the specie on hand, France sends an outflow $-T$ on capital account (ignoring reserve changes), while Prussia has an inflow of equal magnitude. But because current and capital accounts must sum to zero, France has to run a current account *surplus* of T and Prussia an equal deficit for the transfer to be effected. Asking how current accounts can adjust—via devaluation, changes in the level of economic activity, internal income redistribution, inflation,

Table 3.2 Franco-Prussian reparations

	Prussia	France	Rest of world	Totals
1. Current account	$-T+Z$	$T-Z-Y$	Y	0
2. Capital account—reserve changes	$T-Z$	$-T+Z+Y$	$-Y$	0
1 + 2	0	0	0	

$+$ = increase in surplus, $-$ = increase in deficit

and so on—is the crux of the transfer problem. (We will meet it again, for example, in the discussion of economic relationships between the United States and China.) As Hume might have predicted, inflation in Germany and deflation in France helped the transfer go through in the case at hand.

But suppose France doesn't have enough gold. Then it would have to borrow it. One possibility is to raise an amount Z from Prussia. The reverse movement on capital account would reduce France's required surplus and Germany's deficit. Alternatively, France could borrow Y from the rest of the world (mainly Britain). That would allow France to run a smaller trade surplus while still transferring T to Germany.

In practice the French government, headed by Adolphe Thiers, invented the expedient of issuing a large volume of bonds, or *rentes,* to finance the transfer. These were oversubscribed by buyers both inside *and* outside France. Economic historians debate what share of the reparations was recycled abroad in this fashion, but it apparently was substantial. One reason why such *counterfactual* calculations are never credible is that, as noted in Chapters 2 and 8, the current and capital accounts interact in complicated fashion, and ex post it is impossible to sort the linkages out. But recycling in one form or another has played a crucial role in alleviating crises in which the afflicted country has massive external obligations. In repeated debt crises during the last quarter of the twentieth century, developing countries became very familiar with the process.

Reparations and Conflict Inflation: Germany Can't (or Won't) Pay France

Almost five decades after Thiers and his *rentes,* Maynard Keynes at age thirty-five was a junior member of the British delegation at the Versailles Peace Conference early in 1919. He resigned in May, fled to Cambridge and Bloomsbury weekend retreats, and wrote the three hundred–page *Eco-*

nomic Consequences of the Peace in two months. The book's immense popularity made his international reputation. It was due in part to its purple, perhaps somewhat imaginative passages describing the conference's "Big Four": Georges Clemenceau from France, David Lloyd George from Britain, Vittorio Orlando (by far the weakest of the main players) from Italy, and Woodrow Wilson. Wilson was called "a blind and deaf Don Quixote" with "his mind slow and unadaptable," which made him "an old Presbyterian bamboozled by Clemenceau and Lloyd George." The bamboozlers fared no better.

Hyperbole notwithstanding, Keynes's criticism of the proposed arrangements for German reparations was damning. He argued that the Germans could pay at most $10 billion over many years without major social disruption. The obvious numbers to compare are his estimate of $40 billion being discussed at the conference and the $1 billion paid by France in 1871–1873. After negotiation, the total was set at $32 billion (upwards of $400 billion in today's prices) in early 1921. This amount was reduced by about 50% later in the year.

Estimates vary, but worldwide GDP in current prices in the mid-1920s was around $300 to $400 billion per year, with the United States at about $100 billion. Germany's GDP was probably less than $40 billion. Small wonder that the Germans thought their reparations obligations were astronomical! (In an interesting contemporary contrast, in late 2009 Iceland was being asked to pay "reparations" to depositors in "Icesave" accounts offered in the UK and the Netherlands that failed during the crisis. The amount requested was $5 billion, about one-third of 2008 GDP. History suggests that the Icesave obligations will be recycled, or simply not paid.)

Germany's problem was exacerbated by the fact that it could not resort to Thiers's sleight of hand. The United States was the only country in a position to provide massive loans (as Keynes and many others suggested) but was intent on collecting war debts it claimed were owed by its European allies. Perhaps stimulated by Keynes's polemic, the Germans fell behind in obligatory payments in kind in late 1922. In January 1923 French and Belgian troops occupied the Ruhr in an attempt to force deliveries. Commodity price inflation in Germany was already in the range of several hundred percent per year in December, and by mid-1923 there was open hyperinflation.

As Albert Hirschman and other scholars have emphasized, the price spiral was provoked by the social conflict that Keynes had foreseen (although he did not point to its inflationary consequences). Structuralist inflation theory is based on the observations that commodity price increases are driven from the side of costs, and that costs can be pushed up because of conflicting claims to limited real income flows.

To run a current account surplus large enough to meet its reparations obligations, Germany would have had to devalue drastically. Devaluation basically transfers claims on national income from residents of the country concerned to the rest of the world. Real wages in particular are reduced by a weaker currency, and workers may be in a position to defend their real incomes by pushing up money wages, which can then force up prices. Postwar German real wages were in the range of 60–70% of their prewar levels, and labor was expecting to catch up. Moreover unions retained political power after the end of the war. The fact that Germany could not borrow to support a lower trade surplus brought the latent conflict to a head. When the Reichsbank resorted to money creation to support the workers in the occupied Ruhr, inflation took off.

When it becomes self-perpetuating or *inertial* (in a recent coinage from Latin America), a hyperinflation can be halted in its tracks by creation of a new currency *supplemented by supporting policies.* Stopping rapid price increases takes away the inflation tax and forced saving, so contractionary fiscal policy has to be imposed to offset a jump in private consumption and renewed upward pressure on prices. Foreign loans can let the economy operate with a lower trade surplus. On the positive side, the fiscal deficit may come down automatically because inflation no longer erodes real tax revenues.

Such a package became possible in late 1923, when a new currency called the Rentenmark was issued by a new Rentenbank on the basis of a hypothetical mortgage on productive land. The Rentenmark was tied to gold via a fixed exchange rate. One new mark replaced 1 billion of the old money. Inflation was effectively contained, but the situation remained precarious until the United States relented and provided loans under the Dawes and Young plans beginning in 1924. To an extent the capital inflows resolved the social conflict and allowed stabilization to work. By that time aware of the situation, Keynes in his 1923 *Tract on Monetary Reform* emphasized inflation caused by conflict between workers and his favorite evildoers, the rentiers. In Germany, inflation wiped out much of the latter class's wealth and income claims.

Seeing inflation as a consequence of conflicting claims ignores the quantity theory and its equation of exchange. The equation obviously holds as an algebraic identity. Moreover, velocity has never been observed to rise indefinitely. (Even in chronically inflationary Brazil, the ratio of GDP to the money supply reached a level of "only" 65 in the 1990s.) So money creation has to be present to ratify inflation, but seeing it as a basic cause can very often be misleading.

Finally, a word about how debt relates to asset and commodity prices. Commodity price inflation erodes the value of nominal debt owed to rentiers—to pensioners, endowments of nonprofit institutions, and plutocrats—and in extreme cases can liquidate their wealth. Recollections of the 1920s hyperinflation influence Germans' perceptions about the economy to this day. Early in 2009 their politicians were arguing vigorously against economic stimulus packages financed by fiscal deficits because they might set off inflation. In early 2010 they were opposed to low-interest international loans to bail out Greece, at the risk of forcing that unfortunate country into debt deflation à la Irving Fisher.

Asset price inflation, by contrast, feeds on the expansion of debt or other liabilities. As would soon become clear, a debt-supported asset price bubble can end in a big crash.

The Gold Exchange Standard

The 1929 crash was made in the United States but arose in part from imbalances in the global financial system. Early in the 1920s the United States had a strong trade surplus and substantial interest income flows from abroad. The current surplus had to have as its counterpart either lending to other national economies or increases in reserves. Reserves in all countries were made up of both gold and government liabilities of the leading powers in the postwar *gold exchange standard.* U.S. foreign lending was minimal until the Dawes plan but expanded rapidly thereafter, principally to Europe and Latin America.

The gold exchange standard started to emerge before World War I as metallic gold became scarce relative to the overall price level (the equation of exchange again: gold velocity was perceived to be rising). The financial system's response was to reduce the monetary circulation of gold and begin to use dollars, pounds, and German marks as central bank reserve assets. (The mark dropped out after the war.)

Great Britain suffered an immediate postwar recession, which segued into a boom followed by another recession. The Bank of England stopped supporting the pound, which duly fell against the dollar. As noted in Chapter 1, unemployment remained high. At least partly stimulated by nostalgia for the gold standard, pressure developed to return the exchange rate to its historical par of $4.866 per pound from $3.40 at its weakest. Such an appreciation would leave the pound overvalued by 10–20% according to contemporary calculations. British exports would fall and imports increase unless prices in the United States were to rise or Britain could engineer price deflation. Alternatively, lower interest rates in New York could encourage capital movements toward London.

In his *Tract on Monetary Reform,* Keynes characteristically opposed deflation because it would lead to redistribution of wealth from workers and taxpayers toward rentiers (shades of Irving Fisher and William Jennings Bryan!). His arguments failed to convince Winston Churchill, who in 1925 was serving as chancellor of the exchequer. Although Churchill stated, "I do not pose as a currency expert. It would be absurd if I did; no one would believe me," he pushed a Gold Standard Act through Parliament in May. He did acknowledge an article by Keynes published in March asking whether France, with an embarrassingly weak exchange rate, was not better off than Britain, with its high rate of unemployment.

In subsequent speeches Churchill repeatedly linked London's role as a financial center with the empire and lamented the possibility that a *dollar standard* could replace the pound and gold. He did not use those words exactly (Keynes did in the *Tract*), but he was aware that Britain was approaching the end of an era. The ultimate imperialist hoped to retain Britain's role as the global economic hegemon.

The Great Crash

The British and other European economies did not fare well after 1925. One consequence was a visit to New York in the spring of 1927 by the governors of the central banks of the UK, France, and Germany. They wanted the Federal Reserve to reduce interest rates to ease the balance-of-payments situations in their economies.

As noted above, the Fed system had been set up with twelve regional banks and a board of governors in Washington, D.C. How this contraption should work was still up in air in the 1920s. It was unclear whether it would be dominated by the New York Fed or the board (an ambiguity that was resolved in favor of Washington during the New Deal). Mostly appointed by Presidents Harding and Coolidge, the board was widely perceived to be incompetent. Herbert Hoover, then secretary of commerce, called its members "mediocrities." As president of the New York Fed, Morgan's erstwhile deputy Benjamin Strong dominated the system. Hoover thought that Strong had too little fear of inflation and even worse was "a mental annex to Europe" (Galbraith, 1954, 28). In the event, he went along with his European colleagues and pushed through an interest rate reduction.

Did Strong's decision set off a chain of events leading into the Great Crash? As pointed out in Chapter 1, cheap money can certainly facilitate an asset price boom, but there must be other *sufficient* causes. There certainly have been many periods with low rates during which asset prices did not take off. The rate reduction probably helped launch the stock market mania and crash, but several other factors were significant in 1928–29. One was the fact that the real economy appeared to be sliding into recession after mid-1929, which may have unnerved speculators in October.

At the level of the world economy, U.S. lending abroad was reduced abruptly in 1927–28 as finance was redirected toward Wall Street speculation. A credit squeeze in the rest of the world was a consequence as U.S. lending dried up. It became a contributing factor to the international propagation of the Great Depression.

Leverage and Speculation

Within the U.S. financial sector there was notable expansion of *leverage* in various forms. The essential aspect of a leverage (or *gearing*) strategy is to run up liabilities to acquire assets enjoying capital gains. Examples have already been presented in Chapters 1 and 2. Two were important as the stock market boom really got rolling.

One was *borrowing on the margin,* a financial innovation which may have first appeared in connection with the Dutch tulip mania in 1637. In the late 1920s somebody wishing to buy shares could put up a fraction of the cost and then borrow the remainder from his broker using the newly acquired stock as collateral. The buyer's *leverage ratio* would be the value of the shares divided by his initial outlay. If the broker charged a *margin requirement* as low as 10% (not uncommon in those days), then the buyer could invest $10 and borrow $90 to buy $100 worth of shares. His leverage would initially be equal to $100 / $10 = 10$. During the upswing, interest rates on brokers' loans were not low—on the order of 10% or more. But in 1928 some shares appreciated by as much as 500%, so the cost of credit did not matter.

Paradoxically, the buyer's leverage would *fall* with an increase in the price of his shares. For example, if the share price were to rise by 10%, his investment would be worth $110. He would still owe $90 to the broker, so his stake or *equity* in the investment would be worth $20. Because $110 / $20 = 5.5$, his leverage would decrease dramatically, a clear incentive to borrow more from the broker to buy more shares.

By contrast, if the share price were to fall, leverage would shoot up. The investor's equity could become negative, with debt exceeding the value of his collateral. A *margin call* from the friendly broker asking for more money to cover the negative equity would be the likely next step. An attempt by the investor to sell shares in a falling market to recover his position could easily fail.

Just what event(s) triggered the rapid decline in equity prices on "Black Thursday," October 24, and continued freefalls the following Monday and Tuesday will never be known, and in fact it is not important to know. The mania was going to end sooner or later, and manias often end with a crash. Brokers immediately wired margin calls to their clients, requesting them to make up the negative equity. Many of course could not and were summarily wiped out.

In the 1930s legislation was enacted to empower the Fed to set margin requirements. The level of 50% was selected. To look ahead, the famous "irrational exuberance" speech in 1996 by Federal Reserve chairman Alan Greenspan set off a short-lived drop in the market. After the recovery Greenspan notably did *not* raise interest rates *or* increase the 50% margin requirement. In retrospect he might wisely have done both.

To return to 1929, *investment trusts* provided another form of leverage. They were sponsored by existing financial houses, which usually managed them. The trusts were financed by selling bonds, preferred shares, and common stock. The initial offerings were often oversubscribed at their initial price, creating an immediate capital gain for the sponsor. With their new money in hand, the trusts would buy securities in the market. An interesting aspect of the operation is that the value of a trust's holdings was *less* than its outstanding liabilities. The difference accrued to the sponsor.

There was ample room for leverage. If the trust's holdings enjoyed a capital gain and its bonds and preferred shares stayed constant, then all the gain would be credited to the common stock. Its value relative to bonds and preferred shares would rise. Next, the common stock could be held by another trust managed by the same sponsor, with similar leverage. The common stock of the second trust would appreciate by a multiple of the first's. Trusts sponsoring investment trusts proliferated in 1929. Needless to say, they sequentially collapsed when the market crashed.

Goldman, Sachs, and Company was a major sponsor of trusts. They fell apart after the Crash, but as John Kenneth Galbraith dryly remarked, Goldman ultimately "rescued its firm name from its delinquent offspring and returned to an earlier role of strict rectitude and stern conservatism" (Galbraith, 1954, 147). Or at least until 2007–2009. In early 2010 the Goldman Sachs investment bank was awaiting trial in a court case over alleged fraud in transactions involving synthetic collateralized debt obligations based on credit default swaps.

Other Contributing Factors

Beyond leverage, additional factors contributed to the boom. To finance their lending to clients, brokers were borrowing from both New York and out-of-town banks (some of them abroad), often in the form of *call loans,* which could be canceled at any time. There was a massive withdrawal of loans by the out-of-towners after October 24, which New York banks to a large extent made good. Had they not, the crash could have been even worse.

There were also investors' *pools,* a form of insider trading. Members of the pool would agree to put their resources together to buy a certain stock, driving up its price. If other players joined in, the price would rise even further until, at their chosen date and time, members of the pool would sell out, generating a pleasant capital gain. Sometimes spread by its members, rumors abounded about when a pool was likely to be formed.

Finally, in late March 1929 the ineptness of the Federal Reserve Board was amply demonstrated. The board had studiously maintained silence when the market dropped on Tuesday, March 26. Banks began to trim their sails, and the interest rate on call money went to 20%. Charles Mitchell, head of the National City Bank (a precursor to 2009's ill-famed Citigroup), announced that his institution would support the market and if necessary borrow from the New York Fed to do so. Mitchell was a director of the Fed, and perhaps the most powerful player after Strong's death in October 1928. By the end of the day interest rates had declined and the market rallied.

A few days later Mitchell's bank sent out a letter saying: "The National City Bank fully recognizes the dangers of overspeculation and endorses the desire of the Federal Reserve authorities to restrain excessive credit creation for this purpose. At the same time, the bank, business generally, and it may be assumed the Federal Reserve Banks . . . wish to avoid a general collapse of securities markets such as would have a disastrous effect on business" (Galbraith, 1954, 38). It is clear which horn of the dilemma National City preferred.

Ponzi and Successors

One final note is that after all financial crashes, crooks and swindlers emerge from the rubble. Charles Mitchell himself was tried, and to the surprise of contemporary observers acquitted, for tax evasion at the same time that Franklin Delano Roosevelt was being inaugurated in Washington, D.C. As of early 2010 the authorities had begun to bring charges of insider trading and fraud (notably against Goldman Sachs for its manipulation of credit default swaps; see Chapter 4). But the first major example involved a *Ponzi game,* in which the originator delivers promised high returns to initial investors by using the money that subsequent investors pay in.

The name comes from a scheme to make arbitrage profits from differentials between posted exchange rates and the rates implicit in postal "International Reply Coupons" which were in use in the early 1920s. In Boston, Charles Ponzi set up such an operation, which lasted eight months before federal agents locked up his offices.

In 2008–9 the best-known Ponzi schemer was Bernard Madoff, who claimed to have run an operation paying steady "dividends" of 8–12% per year to his clients over nearly two decades. The whole operation apparently cycled more than $60 billion, or roughly 0.1% of world GDP, and as of late 2009 had outstanding liabilities of at least $20 billion.

Relative to world output, Madoff's operations were hugely surpassed in the 1920s and early 1930s by Ivar Kreuger, the Swedish "Match King." He pioneered the techniques of financial engineering that were perfected in the 2000s—the use of funding vehicles not carried on the balance sheets of his central companies and the creation of new forms of hybrid securities and opaque derivatives. These innovations helped him build up an industrial empire based on construction (he was the prime contractor for Stockholm City Hall, where Nobel Prize banquets are held), mining, forestry, pulp and paper, the Ericsson telephone company, banks, and much else besides his matches. He even set up a motion picture company and discovered Greta Garbo, goddess of the silent movies. After his death Keynes eulogized him as "perhaps the greatest constructive business intelligence of his age."

In the late 1920s Kreuger turned increasingly toward Ponzi finance, shifting funds among his myriad companies and raising money with securities and derivatives on Wall Street to lend to foreign governments in exchange for monopoly positions selling matches. His operations unraveled after the Great Crash when he became increasingly desperate for funds and the interest rates he was required to pay went up. He committed suicide in 1932. After his companies went bankrupt, claimed assets of some $250 million turned out to be nonexistent, about the same share of world GDP as Madoff's total operation. But his real-economy empire was also left behind and became the base for much contemporary Swedish industry.

Kreuger's scheme stimulated subsequent financial reforms. His actions and those of others led to Senate hearings between 1932 and 1934 (usually called the *Pecora investigation,* after its last chief counsel, Ferdinand Pecora) which uncovered a wide range of abusive practices including underwriting of unsound securities and conflicts of interest on the part of major banks. The investigation led to the creation of the *Securities and Exchange Commission (SEC)* in 1934.

Seventy years later the SEC failed to prosecute, or even investigate, Madoff's long-running manipulations. Meanwhile, reputable financial advisers were steering their clients away from his clutches. Regulators, had they chosen to do so, could easily have uncovered such a massive scheme. As discussed in Chapter 7, many similar lapses by the SEC helped inflate the financial bubble.

Even more worrisome is that at least through early 2010, ongoing hearings by a congressional Financial Crisis Investigation Commission had extracted apologies of sorts for the crisis from the likes of Chuck Prince and Robert Rubin (more on their roles in Chapters 4 and 7) but had not delved nearly as deep as the Pecora investigation. There is ample journalistic and anecdotal evidence that there was collusion between subprime mortgage lenders and the major banks supporting them in pumping up an enormous expansion of (ultimately) bad debt in the 2000s. It will be a shame if Madoff becomes the only symbol of financial malpractice leading into the crisis.

My wife grew up in Sweden, so perhaps as a consequence we read Swedish mystery novels on long airplane rides and similar occasions. A surprising number of the villains engage in shadowy financial manipulations involving international electronic or nowadays Internet hocus-pocus backed by solid industrial operations. Obviously the authors absorbed a message from listening to their parents' dinner table conversations about the Match King. Alas that financial regulators' and central bankers' memories of the Great Crash were not as retentive as those of Swedish mystery writers.

The Great Depression

While the fundamental cause of the Great Crash—a speculative hypermania that sooner or later was bound to collapse—is relatively clear, the same cannot be said of the depression that followed. More or less plausible explanations abound as to why it happened and why it finally came to an end. Trying to single out one sole cause or cure leads nowhere. There is plenty of blame and approbation to go around.

Many Explanations

What can be done here is to set out briefly the most convincing candidate explanations and discuss how they may fit into coherent macroeconomic analysis. A useful place to begin is with structural factors underlying the slump. The next set of observations focuses on explaining how economic policy was pursued in the United States and what its effects were. A summary of institutional changes under President Franklin Delano Roosevelt's *New Deal* then leads into a brief overall assessment.

The swing downward beginning in mid-1929 in U.S. indicators of real output has already been mentioned. Rough estimates suggest that in current prices GDP fell by around 12% between June 1929 (when the series begins) and June 1930. The decrease in real terms was 8.5%, showing that price deflation was well under way.

As in the run-up to the recent crisis (see Chapters 5 and 9), incomes in the United States had become markedly more concentrated throughout the 1920s, in terms of both the *functional distribution* between wages and profits and the *size distribution* of household income levels. Whether aggregate demand was wage- or profit-led (recall the discussion of these terms in Chapter 2) at the time is impossible to say. But it seems clear that saving from higher incomes at the top of the distribution in part flowed toward the stock market and fed into the boom.

Capital formation dropped after the crash along with consumption of consumer durables. As Keynes emphasized in the *General Theory,* spending on both categories of goods depends on favorable expectations about the future, which vanished. It also depends on the availability of credit, which contracted sharply throughout 1929 and thereafter. At the same time, consumer demand for necessities was not strong, precisely because the income share of people who were not relatively wealthy was low.

A key feature of any banking system is that its component financial firms are highly interconnected by holdings of one another's assets and liabilities. In the United States in the early 1930s the system was fragmented, but its small "independent" banks were still financially *inter*dependent. When a bank with one or a few branches failed because its localized operations could not be sustained, it damaged its counterparties on both sides of their balance sheets. Households and businesses could not recover the deposit liabilities owed to them by the bankrupt institution. Their loans that it held often could not be refinanced elsewhere. At the same time, deflation forced many borrowers to default on their loans, paralyzing the credit system as banks pulled back from new lending. (A similar combination of *counterparty risks* was a major factor underlying the 2007–2009 crash as well, magnified to an international scale.) There were more than two thousand bank suspensions in 1931, the worst year of the depression, up from well under a thousand per year in the 1920s. At a much grander scale, the collapse of counterparty positions in the financial system was an important contributor to the crisis of 2007–2009.

Already in 1928–29 there had been a diversion of bank lending from what Keynes in the *Treatise* called "transaction circulation" to "financial circulation," which contributed to the incipient recession. (Automobile sales fell by *83%* during 1929 as banks rationed consumers to service the market for brokers' loans.) The trend continued for transactions circulation as banks began to fail. Triffin's observation about the prices of raw materials, mentioned above, also came into play. Without credit available to maintain inventories, producers and importers had to cut prices, leading to price reductions on the order of 10–20% in most countries during 1929–30.

International Complications: A Run for Gold

International complications were rife after the crash. The rails leading all countries toward depression were greased by unstable credit, rapidly shifting international capital movements, and falling prices of traded goods. Many of these difficulties were linked to the gold exchange standard. As interpreted in most countries, it had the effect of fixing the exchange rate and also tying the money supply more or less directly to international reserves in the form of gold. Policymakers were hesitant to violate these rules, some of which had the force of law behind them. With hindsight it is easy to argue that heroic, or maybe even just adroit, implementation of expansionary policy by means of overriding the rules could have staved off the depression. There certainly had been precedents: recall Britain's suspension of the Bank Charter Act in 1847, discussed in Chapter 2. After he took office, Roosevelt was at times credited with heroism.

One specific set of events that worsened the international contraction centered on a rush to gold. In 1926 France returned to exchange convertibility at a weak rate. (Recall Keynes's objections to Churchill's return to the gold standard, noted above.) With a strong current account surplus, it amassed large reserve holdings in the form of sterling and dollars. Like the Chinese authorities in the late 2000s, economic policymakers grew concerned about the worth of holdings in the form of foreign assets subject to potential capital losses if the issuing countries were to devalue. In 1931 the Bank of France started selling sterling for gold. Other countries feared that the UK would have to suspend convertibility and also tried to dispose of sterling. The Bank of England did in fact stop supporting the pound in September.

Next there was a rush to convert sterling to dollars and dollars to gold. The Fed had lost $755 million in gold by October. It raised the discount rate from 1.5% to 3.5%, no doubt deepening the depression. By 1932 international monetary reserves had contracted by about a third, putting strong downward pressure on supplies of money and credit. The gold exchange standard did *not* stabilize the system because it failed to provide international financial intermediation.

International Complications: Balance Sheet Mismatches

On the Continent another problem surfaced in national balance sheets, exacerbated by fears about fixed exchange rates. Deposits from foreigners in German banks amounted to 40% of liabilities. After the Nazi Party posted major gains in an election in September 1930, these funds started to be pulled out. There was a full-blown crisis in 1931. The largest Austrian bank, the Creditanstalt, failed, triggering bank runs throughout Mitteleuropa. Contagion ultimately spread through France to Britain, another factor leading the UK to break from the gold standard in September.

There are interesting parallels between these events and the Asian crisis in 1998. Like the economies on the gold exchange standard, countries in that region had largely unregulated capital accounts. National financial actors had run up large short-term liabilities from borrowing abroad while they mostly held long-term assets valued in local currency. The foreign borrowing helped drive up local asset prices for equity and real estate. The boom rested on *mismatches* in both currency and maturity compositions of balance sheets. Although the Continent was in the midst of depression and Asia in a boom, both sets of financial structures collapsed as a result of runs when the mismatches could not be maintained under the fixed exchange rate rules.

Policy Responses and the New Deal

We will get into the details in later chapters, but a convenient quick categorization splits policies into four groups: international (exchange rates, tariffs or other restrictions on the current account, capital account regulation), fiscal (taxes, government spending), monetary (interest rates, control of money and credit, financial regulation), and targeted interventions aimed at industrial stimulation and institutional change. As will be illustrated below with regard to dollar devaluation, all policies interact—that is why macroeconomics is both simpleminded and a fiendishly difficult line of endeavor—but a classification at least provides a place to start.

In the international arena, if the market for some imported good is functioning smoothly (not always the case!), then its price within the buying country will be roughly equal to the product of 1 plus the tariff rate, the exchange rate (as defined in Chapter 1), and the foreign currency price at the border, which includes transportation costs and the like. The approximate cost of a "home" export abroad will be the home price divided by the exchange rate. Increasing an import tariff will drive up the price of the good in question, presumably reducing purchases from abroad and providing an incentive for local production of substitutes. As with any tax, a higher tariff will drive up the price level, absorb purchasing power, and reduce effective demand. This effect will be more or less completely offset by lower imports and higher production of substitutes.

Devaluation will do the same things along with reducing the foreign price of "our" exports. In general, devaluation will be inflationary. If the economy is not strongly wage-led, there is not a large trade deficit, and real exports rise robustly because of their lower prices abroad, devaluation will increase the level of economic activity. It does appear to be *expansionary* in industrialized countries but has often been observed to be *contractionary* in the developing world.

Herbert Hoover was a staunch believer in the gold standard and a deflationist, but (as Schumpeter put it) these beliefs did not prevent him from reaching for the Republican household remedy of tariffs when agriculture began to experience problems in 1930. In Charlie Kindleberger's words, "The action was important less for its impact on the U.S. balance of payments, or as conduct unbecoming of a creditor nation, than for its irresponsibility" (1986, 291). The Smoot-Hawley Tariff Act raised the average level of protection by around 50%. It set off a fairly rapid increase in the level of economic activity—until other countries started to retaliate with competitive devaluation and their own protectionist legislation. As discussed in Chapter 1, a downward spiral of levels of international trade inevitably ensued. Almost every nation did its best to sustain local production and export unemployment to the rest of the world.

When he finally took office in March 1933 after being elected early the preceding November, FDR reached for the Democratic family remedy of pushing up prices. Already in January he had said: "If the fall in the price of commodities cannot be checked, we may be forced to an inflation of our currency.... This may take the form of using silver as a base, or decreasing the amount of gold in the dollar" (Rauchway, 2008, 60). By May he had congressional approval to pursue the latter course, and the exchange rate against an ounce of gold rose from $20.67 to $30. In January 1934, under a Gold Reserve Act, Roosevelt took title to all the monetary gold in circulation and fixed the price at $35 per ounce, which lasted until the demise of the Bretton Woods system in the early 1970s.

As it turned out, the inflationary devaluation experiment succeeded for unexpected reasons. After a 30% drop between 1929 and 1933, real output did begin to rise and deflation (especially for farm prices) abated. The unanticipated consequence was that the combination of a cheap dollar, little prospect of further devaluation because of the gold exchange standard, and political turmoil in Europe stimulated large flows of the metal toward the United States after 1934. The rest of the world suffered from monetary contraction, but the United States began to thrive.

The Fed, now guided by the populist Mormon banker Marriner Eccles and the Keynesian, possibly communist economist Lauchlin Currie, did not sterilize the inflow by pursuing contractionary policy. In response the money supply grew at around 10% per year in the mid-1930s. By the logic of the equation of exchange, there had to be some consequent increase in the value of output. Much of it came in the form of annual double-digit real GDP growth between 1934 and 1937. Prices were effectively stable. Beggar-my-neighbor policy worked well for FDR.

A World Economic Conference was convened in London in June 1933 to try to deal with the worsening depression. Keynes, by that time the consummate insider, covered it as a reporter for the *Daily Mail* while occasionally dining with the prime minister. There were strong attacks on dollar devaluation at the meeting to which Roosevelt felt he had to respond. He was at his estate on Campobello Island on the Maine–New Brunswick border, unaccompanied by economic aides. His July 3 "bombshell" defense of unilateral U.S. devaluation was forceful, but its economic arguments were mutually contradictory or just plain incoherent. Nevertheless, Keynes wrote that FDR was "magnificently right" in defending national currency management instead of trying to stabilize exchange rates according to (in the president's words) the "fetishes of so-called international bankers." This judgment reflected Keynes's dislike of the distributive effects of trending prices—in both directions. From his Wicksellian heritage he was well aware of forced saving and the inflation tax and their ill effects on wage earners and people holding money, but at the same time he deplored debt deflation. The Roosevelt devaluation was not likely to set off a continuing inflation and might help arrest price reductions—hence its magnificence in Maynard's eyes.

Regarding monetary policy and fiscal interventions just after the crash, there is not a great deal to be said. In early November 1929 the New York Fed violated instructions from Washington and created money to buy Treasury bonds, which helped ease the crunch. In a small dose of Keynesianism which would soon be forgotten, Herbert Hoover, by then the president, modestly reduced taxes and asked firms not to cut wages. Thereafter he pushed through Smoot-Hawley and convened what John Kenneth Galbraith labeled "no-business meetings" at which important people fretted publicly about the deepening depression and did nothing else.

In 1963 Milton Friedman and Anna Schwartz published their *Monetary History* of the United States, a monomaniacal brief for a single cause of the depression. The book still has enormous cachet for monetarist economists. The authors argued that the Fed failed to pursue expansionary policy in the early 1930s, at least in part because it no longer was under the sensible direction of Benjamin Strong. They did not talk much about the contractionary international complications mentioned above.

The problem with the Friedman-Schwartz assertion is that it cannot evade the nineteenth-century controversy between the currency and banking schools about whether the money supply is set by policy or responds passively to the needs of trade. According to the latter view, both prices and output were falling strongly in the early 1930s, and the Fed was simply adjusting to that reality. Keynes and Currie both favored active monetary policy and argued at the time that the Fed *should* have acted more aggressively. But after a great deal of econometric to-and-fro running into the 1970s, a Scotch verdict applies regarding whether it *could* have done so with any effect. As discussed in Chapter 4, expansionary monetary policy works by reducing interest rates. But if no one is willing to borrow even at a very low rate, the effort will be futile because it will amount to "pushing on a string." (This phrase is often attributed to Keynes but really surfaced in a question from Congressman T. Alan Goldsborough to Eccles when he was testifying before Congress in 1935.)

Regardless of the direction of causality, the general conclusion drawn from Friedman and Schwartz was that the Fed should intervene aggressively after a financial crash to preclude a big drop in output. So it did after the stock market collapse in 2000 and in the 2001 recession, accompanied by expansionary fiscal policy in the form of the *regressive* (favoring the rich) Bush tax cuts and spending for the "war on terror." These moves certainly contributed to economic recovery but also helped set up the housing bubble and 2007–2009. Insofar as running a macroeconomy resembles driving a car, after a near miss on the interstate at 75 mph you might think you have things vaguely under control. But you never know what horror show may await you just around the next bend in the road.

Fiscal policy, according to the consensus, was broadly neutral during the initial years of the New Deal. In a clear break with Hoover's distaste for intervention to create jobs, the administration and Congress brewed up an alphabet soup of agencies with acronyms, all aimed at relief and public investment. They had enormous political resonance but were not large enough to push up the fiscal deficit by very much. Roosevelt, moreover, had strong prior beliefs in conservative nostrums, not least a balanced budget. Politically weakened by his aborted attempt to stack the Supreme Court with pro–New Deal justices, and fearing that business would not invest under a radical regime, in 1937 he ordered reductions in public works spending. The federal budget switched from a deficit of 3.8% of GDP in 1936 to a surplus of 0.2% in 1937—a large macroeconomic shock. Meanwhile, the Fed had begun to tighten monetary policy in 1936 because of a buildup of "excess" reserves in the banking system. As a consequence of these moves, output fell by about 6%.

In a four-hour session with Roosevelt, Currie tried to convince him that balancing the budget "to restore business confidence" had reduced effective demand. Keynes, with reputation enhanced by the publication of the *General Theory*, wrote that cutting spending was an "error of optimism." He also advised being kind to businesspeople, who after all are a sort of domesticated animal: "If you work them into the surly, obstinate, terrified mood, of which domestic animals, wrongly handled, are so capable, the nation's burdens will not get carried to market" (Rauchway, 2008, 115).

Roosevelt bought into Currie's and at least the first part of Keynes's advice. In the spring of 1938 he called for a resumption of public works activity. The economy recovered into the following year and then was buoyed strongly by *military Keynesianism* as expenditures on armament ramped up into World War II.

Legislation and the Long Run

Institutional changes built into the New Deal were widespread and remain significant today. Before more general considerations, here is a quick list of key congressional acts in chronological order.

The Glass-Steagall Act of 1933 contained two important provisions.

One was the creation of the *Federal Deposit Insurance Corporation (FDIC),* which collects fees from banks to insure deposits in cases of bank failure. The insurance scheme proved its worth seven decades later by precluding bank runs during the 2007–2009 crisis. The FDIC also has the power, which it has recently exercised, to take over and restructure banks that are on the brink.

The second provision was the creation of a *firewall* between commercial and investment banks, with the former restricted to traditional deposit-taking and lending activities, and the latter allowed to trade securities. The financial industry began to chip away at the wall in the 1980s, and it was finally repealed in 1999. As discussed in Chapters 4 and 7, dominant banks began to use their deposits as a base for trading and financial innovation. The disastrous consequences became clear less than ten years later.

The Securities Exchange Act of 1934 set up the Securities and Exchange Commission to regulate financial markets. At times effective in the past, it failed miserably at its task in the 2000s. The Madoff mess mentioned above was fairly minor compared to other errors (see Chapter 7).

The National Housing Act of 1934 set up the *Federal Housing Administration (FHA)* to insure mortgages. The amendments of 1938 created the *Federal National Mortgage Association (Fannie Mae),* with powers to securitize and resell mortgages. The practice spread to deregulated private financial entities in the 2000s, with dire consequences.

The Wagner Act of 1935 established the *National Labor Relations Board (NLRB)* to support collective bargaining and ban unfair labor practices. Union rights were fairly well protected until 1980 but then steadily eroded under the string of conservative administrations beginning with Ronald Reagan in 1980. One consequence was a shift in the income distribution from wages toward profits and from the rest of the population toward the rich (parallel to the changes in the 1920s), as discussed in Chapters 5 and 9.

The Social Security Act of 1935 contained several provisions, but the most important was Title II, setting the current old-age pension system. As revised over the years, it essentially took the form of a pay-to-go or *pay-go* system in which contributions by current employees finance the (modest) pensions of the retired. Roosevelt, however, with his conservative financial instincts, insisted on the fiction that retirees really benefit from running down their previous contributions into a trust fund. A modified version of Table 3.2 would illustrate the deception. Retirees ("Prussia") dis-save, or run a payments deficit with expenditures exceeding non–Social Security income, to accept their pensions. Interest on assets plus previous contributions in the trust fund (Y from the financial sector or "rest of the world") could go directly toward pensions. But the bulk of the payment has to come from the currently employed ("France") in the form of a payments surplus. That part of the transfer is effected in the United States by a payroll tax, which is regressive because it hits low-income people the hardest. The trust fund fiction also confuses discussion about Social Security because of recurrent projections that it will go bankrupt, which is irrelevant in a pay-go world.

Title IV of the Social Security Act, which set up the *Aid to Families with Dependent Children (AFDC)* or "welfare" program, became a hot political issue after Ronald Reagan became president. AFDC was finally abolished under President Bill Clinton in 1996, at which time expenditures were running at around $25 billion per year. It was replaced by a time-limited *Temporary Assistance to Needy Families (TANF)* program.

The Banking Act of 1935 set up the modern Federal Reserve system with powers concentrated in the board of governors in Washington, D.C.

The Fair Labor Standards Act of 1938 established a minimum wage and maximum hours and outlawed child labor. The 2009 U.S. minimum wage was $6.55 per hour, on the order of two-thirds (or less) of similar payments in western Europe.

All of this legislation went a good distance toward bringing an adequate though austere social safety net or welfare state into existence. The key omission at the time was a national health insurance program. Neither the Roosevelt nor the succeeding Truman administration could ever muster up the courage to try to establish one.

On the plus side, the New Deal did create a social contract which held together for thirty or forty years. It broke down in the 1970s during a period of stagnant output and rising prices, or *stagflation*. The 1973 oil shock was a significant immediate cause, along with increasing social conflict. As discussed in Chapters 5 and 6, a conservative ascendancy followed, which ultimately ushered in the economic events of 2007–2009.

Notes

I am no economic historian. This chapter is aimed at setting a background for macroeconomics and is completely based on the work of others. But I have tried to pay attention to my sources.

Hobsbawm (1987, 1994) provides a clear summary of the period under consideration. Kindleberger and Aliber (2005) and Kindleberger (1993) are helpful about its financial crises. D'Arista (2009a) provides an enlightening history of international monetary evolution beginning with the high gold standard. The full text of the "Cross of Gold" speech is at http://historymatters.gmu.edu/d/5354/.

Minsky (1983) discusses the gold standard and subsequent international financial arrangements. (The citation is to a working paper. I have not been able to find a published version.) Triffin (1964) presents his argument about terms of trade movements under the gold standard. Kindleberger (1985) discusses the cyclicality of British long-term foreign investment.

Structuralist inflation theory was formulated in the 1950s and 1960s by economists associated with the Economic Commission for Latin America, responding in part to rather Wicksellian lectures delivered in Mexico City by Kalecki in 1953. Food price inflation was central to their concerns, as in an English-language paper by the Chilean Osvaldo Sunkel (1960). Along with others, the Argentine Roberto Frenkel and the Brazilian Francisco Lopes came up with the idea of inertial inflation, which was the basis for stabilization packages beginning in the 1980s. Taylor (2004) sets out relevant models.

John Kenneth Galbraith (1954) remains a great read on the crash. The discussion of leverage draws on the Princeton financial economist Hyun Shin, and is highly relevant to the events of 2007–209. See Adrian and Shin (2008).

Kindleberger (1986) is essential on the depression. Eric Rauchway (2008) provides a helpful summary of the New Deal and its legislation. Frank Partnoy's (2009) biography of Kreuger is excellent.

Friedman and Schwartz (1963) presents the monetarist take on the depression. There is a large recent technical literature. Cristina Romer (1992) on the monetary expansion under the New Deal is an important example, along with Barry Eichengreen (1996), damning the gold standard.

4

Maynard Ascendant

From the publication of the *General Theory* until the 1960s Keynes dominated macroeconomics. He also headed a remarkable band of younger economists whose ideas appear in the next chapter. The chapter after that describes the counterrevolution that took hold in the 1960s and was overwhelmingly popular until 2007–2009.

The first part of this chapter concentrates on how to think about finance. Keynes's views about financial uncertainty were completely opposed to contemporary orthodoxy. Given recent events, it makes sense to pay serious attention to them. The discussion begins with a brief sketch of his philosophical background and how it led to a youthful excursion into the meaning of probability and fundamental uncertainty. Keynes's ideas in his *Treatise on Probability* are not easy to grasp and are approached via three other interpretations: frequentist, objective theories about probable events; Bayesian analysis; and subjective expected utility. One key question is whether a "complete ordering" of probabilities of future events can be constructed. Keynes thought not, and he emerges as a sort of "qualitative Bayesian."

Three decades later this approach resurfaced in the *General Theory*'s description of financial markets, which broadly overlaps with thoughts from George Soros. Using simple balance sheets, I present the operations of macro-level finance in Keynes's day.

More complicated balance sheets are then used to show how by the 2000s pro-cyclical instability had been built into the system by a proliferation of derivatives, exotic securities, and off–balance sheet vehicles beyond Ivar Kreuger's most inspired creations. The discussion is lengthy but serves as an essential introduction to the events of 2007–2009. Models of financial "cycles" by Soros and by Keynes in the *Treatise on Money* help illustrate the dynamics of the most recent episode of boom and bust. They are complementary to Kindleberger's less formalized analysis. Minsky's real/financial model is also relevant, as discussed in Chapters 5 and 7.

The real side of the economy is the next major topic. After a sketch of the macroeconomics in the *Treatise on Money* and how it relates to the *General Theory,* the latter's model is quickly summarized: structuralist price formation from costs of production; setting the interest rate with liquidity preference; investment and saving determination from the marginal efficiency of capital (or own-rates of interest) and the consumption function; and the emergence of the principle of effective demand from micro-level behavior subject to the income = output or saving = investment macroeconomic balance.

Implications of the basic model are then discussed, including the effects of wage-cutting, the liquidity trap, dynamics of the trade cycle, and other topics. Keynes's views from the 1940s in *How to Pay for the War* and his work with others on national income accounting close out the discussion. A checklist at the end of the chapter sums up.

Philosophy and Probability

Like Bertrand Russell, Frank Ramsey, Eric Hobsbawm, and countless other Cambridge luminaries, as an undergraduate Keynes was an Apostle, or member of the Cambridge Conversazione Society. This "secret" intellectual debating circle was founded in 1820 by a dozen people (hence the name) and has an illustrious membership. Keynes was admitted in 1903, a decade after Russell. Along with the biographer Lytton Strachey, he was the central figure in his time.

Philosophy

Keynes and his cohort of Apostles were heavily influenced by the philosopher G. E. Moore, a charismatic figure who wrote a *Principia Ethica* and contributed with Russell to the creation of analytical philosophy. During his undergraduate years and for some time thereafter, Maynard's deepest intellectual interest was in philosophy. There is a strong ethical strand in all his economics which dates to his formative years.

Initially Keynes's philosophy was a version of *Platonism* absorbed from Moore. The simplistic summary is that concepts such as "green," "ethics," and "probability" have an independent existence beyond our day-to-day experience. Mathematicians are often Platonists. That is why they say that that they "discover" theorems as opposed to inventing them: they already exist in some mathematical reality that, over the centuries, mathematicians gradually explore. Keynes took a similar approach to probability, treating it as the logical relation of hypothesis to evidence.

Another philosophical strand is that already in 1911 Ludwig Wittgenstein, born in Vienna into an immense fortune which he later renounced, arrived unannounced in Russell's college rooms in Cambridge. Almost immediately recognized as a genius, he was sponsored by Russell and Moore and befriended by Ramsey and Keynes. He left Cambridge in 1913 and, after a series of complications too long to set out here, returned in 1929. Keynes was waiting at the station, thereafter writing to his wife: "Well, God has arrived. I met him on the 5:15 train", (Skidelsky, 1992, 291). Keynes and Wittgenstein shared the belief that people had to "see" things the same way before reasoned discussion could be fruitful. In more applied terms, in Chapter 12 of the *General Theory*, shared perceptions among players in financial markets determine how they operate.

Keynes was a major supporter of Ramsey, who traveled to Austria in the 1920s to discuss and help translate Wittgenstein's draft of his *Tractatus Logico-Philosophicus* from German into English. The *Tractatus* became Wittgenstein's doctoral thesis, sponsored by Ramsey and examined by Russell and Moore. Together with Piero Sraffa, the younger philosophers contributed to Keynes's mature views in the *General Theory* about the unpredictability of economic life, which hinge on his earlier ideas about probability.

Inspired by Moore, in the early 1900s Keynes began to investigate the ethical implications of our actions now for well-being in the future. One key issue was how to reason in terms of more or less likely developments to come. He pursued this line of thought in considerable detail, writing the bulk of his *Treatise on Probability* between 1903 and 1913 and finally publishing in 1921. Its content has considerable interest in and of itself but is not easy to decipher. To set the stage, let's look at three interpretations of probability which Keynes did *not* share.

Probability Theories

First, mathematicians usually set up p*robability theory* (which arose historically in the seventeenth century to analyze games of chance) in terms of *frequencies* of well-defined *events* such as tossing a die. If it is cast repeatedly, then any face—say, 1—will show up around one-sixth of the time. If two dice are tossed, then a combination of faces adding up to 7 will show up about one-sixth of the time, and so on. The probabilities for *all* events (thirty-six of them) in the two-dice set are comparable. One can say definitively that the *odds* (or relative probability) against tossing a 5 are greater than those against tossing a 7. In the jargon, a *complete ordering* of the probabilities of events is possible. Further, a number between zero and one can be assigned to the probability of any event, and the probabilities of all the events being considered sum to 1. Finally, probabilities regarding dice are *objective* and would presumably be accepted by anybody who thinks about the issue.

This example involving a small set of discrete events is rather trivial, but the basic logic extends to probabilities over an infinity of events, for instance, the probability that an asset price will change within a certain range at any time. In finance theory, share price movements are often assumed to be described by a *normal* or *Gaussian* distribution, with its familiar bell-shaped curve. This assumption creates practical problems, as discussed below and in Chapter 7.

In the second interpretation, one may have some *prior* probability, derived from experience, about the likelihood of certain events. The prior can be modified to a *conditional* (or *posterior*) probability on the basis of further information. There is a well-known algebraic formula called *Bayes's Law* (after Thomas Bayes, an eighteenth-century English clergyman who figured it out between writing theology and preaching sermons in the countryside outside London), which can be used to compute the posterior. Intuitively, Bayes's formula computes how the probability of an event *A* can be updated after the observation of another event *B*.

To go back to the dice, the prior probability of throwing a 10 is one-twelfth, because only three of the thirty-six possible outcomes add up to 10 (4 and 6, 5 and 5, and 6 and 4). Now suppose you peek at one die and see that it came up with a 6. Then the conditional probability of getting a 10 is one-sixth, that is, the probability that the second die will show a 4.

This example deals with objective frequencies, but one may also use *subjective* numerical information to construct a prior. Suppose for example that an investigator thinks that most people with a certain form of cancer will survive between three and six years, with four years as the "most plausible." He then conducts a study which shows somewhat shorter survival times. Bayes's Law provides a procedure which can be utilized to combine the two sources of information.

In both these examples there is a complete ordering of all the possible outcomes—getting such-and-such a number when throwing the dice and observing how long cancer patients in fact survive—and the relevant probabilities add up to 1.

Finally, as we get closer to Keynes's territory, there is an epistemological question about whether the methods of Bayesian probability can provide a proper justification for beliefs. In particular, in a critique of the *Treatise on Probability* written in 1926 (published posthumously in 1931), Ramsey argued that subjective beliefs must follow the laws of probability if they are to be mutually consistent. This position is an extension of the neoclassical postulate mentioned in Chapter 2 that under instrumental rationality, decisions must be coherent. As usual Ramsey was a few decades ahead of accepted economic theory. The basic ideas were reinvented by the Italian statistician Bruno de Finetti in 1931 and the American statistician Leonard Savage with a Bayesian twist in 1954. *Subjective expected utility* is by now a widely accepted doctrine.

Ramsey made two basic points. The first is that at the end of the day, beliefs about uncertain events are personal to the individual holding them. Second, if the individual makes coherent decisions, these subjective probabilities can be expressed as parameters of preferences over gambles that meet consistency requirements. To put it in a bit more detail, if someone's degrees of belief satisfy the axioms of probability, then it is *not* possible to construct a series of gambles she will accept that will make her strictly worse off. (She will refuse a *Dutch book,* in gambling jargon.) In a comment on the second point Keynes said that according to it, "the calculus of probabilities belongs to formal logic," but his heart may not have been in it. As will be seen, he himself had invented a striking counterexample in the *Treatise on Probability.* He broadly accepted the first point as well.

The *Treatise on Probability*

Keynes's own treatment of probability hinged on a hypothesis (say, H) and evidence E. He considered a "probability relation" H/E. If E makes H certain to occur, the probability relation takes a value of 1. If E makes H impossible, then the value is zero. In his book, probability relations were considered to be objective, although it doesn't make much difference if they are subjective along Ramsey's line. Reasoning in terms of *H/E* was subject to three strong limitations.

First, *H/E* can be assigned numerical values only in certain circumstances, basically when analysis based on frequencies is possible.

Second, if numerical probabilities cannot be assigned, then sometimes it is possible to rank hypotheses as being more or less likely. The available evidence, however, may not permit a ranking. Consider two very English hypotheses about whether or not one should carry an umbrella in case it will rain. Keynes observes that at times "it is an arbitrary matter to decide for or against an umbrella. If the barometer is high, but the clouds are black, it is not always rational that one [hypothesis] should prevail over the other in our minds, or even that we should balance them—though it will be rational to allow caprice to determine us and waste no time on the debate" (8:32).

In a book called *Risk, Uncertainty, and Profits*, also published in 1921, the Chicago economist Frank Knight reasoned along similar lines, drawing an explicit distinction between situations in which *risk* or *uncertainty* rules. In the former, numerical probabilities or odds can be assigned to events, and they can be ranked. There is a complete ordering. Under uncertainty, numerical probabilities and in many cases rankings are impossible. In the *General Theory*, "caprice" in the quotation above became *animal spirits*, which serve as a plausible means for taking decisions under fundamental uncertainty.

Knight's distinction is now common usage. Shades of gray show up in a famous quotation from Keynes in a 1937 article, "The General Theory of Employment," defending his book:

> By "uncertain" knowledge, let me explain, I do not mean merely to distinguish what is known for certain from what is only probable. The game of roulette is not subject, in this sense, to uncertainty; nor is the prospect of a Victory bond being drawn. Or, again, the expectation of life is only slightly uncertain. Even the weather is only moderately uncertain. The sense in which I am using the term is that in which the prospect of a European war is uncertain, or the price of copper and rate of interest twenty years hence, or the obsolescence of a new invention, or the position of private wealth-owners in the social system in 1970. About these matters there is no scientific basis on which to form any calculable probability whatever. (14:113–114)

One can go further in observing that many "matters" or events that may occur in the future are simply unimaginable in the present. Environmental history is full of cautionary tales about societies that unwittingly set up conditions leading to their own collapse; a book by Jared Diamond, *Guns, Germs, and Steel,* is a recent good read. In other examples, in the 1970s nobody foresaw the opening of the ozone holes in response to the emission of chlorofluorocarbon (CFC) gases; at roughly the same time members of the American gay male community did not expect the advent of AIDS. In the military world the events of 9/11 were not on the Pentagon's or CIA's list of pressing concerns.

In macroeconomics, look back, for example, at the *Great Moderation* of economic performance which was being touted heavily by Ben Bernanke and others in the mid-2000s. He obviously did not (could not?) contemplate the possibility that he would have a gale-force crisis on his hands within a few years. Not being concerned with a potential financial collapse is endemic among market players and economists, even in light of the repeated historical recurrence of such events.

In financial markets operating in the contemporary socioeconomic environment, completely unpredictable events can affect capital gains and returns on assets. (Presumably the Easter Islanders had a different set of social arrangements when they provoked an ecological disaster by systematically denuding their small homeland of trees to help build their statues.) To make their machines function, people who built financial models as discussed in Chapter 7 had to impose a complete probabilistic ordering on changes in asset prices. Although they usually assumed otherwise, the distribution cannot be Gaussian because there are too many crashes: for example, in the U.S. stock market in 1987, the bond market in 1994, foreign currencies in 1998, and all the complications of 2007–2009.

There are two possible responses. One route is to stick with numerical probabilities but to assume that changes in asset prices follow a non-Gaussian distribution with *fat tails* which assigns a relatively high probability to large swings. This approach is illustrated in Chapter 7. It permits price surprises or *black swans* to occur, as recently argued by Nassim Nicholas Taleb, who, it must be said, anticipated the 2007–2009 crisis as well as anyone. But he did so by looking at balance sheets rather than applying formal methods. Reliably estimating parameters that specify the form of distributions with fat tails is difficult if not impossible—one reason why this approach has not been widely pursued.

The other response, discussed in detail below, is to follow Wittgenstein,

Keynes, and Soros and treat market behavior as being shaped by *conventions* formed in a social context. They can change rapidly and unexpectedly when there are unforeseen and perhaps unforeseeable events.

Keynes's third limitation on probabilistic reasoning arises because he did not allow a complete numerical ranking of the probabilities of events. That means he cannot have been a Bayesian. Rather he introduced the concept of *weight of evidence.* The basic notion is that we may have more confidence in our probabilistic beliefs in some circumstances than in others. He illustrated the idea with an *urn problem* of the sort often used in discussions of probability theory.

There are two urns with black and white balls in them. In one case "we know that the urn contains black and white in equal proportions; in the second case the proportion of each color is unknown, and each ball is as likely to be black as white. It is evident that in either case the probability of drawing a white ball is 1/2, but that the weight of the argument in favor of this conclusion is greater in the first case" (8:82).

The upshot is that we now have two concepts to grapple with: the probability that a hypothesis is supported by the evidence, and the weight to be attached to that evidence. In Bayesian language, we might become more (or less) sure about a posterior distribution as evidence, or our credence in it accumulates. Bayes's formula permits a calculation. But with only a partial ordering of events and nonnumerical probabilities, the analysis remains up in the air, as Keynes acknowledges in various passages. Daniel Ellsberg, a later commentator, threw up his hands: "When John Maynard Keynes expresses himself with such diffidence on a subject, it is, perhaps, excusable when later theorists shy from committing themselves upon it . . . but it seems incautious of them to try to ignore the subject entirely" (Ellsberg, 2001, 14).

Ellsberg is well known because he independently invented a paradox which extends Keynes's urn problem. It shows that people behave in contradictory fashion (violating the Ramsey–de Finetti–Savage axioms) when presented with a well-defined gamble and then one with more ambiguity involving balls of various colors. Keynes's weight and Ellsberg's *ambiguity* address similar concerns. Purely probabilistic decisions should be complemented with other considerations, as will be seen in Keynes's analysis of formation of expectations, liquidity preference, and own-rates of interest in the *General Theory.* But he never provided quantifiable guidance about just *how* these considerations should be taken into account.

It looks like an oxymoron, but Keynes was in effect a *qualitative Bayes-*

ian, somehow combining prior hypotheses, evidence, and the weight of evidence to arrive at a view about more or less likely future events. Social information and rules of thumb inevitably come into this cognitive process (in Soros's words). Financial markets provide an obvious arena for these ideas to be applied.

Keynes and Soros on Finance

How finance at times can disrupt the macroeconomic system is a central theme of the *General Theory*. The book also explains why at other times markets can be nicely behaved and stable. The discussion to follow draws heavily on insights from Keynes and Soros, two wise and astute participant observers. To a degree their views overlap with ideas from the recently faddish economics subdiscipline *behavioral finance,* which is briefly discussed in Chapter 7. That literature is not pursued extensively precisely because it is academic. When push comes to shove in the policy world, you are better off relying on thoughtful seasoned practitioners and insightful journalists rather than professors.

The word *expectation* appears throughout the *General Theory*. The meaning lies somewhere between prediction and divination of future events. It certainly is *not* probability theory's *expected value* or long-run average of a random variable (for example, 3.5 when one computes the average of many results from rolling one die, or 7 for two dice). Chapter 12, "The State of Long-Term Expectation," provides the most complete discussion.

Chapter 12

Early in the chapter Keynes says, "It would be foolish, in forming our expectations, to attach great weight to matters which are very uncertain," and then adds a footnote: "By very uncertain I do not mean the same thing as 'very improbable'" (7:148). A reference to the chapter on weight of evidence in the *Treatise on Probability* follows. Keynes goes on to say that long-term expectation "does not solely depend . . . on the most probable forecast we can make. It also depends on the *confidence* with which we make this forecast. . . . The *state of confidence* . . . is a matter to which practical men always pay the closest and most anxious attention. But economists have not analyzed it carefully" (7:148).

A useful way to work into this mare's nest is to begin with observations that Keynes made just after the remark about "uncertain" knowledge quoted above from his "General Theory of Employment." He went on to say that to try to make sensible decisions under such circumstances, we can follow three strategies.

One is to "assume that the present is a much more serviceable guide to the future than a candid examination of past experience would show it to have been hitherto" (14:114). Not too promising, in other words.

Second, current prices and output reflect a *correct* summing up of future prospects which can be accepted "unless and until something new and relevant comes into the picture" (14:114). When *rational expectations* became the dominant macroeconomic doctrine in the 1970s, Keynes's caveat was simply ignored.

Finally, we can rely on the "judgment of the rest of the world which is perhaps better informed. . . . The psychology of a society of individuals each of whom is endeavoring to copy the others leads to what we may strictly term a *conventional* judgment" (14:114).

Keynes concludes that the conventions thus established "on so flimsy a foundation" may be subject to sudden and violent changes. The illustration provided in Chapter 12 comes from Maynard's own place and time (although it does show up occasionally on contemporary American television). It is a *beauty contest.*

Keynes was thinking not of Miss Merrie Olde England but rather of 1930s competitions in British tabloid newspapers in which readers were asked to rank photos of young women in the same order of beauty that they thought would be the average preferences of all the competitors. The winning player would not express his or her own preferences or a guess at genuinely average preferences, but rather would reach "the third degree where we devote our intelligences to anticipating what average opinion expects the average opinion to be." In financial markets, professionals dig deeper. "There are some, I believe, who practice the fourth, fifth, and higher degrees" (7:156).

There is no reason to expect a market—a financial market in particular—operating on such principles either to make correct assessments about the "beauty" or somewhat more business-oriented attributes of corporations such as their potential profitability, or to be stable against shocks:

> A conventional valuation which is established as the outcome of the mass psychology of a large number of ignorant individuals is liable to change violently as a result of a sudden fluctuation of opinion due to factors

which do not really make much difference to the prospective yield, since there will be no strong roots of conviction to hold it steady. In abnormal times, . . . the market will be subject to waves of optimistic and pessimistic sentiment, which are unreasoning and yet in a sense legitimate where no solid basis exists for a reasonable calculation. (7:154)

The beauty contest thus acts as a *social* magnification device for Keynes's old fundamental uncertainty about whether or not to carry an umbrella, spread across many "ignorant individuals." It also conforms to Wittgenstein's idea, mentioned in Chapter 2, that cognition, action, and structure of knowledge mutually emerge in a social setting.

Markets driven by average opinion about what average opinion will be demonstrate two special behavioral patterns. As the quotation states, in "abnormal times" they can be volatile and prone to severe loss of liquidity when all opinion shifts the same way. As in 2008–9 the liquidity squeeze can severely limit borrowing, reduce investment, and slow growth in the medium run.

Yet the prophecies of the market can be self-fulfilling: "We should not conclude from this that everything depends on waves of irrational psychology. On the contrary, the state of long term expectations is often steady" (7:162). The contrast with Wittgenstein is that while Keynes's market conventions, though often stable, can drastically and surprisingly change, Wittgenstein's social uses and rules are made solid by practice and tradition.

Soros and Keynes

Soros takes a similar viewpoint. At *any* time, he says, one can contrast a "prevailing bias" in asset prices with "fundamentals." At *most* times, "in the normal course of events [markets] tend to correct their own excesses." But occasionally "prices can influence the fundamentals . . . that they are supposed to reflect. The change in the fundamentals may then reinforce the biased expectations in an initially self-reinforcing but eventually self-defeating process. Of course such boom-bust sequences do not occur all the time. . . . But the fact that they can occur invalidates the theory of rational expectations" (Soros, 2009, 58).

Five conclusions follow from the Keynes-Soros view of financial markets. One is that short-termism will be prevalent. Keynes distinguishes between *speculation,* or "the activity of forecasting the psychology of the market," and *enterprise,* or "the activity of forecasting the prospective yield of assets over their whole life" (7:158). Investors are driven in the direction of speculation because "it is not sensible to pay 25 for an investment of which you believe the prospective yield to justify a value of 30, if you also believe that the market will value it at 20 three months hence" (7:155). To avoid trading centered on short-term fluctuations, he proposes a "substantial" turnover tax on all financial transactions. Besides reducing speculation, the tax has revenue implications that could be quite favorable. We'll return to this idea in discussing financial regulation in Chapter 7.

Second, if one accepts Keynes's view of probability, the concept of financial *risk* cannot be defined in quantitative terms. As mentioned above and described in detail in Chapter 7, mainstream finance theory assumes a complete numerical ordering of probabilities regarding future events. Moreover, the probabilities are supposed to be objective, known to all actors, and "well behaved" in the sense of not having a distribution with fat tails or other quirks. On these assumptions, securitizing and distributing a package of mortgages was supposed to spread its quantum of objective risk across many buyers, diluting each individual's exposure. The 2007–2009 collapse shows that securitization doesn't work that way.

With partial ordering and subjective probabilities, objective risk does not exist. I can't think of a short, snappy synonym in English for *uncertainty* ("puzzle" might be the closest), so following Knight and Keynes, let's stick with that word. Speculators can be viewed as *uncertainty traders* who in 2007–2009 were largely borrowing in the short term to get *trading liquidity* to sweep in capital gains on long-term assets. The infamous observation by Chuck Prince, the subsequently ousted chief of Citigroup—"When the music stops, in terms of liquidity, things will be complicated. But as long as the music is playing, you've got to get up and dance. We're still dancing"—brilliantly captured the mood in July 2007.

What was left unsaid is that the financial world is populated not just by traders like Mr. Prince, who assume that if they cannot fund their assets, they will be able to sell them immediately at prevailing prices, but also by *uncertainty absorbers* which practice enterprise investing, in Keynes's usage. (*Value investors* play a similar role.) Insurance companies and pension funds, for example, have long-term liabilities and relatively assured cash flows from premiums and contributions, and can use these resources to spread market and liquidity uncertainties across time. Warren Buffett's Berkshire Hathaway is reverently mentioned as the premier example.

In 2007–2009 the uncertainty-absorbing financial subsector could not stabilize the system. Money center banks *formerly* helped absorb uncertainty but stopped doing so when they turned toward speculation after the repeal of the Glass-Steagall Act (discussed in more detail in Chapter 7). Most components of the financial holding company AIG were in the insurance business, but the conglomerate went bankrupt after one branch took up extreme speculation. A crucial regulatory question for the future is how to boost the stabilizing market role of uncertainty absorbers and reduce the importance of destabilizing traders. Perhaps better *micro*-level regulation of AIG could have avoided its debacle, but the real problem was that it built up destabilizing *macro* linkages with the rest of the financial system. Discussion of whether or not financial companies with such connections can be effectively regulated appears in Chapter 7.

The third conclusion is that for better or for worse, says Keynes, "the daily revaluations of the Stock Exchange, though they are primarily made to facilitate transfers of old investments between one individual and another, inevitably exert a decisive influence on the rate of current investment" (7:151). A convenient formulation is the ratio of the value of a firm's equity to the market (or replacement) value of its capital stock. It was labeled v (for *valuation ratio*) in the 1960s by Richard Kahn and Nicholas Kaldor in Cambridge, and q by the American Keynesian James Tobin in an independent presentation a few years later. Whatever its symbol, the ratio is often interpreted as a rough-and-ready indicator of the performance of firms. A corporation is in a sort of financial equilibrium when its q (the label adopted in this book) equals 1.

As Keynes points out, if q is bigger than 1, the firm should be building up its capital stock. This is yet another explanation of investment demand in the *General Theory.* The ratio in fact correlated well with U.S. capital formation in the 1950s and 1960s, but then, as often happens in applied macroeconomics, the relationship broke down. If q is less than 1, the firm may be ripe for an external takeover. The American merger and acquisition wave of the 1980s took place during a period when corporate q-values tended to be well below unity.

Fourth, the *state of credit* reflects "the confidence of the lending institutions toward those who seek to borrow from them." A hypothetical collapse in the price of equities ". . . may have been due to the weakening of speculative confidence or the state of credit. But whereas the weakening of either is enough to cause a collapse, recovery requires the revival of *both*" (7:158). The 2007–2009 crash centered on asset prices of houses and the associated securitized mortgages and certainly involved collapses in both confidence and the state of credit. Preventing or limiting destabilizing repercussions between both is the goal of macro-level financial regulation.

Finally, Keynes observes that "philosophically speaking [an existing market valuation] cannot be uniquely correct, since our existing knowledge does not provide a sufficient basis for a calculated mathematical expectation" (7:150). That is, "a weighted average of quantitative benefits multiplied by quantitative probabilities" (7:161) cannot serve as a basis for making decisions. This thought leads to two of his most characteristic observations.

The first is that "most, probably, of our decisions to do something positive, the full consequences of which will be drawn out over many days to come, can only be taken as a result of *animal spirits*—of a spontaneous urge to action rather than inaction" (7:161; emphasis added). Like caprice in deciding whether to carry the umbrella, animal spirits represent a reasonable approach to decision making under fundamental uncertainty.

Pessimism about the ability of animal spirits to support an adequate level of investment pervades the *General Theory,* which after all was a product of its time. A natural corollary was to "expect to see the State, which is in a position to calculate the marginal efficiency of capital-goods on long views and on the basis of the general social advantage, taking an ever greater responsibility for directly organizing investment" (7:164). Recent investment booms in the United States—the dot-com adventure in the 1990s and spending on housing in the 2000s—do not conform to Keynes's vision, although the advances in information technology underlying the dot-coms ultimately were the fruit of government support. It remains to be seen whether private capital formation will recover after 2007–2009. As pointed out in Chapter 5, residential investment may have to be the key.

Financial Market Structure

Fundamental uncertainty is also Keynes's key explanation for *liquidity preference,* or the desire to hold money. Table 4.1 presents a simplified version of how the relevant financial system accounting works out. Observe that the table (harking back to Chapter 1) is set up in terms of financial *stocks,* not *flows.* Liquidity preference replaced loanable funds in the *General Theory* because Keynes started thinking about how the interest rate adjusts to clear markets for outstanding stocks of money and bonds on the

Table 4.1 Financial system balance sheets for the 1930s

Households		Firms		Government		Commercial banks		Central bank	
Money	Net worth	Capital	Loans	"Faith & credit"	Bonds	Loans	Money	Bonds	Bank reserves
Bonds			Bonds			Bank reserves		Int'l. reserves	
Equity			Equity						

financial side of the economy rather than shifting to bring flows of saving supply and investment demand into equality on the real side.

In contrast to Table 2.1, bonds are now (circa 1930) widely in use, issued by the government and business and held by the central bank and households. Strictly speaking, government and (high-grade) corporate bonds are different sorts of securities, but they are usually such close substitutes that for present purposes they can be treated as identical.

Liquidity Preference

The key question is: Why do households hold money? (I omit holdings by government and firms for simplicity.) Partly they use it for *transactions demands,* paying bills and whatnot. This is the sort of money demand built into the quantity theory. But economic actors also hold (or hoard) money as "a barometer of the degree of our distrust of our own calculations and conventions regarding the future. Even though this feeling about Money is itself conventional or instinctive, it operates, so to speak, at a deeper level of our motivation. . . . The possession of actual money lulls our disquietude; and the premium which we require to make us part with money is a measure of the degree of disquietude" (14:116). Liquidity preference is the label that Keynes attached to the desire to hold money to quiet fear.

With money offering security, in uncertain times people will wish to hold onto it instead of bonds. Because at any time there are fixed supplies of money and bonds, the implication is that prices of bonds will be low. The interest that a bond pays is an inverse function of its price, so that bond rates will be relatively high if asset holders are willing to buy them at all. In line with the discussion of own-rates of interest in Chapter 2 (Chapter 17 in the *General Theory*), a whole range of asset prices will fall in response to a high interest rate, reducing incentives to produce new capital goods. *Speculative demand* for money by money-hoarding bears who lack confidence forestalls capital formation.

The classic monetary policy response to this sort of situation is for the central bank to buy bonds from commercial banks by crediting their reserve accounts. This *open market operation* should drive up bond prices and reduce interest rates. Commercial banks in turn will have excess reserves, which will presumably induce them to increase lending. Indeed, the central bank can inject funds into any deposit account it so chooses, to acquire securities of any sort, in the *quantitative easing* maneuvers that began to be practiced in 2008–9. The goal is always to drive interest rates down.

As noted above, however, the state of credit may be so weak that banks are unwilling to lend, exercising their own version of liquidity preference by holding excess reserves even if borrowers are willing to pay high rates.

Recent Wrinkles

Four further observations. First, in practice, only in 2008–9 did the Fed begin to undertake generalized open market operations in the wake of the crash. In "normal" times it would target the *Fed funds rate,* or the rate that banks use "overnight" when borrowing and lending among themselves. The Fed would announce a target rate and then intervene in the overnight market to support it. The transaction vehicle would be a *repurchase agreement,* or *repo,* whereby the Fed would create money to buy a security at a spot price from a bank and agree to sell it back the next day at a slightly higher forward price, with the difference in prices making up the interest. Selling a security in a *reverse repo* would induce an overnight monetary contraction. The price differential is sometimes called a *margin* or *haircut.* The lower the quality of the security in question, the higher the margin. During 2007–2009, margins and haircuts spiked upward by hundreds of *basis points* (or hundredths of a percent).

Second, in the United States (much more than in Europe), firms tend to finance their short-term obligations in the *commercial paper* market, which is based on promissory notes not backed by collateral. Money market funds that are held by households invest in this market. In "normal" times the Fed funds and commercial paper rates are close. But commercial paper transactions froze in the fall of 2008, ramping up the crisis. Highly creditworthy firms simply could not obtain the finance needed to support their day-to-day operations. The freeze started when the Treasury and Federal Reserve did not intervene to prevent bankruptcy of the investment bank Lehman Brothers. It had been a heavy repo borrower, paying a premium rate on some of its loans from other firms to shift dodgy assets off its books at times when it had to file reports with regulators. A major money market fund held Lehman paper, and in the absence of a bailout it *broke the buck* by not redeeming its shares at par.

Third, as a technical matter, own-rates of interest will be affected by the carrying cost and liquidity characteristics of the underlying asset. The discussion above and in Chapter 2 should be extended accordingly (a task taken up at some length with little clarity in Chapter 17 of the *General Theory*).

Finally, in the *General Theory* liquidity takes the form of an *asset,* that is, money, or more recently low-risk assets such as Treasury bills. This interpretation of "liquidity" has changed enormously since Maynard's time. There are now diverse ideas about what it means.

One applies to a *liquid market* in which buying and selling prices for securities are close (that is, *bid-ask spreads* are low). A market that seizes up is obviously not liquid in this sense. Somewhat related notions are that a security should be easy to borrow so that it can be sold short, and that uncertainty regarding its possible default can be easily hedged by using credit derivatives. Whether these latter forms of liquidity contribute to systemic stability is very much an open question.

As observed in Chapter 2, liquidity can also be considered wherewithal. A major contributing factor to the 2007–2009 crisis was the increasing use of *liabilities* to provide trading or *funding liquidity* for speculative purposes. There is also an issue of *market liquidity,* meaning that a firm can easily sell an asset at a stable price. In the fire sales of securities in 2007–2009, both funding and market liquidity went up in smoke.

Finance in the 2000s

The use of liabilities as liquidity has already been mentioned several times. Although the discussion takes us beyond the *General Theory,* it makes sense for future reference to illustrate how the macro-level financial system evolved to allow leverage and liabilities to be used to generate liquidity for the purchase of increasingly speculative assets.

Liabilities and Leverage as Liquidity

Table 4.2 presents a *very* stylized set of balance sheets for a modern rich economy. Before we go into the details of each sector's position, note that they mostly net out; that is, one sector's asset is another's liability. *Primary wealth* in the table is the value of housing or households' residential capital, the capital stock held by firms, and the government's faith and credit in the form of bonds. The value of this wealth is equal to the sum of household, business, and foreign net worth. The rest of the world's net worth is

Table 4.2 Simplified financial balance sheets for the 2000s

Households		Firms		Government		Central bank	
Money	Mortgages	Capital	Loans	"Faith & credit"	Bonds	Bonds	Bank reserves
Bonds	Net worth		Bonds			Int'l. reserves	
Equity			Equity				
Housing			Net worth				

Commercial banks		Special purpose vehicle		Leveraged finance		Rest of world	
Loans	Money	Mortgages	CDOs	CDOs	Loans	Int'l. reserves	
Mortgages	Equity			Repos	Repos		(Net worth)
Bank reserves					Equity		

negative (indicated by the parentheses), because in the table it issues only liabilities held by the central bank as international reserves. In practice in the 2000s it had highly positive net worth built up courtesy of U.S. external deficits over the years. We'll get to that issue in Chapters 5 and 8.

In this chapter Table 4.2 is used to illustrate how securitized mortgages served as a basis for major speculation. Through this and similar institutional changes, strongly *pro-cyclical* behavior got built into the financial system, which ended up destabilizing it completely. The balance sheets illustrate the workings of *collateralized debt obligations* (or *CDOs*), just one of the many types of derivatives that propelled the 2007–2009 crisis.

Households in the table have a stock of residential housing which will have an associated asset price. In the economy depicted in the table, they borrow in the form of mortgages from commercial banks. As noted in Chapter 3, already in the 1930s Fannie Mae got into the business of buying home mortgages and packaging or securitizing them into bonds, which could be sold on to asset holders. This procedure spread to *subprime mortgages* in the 2000s. The "subprime" label is not well defined but broadly means that the loan in question appeared to be so risky that Fannie and its brother agency Freddie Mac would not buy it from the originating lender. Commercial banks and other private financial actors took up the task instead, in *originate-and-distribute* operations which often brought in handsome fees.

A typical ploy was to set up a *special purpose vehicle (SPV)* in effect managed by but *off the balance sheet* of its sponsoring bank. SPVs are similar to the investment trusts that banks set up in the late 1920s and played a central role in the Enron Corporation's financial manipulations around 1990. Too bad the bank regulators didn't pay attention!

The sponsoring bank would take a minimal position in the SPV (not shown in the table) and pass over to it a share of its mortgages as an asset. In turn the SPV would package mortgages of various defined risk categories into a CDO, which was treated as a bond to be sold into the market. The CDO would have an asset valuation ultimately based on the asset prices of its component mortgage risk classes of residential housing. The reason to go through SPVs in the first place was to take the transactions below the bank regulators' radar.

CDOs were well-crafted pieces of deception. They comprised several *tranches* or slices made up of mortgages of different qualities with different attached promises to pay the CDO holders. Asymmetric knowledge led to their rapid spread because the issuer of a CDO earned a commission at the time of issue along with management fees during the life of the security. The payments were front-loaded by *gain-for-sale* accounting, which allowed sellers to book profits when a CDO was first sold. These money flows coupled with the absence of any residual liability skewed the incentives of originators overwhelmingly in favor of loan volume rather than quality. Volume was enhanced by product differentiation through the various tranches.

Like any derivative, a CDO was a synthetic financial instrument which had to be priced. Beginning in the 1990s, *mark- to-market* or *fair value* accounting increasingly became the accepted rule, but markets in which CDOs were traded were often nonexistent or thin. That means their prices at the time of sale had to be "marked" on the basis of statistical models. The procedure was to use historical correlations among mortgage default rates to estimate the probabilistic risk to which a CDO might be subject. Almost all the models were based on a procedure called a Gaussian copula (see Chapter 7). With most players running the same numbers using the same technique, their estimates of CDO valuations generally agreed.

The problem is that when default rates shot above their historical levels, as they did when housing prices fell in 2006 in the first nationwide collapse since the Great Depression, historical correlations became meaningless and CDOs could not be priced. Because they were thinking alike, their holders started to bail out at more or less the same time, precipitating a pro-cyclical positive feedback deleveraging process about to be described.

CDOs appeared to be a way to get around a traditional maturity mismatch for banks. They traditionally operated with retail deposits from small savers as short-term liabilities and held long-term collateralized loans as assets. If they had enough capital (or low enough leverage; see below) to absorb normal fluctuations in asset prices, they could be pretty sure that the amount of their short-term deposit liabilities would be stable (unless of course there was a generalized bank run). This model was gradually replaced by originate-and-distribute securitization, which accounted for roughly 40% of lending by the 2000s. At the same time, however, many banks pursued wholesale deposits and began to borrow in commercial paper markets. If anything, their overall maturity position deteriorated.

Also, the stability of a bank's liability structure was much less assured when it contained a big component of CDOs, even if they were cleverly hidden in the off–balance sheet *shadow banking sector*. Their buyers were free to sell them off at any time. A typical buyer would be a leveraged financial institution such as a hedge fund, an investment bank, or a commercial bank freed by the abolition of Glass-Steagall to engage in trading uncertainty. *Within* this leveraged subsector it was straightforward for any one firm to run up high levels of debt by engaging in repo and reverse repo transactions with its peers. The whole subsector's *net* repo position was small (assumed to be equal to zero in the table), but the underlying, mutually offsetting asset and liability positions of leveraged firms became very large. A firm could readily borrow via repos to buy a CDO.

The repo debt thus served as funding liquidity which leveraged firms could use for speculation. That was the music to which Chuck Prince and his colleagues were dancing. The contrast with Keynes, who thought of liquidity as a safe haven asset, is striking. In the brave new financial world of the 2000s, liquidity in the form of liabilities became a steroid for financial investors' animal spirits.

The process is straightforward but unfamiliar to most people. A sketch is presented here, with additional detail from a Minsky-style financial instability model in Chapter 5. Note that in the table the leverage ratio of an uncertainty-trading firm is the sum of the CDOs and repos it holds divided by the value of its equity. The perverse logic of leverage has already been discussed in Chapter 3, but perhaps it makes sense to go through it again.

Suppose that the asset price of the CDOs goes up. Then if the firm's debt stays (for the moment) constant, the value of its equity has to rise as well. But with high leverage (a ratio of 30 or so in the New York investment banks prior to the crash), the *percentage* increase in the firm's assets will be much smaller than the percentage increase in its equity. The implication is that its leverage ratio will *fall.* That immediately sets up incentives for the firm to run up additional debt to acquire more assets that generate capital gains. Indeed, if most firms act in similar fashion, in a fallacy of composition their joint actions will drive asset prices up and create the gains. The details differ, but the narrative is much the same as in the run-up to the Great Crash of 1929.

The endgame in the recent crisis pivoted on measures of *value-at-risk (VaR),* which can be defined as the level of equity capital a firm must hold to stay solvent with a high probability in the face of adverse shocks. Even if the "high probability" could be assumed to be objective, this definition is not *constructive* because it does not spell out how VaR should be computed. But if as a rule of thumb a firm maintains equity in proportion to VaR, then its leverage will be *inversely proportional*. That is, estimated risk will fall when leverage swings down in a boom, and will rise with induced increases in leverage during a bust.

The 2007–2009 crisis ensued when housing prices started to drop in 2006 after rising strongly since the mid-1990s and fairly steadily since the late 1930s. Asset prices on CDOs and similar paper had to fall off as well. As a consequence, leverage and VaR started to rise. When firms hit regulatory limits on VaR, they tried to sell off their CDOs to reduce debt and build up equity. But they were selling into a falling market, bidding up margins and driving asset prices down further, making a bad situation worse. Wealth holders (including putative uncertainty absorbers such as pension funds which had purchased some tranches of CDOs and were obligated by their regulations to sell when their ratings collapsed) began to flee toward safe assets as a form of Keynesian liquidity. Funding liquidity vanished in the process of *deleveraging*, which continued into 2009. As discussed below, the bear brigade attacked, using short-selling and credit default swaps to drive systemically important financial and insurance companies into bankruptcy.

Finance was thus subject to *systemic risk* (or, better, *systemic uncertainty*), which presumably should be a central concern of prudential regulation because it affects the health of the entire system. Traditionally, microeconomic risk management has been directed toward reducing allegedly quantifiable risk that depends on the characteristics of individual borrowers. But pro-cyclical private-sector behavior of the sort just described can be highly destabilizing, particularly during a boom. If history is any guide, the financial system will take a long time to recuperate and restructure (maybe with another crisis or two along the way), almost certainly in a form much more like Table 4.1 than Table 4.2. Some regulatory implications are taken up in Chapter 7.

Credit Default Swaps

Before we go on to financial cycles, a word should be added about credit default swaps (or *CDS*s), which were major derivative culprits in 2007–2009. Together with CDOs they set up a grand fallacy of composition resting on actions of people thinking along conventional lines and ignoring fundamental uncertainty.

The swaps are a form of insurance, promising to pay out a certain amount of money in the event of default of the reference firm or security. A buyer of a swap does *not* need to have an *insurable interest* in the security in question, for example, by owning it. In traditional insurance practice, only I and not my neighbor can buy fire insurance on my house. The absence of such a restriction is one factor that made CDSs an ideal vehicle for speculation. The *Financial Times* journalist Gillian Tett observes that CDOs of CDSs, which were invented in the late 1990s, gave impetus to the speculative mania which crashed a decade later.

In a refinement of terminology, old-fashioned common garden variety securitizations became known as *cash CDOs*. *Synthetic CDOs* were based on *CDSs* issued against the underlying primary assets. Basically, they allowed players to take offsetting positions about whether the holders of the underlying assets—think of subprime mortgages—would default.

The synthetic CDOs had large *super senior* tranches, which were supposed to have a very low risk of having to pay out for a default. Under existing regulatory rules, financial firms holding them had every incentive to carry minimal backing in the form of capital or reserves. In late 2007 several majors—Citigroup and Merrill Lynch in the United States, UBS in Switzerland—held massive quantities of super senior paper on their own books or had to reabsorb it from staggering off-balance sheet vehicles. These holdings became unsalable except at a huge loss, in turn liquidating the banks' capital. The collapse in values of super senior securities was a major contributing factor to the crisis.

There were other unpleasant surprises as well. One, as Soros points out, is that buying a CDS on a bond is analogous to selling equity short. Short-selling shares is a classic bear maneuver. It involves borrowing stock to sell in the market. (In *naked shorting* the stock is not even borrowed.) The maneuver will succeed if the prices of the shares fall so that the bear can buy back the ones he borrowed and turn a profit after he closes the loan. If prices rise, short-selling can be a disaster.

Despite its name, a CDS can be used in ways not directly linked to the likelihood of a bond defaulting, for example, speculating that the bond's price will fall. The price of the CDS will rise if the bond price does decline, so that the swap can be sold for a profit. Large-scale purchases of CDSs against a specific bond or CDO—"short" positions—are likely to drive down its price, just as widespread short-selling can drive down the price of a specific form of equity. In 2008 bear raids which combined selling their equity short and buying CDSs against their bonds drove the investment bank Lehman Brothers and the insurance company AIG into the ground.

On the other side of the market, selling CDSs—taking a "long" position—offers limited profits but great uncertainty if the buyers decide to cash them in. AIG perhaps thought it was just selling "plain vanilla" insurance when it went long on large quantities of CDSs, but what it really had on offer were *warrants* (contracts it guarantees and agrees to repurchase) to be used for shorting CDOs. When it had to redeem them so the buyers could take their profits, it simply did not have enough reserves on hand. The company's regulators, state-level insurance commissioners, and the Office of Thrift Supervision, which normally oversees the savings and loan industry, had no understanding of the dangers involved.

Another twist is that firms such as Goldman Sachs (accused of securities fraud by the SEC in a suit filed in April 2010), Deutsche Bank, and Morgan Stanley are alleged to have created synthetic CDOs packed with CDSs against mortgages likely to fail. Goldman, in particular, was accused of constructing one such package at the behest of a hedge fund run by John Paulson. His fund made a great deal of money by shorting CDOs based on mortgages, while Goldman received generous fees for setting up the transaction in question. Without mentioning Paulson's role, its sales force persuaded clients to take long positions, which created huge losses when the crisis hit. In its public defense, Goldman argued that as a market maker it had an obligation to take both short and long positions on any transaction. But its bias toward shorting vehicles based on subprime mortgages brought in handsome profits when the market collapsed. Such transactions on the part of Goldman Sachs and other banks were pure speculation. They generated "value added" in the form of profits and paychecks and served as vehicles for smart players to short the mortgage market. The counterparties won or lost large bets on the finances of the hapless souls holding the mortgages (in many cases created fraudulently by finance companies previously backed by the banks) upon which the derivatives were based. By so outmaneuvering the market, Goldman and a few others clearly demonstrated the "higher degree" of insight into expectations that Keynes described in the beauty contest.

In even more extreme cases, default swaps can be an inducement to financial assassination. Suppose that a bank has outstanding loans to a firm but holds a larger CDS position against it. Calling the loans to induce a default becomes an obvious temptation. Such calculations by bondholders may have played a part in forcing the bankruptcy of General Motors in 2009. In the *Financial Times* in April 2009 Gillian Tett reported that it is likely that the investment bank Morgan Stanley made a similar move against BTA, a bank in Kazakhstan which subsequently failed. The bank's or bondholders' positions are not transparent, so there is no possibility for market arbitrage by third parties to alleviate the tension. A *bargaining solution* could involve the creditor blackmailing the firm, but that might not be in the creditor's interest. This problem of moral hazard is the reason why many people call for the abolition or extremely tight regulation of CDS-type derivatives. In late 2009 and into 2010, CDSs on default of sovereign debt issued by Greece were priced at all-time highs. A Greek crisis could concentrate politicians' minds on the possibilities for instability that derivatives create.

Because it involved many mutually offsetting contracts, the nominal value of the CDS market peaked at over $60 trillion, much larger than all the world's bond markets combined. Like CDOs, CDSs were mostly traded as tailor-made (*bespoke* in British) products *over the counter*, which usually meant that they were negotiated over the telephone. Much current debate about regulation centers on whether these and other derivative contracts should be standardized and traded in transparent markets—just like commodity futures, stocks, bonds, and foreign exchange. Creating a market "core" for transactions in derivatives could add stability to other trades, even if they are carried out over the counter.

Soros, Keynes, and Kindleberger on Financial "Cycles"

"Cycle" is the wrong word to describe financial booms and crashes. As already noted in Chapter 1, it implies regularity, while each financial excursion has its own unique character. Nevertheless, a couple of ideas that emerge from analysis of physical or biological oscillations using the mathematical theory of dynamical systems can be helpful in thinking about finance. They were popularized by the mathematician-philosopher Norbert Wiener in his book *Cybernetics* in 1948 and underlie a lot of contemporary discussion about "complexity."

Positive feedback means that a system, or some variable within a system, moves farther on its own in any direction in which it has been pushed. It is a destabilizing response. Negative feedback means that the variable or system moves back against the push, and is stabilizing. A thermostat embodies negative feedback because it stabilizes the temperature in a house. If it loses its little mind and orders the furnace to burn higher when the house temperature goes up, there will soon be a conflagration.

One can also have positive or negative feedbacks between different variables. The classic example is from models about how species interact. If, on the one hand, the population of rabbits (the *prey*) increases, then the population of foxes (the *predators*) is likely to rise—a positive feedback from prey to predator. On the other hand, more foxes mean fewer rabbits—a negative feedback from predator to prey. Fluctuations in the two populations can obviously happen—too regularly in the formal models to be observable in practice, but nevertheless the simplified underlying mechanism is worth bearing in mind. George Soros has a "boom-bust" model of asset prices and leverage along these lines, and in the *Treatise on Money,* Keynes set out a rather more complicated cycle. The two approaches are interesting to compare.

Soros's model focuses on the use of equity to build up leverage. He illustrates it with the conglomerate boom of the 1960s and the proliferation of real estate investment trusts (REITs) the following decade. The essence was that conglomerates or trusts would issue their own relatively high-priced shares to acquire more mundane companies and add the earnings flows to their own. Bigger buyers' earnings per share generated enthusiasm for still more acquisitions. More and more buyers got into the game, setting off a boom.

Figure 4.1, redrawn from Soros's version, shows the dynamics over time. The share price of a buying firm starts to rise, as "price bias" reinforces a "trend" (recall the discussion of Soros's reflexivity model above). There may be a "period of testing" when prices drop off, but if they pass the exam, they can continue to rise. Earnings per share—an index of leverage—also go up, but with a lag. At some point enthusiasm fades and the price begins to fall. Earnings per share continue to rise for a time, but they too decline into a crash. Usually the upswing lasts longer than the decline.

With less emphasis on the timing but more on how the variables interact, they can be plotted in a *phase diagram* (Figure 4.2, a picture that ultimately traces back to J. Willard Gibbs). Omitting the testing period for simplicity, it shows how the trajectories of the two variables run together. The asset price (the prey) leads earnings per share (the predator) upward, with the latter continuing to rise for a while after the price starts to go down. Only later does a "period of deleveraging" begin.

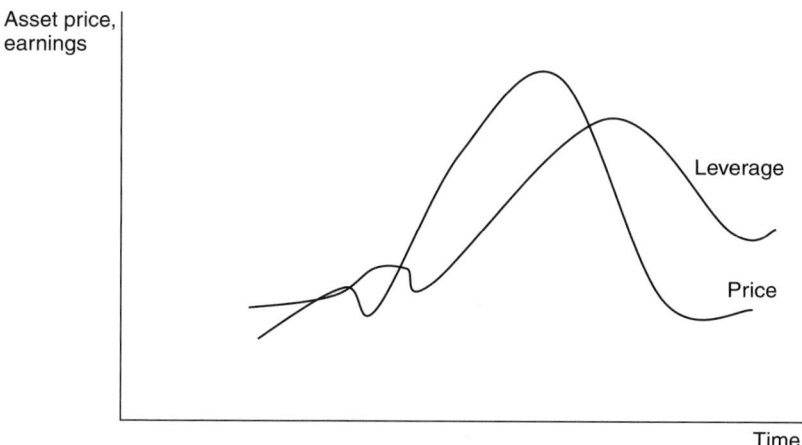

Figure 4.1 Time plot of a Soros financial "cycle"

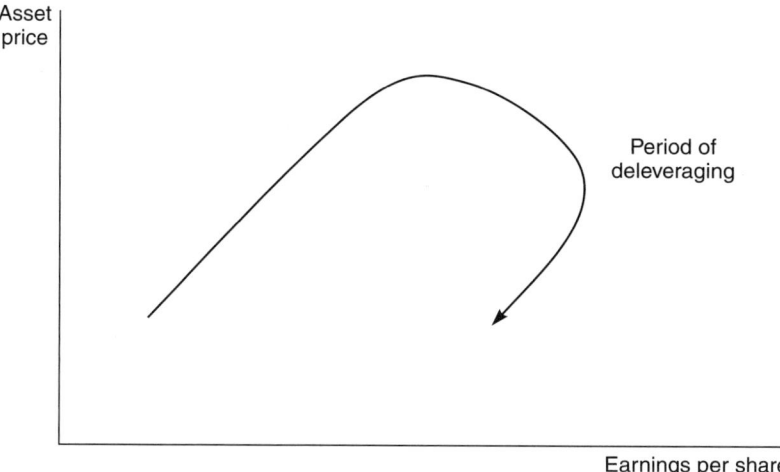

Figure 4.2 Phase plot for a Soros financial "cycle"

Translating Soros's own language into the diagram, we see that a comovement of price bias and trend can be interpreted as positive feedback of the price into its own level. (An asset price increase pushes its own growth rate upward.) Next, "a two-way reflexive connection between market valuations and the so-called fundamentals . . . sets up some kind of short circuit between them whereby valuations affect the fundamentals they are supposed to reflect" (Soros, 2009, 58). The interpretation would be that a share price increase lets a conglomerate or REIT buy more companies to speed up the growth of its own earnings per share. Later in the cycle, "[t]o maintain the momentum of earnings[,] growth acquisitions had to be larger and largerand eventually conglomerates ran into the limits of size" (Soros, 2009, 60). A high earnings level will brake the growth of the asset price. An expanding conglomerate fox cannot find more and more little rabbits to devour.

The slightly puzzling aspect of the diagram in Figure 4.2 is the overshooting or inertia of earnings: if prices break downwards, shouldn't deleveraging get started at once? Soros presents company-level data in support of his model, but it still is of interest to explore the alternative scenario. As it turns out, Keynes in the *Treatise on Money* did almost that. He was concerned with bulls who wish to hold securities and borrow from banks to buy them, and bears who prefer to hold money or else borrow shares to sell equity short. (CDSs which could be used to short bonds had yet to be invented.) Keynes described a cycle in which bulls and bears interact.

Table 4.3 sets out the scenario in his own words. (Ignore the entries about leverage for the moment.) The phase plot in Figure 4.3 is based on the assumption that the table's four "types of speculative markets" run in sequence. In phase (i) asset prices are beginning to rise, and bears are taking profits by closing the positions they opened in a preceding phase (iv). In (ii), which resembles Soros's boom period, bulls are buying and bears move into short-selling in anticipation of a crash. After prices start to fall in phase (iii), bears take profits and bulls back off. Asset prices continue to fall in phase (iv), but bears anticipate an eventual price rise and begin to increase their positions.

It is tempting to reinterpret Keynes's bear position in terms of leverage as practiced by uncertainly trading bulls. In phase (i), for example, asset prices rise and leverage goes down for the reasons discussed above. In (ii) uncertainty traders begin to run up debt to increase their leverage. In phase (iii), after the price reversal they hit VaR limits and cut leverage back. This phase of deleveraging is more abrupt than in Soros's cycle; that is the main contrast between the models. In phase (iv), if investors sense that at low levels asset prices are beginning "to correct their own excesses" (in Soros's words), they may run up leverage to go back into the market and stimulate a new round of price increases. (In more formal terms, asset

Table 4.3 Keynes's financial "cycle" in the *Treatise on Money*

	"We will call the 'bear' position,—including, however, as bears not only those who have sold securities 'short', *i.e.* have sold securities which they do not own, but also those who would normally be holders of securities but prefer for the time being to hold liquid claims on cash in the form of Savings-deposits. A 'bear', that is to say, is one who prefers at the moment to avoid securities and lend cash, and correspondingly a 'bull' is one who prefers to hold securities and borrow cash—the former anticipating that securities will fall in cash-value and the latter that they will rise" (5:250).
	"Now, whilst a tendency of the Savings-deposits (M_3) to increase or decrease is an indication of an increase or decrease of the 'bear' position, there are altogether four possible types of speculative markets:
(i)	A '*bull*' *market with a consensus of opinion, i.e.* security-prices rising but insufficiently so that M_3 is falling, and 'bears' are closing their positions on a rising market."
	Asset price ↑ insufficiently, M ↓, short positions ↓ [Leverage ↓]
(ii)	A '*bear*' *market with a division of opinion, i.e.* security-prices rising more than sufficiently so that M_3 is rising, and 'bears' are increasing their positions on a rising market."
	Asset price ↑ sufficiently, M ↑, short positions ↑ [Leverage ↑]
(iii)	A '*bear*' *market with a division of opinion, i.e.* security-prices falling more than sufficiently so that M_3 is falling, and 'bears' are closing their positions on a falling market."
	Asset price ↓ sufficiently, M ↓, short positions ↓ [Leverage ↓]
(iv)	A '*bear*' *market with a consensus of opinion, i.e.* security-prices falling insufficiently so that M_3 is rising, and 'bears' are increasing their positions on a falling market" (5:252 et seq.).
	Asset price ↓ insufficiently, M ↑, short positions ↑ [Leverage ↑]

prices may be subject to negative own-feedback at low levels and positive feedback when they are high.)

Such simplified descriptions of asset price and leverage movements will of course never be literally correct. There are always too many other things going on. But if John Maynard Keynes and George Soros to a large measure agree about the dynamics of speculative markets, then mere economists

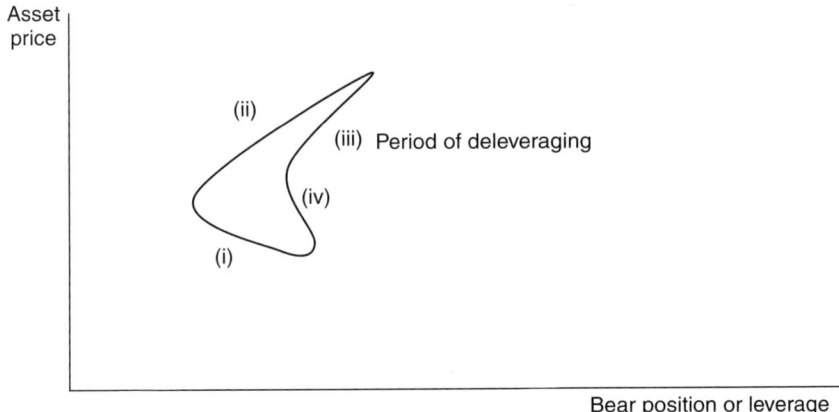

Figure 4.3 The financial "cycle" (updated) from the *Treatise on Money*

and policymakers should take heed. Soros's bias and trend analysis is a reasonable justification for positive feedback of an asset price into its own growth, and the cusp at the of Keynes's cycle shows up in at least some instances.

The continuity in Keynes's ideas about finance between the *Treatise on Money* and the *General Theory* is clear. In the *General Theory* he reformulated his old ideas about probability to refine his insights into the behavior of bear speculators. In the *Treatise* he accepted Say's Law, and in the *General Theory* he did not. Bears and bulls have different impacts on the real economy in those two worlds. That is the topic to be taken up after a brief discussion of Kindleberger's financial cycle scenario in Chapter 2 of *Manias, Panics, and Crashes*.

Kindleberger credits Minsky for emphasizing the expansion of credit as a major causal factor underlying a mania, bubble, or asset price boom. He attaches great importance to the behavior of heavily indebted borrowers, those practicing what Minsky calls *Ponzi finance*, as discussed in Chapter 5.

Asset price growth gets under way as a result of some sort of *displacement* of the system, rather like Soros's concatenation of a price bias with a trend. As asset prices start to rise, players increasingly engage in what Adam Smith and his contemporaries called *overtrading*. More investors get drawn in, with insiders taking profits by selling assets to them. Sooner or later it is likely that interest rates and the speed of transactions will go up. Sellers become more eager than buyers, and prices begin to slip in a period of *financial distress* in which borrowers cannot keep up with their debt servicing commitments. A panic begins, which might be better described by Keynes's than Soros's dynamics. To use a nineteenth-century word, *revulsion*, or a flight to liquidity in the form of "safe" assets, ensues. Banks become much more cautious about collateral for loans, practicing *discredit*, another word that is two centuries old.

Words like "overtrading," "revulsion," and "discredit" sound as if they just emerged from some musty attic, but they do give a graphic description of a boom followed by a collapse or crash. Ultimately some lender or market maker of last resort has to appear to resuscitate the financial system, quite possibly with extremely large injections of credit as in 2008–9.

Macroeconomics of the Real Side

Insofar as the label can apply to such a master of multitasking, Maynard didn't become a "full-time" economist until he was in his late thirties, after the *Economic Consequences of the Peace*. Much of his work was concerned with economic fluctuations, but it differed from a lot of Cambridge trade cycle theory in the 1920s, which emphasized swings in business psychology. A 1929 book called *Industrial Fluctuations* by Keynes's friend and rival A. C. Pigou is a typical example.

Although, as we have seen, Keynes came back to market psychology in the *General Theory*, he initially adopted a more abstract approach, exploring inflationary dynamics in terms of class conflict and the quantity theory of money in his *Tract on Monetary Reform*. He also invented the idea of interest rate parity linking changes in the exchange rate to interest rate differentials across countries, a key part of open economy macroeconomics, discussed in Chapter 8.

Subsequently, for the commodity price–real output side of the macroeconomy he produced a complicated neo-Wicksellian two-sector model in the *Treatise on Money* and a sleek, elegant machine in the *General Theory*. Thank heaven for the Ricardian vice! There is an enormous specialist literature on Keynes's transition between the two books which cannot be addressed here, but it does make sense to look briefly at linkages between the financial and real sides in the *Treatise*.

Real-Side Macro in the Treatise on Money

Two sectors produce consumption and capital goods respectively. Their interactions are analyzed in a set of *fundamental equations* which are baroque versions of the ones presented below for a single sector producing aggregate output in the *General Theory*. The equations involve a price for consumer goods *and* both a cost and a selling price for capital goods. The value of consumption (price times quantity) is equal to labor earnings minus saving. The selling price for capital goods is closely related to the asset prices discussed in connection with Table 4.3.

In full equilibrium the two prices for capital goods are equal. Also saving from earnings is equal to investment valued at its cost price. Outside of equilibrium, the latter condition does not apply. If at an initial equilibrium rising asset prices stimulate investment demand, then the selling price of capital goods will rise, producing windfall profits in that sector. Spillover demand for consumer goods will bid up their price too, raising profits in that sector as well. Added to labor savings, the extra profits provide enough finance to meet investment demand. That is,

Saving from labor earnings + Windfall profits in both sectors =
Value of investment at its selling price.

One step of the transition to the *General Theory* was the replacement of windfall profits by *business saving* or retained corporate earnings, which can take either sign. Suppose that saving from both wages and profits responds to changes in output. If investment increases, we can then drop the *Treatise*'s forced saving response based on jumps in the consumer and capital goods prices and replace it with the *General Theory*'s adjustment of the level of economic activity obeying the principle of effective demand. Schumpeter and Wicksell would have stayed with Say's Law, especially the latter, because in the *Treatise* Keynes argued that monetary policy could be used to drive investment and savings from earnings toward equality.

Indeed, Say's Law lurks in the background of all the *Treatise*'s reasoning. Keynes *was* concerned with the possibility of declining output if investment fell short of saving but could not deal with it effectively. He even had a "banana plantation" example, in which output fell to zero in response to a higher saving rate. The problem of how to determine a macro equilibrium with less than full employment was only resolved in the *General Theory*.

Finally, the most interesting analytical aspect of the *Treatise* was not treated very explicitly. In the model of the real side, the selling price of capital goods refers to commodities, but presumably it rises along with the asset price of equity issued by producers. Then we can get into financial developments like those illustrated in Table 4.3 and Figure 4.3. Rising asset prices might then feed back into higher investment demand along the lines of Tobin's *q*, and so on.

A formal *Treatise*-type model built on both the real and the financial sides would be fascinating but intractable because it would be too complicated. Minsky's model, discussed in Chapter 5, takes up the task of building asset price effects into the business cycle model of the *General Theory*.

The Basic Model in the General Theory

The experts naturally disagree about the timing, but a summary view is that Keynes took about five years, from fall 1930 until 1935, to traverse from the *Treatise on Money* to the *General Theory*. (As an aside, the title of the later book was in part borrowed from Einstein's general theory of relativity, which was very much in the air at the time. He took ten years to get from special to general relativity.)

Keynes was helped by comments from his professional contemporaries, including Ralph Hawtrey at the Treasury (who had his own business cycle model driven by monetary expansion in the upswing and then contraction at the top), Dennis Robertson in Cambridge, and F. A. Hayek at the London School of Economics. He also interacted with a younger "Cambridge Circus" made up of Sraffa, Joan and Austin Robinson, James Meade visiting from Oxford, and Richard Kahn, who served as organizer.

There were key simplifying changes between the two books. The *Treatise*'s fascinating but elusive bull and bear financial ballet was replaced by liquidity preference. Output adjustment and the principle of effective demand replaced forced saving, requiring the specification of mechanisms for determination of consumption (and saving) and investment. Because commodity prices no longer could respond to an investment-saving gap in a forced-saving Say's Law world, the *General Theory* switched to cost-based structuralist price formation instead. Behind all the new apparatus (especially liquidity preference and investment demand) lay the disturbing presence of fundamental uncertainty, but Keynes took that largely as exogenous to the workings of his real-side macroeconomics. Of course the relationships could always shift unexpectedly in response to financial developments.

To follow largely the Italian Keynesian Luigi Pasinetti, it may help to set out the key linkages in terms of symbols (no significant mathematical manipulations involved!). Figure 4.4 shows the details.

Over to the left is the *money* (or *nominal*) wage rate *w* in units of dollars per hour (or per period of pay). At the macro level, the money wage would have to be defined by an index of observed wages across the economy. Keynes saw the money wage as being determined by institutional factors such as law and custom and the extent of unionization. Although the point is not emphasized, the wage-price relationship could also be influenced by the level of economic activity (see below). He explicitly rejected a standard neoclassical or *second classical postulate* (his own label) saying that the real wage is set by the "marginal disutility" of work. As discussed in Chapter 6, this idea unsurprisingly reappeared with vigor in the mainstream reaction to Keynesianism.

A simple but robust theory of price formation can be based on *unit labor cost* or $\frac{w}{\lambda}$ where λ is *labor productivity* defined as output per worker-hour. That is, the cost of each unit of output is the wage multiplied by the amount of labor needed to produce it. Kalecki proposed that firms set an aggregate price level as markup at rate *m* over unit labor cost

$$P = (1 + m)\frac{w}{\lambda}.$$

He assumed that the markup stays fairly constant when output changes, which is a pretty good first approximation (to be relaxed below and in Chapter 5).

One can define a real wage ω as

$$\omega = \frac{w}{P} = \frac{\lambda}{1 + m}.$$

This equation is a variant on the wage-profit relationship introduced in Chapter 2. It embodies Peter Flaschel's two souls problem mentioned there. If productivity stays constant and the money wage is fixed institutionally, there is no room for independent determination of *both* the real

```
w ⇒ P             C          PC + PI + PG − PX = 0
   ⇒ i ⇒ I ⇒    Y    from   Y = PX = wL + rPK
   H              X          PC = [1 − s(ω)] (1 − t)Y with ω = w/P
```

Figure 4.4 Causal links in the *General Theory*

wage *and* the markup rate. Fix one and you get the other. Kalecki thought that firms utilize monopoly power to set their chosen markups and so determine the real wage.

As noted in Chapter 1, to assuage professional opinion Keynes adopted a neoclassical approach to income distribution in the *General Theory*. He assumed that the real wage falls as output increases because of decreasing marginal productivity (the *first classical postulate*). With a fixed money wage the markup and the price level would thereby have to rise when output goes up. He was wrong empirically, as discussed in more detail below. In either the Kalecki or Keynes version, the overall price level P is largely set from the cost side by the money wage. That is the first key linkage in Figure 4.4.

The second linkage follows from the price level together with the money supply H. Money supply is regulated by open market operations (not described in detail in the *General Theory*) on the part of the monetary authorities. For applied macroeconomics, Keynes set up liquidity preference as an inverse relationship between *real balances* $\frac{H}{P}$ and the interest rate i. Real balances are relevant because rational actors should not suffer from *money illusion*, or confusion of a nominal quantity of money with its real purchasing power. If $\frac{H}{P}$ goes up, people will presumably divert some of their increased real money wealth toward holding bonds, meaning that bond prices will rise or the interest rate will go down. This mechanism will reappear below as part of the *Keynes effect* of cutting money wages.

Reading the causal scheme in Figure 4.4 from left to right, we see that the money supply and the price level jointly determine the interest rate. The next linkage shows that real investment I follows from the interest rate via the marginal efficiency of capital or own-rates of return. As discussed below and in Chapter 5, left-Keynesian (or, really, Kaleckian) models typically assume that investment or its rate of growth also responds to economic activity and the income distribution. These extensions lead into possible wage-led or profit-led aggregate demand regimes, as introduced in Chapter 2.

The equations to the right in Figure 4.4 support the principle of effective demand.

The first one,

$$PC + PI + PG - PX = 0,$$

applies in an economy closed to international transactions and says that the value of domestic demand is met by the value of output PX with X as real output. Besides capital formation I, demand is composed of real private consumption C and real purchases G of goods and services by the government. (As an aside, in the U.S. government, outlays split into three roughly equal portions: purchases from business, payments to government employees, and transfers to households via Social Security, Medicare, and so on.)

Keynes's fundamental postulate is that income Y is equal to the value of output PX. In the simplest distributive accounting, income or value added is equal to payments to labor and capital,

$$Y = wL + rPK,$$

with L as employment, PK as the capital stock valued at market prices, and r as the rate of profit. This decomposition is basically Adam Smith's adding-up theory of value. We will not use it at present, but it will provide the basis for analysis of productivity growth in Chapter 5.

To keep things simple, assume that income is taxed at a single rate t (around 30% in the United States, higher in western Europe). Then *disposable income* is $(1 - t)Y$. Let $s(\omega)$ be the rate of saving from disposable income. The notation is meant to suggest that the saving rate depends on the real wage ω, presumably *decreasing* as ω goes up because distribution shifts against profit incomes from which a higher proportion is saved.

Such distributive effects on saving are observed empirically. They are always present in left-Keynesian analysis but are abhorred by the mainstream, which does not include them in its models. Keynes was certainly conscious of them in the *General Theory* but chose to emphasize the fact that only a fraction of disposable income gets consumed. The version of his consumption function in Figure 4.4 is

$$PC = [1 - s(\omega)](1 - t)Y,$$

with the factor $[1 - s(\omega)]$ as the *propensity to consume* from disposable income (equal to 1 minus $s(\omega)$, which is the saving rate or *propensity to save*). Empirically, consumption also seems to respond to changes in wealth, a linkage not analyzed in detail by Keynes but taken up below.

If saving is positive, the propensity to consume will be less than 1, a property that Keynes considered to be a "fundamental psychological law" (7:96). He also thought it would be a "fairly stable function," making changes in consumption depend directly on changes in income. If that is the case, then one can plug the consumption function into the accounting balance

$$PC + PI + PG - PX = 0$$

to determine the level of output as a function of investment and government spending, which is assumed to be set by fiscal policy. This maneuver constitutes the principle of effective demand. As shown in Figure 4.4, it completes the basic model of the *General Theory*.

Implications of the *General Theory*

From the real and financial analysis in the *General Theory*, Keynes arrived at recommendations that guide macro policy more than seventy-five years after he first laid them out. Implications of the theory about the structure and functioning of the macroeconomy provide background for the policy debate. These issues are the focus of this section.

Avoiding Pro-cyclicality

Just three more equations and then we are done with them. The first one is not discussed by Keynes but provides background for later discussion. To set it up requires a bit of high school algebra. Always assuming that income = output, you can plug the consumption function into the macro balance equation and simplify to get

$$[PI - s(1 - t)PX] + [PG - tPX] = 0.$$

The two terms in brackets to the left of the equals sign represent net borrowing at current prices (because the price level P is not canceled out of the equation) by the private sector and the government respectively. As discussed in Chapter 1, the income = output postulate means that they have to sum to zero. The positive terms in the expression, PI and PG, are sometimes called demand *injections*. Saving $s(1 - t)PX$ and tax receipts tPX are *leakages*. Macroeconomic balance requires equality between injections and leakages.

Governments typically run deficits, so that in an economy closed to foreign trade the private sector would have to run a surplus. (In the United States prior to 2007–2009 both sectors often ran deficits, so the economy ended up borrowing from the rest of the world.) A key question is how the overall net borrowing flow responds to *changes* in the level of output. Suppose that for some reason X jumps downward. If the sum of the two net borrowing flows were to fall in response, then aggregate demand would decline. Output would presumably drop further, maybe even to zero as on the banana plantation in the *Treatise on Money*.

This destabilizing positive feedback loop would not occur if overall net borrowing were to rise in response to lower output. That is, borrowing should vary *counter-cyclically* to ensure that a *Keynesian stability condition* is in place. The minus signs on their entries in the equation above indicate that both saving and taxes vary counter-cyclically. If, however, the causal scheme in Figure 4.4 is extended to include a positive effect of output on investment (observable in the data), then private net borrowing could decrease *pro-cyclically* in response to a jump downward in output. For overall system stability, government borrowing would have to increase strongly through lower taxes and possibly increased spending as well. As will be seen in Chapter 5, private-sector net borrowing on the part of households (especially) and business is pro-cyclical. Government borrowing is counter-cyclical and serves to stabilize the system. The big expansion of government spending coupled with some tax reduction in the wake of the events of 2007–2009 is only the most recent example.

The Multiplier

The *multiplier* figures prominently in the *General Theory*. The "story" is that an increase in (say) real investment will raise output one-for-one. But then some of the income generated by the output increase will be spent on consumption, which will generate more output and so on. These successive rounds of demand will not blow up if the Keynesian stability condition is satisfied. They are supposed to play out rapidly, so that the final result can be expressed as in the equation just below.

This idea, first stated by Kahn, was another steppingstone in Keynes's transition from the *Treatise on Money.* Milton Friedman's permanent income hypothesis aimed at derailing the multiplier by asserting that consumption does not rise in response to "transitory" growth of income.

For a version in algebra, the net borrowing equation can be restated as

$$X = \frac{I + G}{s(1 - t) + t}.$$

The denominator in this expression is less than 1, meaning that an increase in investment or government spending will raise output more than in proportion. This response gives a multiplier with an algebraic value of $\frac{1}{[s(1-t)+t]}$. One last equation follows if we assume that an increase in government spending is offset by higher taxes collected via an increase in the tax rate *t*. This *spend-and-tax* policy yields the expression

$$X = G + \frac{I}{s}$$

for output. It shows that real GDP goes up only one-for-one with an increase in G. In the jargon, the *balanced budget multiplier* on government spending is equal to 1. This reasoning may be relevant to the United States if, as is likely, national health insurance has to be financed by higher taxes.

Alternatively one could consider a *tax-and-spend* policy in which the proceeds from a higher tax rate are spent by the government. In that case the multiplier on investment becomes $\frac{1}{[s(1-t)]}$, higher than the value quoted above. This scenario is closer to the pre-1970s situation in the United States, when income taxes were not adjusted for inflation. As nominal incomes went up, *bracket creep* in the then more progressive income tax system provided additional real revenue, which Congress was usually quite happy to spend.

Money Wage Cuts

The *General Theory*'s dismissal of money wage cuts as an effective means to alleviate unemployment rested on two arguments. The first was practical ("not theoretically fundamental" in Keynes's words). Wage reductions would have to be negotiated in piecemeal fashion, but each such attempt would be resisted by the affected group because not only its real but also its *relative* income position would be eroded. Even if, as Keynes accepted in the *General Theory*, a lower economy-wide real wage is needed to permit more employment, "wage-wage" conflicts will make this goal very difficult to achieve by bargaining over contract revisions.

The more "fundamental" argument can be illustrated with Kalecki's markup pricing equation,

$$P = (1 + m)\frac{w}{\lambda}.$$

For any value of the markup rate m a reduction in the money wage w will lead to a *proportional* fall in the price level P, so that the real wage $\omega = \frac{w}{P}$ will not be affected. Hence there will be no incentive for employers to hire more workers or for the level of aggregate demand to change if it is wage- or profit-led. One can see this result directly in the equation for the real wage,

$$\omega = \frac{w}{P} = \frac{\lambda}{1+m},$$

which does not involve w or P explicitly.

Pro-cyclical Real Wage

In his book Keynes said that the markup rate m would be an increasing function of the level of output, but as noted in Chapter 1, he later realized that this assumption is not required for the basic argument to go through.

In practice it is not easy to define a "real" wage by using the data; too many technical details are involved. But evidence suggests that the wage certainly does not vary counter-cyclically, as was pointed out by the young labor economists Lorie Tarshis and John Dunlop in the late 1930s. Keynes agreed and said that he could live happily without the first classical postulate. (Dunlop later went on to become a leading institutionalist student of the labor market who developed Keynes's ideas about wage-wage competition into *wage contours* for the U.S. economy. Tarshis wrote the first

Keynesian textbook in the United States, but it ran into McCarthyite problems and disappeared from view.)

Wages and Prices

Keynes's reasoning is spelled out in detail in Chapter 19, "Changes in Money-Wages." It is summarized in Figure 4.5. The "Effective demand" curves in both diagrams illustrate the case in which demand is profit-led: a higher real wage generates a lower level of economic activity. In the upper diagram the first classical postulate applies along the "Wage curve," with the real wage falling (that is, the money wage goes down and/or the price level goes up more strongly than the wage) when output is higher. The lower diagram shows a Dunlop-Tarshis pro-cyclical real wage (meaning the money wage goes up and/or the price level does not increase as strongly).

In both diagrams the intersection of the curves determines both the real wage and output. A rightward shift of the demand curve (say, from higher government spending or tax cuts) would affect both variables. In the more realistic lower diagram, higher output from the demand shift could well be associated with higher wages and prices, with market institutions determining the strength of the responses. In Chapter 5 we will see how wage, price, and productivity dynamics can fit into a model of cyclical growth consistent with the lower diagram.

A further point is that the Chapter 19 macroeconomics of the *General Theory* is perfectly capable of dealing with varying wages and prices. It is not handicapped by nominal rigidities as was argued after World War II. Keynes did not go into the details of wage and price dynamics, but they certainly fit into his model.

Finally, in Figure 4.4, just how strongly the money wage as the principal component of costs affects the price level will itself depend on the level of effective demand. Only in Kalecki's constant markup case is this linkage irrelevant.

Keynes Effect

In Chapter 19 Keynes did recognize one possible channel though which cutting the nominal wage could stimulate employment. It came to be known as the *Keynes effect*.

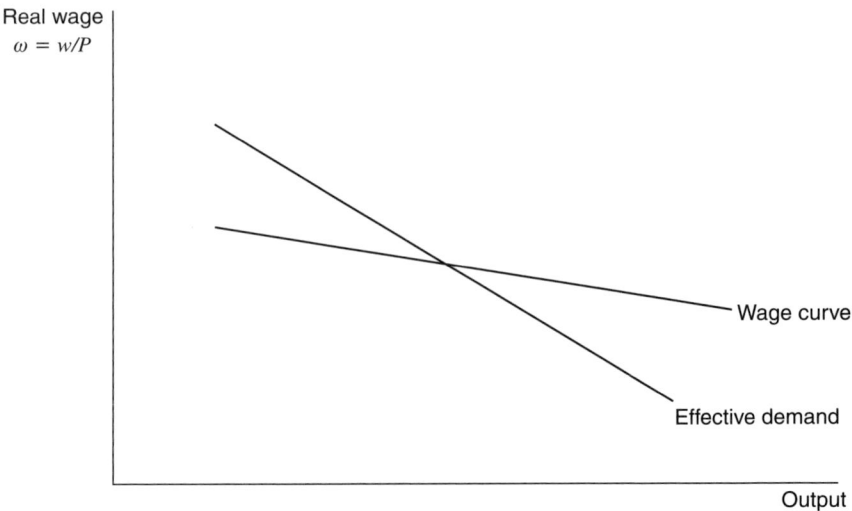

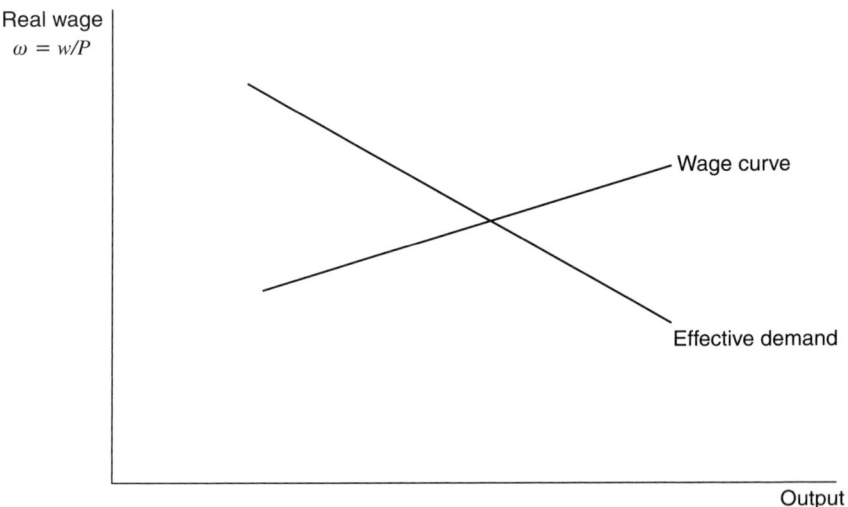

Figure 4.5 Macro equilibrium in the *General Theory's* Chapter 19 model with profit-led effective demand: the first classical postulate in the upper diagram's wage curve and a pro-cyclical real wage in the lower diagram

If lower wages bid down prices, then the level of real balances will rise. As noted above, the interest rate could be expected to fall and stimulate investment demand. But you could get the same result without the hassle of renegotiating wage contracts just by increasing the money supply—a far simpler maneuver.

Moreover, if higher real balances were to be attained by wage and price reduction, then the real burden of debt would increase and potentially exacerbate a recession through its (negative) *wealth effect* on consumption demand, as discussed below. Finally, a functioning capitalist economy *requires* relatively stable nominal payment flows to maintain a social contract. Cutting one particular means of payment, such as money wages, will upset the social balance with respect to other payments, such as pensions, salaries, and many forms of rentier income. Workers will resist changes in pay differentials not just among themselves but also with respect to the other social classes.

Pigou Effect

In the *General Theory,* A. C. Pigou was Keynes's favorite example of a classical economist who failed to grasp the new truths that were being unveiled. Nevertheless Pigou and Keynes were Cambridge colleagues and remained friends. Pigou was a few years older and strongly supported Keynes's early work on probability. Decades later he invented the *Pigou effect* (or *real balance effect*), which became the principal mainstream argument against effective demand. The effect is not mentioned in the *General Theory,* but since it resembles the Keynes effect, now is a good time to bring it in. It will figure centrally in the neoclassical reaction to Keynes described in Chapter 6.

Fortunately for Keynes, the Pigou channel has minor practical importance. Unfortunately for economics education, along with the discredited first classical postulate it is a fundamental component of the *AS/AD model* (for aggregate supply/aggregate demand) discussed just below, which dominates all elementary textbooks.

Recall from Wicksell that because inflation reduces real balances, it will induce people to raise their saving rate to restore the wealth that it has destroyed. Inflation is the *growth rate* of a price index. Pigou restated the inflation tax argument in terms of jumps in the price *level.* To run the thought experiment in the other direction, suppose that a reduction in the money wage bids down the price index. Then real balances will increase and people will consume more or save less, boosting aggregate demand via the paradox of thrift. Wage-cutting does work, and can drive the economy toward full employment! The linkage is more direct than the Keynes effect, not requiring an intermediary reduction in the interest rate and increase in investment demand.

A numerical example is a good way to illustrate the irrelevance of the Pigou effect. Table 4.4 presents numbers broadly illustrative of a middle-class household in the United States before 2007. The family's disposable income is $50,000 (or 50 for short). They own a house worth 300, with a mortgage of 130. They also hold 30 of "money" (cash, deposits, CDs, money market funds, and so on). Their net worth works out to be 200.

A plausible consumption function has a propensity to consume from income equaling 0.8 *and* a propensity to consume from wealth of 0.05; that

Table 4.4 Effects of price changes on consumption

Household balance sheet (thousands of dollars)			
House	300	130	Mortgage
Money	30	200	Net worth

Propensity to consume from income = 0.8
Propensity to consume from wealth = 0.05
Income = 50   Consumption = 50   Saving = 0

Effect of a 25 percent reduction in value of house	
Wealth ↓ by 75 (37.5%)	Consumption ↓ by 3.75 (7.5%)

Effect of a 5 percent reduction in the price of goods and services	
Real balances ↑ by 1.6	Consumption ↑ by 0.08 (0.16%)
Real debt ↑ by 6.8	Consumption ↓ by 0.34 (0.68%)
Real income ↑ by 2.6	Consumption ↑ by 2.1 (4.2%)

is, 80% of current income and 5% of current wealth are directed toward consumption. (Rationales for the *wealth effect* are presented in Chapter 6.) With these parameters, the household's saving level is zero.

For this household the big economic event of 2007–8 was a 25% (roughly) reduction in the value of their home. Because of the negative wealth effect, their consumption should fall by 7.5%. Such a change is the basic cause of the recession that began in late 2007.

Because most wealth in the United States is *not* held in the form of money, the Pigou effect turns out to be distinctly second order. The table shows that a 5% reduction in the price level (quite a large deflation) acting through the Pigou channel would make consumption rise by only 0.16%. On the other side of the balance sheet, the household's real burden of debt would go up, cutting consumption by 0.68%. That is, when nominal liabilities exceed the amount of money the household is holding, the Pigou effect runs the "wrong" way (as Keynes pointed out in Chapter 19 in discussing his own eponymous effect).

Finally, if the household's nominal income is not linked to the price level, its real income will rise and consumption will go up by 4.2% because *negative* forced saving kicks in. If, as with William Jennings Bryan's prairie farmers in the late nineteenth century, the household's income *is* linked to a falling price level, it suffers from debt deflation.

The AS/AD Model

The AS/AD model is one of many attempts to move the microeconomic analysis described in connection with Figure 2.1 into the macro realm. The diagram features aggregate output on the horizontal axis and the corresponding price index on the vertical axis. It is presented in Figure 4.6.

The AD relationship says that aggregate demand will increase when the price level falls, that is, when the curve has a negative slope. This linkage could reflect the Pigou or, perhaps more plausibly, the Keynes effect. Table 4.4 shows that when debt levels are high, there is every reason to expect the opposite response: a lower price level can reduce demand by increasing the burden of debt.

Curiously enough in standard practice, the Pigou and Keynes effects are treated as being *very* powerful. Aggregate demand is said to be determined

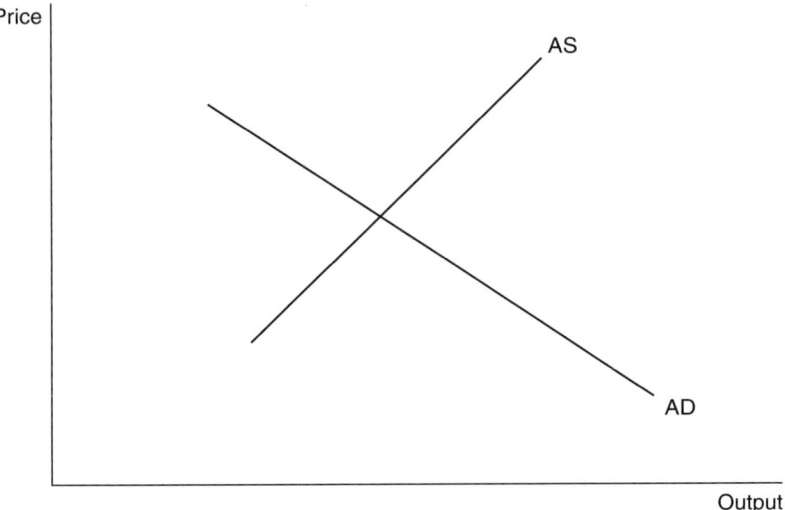

Figure 4.6 The standard AS/AD model

by a version of Chapter 2's ever adaptable equation of exchange written in the form

$$\text{Demand} = \text{Money} \times \text{Velocity} / \text{Price level}.$$

According to this formula, a 5% price cut will lead output to increase by 5%. This response is over thirty times stronger than the one in Table 4.4. It is ridiculously high.

The AS relationship is built around the idea that a higher price level will reduce the real wage and so create incentives for firms to raise employment and output. The curve will have a positive slope in the diagram. But the first classical postulate is not supported by the data, which suggest that a lower level of output leads to a lower real wage. Both the AS and AD relationships could easily slope the "wrong" way.

The same result occurs for the economy depicted in the lower diagram of Figure 4.5 if we think in terms of the price/wage ratio, say, $R = \dfrac{P}{w}$. When the price level increases relative to the wage, effective demand rises because profits rise. At the same time, higher output will raise labor's relative bargaining power, and R will fall in a supply-side response. Both curves have improper slopes.

So much for economics education.

Liquidity Trap

In Chapter 15 Keynes introduced an idea that Dennis Robertson christened the *liquidity trap*. The trap supposedly opens when the interest rate is low. The central bank can try to force the rate down further by buying bonds, but it remains obstinately stuck at some level. The trap may be empirically relevant, but Keynes's argument for its possible existence is one of the few places in the *General Theory* where he sounds distinctly antiquated, for a couple of reasons.

His thinking rests on the well-known inverse relationship between the price of a bond and its current interest rate. Suppose that somebody expects the interest rate next "period" to be higher than it is now, which implies that the bond price has to be lower. Then if the player buys a bond today, she will anticipate a capital loss that may be big enough to offset the bond's coupon payment or running yield. Working through the math shows that the loss will be greater the lower the current rate. So if the rate is low, it may be wiser not to buy at all and stay liquid by holding money instead. After all, the bond is expected to cost less in the future.

Robertson neatly summarized the gist: "[T]he rate of interest is what it is because it is expected to become other than it is" (Skidelsky, 1972, 563). A more generous interpretation à la Soros is that liquidity preference involves bootstrap dynamics whereby the "tone and feel" of the financial market evolve over time, with changing perceptions about future interest rates affecting current preferences for liquidity.

Keynes's specific argument is out of date, because a market player can now engage in derivative operations to protect herself against the expected capital loss. For example, she can simply buy the bond now and also purchase a *put option* or *put warrant* to sell if the price falls by a certain amount. Keynes's general view remains in force, however, because financial actors may simply choose not to engage in certain transactions—not to enter the Fed funds or commercial paper markets in 2007–8, for example.

From a contemporary perspective Keynes's analysis is also deficient because he did not take up CDSs, which were at the center of the 2007–2009 crisis. Given his views about the uselessness of calculations built around complete orderings of probabilities of defaults (or falling bond prices), he would have resisted currently fashionable formal models, but it would have been good if he had set down his qualitative Bayesian views about these issues.

A loanable funds version of the liquidity trap can be constructed by assuming that the natural rate of interest at which savings equals investment is less than zero. Desired saving has risen and planned investment fallen to such an extent that even if the rate is zero, there will be excess saving and low aggregate demand. A "solution" is for the central bank to create money aggressively enough to set off price inflation and force the real interest rate into negative territory. Or else inflation might be induced by other means such as Roosevelt's devaluations in 1933. The inflation strategy was recommended to Japan, mostly by foreign experts, during its 1990s stagnation. The Bank of Japan ignored them, and the government finally got the situation more or less under control by restructuring the banking system in an exercise likely to be relevant for the United States in the 2010s.

Finally, as discussed in the following chapter, Minsky's ideas about financial cycles suggest that the interest rate may in fact be quite stable when both its own level and aggregate demand are high.

Trade Cycle

Keynes leads Chapter 22, "On the Trade Cycle," with the observation that "[s]ince we claim to have shown in preceding chapters what determines the volume of employment at any time, it follows, if we are right, that our theory must be capable of explaining the phenomena of the Trade Cycle" (7:313). He came pretty close to the mark, but as will be seen in Chapter 5, the devil of the cycle lies in understanding the details. He left some of them out.

A useful place to begin a quick sketch is with the multiplier formula presented above for output determination:

$$X = \frac{I + G}{s(1-t) + t}.$$

With unchanging fiscal policy (fixed values of G and t), the level of output X is determined by investment I and the saving rate s. As in Figure 4.4, investment is set by the marginal efficiency of capital, in turn influenced by the interest rate, which follows from liquidity preference. The saving rate emerges from the consumption function.

Keynes sees shifts in the marginal efficiency of capital as the main driving force underlying the cycle. The other two relationships serve as amplifying or damping factors. As in Roy Harrod's growth model, discussed in Chapter 5, positive feedback is likely to be involved. Higher investment increases output, which, with vibrant animal spirits, can push investment up further. (On the way down, with spirits sagging, the process will run in reverse.)

Liquidity preference may lag investment, so that higher output means that the interest rate increases faster. As in Kindleberger's financial cycle, at some point during a cyclical upswing the rate may rise to a level high enough (in conjunction with other factors such as the income distribution, as discussed in Chapter 5) to switch the growth rate of investment from positive to negative, initiating a downswing. If the interest rate continues to rise after the fall-off in investment growth (in the same way that earnings per share overshoot the falling asset price in the Soros cycle of Figure 4.2), then it will worsen the fall.

Keynes further thought that shifts in the saving rate could exacerbate the cycle. If asset prices fall in advance (as a *leading indicator*) or along with the growth of investment, then the saving rate could increase, reducing output and investment demand. In the mid-1930s, "[w]ith a 'stock-minded' public, as in the United States to-day, a rising stock-market may be an almost essential condition for a satisfactory propensity to consume" (7:319). No doubt rising housing prices in the United States beginning in the 1990s helped generate a satisfactorily high level of consumption.

Recovery from a recession calls for a renewal in animal spirits, which may not easily happen. A low interest rate is probably a necessary but by no means a sufficient condition. In an Austrian or Marxist twist, Keynes argues that there may have been excessive or misdirected investment during the preceding boom, which has to be worked off. The implication is that a slump may be deep and long-lasting—like the Great Depression!

In practice, post–World War II recessions in the United States have been rather brief, with a peak-to-trough period usually running for a few quarters. In most instances GDP growth coming out of the trough has been quite rapid. Depending on how one defines the length of a slump, the worst one after the war ran in "double-dip" fashion from 1980 through

1982, accompanied by financial sector retrenchment in the wake of the 1979 interest rate shock and the developing country debt crisis, which impacted strongly on the larger banks. The unemployment rate (a *lagging indicator*) peaked at 10.8% late in that year. The recession that began in December 2007 could be as deep on the real side, accompanied by far more serious financial dislocation than in the early 1980s. Only economic performance in 2010 and beyond will tell us how severe the real recession turned out to be.

As a general view of the cycle Keynes's description makes sense. He did not, however, bring up the fact that, for the United States at least, both residential investment and changes in saving by households appear to be more volatile than business net borrowing. There are also fairly regular distributive shifts over the cycle—pro-cyclical real wages interacting with profit-led demand—which help keep it under way. These additional mechanisms fit readily into analysis based on Chapters 19 and 22 but were not stressed by Keynes himself.

Macro after the *General Theory*

Winston Churchill, being concerned with empire, military strategy, and breaking German codes based on the Enigma machine, had little time and less patience for economics during the war. He scarcely mentions Keynes in his five-volume history. Maynard himself, meanwhile, moved into a pivotal advisory post in the Treasury, virtually acting as de facto chancellor of the exchequer. He dominated wartime economic policy. His role in international economics has already been briefly described and is pursued further in Chapter 8. Two other pieces of analysis are relevant for later discussion: a 1940 pamphlet, *How to Pay for the War*, and his work with others on formulating the national income and product accounts.

How to Pay for the War

The pamphlet was a brilliant attempt to kill many birds with one stone. All economists agreed that Say's Law would apply in wartime. Output would be pushed to the highest possible level, and aggregate demand, including military spending, would have to accommodate. If policies could not be designed to restrict civilian demand to the supply available after military needs were met, then inflation was likely to take off. Keynes despised the adverse effects of the inflation tax and forced saving on the working class, and feared they would ignite a wage-price spiral. Not grasping how pent-up demand and the joy of victory would boost consumers' animal spirits and lead to a postwar boom, along with most economists he thought there would be a recession. He was concerned with how to avoid it.

Keynes was neoclassical enough to emphasize that rationing was a poor way to control demand. Partial rationing would just divert spending toward non-rationed goods, and universal rationing would be a bureaucratic nightmare. If inflation was ruled out, then the only policy tool available was more taxation. Maynard's clever stroke was to propose that higher taxes on lower incomes should be partially converted to compulsory savings bonds, which would be repaid later to offset the expected postwar slump. Inflation and rationing would be avoided and provision made for the future.

For better or worse, the proposal got nowhere, in part because the Labour Party opted for a combination of inflation and rationing to restrain demand. The book's ideas did seep into postwar mainstream macroeconomics in the form of an *inflationary gap* which could open up if expansionary policy were to be pushed too aggressively. But the mainstream did not pick up on the inflation tax and forced saving, the gap's Wicksellian forebears, which for reasons discussed in Chapter 2 have faded from the literature. That leaves obscure the adjustment process that is supposed to apply if aggregate demand is pushed above a fixed level of supply. Some actors have to take a real income or wealth reduction to force them to reduce their levels of demand, but in post–World War II inflationary gap analysis, just who the losers are is never made clear.

National Accounts

Attempts to construct national income accounts date back to the Puritan polymath William Petty in mid-seventeenth-century England (he also came up with calculations very similar to the Kahn-Keynes multiplier) and the physiocrats in late-eighteenth-century France. There were several versions in England in the early twentieth century. In the 1930s Colin Clark in Cambridge put considerable effort into constructing accounts consistent with the fundamental equations of the *Treatise on Money.*

The key steps toward the present-day NIPA system with its explicit income = output balance, however, were taken by Keynes and the German émigré Erwin Rothbarth at Cambridge in the late 1930s and then by

Keynes himself in *How to Pay for the War*. After his move to the Treasury, the first "official" accounts came out in a white paper in 1941. They were worked up by James Meade and Richard Stone (both later got Nobels) under Keynes's direction. Parallel efforts in the United States also produced accounts along NIPA lines in the early 1940s.

Flows of funds accounts were set out by the American institutionalist Morris Copeland in 1952. Under United Nations auspices, Stone took the lead in integrating NIPA, FOF, and input-output accounting into the integrated system which is in virtually universal use today.

Maynard's Lessons

Keynes offered many lessons for his successors. Here is a brief summary.

The foremost idea is that all economic decisions are taken under conditions of fundamental uncertainty—not "risk" in the sense that possible events in the future can be fully described by an objective probability distribution known to at least some (and possibly all) participants in the market. For example, from Keynes's point of view the idea that subprime mortgage borrowers' probabilities of default could be quantified on the basis of historical data during a period in which housing prices rose at an unprecedented rate was nonsense. Of course prices could always go down, as demonstrated after 2005.

Two Sets of Prices

The recent significance of housing price fluctuations points to the fact that a capitalist economy has two sets of prices: for assets such as housing and securities, and for goods and services. In the *General Theory*, Keynes broke from the quantity theory that he had espoused in his *Tract on Monetary Reform*. Rather, he assumed that prices of goods and services are driven by costs—notably the wage and exchange rates as costs of labor and imports respectively. In the full model of Chapter 19, the price level or price/wage ratio could also respond to effective demand.

Regarding asset prices, and housing prices in particular, Keynes would say that thinking that securitizing the increasing volume of mortgages and selling them into the financial market would "diversify" default risk was nonsense upon stilts. So long as housing prices kept rising, consumers increased their borrowing. Financial traders ran up more debt with one another and the rest of the world to buy more securitized mortgages. When housing prices stalled and started to drop, an unexpectedly high number of borrowers walked away from their mortgages, and the whole highly leveraged and securitized house of cards came down. Keynes did not discuss bubbles based on linked increases in asset prices and leverage, but Charles Kindleberger—a true-blue Keynesian—certainly did. Soros's model of financial cycles follows a similar line.

For the real side of the economy, Keynes used psychological and sociological observation to frame hypotheses about how market actors operate—hence his assumed dependence of saving on income and of investment on interest and profit rates along with asset prices. He also thought that saving and investment decisions were strongly affected by current economic perceptions, or "expectations."

He argued vigorously that Say's Law of markets does not apply. With his principle of effective demand operating, there is no natural tendency for the economy to arrive at full employment.

Keynesian Categories

One Keynesian category involves setting up models with collective social actors instead of "rational" agents which act individually. The quotation marks are meant to signal that most people's understanding of rationality lies light-years away from the standard macroeconomists' assumption that it amounts to behaving consistently with a "true" model of the economy, which on the basis of Keynesian ontology cannot possibly exist.

The justification for thinking about collective actors is that the socioeconomic circumstances in which groups of people operate—be they sweepers in Mumbai or traders on Wall Street—impel them toward shared economic attitudes and patterns of behavior. Even after 2007–2009, the fact that financial sector leaders in both Europe and the United States seemed to think that the system that had failed should be largely reinstated with their same income levels as before demonstrates the strength of collective patterns of belief.

Fallacies of composition can easily arise in which apparently rational decisions at the level of individual or collective actors create a macroeconomically unsustainable situation.

Considering broad social classes of collective actors means that macroeconomic models can conveniently be based on the sectoral/functional income distribution built into the national income and product accounts (largely by Keynes and his followers James Meade and Richard Stone at the

U.K. Treasury in the early 1940s). Distributive issues are described in terms of the functional rather than the size distribution of income because the former fits more easily into macroeconomic discourse.

There is always distributive conflict among classes, at times latent and at other times painfully visible. It may lead to overt hostility or be displaced into other areas. Inflation has been a common outcome of conflicting income claims worldwide. As recognized by Keynes, the German hyperinflation in the early 1920s can be traced to workers' attempts to restore their pre–World War I real income level by pushing up money wages abetted by a compliant central bank. U.S. stagflation in the 1970s is another example, which was ended by tight money and union-busting under Reagan. Running up debt can be another outcome of conflict (a point raised by Albert Hirschman among others).

On the financial side, Keynes's villains in the *General Theory* were high savers and bear speculators holding out for high interest rates. He thought that these groups, probably broadly overlapping in terms of social background, would cause long-term stagnation by holding down aggregate demand. Both groups were conspicuously absent in the United States during the 1990s while investors' animal spirits were high. The dot-com asset price crash ended a very Keynesian boom, a possibility that he did not fully consider.

Rather, Keynes proposed a business cycle theory with output swings upward and downward led by investment. Along with shifts in the level of saving, he thought that changes in the interest rate rather than asset prices would be the main factor amplifying or dampening the cycle. The basic framework fits the recent period, but with movements in debt (which did not enter into his cycle theory) and asset prices playing central roles.

Finally, Keynes devoted a lot of effort in the 1920s to formulating industrial policies to deal with structural unemployment in Britain's lagging industries such as coal. In the 1940s he labored long and hard to set up a stable, balanced global macroeconomic system. How such ideas can be updated to deal with contemporary problems is a pressing issue.

Macroeconomics in Practice

Fundamental uncertainty means that expectations about the economy can shift rapidly. But if they are stable, as they can be for extended periods of time, then Keynes's basic macro model is well defined. Even in crisis the basic income = output accounting framework applies. That is the key reason why the Obama stimulus package of 2009 had traction. By generating public demand for output by tax cuts and government spending at a time when private investment and consumption were contracting, it gave enough support to income to rule out a very deep recession (or depression).

That is, on the real side, the principle of effective demand is intact. Say's Law is not enforced. Standard econometric tests show that saving does not drive investment, and full utilization of labor and installed capacity is not observed. On the whole, the private sector behaves pro-cyclically, so fiscal and monetary policy have to be deployed as counter-cyclical stabilizers.

Observed macroeconomic linkages follow the pattern of Figure 4.4. Cost-based structuralist inflation models apply. Kalecki's first approximation of a constant markup was never fully accepted by Keynes, who was well aware of the possibility of changes in nominal wage and price levels and their distributive effects. Prices can respond to the level of demand, for example, although their overall level is anchored by costs.

The monetary authorities intervene in the market for overnight interbank debt to influence the interest rate, usually counter-cyclically. For the past decades in the United States at least there has been no clear association between the growth rate of the money supply and price inflation for goods and services. The quantity theory does not rule.

Investment demand shifts in line with own-rates of return and the marginal efficiency of capital. It responds positively to profitability and the level of economic activity as posited by Kalecki and Steindl, and negatively (usually weakly) to the interest rate.

Aggregate consumption responds positively to output and negatively to profit income flows, consistent with different propensities to consume from wage and non-wage income. Consumption and saving react weakly if at all to changes in the interest rate but do appear to be influenced by movements in wealth.

In Keynes's view, business cycles are driven by shifts in investment demand with changes in saving and the interest rate serving as amplifying or damping factors. Animal spirits may turn growth of investment into a positive feedback process in an upswing. The expansion may be cut off by rising interest rates and the downswing exacerbated by increasing saving rates if asset prices decline.

Economic Policy

Keynes's mature ideas about economic policy were never set out in a coherent form and remain subject to substantial debate. A quick sketch can be based on Chapter 3's four-way breakdown of monetary and fiscal maneuvers, targeted interventions, and international policies.

On the international front, toward the end of his life Keynes backed the Bretton Woods system with fixed exchange rates and heavy capital controls. He also wanted an international reserve currency which could be expanded to support deficit countries, but the United States would have none of that. The system as it was created lasted for more than two decades—not a bad run. Early in his career he espoused free trade on Ricardo's lines but gradually drifted toward soft mercantilism aimed at boosting national income by export promotion and import substitution—a policy line promoted enthusiastically by some of his Cambridge successors.

He supported industrial policy and thought that the state should take control of most investment decisions. He also was in favor of taxes or other restrictions on financial transactions.

In general Keynes favored easy money, thinking that low interest rates were essential to put a floor under investment demand. But he had his doubts about the effectiveness of monetary policy, for example, with his invention of the liquidity trap. He did not take on board Austrian ideas that low rates may stimulate overinvestment and/or set off asset price inflation.

"Increase G," or if in doubt boost government spending, is the simplistic version of Keynes's fiscal message. In fact he *never* said that. The idea was the invention of his mainstream followers as discussed in Chapter 6. Keynes himself was dubious about heavily unbalanced budgets, as in *How to Pay for the War*. He thought that the government's current and capital accounts should be separate, with the current budget kept in balance. The capital budget should support industrial policy as mentioned above, and public works expenditures could be used counter-cyclically (as he advised Roosevelt in 1938 after New Deal public works spending was cut back). He did not anticipate the post–World War II jump in spend-and-tax interventions to construct the welfare state but probably would have counseled prudence.

The significance of Keynes's impish observation that in the long run we will all be dead is easy to overrate. Consistent with Ramsey's original version of his growth model, Keynes did have a long-run view of where the economy was going. He thought that consumption demand per capita would stabilize at a high level while the return to capital would tend toward zero; that is why rentiers could be euthanized and the state would have to support investment. That forecast turned out to be wrong. The profit rate has remained high (and recently rising), and modern capitalism continues to produce new goods which people want to buy. (It is a lot easier to write this book on a computer than on a balky mechanical typewriter, for example!) We will see in the next chapter that if there is ongoing labor productivity growth, then demand per capita must increase to prevent ever-growing unemployment (an idea emphasized by Luigi Pasinetti). Like Ricardo and Malthus, Keynes did not fully take in the long-run implications of continuing productivity growth.

The key point, however, is that when it is restated in terms of the economics of growth, Keynes's demand-driven macro framework remains valid. It has also been remarkably durable. In the short to medium run it provides the only approach that exists that can deal with macroeconomics after 2007–2009.

Notes

There is now a large academic industry focused on Keynes's early work on philosophy and probability. The collection of papers edited by Jochen Runde and Sohei Mizuhara (2003) is a good introduction.

Daniel Ellsberg (2001) is a belated publication of his 1962 Harvard Ph.D. thesis, with the paradox mentioned in the text and much discussion of Keynes. Alberto Feduzi (2007) gives a clear analysis of the complications. Ramsey's essay "Truth and Probability" is available at http://socserv.mcmaster.ca/~econ/ugcm/3ll3/ramseyfp/ramsess.pdf. Frank Knight (1921) gives his views on risk and uncertainty. Jared Diamond (2005) discusses the options for societal collapse. Nicholas Taleb (2007) describes his black swans. For Ben Bernanke's take on the Great Moderation, see http://www.federalreserve.gov/boarddocs/speeches/2004/20040220/default.htm.

The quotation from Chuck Prince was in the *Financial Times,* July 10, 2007.

For discussion of leverage and liquidity and other topics in regulation, see Brunnermeier et al. (2009). As noted in Chapter 3, the leverage analysis in the text is inspired by Hyun Shin, one of the co-authors. Soros (2009) and Tett (2009) navigate the roiled waters of CDOs and CDSs with great aplomb. Goldman Sachs's synthetic CDO maneuvers are described in a report from the Senate Permanent Subcommittee on Investigations available at http://graphics8.nytimes.com/packages/pdf/business/2010April26_MemorandumonWallStreetCrisis.PDF.

Norbert Wiener's *Cybernetics* (second edition, 1961) is fascinating but not an easy read. Kaplan and Glass (1995) leads fairly gently into predator-prey differential equations.

Luigi Pasinetti (1974) presents a schematic of the *General Theory* model similar to the one in Figure 4.4, and congratulates Keynes on his Ricardian vice. The Keynesian stability condition with its injections and leakages is implicit in a 1939 paper by Paul Samuelson and also in Keynes's *How to Pay for the War,* from 1940. Pigou (1943) presents his anti-Keynesian effect, which led into Modigliani's pivotal model from 1944. Dutt (2002) recounts the tangled history of the AS/AD model. Mitra-Khan (2009) reviews the origins of the NIPA system on both sides of the Atlantic. Copeland (1952) lays out his flows of funds accounts.

Papers in the collection edited by Backhouse and Bateman (2006) present broadly consistent interpretations of Keynes's views on policy.

— 5 —

Keynesian Growth, Cycles, and Crisis

This chapter is devoted to economic growth and business cycles as analyzed by two generations of Keynes's successors, most with close Cambridge connections: Michal Kalecki, Josef Steindl, Roy Harrod, Nicholas Kaldor, Joan Robinson, Evsey Domar, and Richard Goodwin from the first wave; Hyman Minsky, Luigi Pasinetti, and Wynne Godley from the second. The first three-quarters of the chapter are devoted to their various contributions. The last part pulls many of them together to describe significant changes in the U.S. economy after around 1980, and how they combined to create the crisis at the end of the 2000s. After financial and international complications are discussed in Chapters 7 and 8, Chapter 9 provides a final summing-up.

Joan Robinson pointed to an important distinction between *history and equilibrium*, or between thinking in historical and logical time. Growth and cycle theory operate in the latter domain and occupy space in this chapter. But the theory is useless unless it can also shed light on observed historical changes and future prospects. Those topics are taken up as well, here and in Chapter 9. More high school mathematics than in other chapters is used to describe the logic of the models, but the discussion should still be fairly straightforward.

Economists use two key variables to analyze growth of real output per capita. One is investment, or gross fixed capital formation; the other is the rate of growth of labor productivity. Investment adds to the existing capital stock and serves as a vehicle for new technologies that boost productivity.

Expectations based on animal spirits suggest that at least at times, investment can be subject to positive feedback; an increase in its level boosts output through the multiplier, raises expectations, and speeds up its own rate of growth. If that were the only force driving output expansion or contraction, then the macroeconomy would be drastically unstable. This potential instability was at the center of Harrod's pioneering growth model from 1939. If positive feedback is present, then some other variable(s) must act to stabilize the growing economic system, probably cyclically as in Keynes's and Soros's financial models described in Chapter 4 and revisited below. In 1946 the MIT economist Domar produced a complementary analysis of stabilizing negative feedback in the investment decision based on the effects of capacity utilization.

In 1967 Goodwin (with echoes of Marx) pointed out that changes in income distribution may support a "growth cycle." Goodwin's model assumed that investment is determined by available saving. Dynamics in a demand-driven version with investment following either Harrod or Domar hinge on whether growth is wage- or profit-led—the Kalecki-Steindl connection. Distribution will also respond to the pattern of productivity growth, which is likely to be linked to economies of scale as in Kaldor. Because employment growth is the difference between output and productivity growth rates, their behavior over time strongly affects the labor market.

The next topic is how the interest rate and debt can affect the real side of the economy over time, extending Keynes's own analysis in the *General Theory*'s Chapter 22 on the trade cycle. The focus is on the financial instability model set out by Hyman Minsky. He concentrated on how shifts in a liquidity preference schedule which depends on asset prices as well as the interest rate can generate large swings in investment demand and output. But the dynamics of his model are quite general; it can also be used to illustrate the sorts of financial cycles discussed by Soros and Kindleberger.

Cyclicality is also linked to shifts in levels of net borrowing, pro-cyclical on the part of the private sector and counter-cyclical on that of the government. Godley and Steindl independently proposed a useful way to summarize the details. To think about the long-run configuration of the economy, it helps to bring in sectoral productivity and employment dynamics. Recently in the United States the finance, insurance, and real estate *(FIRE)* sector has played a significant role in productivity (though not employment) growth. It may not continue into the future.

The final topic is whether all these models can shed light on the run-up to the crisis of 2007–2009, on both the real and financial sides. A provisional assessment suggests that in fact they can.

Accounting for Economic Growth

A striking feature of capitalism in the now rich economies is that for over two hundred years it has generated rising levels of real income per capita—in the range of 2% per year or a 7.25-fold increase per century according to the standard calculations. Beginning with Harrod's paper, economists have been trying to get their heads around this phenomenon. Their success has been limited, but some lessons have been learned. They can help focus thinking about recovery from the crisis of 2007–2009.

Most results in growth theory come from extending Keynes's accounting for *levels* of flows of income, output, and their components to their *rates of growth*. For example, the growth rate of GDP is the change in its level over some period (a quarter or a year), divided by the level at the beginning of the period, giving a number such as 3% per year. Before we get into cyclical growth involving both output and distribution, it makes sense to spell out how simpler one-dimensional models operate.

Growth Accounting I

Harrod and Domar started (independently) from Keynes's postulated equality between saving and investment, both expressed in real terms. They assumed that it is possible to estimate the real stock of capital (say, K) by a *perpetual inventory* method, which boils down to summing flows of real investment in gross fixed capital formation from the NIPA estimates over time and subtracting reductions in capital due to depreciation and scrapping.

To keep things simple, ignore depreciation. Then in a first pass at the accounting, the growth rate (say, g) of capital will be investment during the current period divided by the level of the capital stock at the beginning. Suppose that saving, following Keynes, is proportional to output X. Then Keynes's condition for short macroeconomic balance is that investment minus saving is equal to zero,

$$g - su = 0,$$

with s as the *saving rate* (level of saving divided by output, say, s) and $u = \dfrac{X}{K}$ as the *output/capital ratio* (u for "utilization"). Output and utilization are supposed to adjust to bring saving in line with investment. Another version of this formula is

$$su = g.$$

This relationship is known as the *Harrod-Domar equation*. Harrod called the su term on the left-hand side the *warranted growth rate*. The equation provides a useful way to categorize theories of growth.

Neoclassical growth theory is based on a J. B. Clark aggregate production function and associated marginal productivity rules about income distribution (recall Chapter 2), assumed full employment of labor and capital, and Say's Law in all their combined glory. For a given saving rate (see below), these assumptions nail down the su term in the Harrod-Domar equation, so that the growth rate g on the right-hand side is determined by forces of *productivity and thrift*. Suppose that the economy starts off with a low endowment of capital, or a low ratio of capital to labor. Then it will build up its capital stock so that the output/capital ratio u will decrease over (logical) time. At some point the warranted growth rate will equal the *natural* growth rate n of the labor force. The system will then stay forever at a *steady state* with equal growth rates of labor and capital and a constant value of u, determined by the equation

$$su = n.$$

This convergence scenario will be extended to incorporate labor productivity growth below. It is similar to the ones already discussed for Ricardo's and Ramsey's models, and summarizes the neoclassical vision of the long run. Toward the end of this chapter we will see that after 1980, the U.S. economy appeared to be running *away* from a steady state.

There are in fact two versions of the model. One is the contemporary restatement of Ramsey's original set-up, already sketched in Chapter 2 and taken up again in Chapter 6. Because of the Keynes-Ramsey rule, its consumption growth rate falls over time as the capital/labor ratio rises and the economy approaches the steady state. The other variant, which was proposed independently by the Australian Trevor Swan and the MIT economist Robert Solow, assumes a constant (or maybe exogenously changing) saving rate. Take your choice. Optimal growth fits the fancy of the contemporary mainstream.

Between the two versions my own preference is for Solow-Swan because the assumptions underlying the Ramsey *optimal growth* model are even more bizarre than Say's Law and J. B. Clark. Better still, Solow's and Swan's neoclassical production apparatus is not really needed. Using growth accounting based solely on NIPA numbers (see below), one can come up with convergence results similar to theirs. The macroeconomy can get along without a neoclassical aggregate production function after all!

In the 1950s and early 1960s Kaldor set up a hybrid model obeying Say's Law which traces directly back to forced saving macroeconomic adjustment in the *Treatise on Money*. He based it on what he called *stylized facts* about the process of economic growth. An advanced economy is supposed to have full employment of labor and a stable output/capital ratio and profit rate, at least across business cycles. These conditions are combined with steady increases in labor productivity and capital/labor ratios over time. To describe the details requires another excursion into growth accounting.

Growth Accounting II

Recall the *adding-up* breakdown of income into payments to labor and capital from Figure 4.4,

$$Y = PX = wL + rPK,$$

in which Y is income, P the price level, PX the value of real output, w the money wage, L employment, r the profit rate, and the value of capital is PK.ABtaining both sides by P gives

$$X = \omega L + rK$$

with $\omega = \dfrac{w}{P}$ as the real wage.

To transform the accounting into growth rate form, it helps to define the *labor share* $\psi = wL/Y = wL/PX$ and *capital share* $\pi = rPK/Y = rPK/PX$. Another version of the two souls problem immediately follows:

$$\psi + \pi = 1.$$

If one share goes up, the other has to go down.

Using the notation introduced in Chapter 4, let $\lambda = \dfrac{X}{L}$ stand for average labor productivity, and we can also interpret capacity utilization $u = \dfrac{X}{K}$ as capital productivity. We then have the labor and capital share as $\psi = \omega/\lambda$ and $\pi = r/u$ respectively. The two souls equation can be restated as

$$\frac{\omega}{\lambda} + \frac{r}{u} = 1.$$

To maintain the equality, an increase in either labor or capital productivity would have to be offset by a jump in the real wage and/or the profit rate. Productivity growth translates immediately into an increase in some form of income, subject to distributive rules that remain to be specified. After some algebraic sleight of hand, a growth rate version emerges as

Surplus = ψ × (growth rate of λ) + π × (growth rate of u) = ψ × (growth rate of ω) + π × (growth rate of r).

The *Surplus* term at the beginning of the equation is a flow of real output growth resulting from productivity increases. It must be split between growth of real wages and profits after the second equals sign—the two souls problem in growth rate form. As will be seen, labor in the United States has been losing in this conflict over the past three decades—the fruits of productivity growth have mostly gone toward profits—especially during the run-up to the crisis.

Looking at overall growth of output, one can further show that

Growth rate of X = ψ × (growth rate of L) + π × (growth rate of K) + Surplus.

Output growth decomposes into a weighted average of growth rates of labor and capital plus the surplus. Following a 1957 paper by Solow, the surplus is often called *total factor productivity growth,* or *TFPG*. Neoclassical economists stress how they can derive the foregoing equations from the J. B. Clark machinery, but they really just follow from national income accounting.

For the United States the stylized facts are that the output/capital ratio is stable across business cycles, and trend growth in labor productivity is around 2% per year. Productivity growth speeds up coming out of a recession. In recent history in East Asia, capital productivity has been steadily declining while labor productivity growth has been very fast—at times nearly 10% per year—as labor moves from agriculture to sectors with higher average productivity (the U.S. case is discussed below) and the high-productivity sectors approach the world technological frontier. It seems moderately more enlightening to think in terms of separate rates of labor and capital productivity increase rather than bundle them up into TFPG, but mainstream economists analyzing *sources of growth* invariably do the latter.

Kaldor Mark I

To get back to Kaldor, in order to "explain" his stylized facts, he set up a growth model with an independent investment demand function *and* full employment of labor. We will see shortly how he sidestepped the usual implication of Say's Law that saving determines investment.

Along Adam Smith's lines, he thought that economies of scale were an important contributor to labor productivity growth and postulated a specific from of a *technical progress function*. (We can call it Kaldor Mark I.) He assumed that labor productivity is an increasing function of the capital/labor ratio because of *capital deepening*.

With the labor force and its productivity both determined at any point in time, we find that output = employment × labor productivity. If output, investment, and the capital stock are all set, then the only way the Harrod-Domar equation

$$su = g$$

can be satisfied is by adjustment in the saving rate s. Like Schumpeter in his *Theory of Economic Development*, Kaldor assumed that s would change because of forced saving in the short run—a rare postwar application of this mechanism in explicit form. The income distribution would shift in favor of high-saving profit recipients when investment demand goes up.

The model will converge to a steady state if demand is wage-led. If it were profit-led, then an increase in the profit rate due to higher investment demand would bid up demand still further. There is always a distributive twist like this in Kaldor's macro models. At the steady state Kaldor's stylized facts as recited above apply. It is also true that

$$\text{Capital stock growth rate} = \text{employment growth rate} + \text{labor productivity growth rate},$$

so that the natural rate of growth on the right-hand side now includes both population and productivity increases.

At a steady state with constant labor and capital shares, the real wage will grow at the same rate as labor productivity because the labor share ψ is the ratio of the former to the latter ($\psi = \dfrac{\omega}{\lambda}$ with ω as the real wage and λ as productivity). This 100% pass-through of productivity gains into real wages rules out a Luddite scenario with a trending distribution between labor and capital. (We will see shortly that no such stability is observable in the United States over the past thirty years or more.) It shows up in Ramsey and Solow-Swan steady states as well, and explains why many economists are partisans of productivity growth. Capitalism is supposed to benefit the masses in the long run, even if the 100% pass-through is no more than a corollary of steady state growth accounting.

Demand-Driven Growth

The next task is to work out the details about how effective demand can be brought into the picture. Harrod and Domar thought along those lines, as did Robinson and then Kaldor in a second growth model in the 1960s which also emphasized the effects of productivity growth.

Harrod and Domar

Harrod's paper is notoriously difficult to read; he is basically trying to talk though complicated and tedious (though not particularly difficult) growth rate algebra in English. Here is a shot at explaining what he had to say.

His argument hinges on an expectational mechanism called the *accelerator*. Expectations of future profitability are supposed to increase when current output and profits are high. They in turn will stimulate higher investment demand. In a bit more detail, the Harrod-Domar equation can be written in multiplier form as

$$u = \frac{g}{s(\psi)}$$

with the saving rate depending inversely on the labor share ψ because wage-earners save less than recipients of profit income. Capacity utilization u is determined from the demand side by the investment injection g and the saving leakage $s(\psi)$. Harrod's accelerator can be interpreted as saying that the *growth* of the capital stock growth rate g will increase with a higher value of u. From the equation just above, this linkage generates positive feedback from g to its own rate of growth.

An increase in the labor share ψ will reduce the saving rate and increase u. Via Harrod's accelerator, the growth of investment increases as well. Both u and investment growth are wage-led or subject to the paradox of costs as discussed in Chapter 2. The investment and savings functions interact to generate the wage-led outcome.

The system can also be profit-led, for at least two reasons. Considerations of the marginal efficiency of capital suggest that besides capacity utilization, an increase in the profit share π should have a direct positive effect on the growth rate of g (or ψ should have a negative effect). Second, the wage share $\psi = \dfrac{\omega}{\lambda}$ is also an index of unit labor cost. In an economy open to trade, if ψ falls, it will reduce the cost of home exports and presumably increase their volume, raising home's internal aggregate demand and moving the economy in the direction of being profit-led.

After calculating through all the linkages (a tedious exercise in high school algebra which I usually get right after the third or fourth try), we find that the same conclusions apply to capacity utilization itself: an increase in its level could very well stimulate its own growth rate. An increase in the labor share could push the growth of utilization in either the wage- or profit-led direction. Regardless of the distributive twist, however, we are still talking about highly unstable positive feedback dynamics for u.

Domar took a more restrained approach to the investment decision, concentrating on the conditions required for the economy to operate at full capacity utilization. One can read a dynamic specification into his model which generates the full capacity result.

Suppose that $\bar{u}$ (pronounced "u-bar") is a "normal" or "target" value of u. Let D stand for the current degree of utilization and define it as

$$D = u/\bar{u} = g/s\bar{u}.$$

If D is less than 1, for example, the current utilization rate lies below its target value. An investment theory which supports full capacity utilization says that the growth rate of g will respond to $1 - D$. If D is less than 1, investment will speed up; if D exceeds 1, investment will slow down. There is negative feedback around normal capacity utilization.

Whether Harrod or Domar was right is an open question. Soros's reflexivity ideas suggest that Domar may be correct "much" of the time, but Harrod can always barge in, for example, in the overinvestment boom in fiber optic cables and similar artifacts in the United States in the late 1990s. It remains to be seen how both approaches fit into cyclical growth incorporating shifts in the income distribution between capital and labor.

Joan's Banana

In 1956 Joan Robinson took a step toward showing how distributive changes can stabilize capital stock growth driven by a strong accelerator. She assumed that the saving rate from profit income is s_r and saving from wage income is zero. With r as the rate of profit (defined above as profit income divided by the value of the capital stock), then the Harrod-Domar equation can be restated as

$$s_r r = g.$$

This formula is commonly known as the *Cambridge equation*. Saving per unit of capital is the saving rate from profits multiplied by the profit rate itself. It equals investment per unit of capital.

Robinson thought that planned investment should depend on the expected profit rate. During times when financial conventions about profits are stable, the expected rate presumably will be close to the observed rate r. Investment will respond positively to an increase in r, with a stronger effect when the profit rate is low. This relationship appears as the "Animal spirits function" in Figure 5.1. It shows the planned rate of the growth as a function of r. Meanwhile, the economy always operates along the line la-

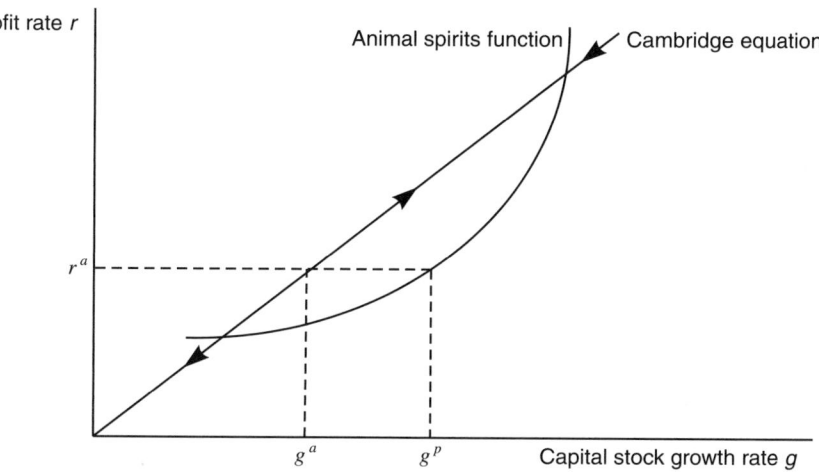

Figure 5.1 Joan Robinson's banana

beled "Cambridge equation" because it represents the saving = investment equality.

At any point in the model's logical time, the growth rate g has been set by "history," and determines r from the Cambridge equation. Robinson's dynamic assumption is that growth will accelerate when the planned rate g^p from the animal spirits function exceeds the historical or actual rate g^a, which gives a profit rate r^a. (The letters upstairs are "superscript" labels, not exponents. The dashed lines in the diagram indicate how g^a determines r^a and thereby g^p.)

As drawn, the diagram becomes *Joan Robinson's banana*. The steady state with $g^p = g^a$ at the lower end where the two curves cross is unstable; the upper steady state is stable. From a low level (but not a *very* low level less than the one at the lower steady state) the profit rate would increase over logical time; from a high level it would decrease. Because $r = \pi u$, the change in r would involve shifts in both the profit share π (forced saving, in effect) and capacity utilization u—probably a bit of both.

There is positive feedback, and growth is profit-led in this model. Ultimately a changing income distribution steers it toward a steady state. Also note that more robust animal spirits will shift the relevant curve to the right, raising growth and profit rates at a new steady state "in the long run." The next step is to show how somewhat similar dynamics play out with regard to technical change.

Nicky and Productivity Growth

When it came to changing his mind about the details of the theory while maintaining the basic underlying vision, Nicky Kaldor was almost as agile as Maynard Keynes. Sticking to his views about the importance of rapid growth in stimulating increases in productivity, he switched from a Mark I to a Mark II technological progress function in the 1960s. In the later version he said that the growth rate of labor productivity depended on the growth rate of output (replacing the growth of the capital/labor ratio in Mark I). The rationale was that more rapid output expansion leads to the introduction of more productive technologies and the realization of economies of scale of both static and dynamic character (learning-by-doing and induced innovations in the latter case).

This relationship, usually known as the *Kaldor-Verdoorn equation* (Petrus Johannes Verdoorn was a Dutch economist who came up with similar ideas in the late 1940s), is empirically well supported. Another version due to the American economist Arthur Okun is called *Okun's Law* and focuses on cyclical relationships between employment and productivity. He thought in terms of the *Okun gap* between actual and potential or full capacity output. The law states that a 1% increase in output will increase employment by only about half a percent (a third of a percent in Okun's day) because of rising productivity.

The essentials of Kaldor's later growth model are presented in Figure 5.2. Besides the positively sloped Kaldor-Verdoorn linkage *from* output growth (horizontal axis) *to* productivity growth (vertical axis), it incorporates a line labeled "Output growth" representing a causal relationship running the other way. A positive slope signals profit-led growth because a faster rate of productivity growth cuts unit labor cost and bids up the profit share, stimulating more export and investment demand (another distributive linkage lurking within a Kaldor model). It could also be true that there is a direct effect of productivity growth on investment which could complement the distributional linkage.

The upper diagram in Figure 5.2 shows a case in which effective demand is *weakly* profit-led. That is, with the steep "Output growth" schedule, a big change in the productivity growth rate does not stimulate much growth in demand. Demand is strongly profit-led in the lower diagram, in which the "Output growth" schedule has a shallow positive (upward) slope. Wage-led demand would generate an output growth curve with a negative or downward slope.

5 ▪ Keynesian Growth, Cycles, and Crisis

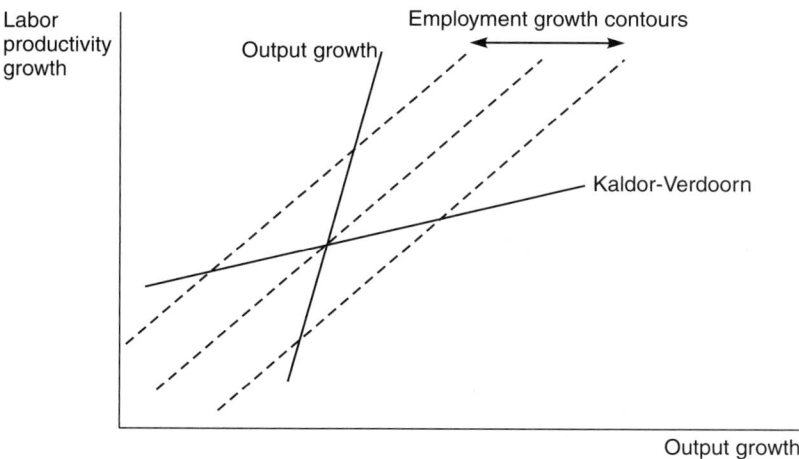

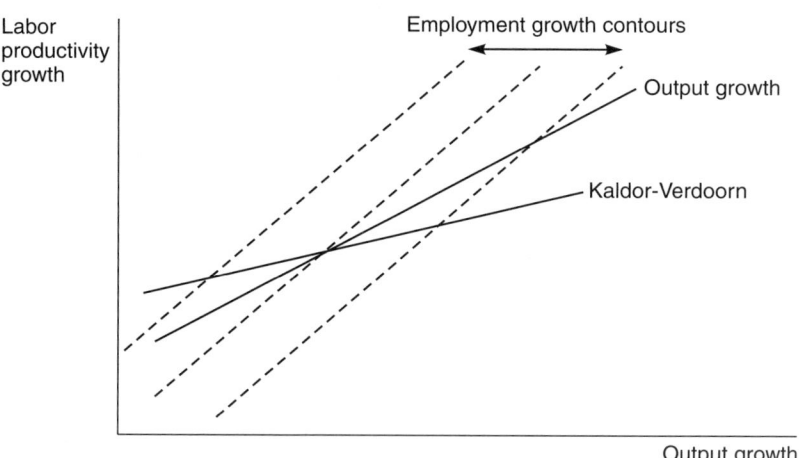

Figure 5.2 Kaldor model with weak (upper) and strong (lower) profit-led demand

In both diagrams an upward shift in the Kaldor-Verdoorn line due to an exogenous speedup in the rate of technical change would boost both output and productivity growth. A rightward shift of the "Output growth" schedule due to expansionary policy would raise both growth rates as well.

Because employment is always an issue, it makes sense to look at that variable as well. Along each of the dashed "Employment growth contours" the employment growth rate stays constant. The contours are based on the relationship

Employment growth = Output growth − Labor productivity growth,

which implies that a given rate of employment growth can be generated by different combinations of output and productivity growth rates. The slopes are positive because an increase in labor productivity growth would have to be matched by an increase in output growth to hold employment growth constant.

Along each contour line (with a slope of unity or 45 degrees), if the output growth rate is high, then productivity growth must be low and vice versa. Contours farther to the southeast correspond to faster output expansion and therefore higher employment growth rates.

Now consider an upward shift in the Kaldor-Verdoorn schedule, due to an underlying acceleration of technical change. In the upper diagram the equilibrium point where the two schedules cross will move up from its initial position, signaling a slowdown in employment expansion or "jobless growth" with associated Luddite fears. (Recall Ricardo's analysis of the effects of productivity growth in Chapter 2.) In the lower diagram, faster technical change gives rise to employment expansion as the equilibrium point moves below the initial employment growth contour.

Great flexibility in the economy is required if it is to generate both sustained productivity growth and acceptable employment growth over time. Over the past ten or twenty years or so, many rich economies have not created sufficient employment expansion to keep pace with population growth. We'll get back to this problem later.

Cyclical Growth

Now we come to a central theme of this chapter: how distributive cycles interact with growth in effective demand. The first explicit statement came from Goodwin, an American who ended up in Cambridge for political reasons during the McCarthy period. He also spent time in Siena, where, bathed in Tuscan light, he flourished as an eminent abstract painter.

Goodwin's Growth Cycles

Goodwin set out his model in 1967, in part following Marx, who as described in Chapter 2 had sketched the basic mechanism in volume one of

Capital a century before. Goodwin introduced predator-prey mathematics from biology into economics to undertake the task.

He assumed that a version of Say's Law applies, with the levels of output and employment being determined by the available stock of capital. The labor force grows at rate n. The *employment ratio,* or the level of employment divided by the labor force, changes over time, with the growth of employment being driven by capital formation. Investment is equal to the profit share times output, if all profits are saved (and automatically converted into new capital) and all wage income is consumed, as in the Cambridge equation with $s_r = 1$.

The wage share is assumed to increase in response to the employment ratio because of increasing tightness in the labor market. A higher wage share forces the profit share and thereby the growth of the capital stock and the employment ratio to slow down. In other words, the employment ratio is the prey for the predatory wage share. Growth of the wage share decreases when the employment ratio falls.

Neither variable has any direct effect on its own growth rate. In this degenerate case in which all one variable does is feed into fluctuations of the other, the mathematics shows that they cycle in *closed orbits,* illustrated in Figure 5.3. Which orbit the variables select depends on *initial conditions* or where they are in the phase diagram when the model takes effect.

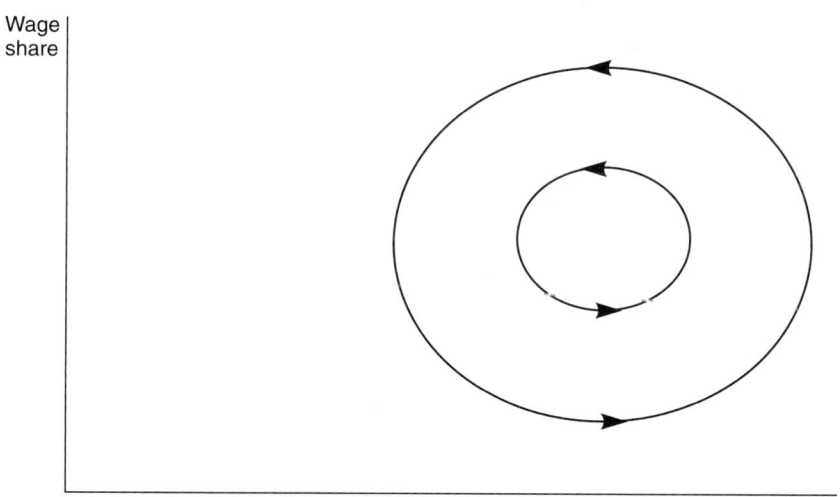

Figure 5.3 Closed orbits in the Goodwin model

Cyclical Growth with Productivity and Real Wage Dynamics

Translating Goodwin (or Marx, Keynes, Kaldor, or Robinson) from logical to chronological time is difficult. Goodwin's machine lacks traction, but its basic logic carries over into econometric models driven by effective demand in which there is productivity growth and distributive conflict. For the United States at least, counterclockwise cycles like the ones in Figure 5.3 between the level of economic activity and the labor share continue to appear. The problem for applied macroeconomists is to discern how the patterns suggested by the theory show up in the data and then say something sensible about policy implications.

For a full-blown cyclical growth model incorporating effective demand and the income distribution, we need to unravel the dynamics of two variables: capacity utilization $u = \dfrac{X}{K}$ and the labor share $\psi = \dfrac{\omega}{\lambda}$. The Harrod-Domar discussion above suggests that the growth rate of capacity utilization may respond with either sign to a change in the labor share; that is, it can be either wage- or profit-led. The growth of utilization would be subject to positive own-feedback according to Harrod and negative feedback following Domar.

In principle the growth of the labor share could respond with either sign to an increase in capacity utilization. Slower growth would amount to a version of forced saving or a *wage squeeze*. In Goodwin's version the share grows faster and creates a *profit squeeze*. He does not, however, address the dynamics of productivity growth which crucially affect how the share changes.

Keeping all these possibilities in mind is not easy. Table 5.1 gives a partial summary, omitting the Harrod versus Domar distinction, which is taken up below. Two of the four scenarios will be unstable because changes in the two variables reinforce one another. For example, if there is a profit squeeze, the wage share will grow faster when capacity utilization goes up. If demand is wage-led, utilization itself will rise in a destabilizing re-

Table 5.1 Four possible scenarios for cyclical growth

	Profit-led demand	Wage-led demand
Profit squeeze	Stable (counterclockwise cycle)	Unstable
Wage squeeze	Unstable	Stable (clockwise cycle)

sponse. The stable profit-squeeze/profit-led scenario is a generalization of Goodwin.

Stable wage-squeeze/wage-led dynamics would show up in a cyclical growth version of Kaldor's model from the 1950s or, for that matter, the *Treatise on Money*. In contrast to Goodwin it would generate clockwise cycles in a phase plot with capacity utilization on the horizontal axis and the wage share on the vertical. Rich capitalist economies have falling wage shares when output rises from a cyclical trough. They do not demonstrate extreme instability, so insofar as a simple two-dimensional model applies, they are not likely to have wage-led aggregate demand.

Productivity dynamics are crucial to the evolution (again in logical time!) of the labor share. The interaction of productivity growth with real wage growth is pretty complicated. The general view is that on top of its long-term upward trend (the 2% growth rate over centuries mentioned above), labor productivity growth tends to speed up as the economy emerges from a recession, following the short-term dynamics emphasized by Okun. The usual rationales are blue-collar labor hoarding by firms at the bottom of the cycle, or else the presence of overhead labor as a fixed cost. Figure 5.4 shows the pattern for deviations of productivity from its trend in the United States. The shaded sections represent recessions as defined by the National Bureau of Economic Research (NBER). The deviations typically decline and turn negative toward the end of an upswing. They remain negative going into or during a recession, and then become strongly positive as output starts to grow again. As of early 2010 the rise in productivity through the recent recession did not bode well for growth in employment.

The labor market is not tight as the recession ends, so real wages don't increase until later in an upswing. The implication is that the labor share declines as a result of the productivity jump, stimulating demand if it is profit-led. Along with low interest rates (see below), this interaction between distribution and demand contributes to a recovery. Subject to fluctuations, real wages start to grow as recovery proceeds. With productivity growth leveling off, the labor share starts to rise. Its increase along with rising interest rates are among the factors slowing growth in demand at the top of the cycle. Utilization usually peaks just before an NBER recession, then drops off rapidly before recovering.

Figure 5.5 presents a time plot of the Goodwin process for the United States. A V- or U-shaped pattern for the labor share shows up in most upswings. The upward movement usually lags capacity utilization in its recovery phase, broadly consistent with Goodwin's predator-prey dynamics.

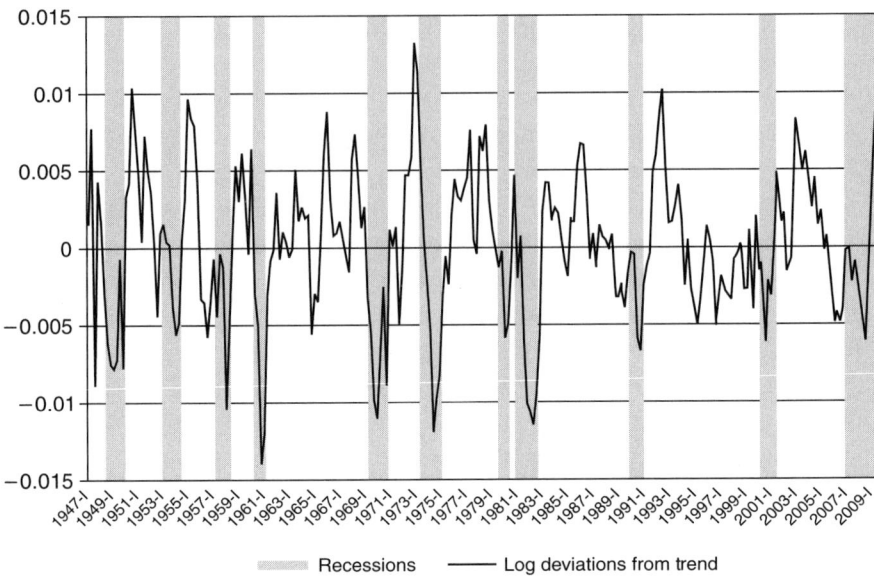

Figure 5.4 Deviation of actual labor productivity from its trend (log of quotient) for the U.S. business sector

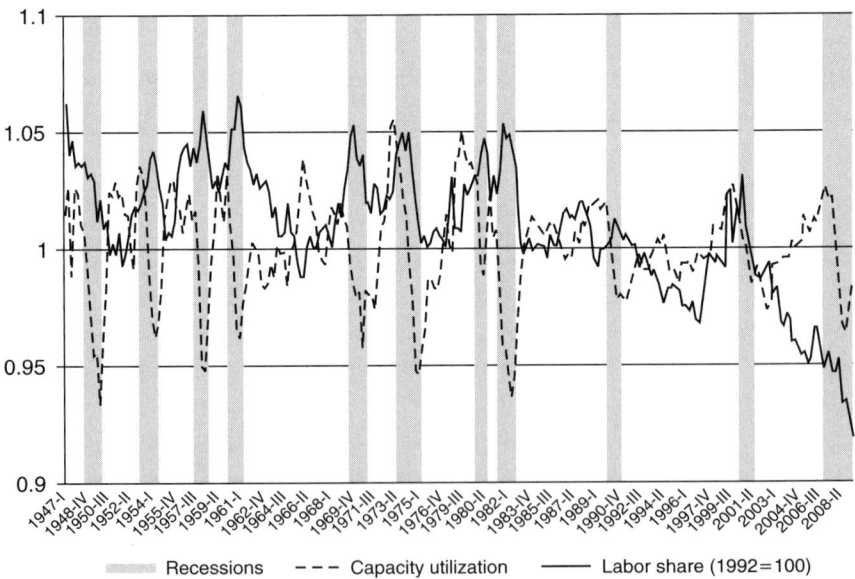

Figure 5.5 Time series for capacity utilization and labor share

Details of the Dynamics

It may be of interest to notch up the technicalities to explore Goodwin-style dynamics a bit further in logical time. The details are illustrated in Figure 5.6. It extends the Keynes-style Chapter 19 model shown in the lower diagram of Figure 4.5 from a static to a dynamic specification. The wage share ψ and capacity utilization u are the relevant variables to consider because, as opposed to the real wage and output in Figure 4.5, they are ratios which do not have strong time trends. (The math doesn't really work unless they are completely non-trended, which as we will see they are not, but we'll ignore that complication to keep things simple.)

The new trick is to introduce *nullclines* for the growth of both utilization and the share in a phase plot between the two variables. ("Cline" comes from a Greek word meaning slope, and "null" refers to the assumption that one of the variables is not changing over time when both of them lie along its nullcline.) The nullcline labeled "Stable wage share" depicts combinations of ψ and u that hold ψ constant. In an economy with a profit squeeze

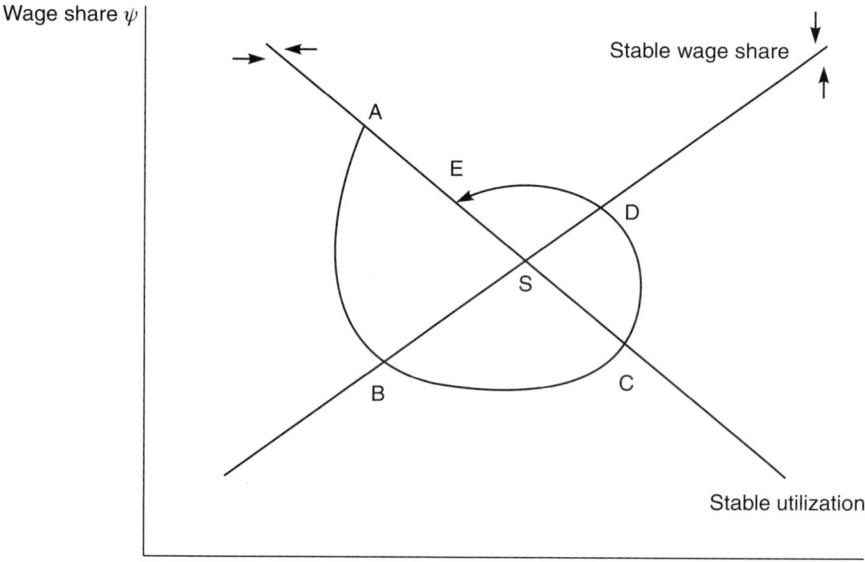

Figure 5.6 Stylized version of a Goodwin cycle for the wage share and capacity utilization

it has a positive slope because an increase in the steady state level of the capacity utilization rate has to be met by a higher wage share to hold the share itself steady. The little arrows at the top right show that the share falls when its value lies above the nullcline and rises in the opposite case. Similar reasoning applies to the "Stable utilization" nullcline. The small arrows at the top left signal that if there is Domar-style negative investment feedback, then utilization decreases when its level lies "above" (to the right of) the line.

Imagine that the economy initially has low utilization and a high wage share at point A. The arrows beside the nullclines signal that the wage share will start to fall while utilization goes up. The share will start to recover at point B, inducing a profit squeeze which ultimately begins to drive down utilization at C. The share overshoots and finally begins to fall at point D, with a new cycle beginning at E. As drawn the spiral will converge toward steady levels of u and ψ at S, but continuing shocks to the system can keep its cycles going.

Econometric estimates in chronological time usually support this Domar-style interpretation, which is broadly consistent with Figure 5.5. Because the real wage is $\omega = \dfrac{w}{P}$, the models have to estimate separate inflation equations for the money wage w and the price level P. Typically both the wage and price levels grow faster when economic activity increases, with the wage response being stronger. A higher labor share slows wage growth but weakly pushes up the price level because it represents an increase in unit labor cost. These results are consistent with Keynes's treatment of variable prices in Chapter 19.

Finally, what can Goodwin cycles say about recovery from 2007–2009? Figure 5.5 shows a pronounced fall and weak recovery of the wage share prior to 2007. At the same time, capacity utilization was rising. With the arrival of the financial crisis, capacity utilization plummeted and recovery of the labor share was cut off. As of early 2010, whether a relatively high profit share would stimulate a recovery in output remained to be seen.

Minsky's Endogenous Finance and Cycles

The next step is to bring in the financial side of the economy. Hyman Minsky is the appropriate guide.

Minsky looked like an Old Testament prophet and relished the effect. He spent many years teaching at Washington University in St. Louis, and was a director of the Mark Twain Bank. As with Keynes and Soros, firsthand experience in the financial system shows through in his writing.

Minsky's "moment," announced in the financial media in 2008, came after his death and that of Charles Kindleberger, whose analysis of crises was equally insightful. Minsky's claim on the moment emerged from his historical analysis of *endogenous finance* and (to an extent) his core macro model, which links the financial side of the economy with output cycles as described by Keynes in Chapter 22 of the *General Theory*. As will be shown, the model can also be reinterpreted to illustrate the purely financial cycles between asset prices and debt or leverage of the sort discussed by Soros and Kindleberger. The modeling fits into the discussion here. Endogenous finance features as a counterweight to mainstream finance theory in Chapter 7.

Finance

Minsky's "micro foundation" for both lines of thought is that economic actors are constrained by their inherited financial positions, which he describes as *hedge, speculative,* or *Ponzi*. A unit is practicing hedge finance when a "reasonable" lower bound on its anticipated cash flows from operations exceeds anticipated commitments at all future times. ("Anticipated" is used in a Keynesian sense. Expected values over well-defined probability distributions on all future events are as alien to Minsky's worldview as to Maynard's.)

Speculative units anticipate that cash commitments will exceed cash flows at some points in the future, for example, when principal repayments on short-term debt fall due. They can run into trouble if the money or commercial paper market does not function normally at critical times, such as when debt has to be refinanced. If speculative positions are common, the whole system may be moving toward *financial fragility*.

Fragility is much more likely if many firms are engaging in Ponzi finance, with anticipated cash inflows falling short of obligations at most or all future times. Like their namesake, described in Chapter 2, Ponzi units have to borrow to pay interest as well as principal on their debts. Were they wise, they would carry big stocks of liquid assets, but often they do not. An enterprise with highly fluctuating sales, for example, may hope that some year's bonanza will carry it through the next few. Prior to 2007–2009 the

Enron Corporation, the most notorious example from the 1990s stock market boom, had marked-to-market anticipated energy-trading revenues far into the future, thereby providing nonexistent collateral for its Ponzi mountain of liabilities.

There are several versions of Minsky's cycle or crisis model. The one in his 1975 book *John Maynard Keynes* (republished in 2008) is as easy as any to understand. It can be set up as a cross between the *General Theory*'s discussion of trade cycles and Harrod's growth model. Minsky's presentation lacks clarity. The following discussion reflects my attempt to figure out what he is saying.

His reasoning rests squarely on Keynes's idea that the *speculative demand* for money arising from liquidity preference is high when times are uncertain or simply bad. In contrast, "during a boom the speculative demand for money *decreases*" (Minsky, 2008, 121; emphasis added). Minsky goes beyond Keynes in assuming that speculative demand depends on both the interest rate *and* capital asset prices. At any point in (logical) time it decreases with the interest rate and *increases* with asset prices. A similar asset price linkage was introduced by Keynes in phase (ii) of the financial cycle in the *Treatise on Money*, summarized in Table 4.3. Bears increase their money holdings and short positions in anticipation of future decreases in asset prices.

The money supply minus transactions demand must equal speculative demand. For a given level of transactions demand, an increase in the money supply will reduce the interest rate and increase asset prices because both such changes push up speculative demand. The speculative demand function is also supposed to shift over the cycle, as in the transitions between phases (i) and (ii) of the bull-bear scenario in Table 4.3.

Higher output means that transactions demand increases. With a fixed money supply, speculative demand would have to be forced downward by a higher interest rate and/or lower asset prices. But if a boom is under way, "increasing the surety of income from capital-asset ownership, then the liquidity preference function will shift" (Minsky, 2008, 73), presumably downward. The interest rate does not have to increase very much as output rises. (This stability of the interest rate is a key linkage in Minsky's dynamics, as discussed below.) The price of capital assets, or the value of q in James Tobin's usage, can also rise. At the beginning of an upswing the economy acts as if it is in phase (i) in Table 4.3: bear positions are being wound down and asset prices are increasing.

The Real Side

To trace the dynamics over to the real side, recall from Chapter 1 that that value per unit of an asset "should" be equal to its capitalized return, so that q can be determined according to the formula

$$q = \frac{r}{i},$$

with r as the profit rate and i as the interest rate. Higher investment g pushes up q because from equations presented above, $r = \pi u$ and $u = \frac{g}{s}$. Minsky can be interpreted as saying that because there is a stable interest rate when economic activity is increasing in response to a higher level of g, then r will rise more than i, increasing q. With a Harrodian investment function which says that the growth of g depends on q, investment will feed back positively into its own rate of growth. A firm will typically have debt as well as equity, so it is reasonable to assume that it will reduce investment when its debt/capital ratio goes up.

The next step is to set up nullclines for Minsky's dynamics. If the firm does not issue new equity to finance investment (for decades prior to 2007–2009 corporations in the United States mostly ran up debt to buy back shares instead of issuing new ones), then its debt/capital ratio will grow in response to an increase in g and decrease when retained earnings resulting from higher output go up. At the macroeconomic level, total profits and retained earnings will be driven by g through the multiplier, but working through the numbers suggests that an overall positive response of the debt ratio to g is likely.

If the interest rate is not "too high" (specifically if g exceeds i), the ratio will be self-stabilizing: an increase in its level will slow its growth. (The inequality $g > i$ is sometimes called a *solvency condition*. It states that if a debtor borrows a fixed proportion of income, and if its income growth exceeds the interest rate, then the debtor can "outgrow" its borrowing in the sense that the debt/income ratio will stabilize at some level. Domar introduced the basic accounting relationships in the mid-1940s. Fiscal implications are sketched in Chapter 6.)

On all these assumptions, Figure 5.7 illustrates how the dynamic model works in logical time. The nullcline labeled "Stable debt/capital" depicts combinations of the variables that hold the ratio constant over time. It has a positive slope because an increase in the capital stock growth rate has to be met by a higher debt/capital ratio to hold the ratio constant. The little arrows over to the left show that the ratio falls when its value lies "above" (to the right of) the nullcline and rises in the opposite case.

Similar reasoning applies to the "Stable growth rate" nullcline, except that the small arrows at the top signal that with Harrodian positive feedback, the growth rate speeds up when its level lies above the line. Because of the Harrod linkage the economy could very well be unstable. The figure shows a configuration of the nullclines in which debt dynamics stabilize the explosive investment response.

Both the growth rate and debt/capital ratio would stay constant at the steady state at point A, where the nullclines cross. Suppose that firms suddenly lose confidence at the steady state, so that the growth rate jumps down along the dashed line to B. After the fall, firms will start to pay back debt and further reduce investment until the solid trajectory crosses the "Stable growth rate" nullcline at C. At that point enough debt has been repaid to give firms an incentive to increase the capital stock growth rate. When the trajectory crosses the nullcline for the debt/capital ratio at D, they start to run up debt again.

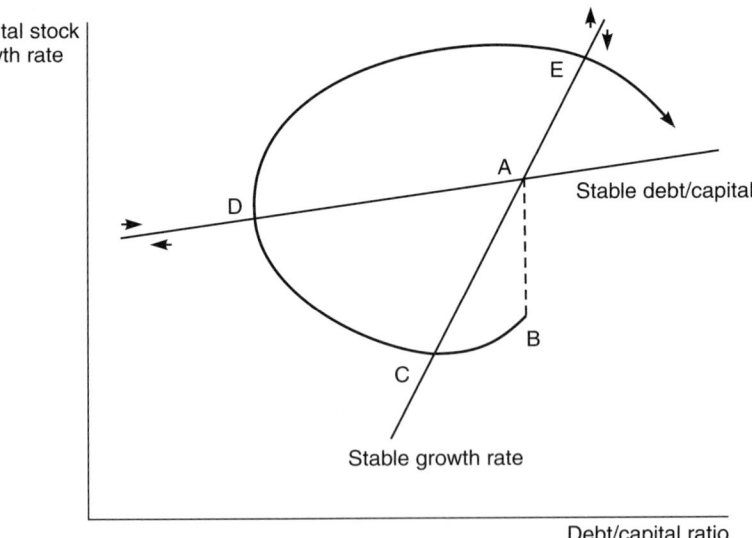

Figure 5.7 Minsky's real/financial cycle

Because of the rise in the profit rate relative to the interest rate sketched above, this phase of expansion may last for a considerable time. Meanwhile the financial system becomes increasingly fragile as individual actors shift from hedge toward speculative and Ponzi positions. With rising asset prices, Minsky's version of speculative demand suggests that interest rates will have to rise. An increase in bear positions as in phase (ii) of Table 4.3 will have a similar effect.

With higher debt/capital ratios and interest rates, the increase in the capital stock growth rate will slow down. Sooner or later the trajectory will cross the growth rate nullcline at E and investment will fall. Whether the collapse will be gradual as in Figure 5.7 and the Soros cycle in Figure 4.2 or abrupt as in the Keynes cycle in Figure 4.3 (which takes a fancier set of nullclines to describe) is an open question.

Minsky and Soros

Minsky's model can serve as a generic description of financial crises. For example, Figure 5.7 looks like Figure 4.2 for the Soros model, which depicts a financial cycle between an asset price and earnings per share as a measure of leverage. To pursue the similarity, suppose that in Figure 5.7 the variable on the horizontal axis is reinterpreted as leverage (measured in the usual fashion as the ratio of assets to net worth) and an asset price replaces capital stock growth on the vertical.

To set up a simple model, a financial firm's balance sheet can be written as $P_A A = B + E$, with A as its assets, P_A as the asset price, B (for "bonds") as its debt, and E as equity. The firm's leverage ratio Λ is $\Lambda = \dfrac{P_A A}{E}$. As discussed in Chapter 3 and in connection with Table 4.2, if the firm holds its debt level constant, then it is easy to see that its leverage *decreases* when the asset price goes up. A common response is to increase debt to run leverage back up to seek additional returns. Similarly a reduction in P_A raises leverage and may induce the firm to try to shrink its balance sheet because VaR restrictions begin to bind. Growth in leverage thus responds positively to the asset price and negatively to the level of leverage itself. Its nullcline in a phase plot with Λ on the horizontal axis and P_A on the vertical slopes upward.

There may well be positive feedback of the level of the asset price into its own growth rate, as in Soros's cycle. Higher leverage, by contrast, will cut into demand for the asset and induce the price to decline. The implication is that there may be a steep positively sloped nullcline for P_A.

The nullcline for the asset price would shift to the right if positive feedback gets stronger, as in Soros's discussion of price bias and trend, or if the effect of higher leverage in slowing price growth gets weaker (for example, after the SEC's relaxation of leverage limitations for investment banks in 2004, as discussed in Chapter 7). After the shift it is easy to see that leverage and the asset price would follow a clockwise trajectory like the one in Figure 4.2 with leverage continuing to rise for a time after the price breaks downward.

A Kindleberger Moment

Charlie Kindleberger generously credited Hy Minsky for inspiring his own ideas about manias, panics, and crashes, summarized in Chapter 4. No doubt he was sincere, but it is also fair to say that Minsky's main concern was with destabilizing interactions between the real and financial sides of the economy rather than financial crises per se. The cycle depicted in Figure 5.7 can be seen as an extension of Keynes's Chapter 22 analysis of the trade cycle, with more emphasis on the role of asset prices and liquidity preference. Although Minsky does not use Tobin's notation, his key asset price is q, the valuation ratio for physical capital.

Kindleberger, however, pays much more attention to asset prices for securities and how they can set off a mania nourished by increasing debt. In 2007–2009 the central asset prices were for residential housing *and* the securitized synthetic assets constructed from mortgage loans. The scenario is similar to the reinterpretation of the Minsky diagram just discussed. In that regard the panic and crash were more a Kindleberger than a Minsky moment.

Net Borrowing Trends and Cycles

Wynne Godley was a macroeconomic modeler who operated very much in Keynes's tradition of setting up and analyzing NIPA and related accounts, with minimal attached mathematical theorizing. In a preface to a recent book, *Monetary Economics* (co-authored by Marc Lavoie), he recalled that in early 1974 he "first apprehended the strategic importance of the accounting identity which says that, *measured at current prices,* the government's budget deficit less the current account deficit is equal, by definition, to private saving minus investment" (Godley and Lavoie, 2007, xxxvi). Another way to say the same thing is that after the raw data have been massaged (or cooked, or mangled) to fit into Keynes-Meade-Stone NIPA/FOF accounting schemes, the numbers satisfy the balances described in Chapter 1 and set out in algebra in Chapter 4. Macro equilibrium is built into this basic information that modelers use. Recognizing that fact and bringing plausible economic analysis to bear on it was one of Godley's main accomplishments. Josef Steindl independently came up with similar ideas in the early 1980s.

One example that has come to the fore in recent years is the widespread use of diagrams, designed by Godley, showing net borrowing flows as shares of GDP for households, business, government, and the rest of the world. From NIPA accounting, the four flows must sum to zero. Figures 5.8 and 5.9 display the data for the United States, with the series presented separately in Figure 5.8 and superimposed (to highlight comparisons) in Figure 5.9. The shaded areas are periods of peak-to-trough recessions according to the NBER methodology. Similar diagrams show up in policy analyses by Godley and colleagues (often for the Levy Economics Institute at Bard College), and with cyclical regularity in the *Financial Times.*

The diagrams are useful for thinking about both economic trends and cycles. A few immediate observations stand out.

There was a notable shift in the patterns of the curves around 1980. One observation is that periods between recessions became longer, perhaps because of increasing access to finance as discussed below. More important, the United States usually ran a current account surplus (positive foreign net borrowing with the United States lending to the rest of the world) before 1980. Thereafter the economy embarked on an external deficit with a strongly increasing trend from 1991 until 2007–2009. The transient external recovery beginning in the mid-1980s was due to dollar devaluation (the Plaza Accords), a recession, and American export of military services during the Gulf War. It did not persist.

In the diagrams, household net borrowing is approximated by the difference between residential investment and household saving. Before 1980, increasing household net lending (more negative levels of net borrowing across business cycles) offset the mildly upwardly trending government and business deficits to support the surplus on current account. Starting in

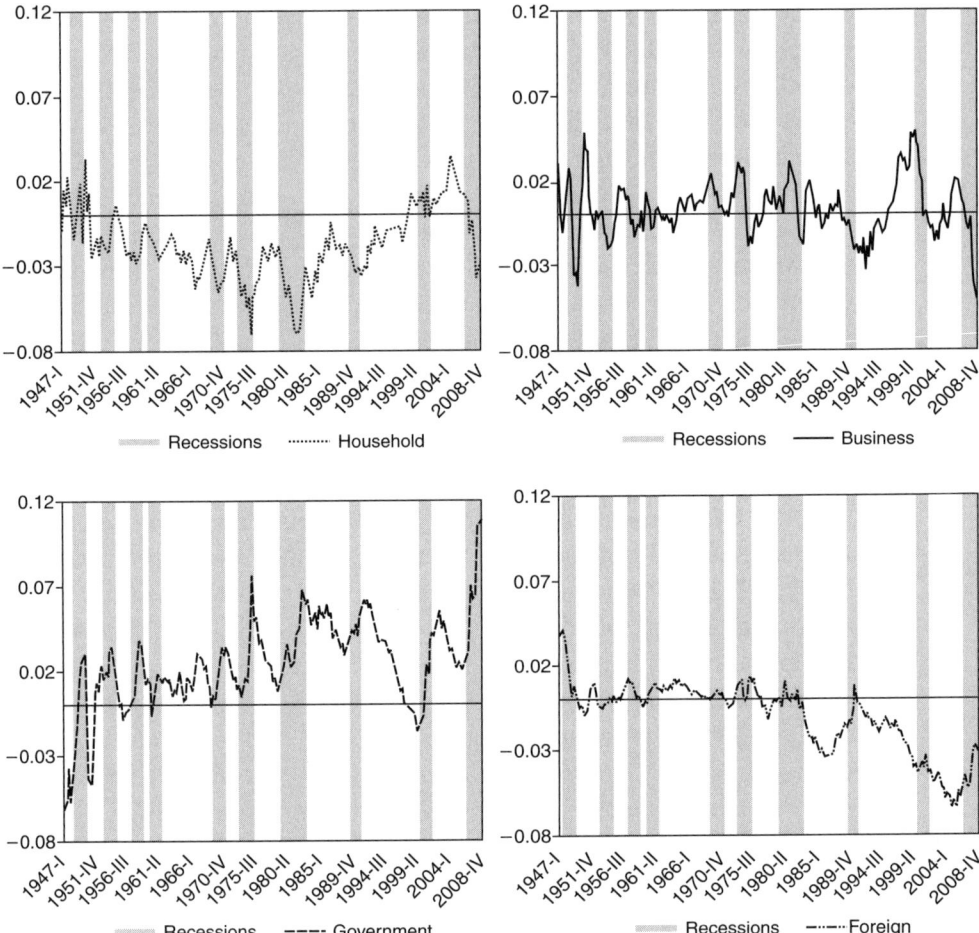

Figure 5.8 Sectoral net borrowing flows normalized by GDP and NBER reference cycles

the 1980s, although the fiscal position certainly mattered, an upward trend in household deficits maintained a steadier relationship with the almost uninterrupted decrease in foreign net borrowing (or increase in foreign lending).

One underlying factor was the substantial rise in household consumption expenditure as a share of disposable income, shown in Figure 5.14 below. Most of it was directed toward services in general, and health care in particular. Another important cause was the relaxation of regulation of household borrowing, which led to a massive expansion of credit card and mortgage debt beginning in the 1980s. The ratio of household debt to GDP more than doubled to over 130%, while *personal saving* or total household saving net of depreciation fell from 12% of personal income to near zero. (Rates in the euro area and Japan are around 10% and 5% respectively.) This trend reversed abruptly in 2007, with household net borrowing falling by nearly 7% of GDP (and business borrowing by 6%) into fall 2009. A large recession was the unavoidable consequence. As noted in Chapter 1, already in the 1990s Godley warned about these adverse trends; it took a decade for his predicted disaster to play out.

A somewhat related point is that aside from the Reagan and Bush II periods, U.S. data do not reveal "twin" fiscal and foreign deficits. There is a more apparent linkage between private and foreign net borrowing. Twin deficits (their rationale is sketched in Chapter 2) are a long-standing orthodox dogma and are often invoked in support of contractionary fiscal policy in response to balance-of-payments problems—the International

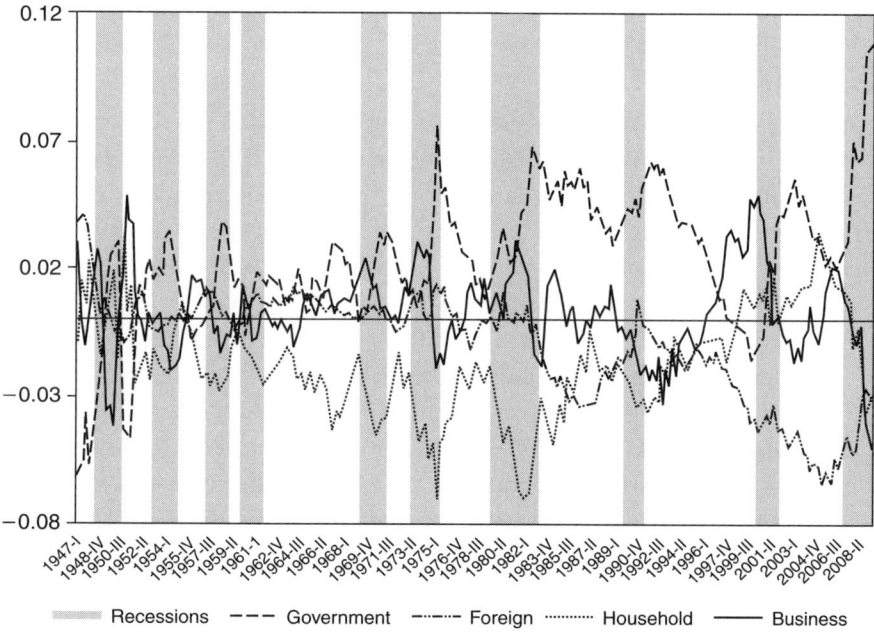

Figure 5.9 Superimposed net borrowing flows normalized by GDP and NBER reference cycles

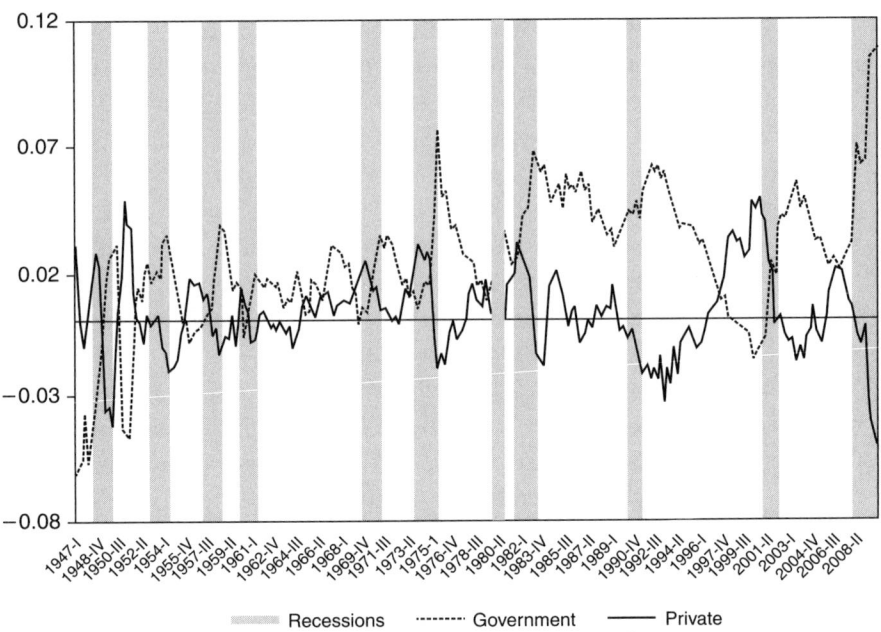

Figure 5.10 Government and private net borrowing flows normalized by GDP and NBER reference cycles

Monetary Fund's household remedy dating back to U.S. dominance at the 1944 conference at Bretton Woods. The problem with the theory is that it does not fit the data. In the latest crisis, the increases in household and business net lending mentioned above were clearly associated with an increase of foreign net borrowing by over 2% of GDP. Capital inflows were still strongly positive but diminished in magnitude.

With regard to cycles, Figure 5.8 shows that household net borrowing has typically gone up as the economy emerges from a recession and peaked prior to or during the slump that follows, as households begin to repair their balance sheets. The rapid decrease into the latest recession is typical. Business net borrowing has tended to peak later in the cycle—an example of the accelerator investment response that Harrod emphasized. This pattern was repeated going into 2007.

Household borrowing over the cycle is not consistent with the "consumption-smoothing" or pro-cyclical saving behavior built into mainstream macroeconomics. The consumption share of household income does vary counter-cyclically, but it is offset by higher taxes and not more saving, as theory from Keynes (7:120) to *Ricardian equivalence* and real business cycles suggests (details in Chapter 6). The absence of *expenditure smoothing* by households in the data has not been widely discussed because economists have tended to ignore their role in capital formation. Residential investment is a key contributor to pro-cyclical private net borrowing. It fell by 20% during 2008—an ominous sign for the future.

Figure 5.10 compares the private or combined household and business net borrowing share of GDP with the government's share. As business borrowing began to tail off, the overall private share started to decline before the recession was officially under way. Government net borrowing varies counter-cyclically, as in traditional fiscal analysis of automatic stabilizers, pro-cyclical tax revenues, and so on. Historically it has risen through recessions and peaked as recovery gets going. It spiked by 8% of GDP after the economy entered into recession in late 2007. Historical patterns suggested that the government's share would rise through 2010 at least.

Productivity and Employment Growth

Kaldor's model sketched above (see Figure 5.2) underlines interactions among labor productivity growth, distribution, and employment. Another angle is provided by sectoral disaggregation. Questions to be addressed include:

How should gains in productivity at the sectoral level as usually calculated be interpreted?
Which sector(s) have contributed most to overall productivity growth? Through which channels?
Which sector(s) have contributed to employment creation?

This section first presents empirical results for the United States regarding the second and third sets of questions and then comes back to interpretation. In line with the diminishing importance in the U.S. economy of agricultural, manufacturing, and other activities which produce physical goods (see Table 5.2), I work with three sectors: finance, insurance, and real estate, or FIRE; "Other services"; and "All other."

An individual sector will have its own level of productivity, defined along the lines presented above as the ratio of its real output to employment. FIRE's employment and output shares in Table 5.2 have stayed relatively constant. The fact that its output share substantially exceeds its employment share means that its labor productivity exceeds the economy-

Table 5.2 Three-sector output and employment shares

	1975	1985	1995	2005
Output shares				
FIRE	0.246	0.237	0.227	0.228
Other services	0.458	0.489	0.509	0.535
All other	0.296	0.274	0.264	0.237
Employment shares				
FIRE	0.064	0.072	0.068	0.072
Other services	0.471	0.514	0.570	0.650
All other	0.465	0.414	0.362	0.278

wide average. The other two sectors are in the opposite situation. Both shares for "Other services" went up, while they declined for the goods-producing sector. For the latter, the output share declined a lot less than the employment share, meaning that its productivity level went up.

A sector's own-rate of productivity growth can be calculated over time. In addition, at any time the sector may have (say) an above-average level of productivity. Then if its employment level is increasing, there will be a *reallocation gain* which will contribute to productivity growth economy-wide. (There will also be a positive contribution from a sector with below-average productivity which is losing employment.) One can write out a formula in which economy-wide labor productivity growth can be expressed as an average of own-rates of productivity growth of the three sectors, weighted by output shares, along with reallocation effects based on sectoral labor force growth rates multiplied by weights reflecting average productivity across sectors.

This sort of decomposition is used in development economics. The results for developing countries which have sustained output growth (by no means all of them!) typically show that if real per capita income rises, then manufacturing is the main motor for overall productivity growth, but that there can be visible reallocation gains as labor moves out of low-productivity sectors such as agriculture. A slightly different pattern shows up over recent decades in the United States.

First, Figure 5.11 shows indexes of own-productivity levels (1980 = 100) for the three sectors. Since 1980 all sectors have seen productivity increases. As noted in connection with Table 5.2, the "All other" sector has

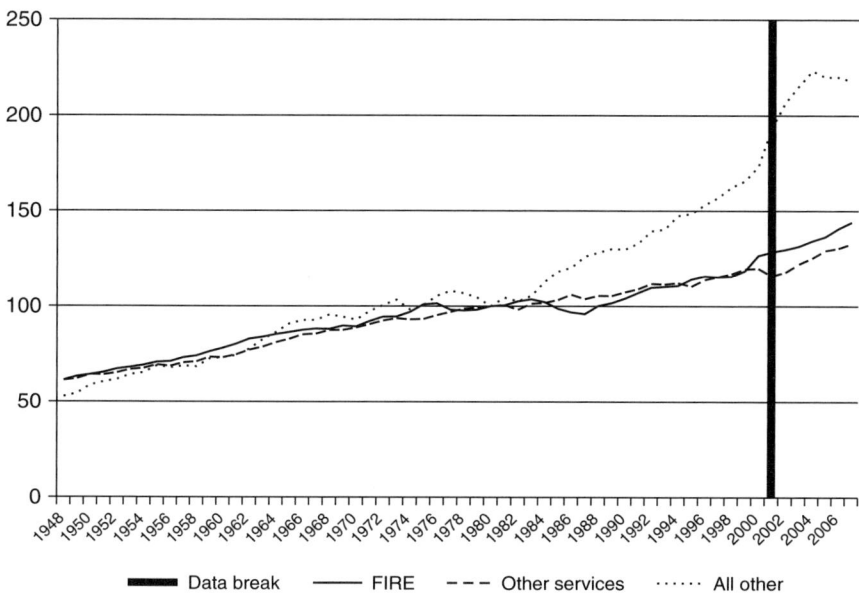

Figure 5.11 Sectoral productivity levels (1980 = 100)

had faster own-productivity growth than the other two. The United States still resembles developing economies in that productivity growth in the goods-producing part of the economy is relatively high.

Figure 5.12 presents the *contributions* of the sectors to overall productivity growth between recessions (skipping the one in the early 2000s because there are too few observations thereafter). The lengths of the bars represent weighted contributions of sectoral own-rates of productivity growth and gains from reallocation.

FIRE stands out for a couple of reasons. In all periods it made substantial direct and reallocation contributions to economy-wide productivity increases. The latter occurred because the sector had positive employment growth and (as noted above) an above-average level of productivity. Reallocation gains or losses in the other two sectors were not large. Both had positive direct contributions, more from "All other."

Next I take up employment expansion. Kaldor's model suggests that productivity growth can create *un*employment unless effective demand grows to meet a higher level of real output per unit of labor. As it turns out, the growth rate of the economy-wide employment ratio (employment di-

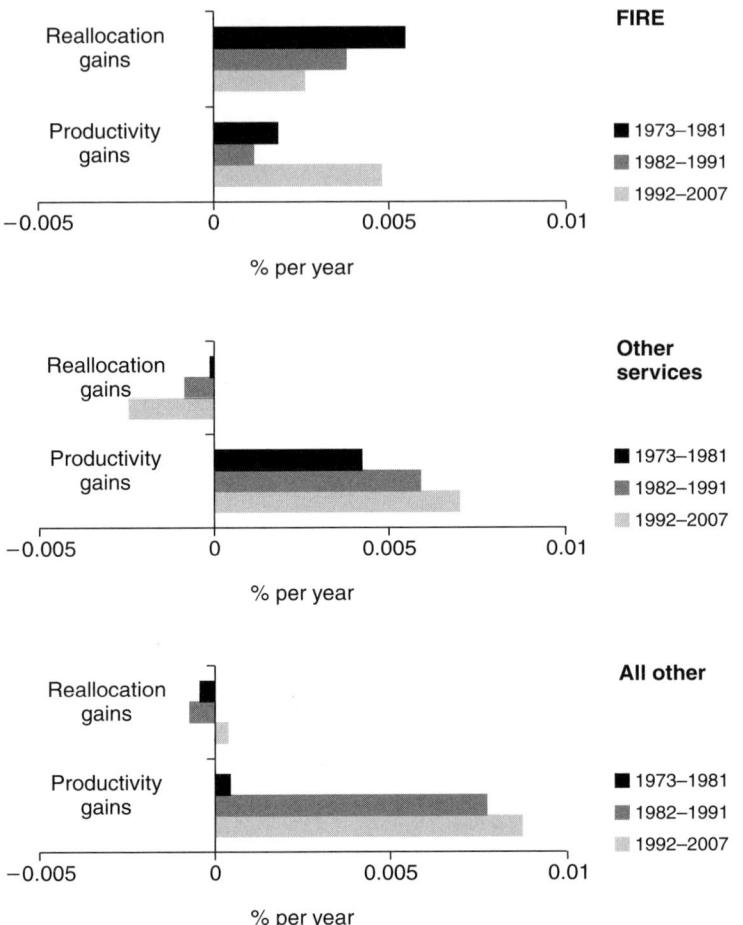

Figure 5.12 Sectoral direct and reallocation contributions to overall productivity growth

vided by the labor force) can be decomposed into an average of growth rates of that ratio in the three sectors, weighted by their shares in total employment. At both the national and sectoral levels, the employment ratio will rise if the growth rate of output per capita exceeds growth of labor productivity.

Figure 5.13 presents results for the United States. During 1973–1981, the stagflation period, the overall employment situation deteriorated, especially for the "All other" sector. In subsequent periods, other services provided most employment generation, as is the case in most economies. In the United States this result reflected the rapid growth of household consumption of services mentioned above. It also might be called the *Wal-Mart effect*. That company and other high-volume retailers had rapid productivity growth due to appropriation of economies of scale in volume purchasing and inventory management, but at the same time demand for their products grew rapidly. Goods-producing sectors shed jobs. FIRE made minor contributions to job creation.

For interpreting these results, the main difficulty is posed by FIRE. Labor productivity increases in a sector if its real wages and/or profits per unit of labor go up. In most sectors one can usually point to specific technical or institutional changes underlying growth in real value added. Over

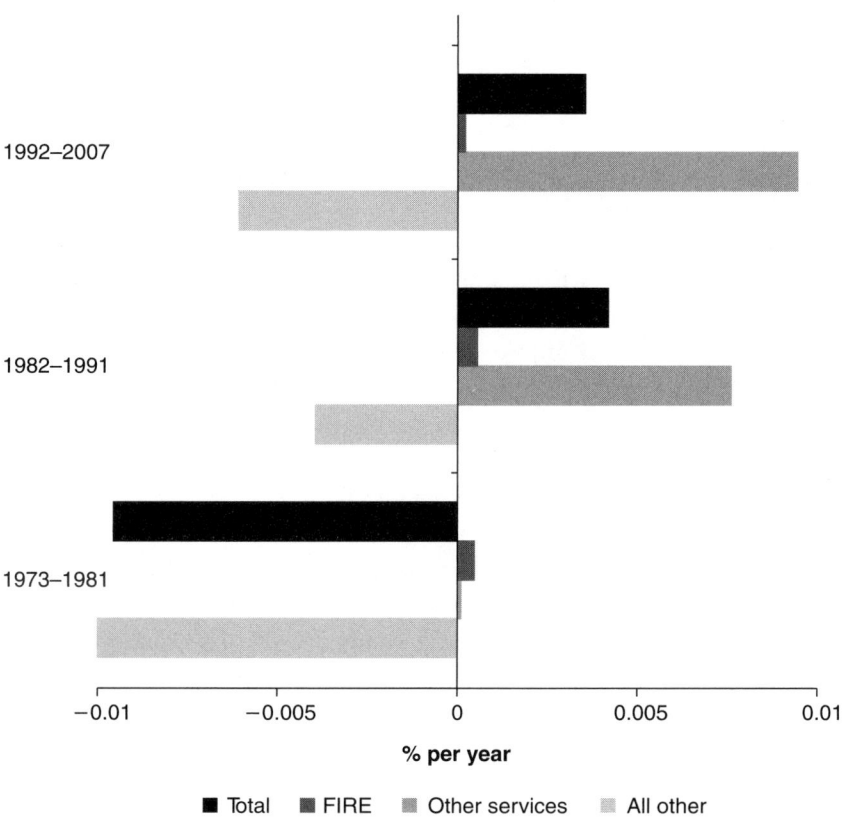

Figure 5.13 Sectoral contributions to employment growth

the centuries the causes have ranged from increasing division of labor in the pin factory to computerized inventory management in the volume retailers. FIRE, however, is an exception. Although the efficiency of its back office operations has dramatically improved (or costs have been slashed by foreign outsourcing), much of its observed increase in value added has been the translation of capital gains on asset prices during the equity and real estate booms into higher real labor payments (bonuses and fees) and profits.

The bottom line is that a significant proportion of FIRE's own productivity gains depicted in Figures 5.11 and 5.12 represent money illusion based on spiraling asset prices. In the future the sector's labor payments and profits per unit of labor deflated by a price index for goods and services might be expected to go down even as its employment shrinks. If it appears, the resulting negative productivity growth will be just as "real"— or fictional—as the positive growth observed after 1980. The huge bonuses announced by Wall Street in late 2009 go against this analysis, but it remains to be seen how long they will persist.

Keynesian Thinking and the Crisis

In Chapter 22 of the *General Theory* Keynes stressed how shifts in investment demand (or the schedule for the marginal efficiency of capital) were in his view the main driving force behind economic fluctuations, with movements in the consumption function and liquidity preference playing amplifying or damping roles. He did not analyze shifts in distribution and the implications of rising debt very deeply (although there are useful remarks in Chapter 19 and elsewhere).

As mentioned above, there were major changes in the U.S. economy after the early 1980s; others are discussed immediately below. A relatively stable pattern of cyclical growth with rising inflation that emerged after the war ended at that time, to be replaced with a combination of real and financial trends that supported fairly steady growth with moderate inflation on the one hand and increasing income inequality and financial instability on the other.

These developments fit into the framework designed by Keynes, but the details differ from those he emphasized in his book. Distributive changes have been striking. The consumption function has shifted dramatically. The financial system has played a highly destabilizing role, centered on asset price fluctuations and the accumulation of debt. Movement in residential investment has been important but was not the key factor driving the financial crisis—that is, until it broke.

The causes behind the 2007–2009 events were outlined briefly in Chapter 1. Now we can use the analysis in this and previous chapters to fill in details. Important changes over time are illustrated on Figures 5.14 and 5.15. (The latter reproduces Figure 1.4 with NBER recessions shaded in for easy reference.) Additional details about finance are presented below.

In Figure 5.14 the first thing to observe is the persistence of the Goodwin cycle in an index of the wage share. But note how the share trends downward beginning in the early 1980s. Its counterpart is the big increase in the profit rate shown in Figure 2.2. These shifts in the functional distribution fit more easily into macro models than changes in the distribution of income by size, which followed a similar pattern, as sketched in Chapter 9.

So the U.S. economy underwent a substantial distributive shift against

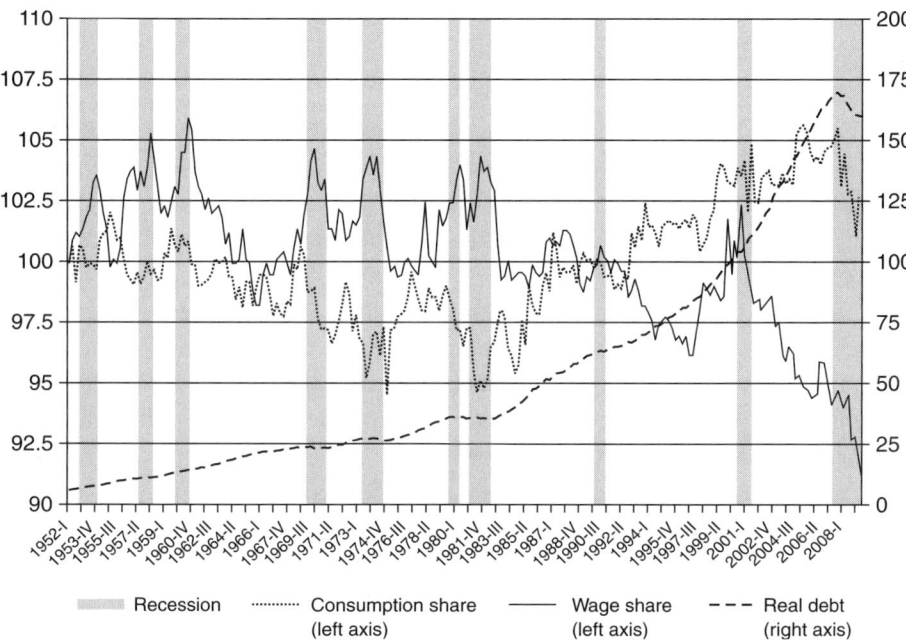

Figure 5.14 Wage share of value added, consumption share of disposable income, and household debt-to-income ratio with NBER reference recessions

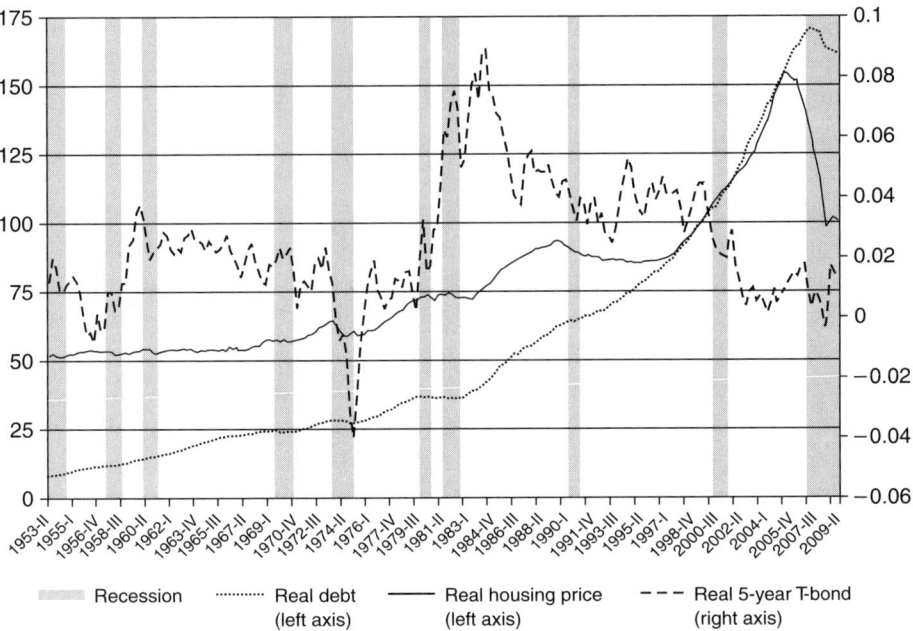

Figure 5.15 Real medium-term interest rate, housing prices, and real household debt with NBER reference recessions

labor and, effectively, the middle class. In Peter Flaschel's image from *Faust*, the soul of capital became more potent than the soul of labor, very substantially aided by the coming to power of economic and political conservatives under Ronald Reagan and the unwinding of New Deal labor market reforms.

Thorstein Veblen, as pointed out in Chapter 2, emphasized the social significance of striving to maintain and increase consumption levels. In the 1940s the economist James Duesenberry came up with a *ratchet effect* (described in its historical context in Chapter 6) whereby households tend to raise consumption in affluent periods but do not cut back very much when their absolute or even relative income falls. Veblenesque conspicuous consumption and social emulation are at the root of the phenomenon. As their income position deteriorated before and after the turn of the twenty-first century, American households did indeed keep on consuming. Note the rising share of consumption in disposable income in Figure 5.14. (As pointed out previously, rising health care costs contributed to this trend.)

So how did households pay for more consumption? By running up debt, of course. We are back to Albert Hirschman's observation from Chapter 1 that distributive conflict can spill over into inflation or escalating debt. The latter option came to the fore in the United States, as shown by the more than doubling of the household debt-to-income ratio in Figure 5.14.

This increase was made possible by several factors. One already mentioned was a significant relaxation of lending standards for households—smaller required down payments, less aggressive checking of income levels and assets (the famous *ninja mortgages* required no income, no job, and no assets), aggressive promotion of credit cards, and so on. Also important was the rapid reduction in interest rates in the 2000s (Figure 5.15). The rate reductions were initially targeted at alleviating the recession early in the decade. Along with the Bush II jump in government net borrowing shown in Figure 5.8, they were successful. But then with some fluctuations, low rates were maintained after 2001 (in part because capital inflows held them down; see Chapter 8). As shown in Figure 5.15, housing prices (depending on which index one chooses; see Figure 1.2) continued to grow through the middle of the decade. Real household debt kept pace, overshooting the housing price break along the lines of the Minsky-Soros model of Figure 5.7.

Financial engineering, the originate-and-distribute lending model, and proliferation of off–balance sheet vehicles led to the spread of CDOs, CDSs, and other incomprehensible derivatives, as discussed in Chapter 4. They magnified as opposed to diversifying Keynesian uncertainty and made the 2007–2009 unraveling far more severe than it might otherwise have been. Post–World War II finance theory provided an ideological justification for these trends, as discussed in Chapter 7.

There were also international complications, as shown by the mirror-image movements of household and foreign net borrowing in Figure 5.9. The implications will be discussed further in Chapter 8.

In sum, to repeat an observation from Chapter 1, cognitive misperceptions and inappropriate actions at many levels worked together to create the crisis. Its unfolding can certainly be understood from the Keynesian perspective encompassing distinct groups of social actors with highly imperfect knowledge.

On the side of political economy there was effectively an alliance between (mostly) non-affluent households, finance, and politicians in power in support of more debt. Even if each group could be seen as pursuing its own self-interest (for example, see the discussion just below of household financial behavior), macroeconomically they created an unsustainable situation. The fallacy of composition came into play once again.

Its effects were amplified in a profit-led economy in which slower real wage than productivity growth over time supports employment and output expansion. On the one hand, this linkage may be beneficial. Faster growth of output and (possibly) employment can help defuse Luddite objections to productivity increases.

On the other hand, rising inequality becomes almost a precondition for robust economic performance. After the early 1980s, increasing debt served as a social safety valve that helped prevent distributive tension from spilling over into the political arena. The process ultimately broke down on the financial side because of its internal contradictions, but it did survive for a few decades.

A neoclassical economist might well ask how a macroeconomic requirement of output determination by effective demand combined with a shifting income distribution could translate into incentives for millions of individual households to increase their spending and go into debt, aided and abetted by financial innovation. But it happened. So much for the methodological individualism and instrumental rationality with their destabilizing effects nullified by Say's Law that are built into neoclassical theory.

The Financial Side

It makes sense in closing to add a few details about financial developments, to supplement the foregoing discussion and provide background for a fuller discussion in Chapter 7.

Figure 5.16 shows household debt and total expenditure (consumption plus investment) as ratios to net worth. Household spending rose as a share of income after around 1980, but on trend it *fell* relative to net worth. The main reason is that households enjoyed capital gains on equity (directly and through mutual funds) and housing. Neoclassically speaking, it was not obviously irrational for them to convert capital gains into more debt to support higher spending. Their debt/net worth ratio rose "only" from around 15% in the early 1980s to a bit more than 20% in the early 2000s.

But also note how the ratios were whipsawed by changing asset prices. They dropped fairly sharply in the late 1990s with the stock market boom and then jumped up when equity prices collapsed. A similar pattern re-

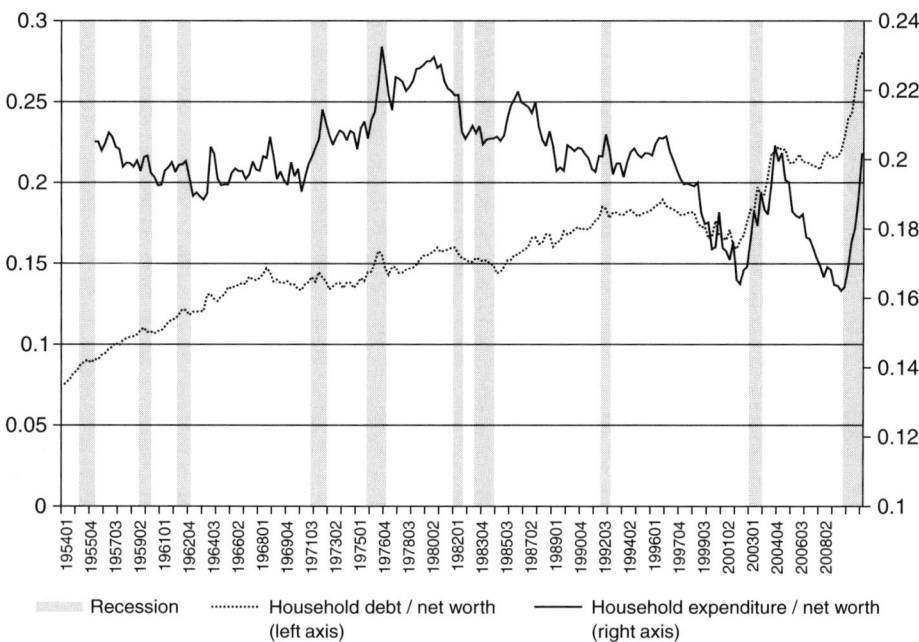

Figure 5.16 Household debt and expenditure relative to net worth

peated in the 2000s with housing prices as the driving force. The big jump in the debt ratio after the middle of the decade helps explain why households' net borrowing drops so rapidly in Figures 5.8 and 5.9. Their balance sheets took a big hit, and they sharply reduced their net borrowing (Figure 5.8) to try to build them back up.

Recall from Chapter 4 that primary wealth in the economy is the value of its capital stock plus government debt. Since around 1950 the ratio of GDP to wealth in the United States has been close to one-quarter. Because government debt is a fraction of the capital stock, this observation means that the U.S. capital/output ratio fluctuates around a level of four, consistent with the range of variation in capacity utilization shown in Figure 5.5.

Despite this long-term stability, the financial superstructure of the economy has changed dramatically—especially since 1980. The changes show up clearly in Figure 5.17, which shows ratios of financial positions to primary wealth for households, the rest of the world, the financial sector, and nonfinancial business.

The most striking change is the growth of total assets and liabilities of

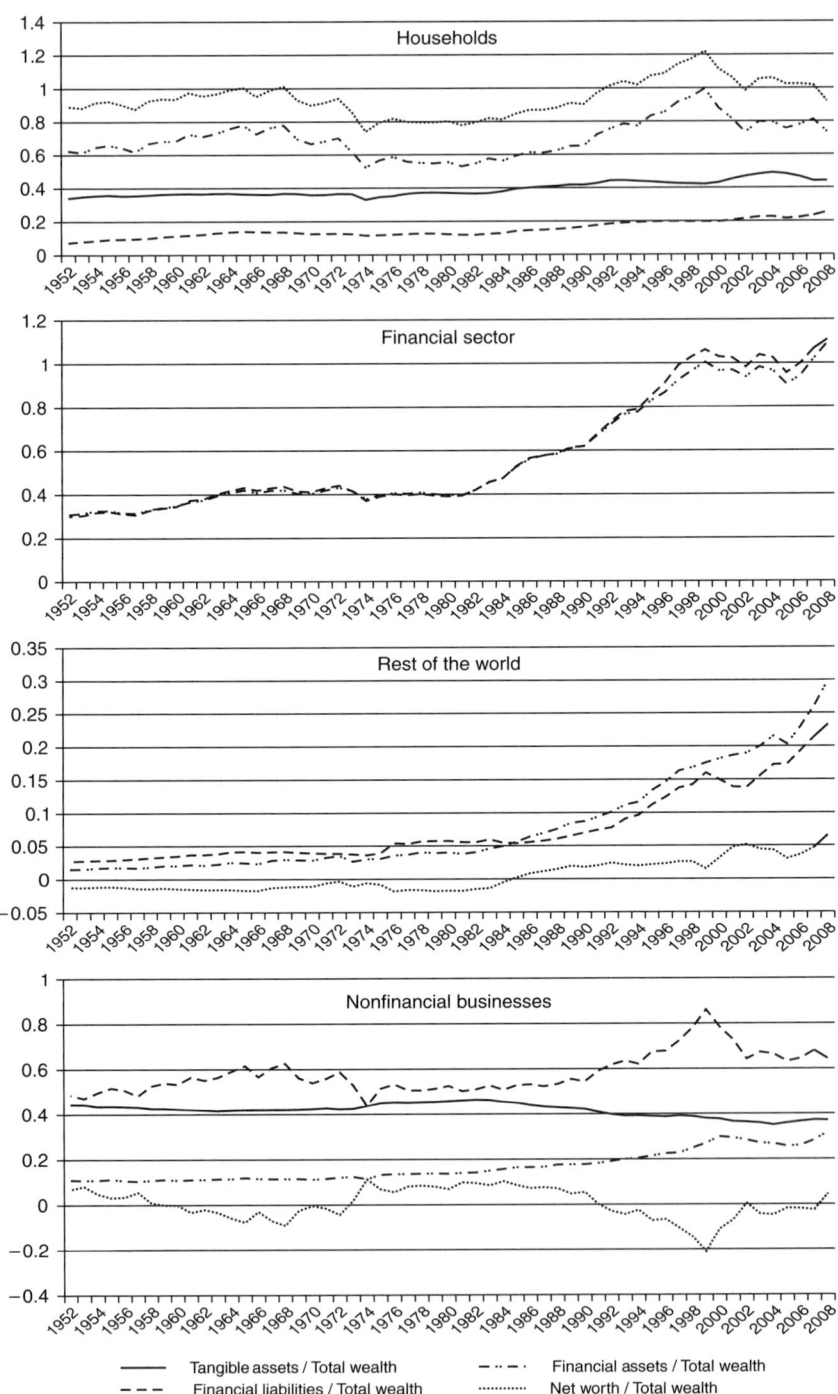

Figure 5.17 Financial positions of households, rest of the world, financial sector, and nonfinancial business relative to total wealth

the financial sector from around 40% of primary wealth in 1980 to over 100% in the late 2000s. Much of the shift can be explained by the expansion of mutual and retirement funds. But it also reflected the explosion of securitization. There was a major reallocation of sources of the nonfinancial sector's debt from the balance sheets of banks (mortgages, credit cards, and so on) to securities markets (for example, corporate bonds, commercial paper, and asset-backed securities). The banks' share fell from over 45% to 30% and the securities markets' participation rose correspondingly. More on the implications in Chapter 7.

The asset and liability positions of the rest of the world rose by around 20% of total wealth. More important, the sector's net worth rose by more than five percentage points, building with the flow of current account deficits that began after 1980.

The share of net worth of households fluctuated parallel to the value of their financial assets. The value of tangible assets rose in line with the price of residential capital, and as already illustrated in Figure 1.4, debt rose a bit faster. The nonfinancial business borrowing binge during the 1990s, shown in Figure 5.8 (the dot-com episode), was reflected in a rising share of debt before 2000.

These financial movements provide another angle to view the economy after 1980. Divergent trends emerged, with contradictions that became apparent during 2007–2009. How they will shift in the 2010s remains to be seen.

Lessons from the Disciples

Fundamental uncertainty, the absence of Say's Law, and the presence of tensions between collective social actors characterize Keynesian economics. As described in this chapter, useful applied models can be based on these ideas. Here is a quick summary bringing in some additional thoughts from Chapters 7 and 8, all to be drawn on in Chapter 9.

Macroeconomic Growth

Kaldor argued that like the level of economic activity, the rate of economic growth is driven from the demand side. In his models from the 1960s the growth rate may or may not converge to a steady state, and full employment is not guaranteed. Because of economies of scale and technological advances embodied in learning processes as well as new capital goods, the growth rate of labor productivity responds positively to output growth, especially in industry. (An increase in the output growth rate of 1% may be associated with an increase of 0.5% in productivity growth.) Like all Cambridge economists including Keynes (though he downplayed it in the *General Theory*), Kaldor assumed that saving is influenced by the income distribution. In a convenient formulation, the private-sector saving rate is a decreasing function of the wage share of total income.

Kalecki proposed a theory in which investment is driven by the rate of profit. Steindl added the level of economic activity (herein measured as the rate of capacity utilization) as an additional determinant. A model can be set up in terms of the output/capital ratio as a measure of utilization and the wage share (equal to the real wage divided by the level of labor productivity, with profit share + wage share = 1) representing distribution. In an economy open to foreign trade at a given exchange rate, exports are likely to respond positively to the profit share because an increase signals a reduction in unit labor costs.

With these investment and export functions and a Cambridge-style saving function in force, both output and capital stock growth as determined by aggregate demand can respond either positively or negatively to an increase in the wage share. The alternative possibilities have come to be called "wage-led" and "profit-led" respectively.

Distributive Cycles in Effective Demand

Goodwin's dynamic specification borrowed from models of predator-prey dynamics. The resulting cycle resembles one proposed by Marx in volume one of *Capital*.

The original model is not Keynesian because its level of investment is determined by available saving, following Say's Law and Marx. Its pattern of cyclicality, however, can easily be extended in a Keynes-Kalecki-Steindl direction by incorporating dynamics of the wage share. In this setup Kaldorian productivity dynamics come to the fore. As an economy emerges from a recession, labor productivity usually rises because firms have been hoarding labor during the trough in anticipation of rising output in the future. When that happens, productivity or the output/labor ratio goes up. This jump forces the labor share downward, stimulating aggregate demand in a profit-led economy.

As output rises, productivity growth tails off, and the real wage starts to rise as the labor market tightens. The income distribution shifts against profits, slowing demand growth near the upper turning point. Such a system with profit-led demand and a "full employment profit squeeze" is not a bad fit for the business cycle in the United States.

Macro Accounting Restrictions

Chapter 1 stresses how Keynes built his macroeconomic system around the postulate that the value of output is always equal to income. This "identity" serves as the foundation for all contemporary national accounting. Godley and Steindl emphasized three important implications.

One is that the excess of spending over income can take either sign for any individual or socioeconomic group (say, households, nonfinancial business, financial business, government, and the rest of the world), but that the economy-wide sum of these "net borrowing" flows must be zero. A decomposition of net borrowing provides a convenient means for analyzing macro cycles and trends.

Second, in a complete accounting setup with no "black holes," one can see how shifting ratios of macro flows (for example, investment in new capital goods, saving) and stocks (the capital stock, net worth or wealth, and so on) can either stabilize or destabilize the system. The fiction built into economic growth theory is that all flow/flow, flow/stock, and stock/stock ratios converge to "steady state" levels (or perhaps cycle around them as in a Goodwin model). Contrary to this theory, over the recent political economy cycle, key variables in the U.S. economy have demonstrated divergent trends.

Finally, global macroeconomic accounting without black holes reveals that there is not much room for variables such as exchange rates and external deficits to adjust independently of one another (in the jargon, the system has very few "degrees of freedom"). How one can ascertain directions of macroeconomic causality when they are so circumscribed has been subject to fierce debate.

As I discuss in Chapter 8, suppose that two countries with output determined by effective demand share a current account balance (that is, one's surplus equals the other's deficit). Its level responds to the exchange rate between the two currencies. So either the level of the balance could be (somehow) fixed, or else shifts in the exchange rate could drive the balance.

More generally, for N countries there will be $N-1$ degrees of freedom on current account.

Now consider national balance sheets, which can adjust rapidly to capital movements. Without capital controls, one can show that if central banks are fixing interest rates, then the exchange rate will be stable *unless* one country intervenes in markets to control its level of international reserves and the other country acquiesces. Then the rate will have to float. This game also generalizes to N countries with $N-1$ degrees of freedom on capital account.

The bottom line is that with rapid adjustment in capital markets and much slower adjustment in trade, among N countries $N-1$ bilateral exchange rates are determined on capital account, which in turn, all other factors held equal, determine current account balances. The rates can either float or be fixed by policy interventions (which can include controls on capital movements, as in China), with at least one country accepting the consequences.

Finance

To turn to the financial side, Kindleberger's historical discussion of asset price booms fueled by increasing debt is a good description of the run-up to the 2007–2009 crisis (also noted by Soros). Keynes paid little attention to such phenomena. Nor did he discuss increasing financial fragility due to rising debt-service burdens in an upswing, as emphasized by Minsky, though his macro model is a natural extension of Keynes's trade cycle theory. Besides debt burdens, Minsky emphasized the influence of changing asset prices on financial decision making over the cycle.

As described in Chapter 7, Minsky also argued that financial evolution linked to fragility can be destabilizing. Via changes in asset and commodity prices and its political efforts to remove regulatory controls, a growing financial sector can upset the rest of the system in several ways.

Bailing out finance in recurring crises encourages the surviving institutions to move into more fundamentally uncertain territory because they are less inhibited by regulatory restriction. Traders always respond to short-term incentives for high-uncertainty/high-return trading, and management may not be able to stop their games. Responsible boards of directors of aggressive firms might wish to rein in their traders but do not do so for fear of "losing talent." Every financial shakeout in which at least some institutions get rescued seems to worsen these problems of moral hazard.

Cutting interest rates to support the level of output when inflation is low may stimulate an asset price bubble, feeding into output expansion. On the fiscal side, a stimulus package could provoke commodity price inflation, especially if labor is in a position to meet price increases by successfully bargaining for higher wages, which could lead to further increases in prices, and so on.

But then if the central bank raises rates to slow the economy, it could provoke an asset price crash and major recession, creating a need to bail out the system once again.

Notes

G. C. Harcourt (2006) gives a helpful review of much of the material in this chapter. See Joan Robinson (1974) for her views on history versus equilibrium.

The growth accounting in this chapter appears in algebra in Rada and Taylor (2006) and Taylor (2010), including a demonstration that a growth model based solely on accounting relationships will converge to a Solow-style steady state. Fairly high-tech treatments of growth theory complementary to the presentation here are by Duncan Foley and Thomas Michl (1999), Peter Skott (2008), and Peter Flaschel (2009). I have borrowed liberally from all three.

Harrod (1939) and Domar (1946) are the original economic growth papers. Solow (1956 and 1957) sets out the neoclassical gospel. Kaldor (1961) recites his stylized facts and a version of his Mark I model. Robinson (1969; originally published 1956) presents an intriguing review of the early development of growth theory, and Robinson (1962) unveils the banana diagram. Kaldor (1978) describes his Mark II technological progress function, which had its debut in the inaugural lecture for his professorial chair at Cambridge in 1966. Okun (1962) proclaims his gap and law.

Goodwin (1967) sketches his model of growth cycles. Taylor (2004 and 2010) introduces the cyclical growth model described in the text. Econometric estimates appear in Flaschel (2009) and Barbosa-Filho and Taylor (2006, based on the lead author's New School Ph.D. dissertation). Minsky (2008) is the reissued version of his 1975 book on Keynes.

Godley and Lavoie (2007) is the latest summary of the first author's approach to macroeconomics. Analysis of net borrowing was introduced in an earlier book by Godley and Cripps (1983) and in papers from the early 1980s collected in Steindl (1990). Barbosa-Filho et al. (2008) present U.S. data and discussion.

Ocampo, Rada, and Taylor (2009) outlines the analytics of the labor productivity and employment decompositions reported here, along with empirical results for developing countries. The basic ideas come from Moshe Syrquin (1984) and Luigi Pasinetti (1981).

— 6 —

The Counterrevolution

The economists discussed in Chapter 5 were like the Old Believers in the Russian Orthodox Church from the late seventeenth century onward. They didn't quite follow their Russian counterparts in making the sign of the cross with two fingers but certainly did believe in fundamental uncertainty, animal spirits, the potential instability of capitalism on both the real and financial sides, and class conflict. When they set up formal models, it was understood that the machinery could easily break down because of all the potential instabilities and uncertainties emphasized in the *General Theory*. Their basic causal scheme remained that of Figure 4.4, extended by feedbacks from output to the growth of investment (Harrod and Domar); from distribution, productivity, and employment into effective demand and price-cost relationships (Robinson, Kaldor, Kalecki, and Goodwin); and from finance (Minsky).

The Old Believers and their successors form a distinct sect, nowadays called *post-Keynesian, heterodox, or structuralist.* (I prefer the last because of overlaps between Keynesianism and economic thought using the structuralist label in developing countries.) Even among economists who still consider themselves Keynesian, the "post-" group make up a distinct minority. It remains to be seen if this situation will change in the wake of the 2007–2009 crisis.

As observed in Chapter 1, reactions against the *General Theory* began soon after it was published. Several were incorporated into mainstream Keynesianism from the 1930s through the 1960s. It was a blend of Walrasian formulations with effective demand, at times called the *neoclassical synthesis* (a label coined by the MIT economist Paul Samuelson). Invoking the mother superior of the Old Believers, Robert Skidelsky summarized the situation well: "These early theoretical models incorporated features which were not at all evident in the *magnum opus,* but which conformed more closely to orthodox theory. The constructors of these models also thought they were improving the original building. Joan Robinson, no slouch with insults, would later label the result 'bastard Keynesian.' But Keynes was the bastard's father" (Skidelsky, 1992, 538). The bastard's anatomy and metabolism are the first topics considered here.

The great battles of the 1950s and 1960s were between old and mainstream Keynesians and monetarists marshaled by Milton Friedman. The monetarists operated within a Wicksell-Keynes framework, with emphasis on Wicksell. They argued that macro policy interventions may appear to work for a while but ultimately will be ineffective. Keynesians did and do think that policy interventions have their limitations but can exert traction on the system. Later analysis of the monetary system also moved toward Wicksell (and some post-Keynesians) by concentrating on the interest rate instead of the money supply as the key policy indicator.

The monetarists were soon overshadowed by more radical revolutionaries, the *new classical* economists, who simply proclaimed very loudly that Say's Law applies in a world in which there are random shocks to supply which obey an objective probability distribution known by all economic actors. *Rational expectations* of the shocks operate to make policy ineffective even in the very short run. Exaggerating the size of Chapter 2's little triangles, a down-market version called *supply-side economics* argued that reducing taxes can unleash enormous gains in economic efficiency.

These debates played out in the 1970s. Since then academic fads (described briefly below) and empirical work have dominated macroeconomics. There has been a degree of convergence between the new classicals and the new Keynesian inheritors of the neoclassical synthesis. The Walrasians won the professorial battles. The neoclassical synthesis and rational expectations models also influenced thinking about open economy macroeconomics, discussed in Chapter 8.

Mainstream Keynesianism

Restating the *General Theory* in terms of algebra and equations while minimizing the significance of fundamental uncertainty and all the rest got under way in September 1936 at an Oxford meeting of the Econometric Society. (Kahn and the Robinsons from the Cambridge Circus were not there.) Roy Harrod and James Meade were driving forces behind extending the causal scheme in Figure 4.4 to (1) emphasize the importance of economic transactions as summarized by the value of output *PX* in the determination of the demand for money along the lines of the quantity theory, and (2) bring in, with scant empirical justification, the rate of interest together with output as a determinant of consumption and saving.

The late 1930s restatement pushed Keynes's crisp causal scheme back toward a general equilibrium formulation, albeit still incorporating the principle of effective demand. At that point macroeconomics contracted a deep Walrasian infection which finally flared up as the new classical school in the 1970s.

IS/LM

Meade's contemporary John Hicks drew the *IS/LM diagram* worth a thousand words which came to serve as the main teaching device for mainstream macro before it was supplanted by AS/AD. As illustrated in Figure 6.1, it has output on the horizontal axis and the interest rate on the vertical. There are two curves, with names later supplied by the Harvard Keynesian Alvin Hansen.

The IS or "investment-saving" curve shows the level of output as deter-

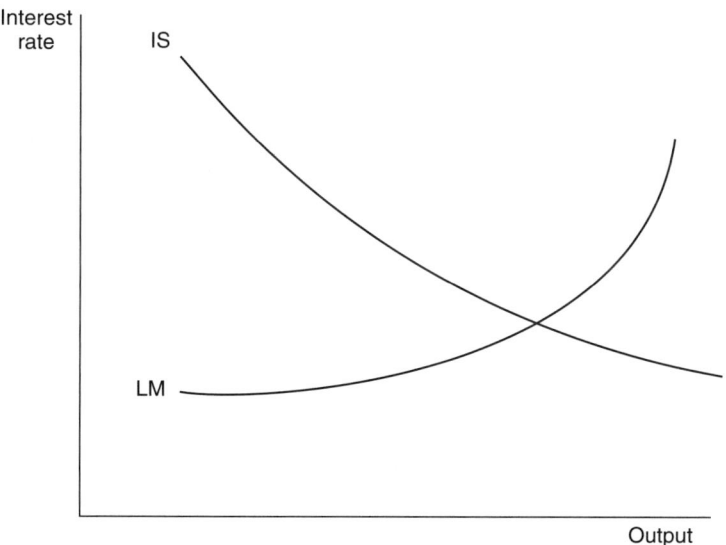

Figure 6.1 The Hicks-Hansen IS/LM diagram

mined by the interest rate through the investment and saving functions. It slopes downward because a higher interest rate cuts back effective demand.

The LM or "liquidity-money" curve shows how the interest rate responds through the speculative demand function for money to higher transactions demand due to larger output (with a fixed money supply equal to the sum of the two forms of demand, as in Minsky's model presented in Chapter 5). If we ignore equity in the balance sheets in Table 4.1 and treat bonds and loans as being very similar, then there are two financial markets to be cleared—for money and for bonds and/or loans. If one market clears, however, then so will the other because of the adding-up restrictions built into the balance sheets. If the rate is seen as adjusting to clear the market for bonds and loans, then the money market will clear automatically and vice versa. This observation has implications for open economy macroeconomics as discussed in Chapter 8.

A more contemporary justification for the LM curve would be that it simply describes central bank interest rate policy. If the bank pegged the rate at some level, the LM would just be a horizontal straight line. If the curve is supposed to describe a central bank interest rate response function to higher economic activity, it should have the conventional upward slope.

Macro equilibrium is determined at the point where the curves cross. They can move for various reasons, but the usual focus is on policy analysis: expansionary fiscal policy will shift the IS curve to the right, pushing up both output and the interest rate. Suppose that the LM on the traditional interpretation has a steep slope at a high, "full-employment" output level because the effect of output on transactions demand is strong and/or the effect of the interest rate on speculative demand for money is weak. (The relative strengths of these effects at high output are reversed in Minsky's model described in Chapter 5. If they are reversed at *low* output, then we have Hicks's version of the liquidity trap with a nearly horizontal LM.)

With a steeply sloping LM, the attempt at fiscal expansion will be offset by a higher interest rate, which will reduce investment and consumption demand along loanable funds lines. Government spending *crowds out* private outlays. As will be seen, a jump in inflation plays a similar role in Friedmanite monetarism. Expansionary monetary policy will shift the LM downward. It won't have much bite if the IS is steep, meaning that big interest rate changes are required to induce an appreciable change in output via the saving and investment functions. As the diagram is drawn, that circumstance applies at low output levels, but other configurations of the IS curve are certainly possible.

Historically the AS/AD model discussed in connection with Figure 4.6 emerged from IS/LM. If the price level falls (say), real balances will go up, shifting the LM curve down. The resulting lower interest rate will stimulate demand through the Keynes effect. This rationale for a downward-sloping AD curve is consistent with the entrenched mainstream view that if reducing the money wage bids down the price level, then it will increase employment. As discussed in Chapter 4, Keynes's response is that it is much easier to generate the same outcome by increasing the money supply.

If the LM represents central bank policy, the authorities would presumably move it downward when the price level falls, in an exercise in *inflation targeting* (discussed below). Output would increase along the IS curve as a consequence. In this case the authorities would be intervening actively to make wage reduction feed into higher employment. So why not just shift the curve down anyway?

Fiscal Complications

Beyond IS/LM, a few other ideas of the early mainstream Keynesians carry over to current debate. One is Alvin Hansen's emphasis on *secular stagnation*. Borrowing a thought from Keynes, he argued in the late 1930s that future investment demand was likely to be weak because population growth was apparently slowing, and no new demand-inducing technological breakthroughs like the railroads after the Civil War seemed to be in the cards. As observed in Chapter 3, military Keynesianism in the form of arms and personnel spending for World War II soon overcame short-term concerns over stagnation. The postwar baby boom took care of the population worries, and for better or worse there has been vigorous technological innovation.

Hansen did not foresee these trends and so was empirically incorrect. He also stressed that the government could always support demand by public works and other forms of spending. As noted in Chapter 4, this "Increase G" interpretation of Keynes may not be faithful to the master but it lives to this day, for example, in the 2009 Obama stimulus package.

A second idea (already noted in Chapter 1) that some early Keynesians introduced is that there is a *government budget constraint* which says that if fiscal spending exceeds tax revenues, then public debt is going to go up. If the fiscal deficit is roughly proportional to GDP and the real interest rate exceeds the GDP growth rate, then the government will be violating the solvency condition introduced in Chapter 5. It will be heading into a *debt trap*. Further implications are developed below. (Many Old Believers of the Increase G or *fiscalist* persuasion considered this line of thought dangerously counterrevolutionary. Richard Kahn wanted to read Wynne Godley out of the movement for bringing it up.)

Consumption Function

Keynes's consumption function was redesigned because it had empirical problems, as pointed out by Simon Kuznets and others. As discussed in connection with household net borrowing in Chapter 5, the marginal propensity to consume appears to vary counter-cyclically, falling in booms and rising in slumps. Over longer time spans a companion finding was that consumption is a constant proportion in the range of 90–95% of income. The reason is that the change in household wealth is just income minus consumption (ignoring interest, taxes, and so on). Over a long run of averaged data, the wealth/income ratio is stable, meaning that the consumption/income ratio must be stable as well.

In Figure 6.2 the "Keynes" consumption function crosses the long-run relationship. Over periods of quarters or a few years, data points may (or may not) cluster along the "Keynes" relationship. But if per capita income is growing, the schedule itself has to shift upward over time to permit the long-run average consumption/income ratio to remain constant.

Beginning in the late 1940s, an active cottage industry grew up attempting to explain these findings. First, the Harvard economist James Duesenberry argued on sociological grounds that each household's consumption behavior is the result of learning, custom, and habit (points already made in *The General Theory* and, for that matter, Veblen's *Theory of the Leisure Class*). People do watch one another as well as the movies and TV, and they shape the level and composition of their spending accordingly.

Second, consumption is somewhat inertial. When income swings up, consumption rises, but at a lower rate of growth. When income declines, households try to retain existing real standards of living, so that consumption drops off with a lag, giving rise to a *ratchet effect*. In an upswing, consumption moves along the "Keynes" curve in Figure 6.2, but it doesn't fall very much when income declines. Thus in the next upswing the "Keynes"

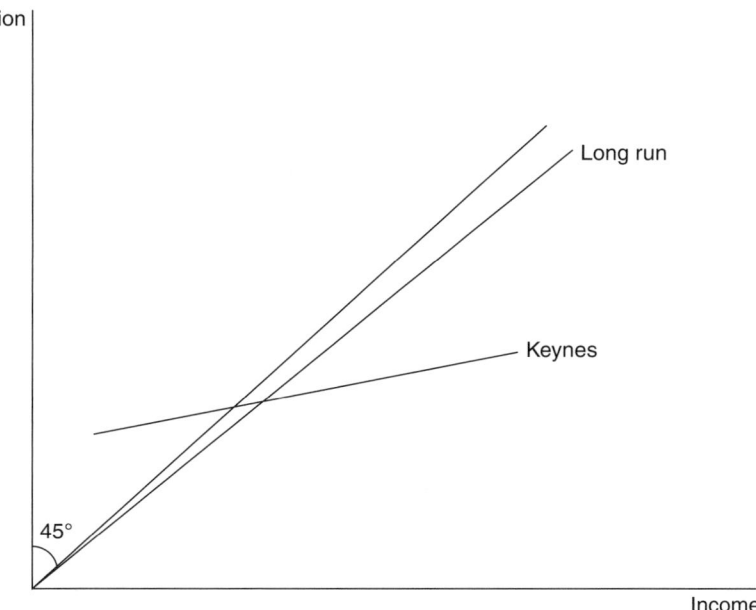

Figure 6.2 Alternative consumption functions

schedule drifts up, providing a mechanism for its movement along the "Long run" line over time.

Duesenberry's model explained the stylized facts of its time parsimoniously and with a bit of flair. As noted in Chapter 5, it helps provide an explanation for the dramatic fall in the U.S. household saving rate after the income distribution began to shift against wages in the early 1980s. But it lacked rational actor "foundations," which is the main reason why it has almost completely disappeared from view.

The introduction of wealth effects by Franco Modigliani and colleagues, by contrast, remains influential. His *life cycle* consumption model tried to describe the ways in which people plan their economic lives. The households considered, however, are of a certain age and kind. As the Harvard economist Stephen Marglin observes: "People whose employment prospects are reasonably certain, who follow a reasonably predictable career path, and whose lives are otherwise sufficiently ordered that long-term planning makes intellectual and emotional sense might . . . make decisions according to the life-cycle hypothesis. . . . (A colleague of mine once remarked that the life cycle hypothesis is just what one would expect of a tenured college professor!)" (Marglin, 1984, 431). That colleague was almost certainly Duesenberry.

Such a well-ordered person might be T years old, expecting to live to age L and to work to age $N < L$. Let ω be expected yearly average wage income (assumed constant) for the rest of his working life and W be his wealth. Then if he spreads out his consumption over time, the level at age T could take the form

$$C_T = \frac{W + \omega(N - T)}{L - T},$$

where it is understood that the term $\omega(N - T)$ drops out when the person retires (that is, $\omega = 0$ when $T > N$). Somebody aged forty-five who expects to work to sixty-five and die at seventy-five will aim at smoothing consumption over his expected life cycle, at age forty-five consuming 3.33% of his wealth per year and 66.67% of expected average wage income. Evidently these shares will change over a person's life cycle, but the population-wide numbers add up to something like the parameters used in the illustrative consumption function discussed in connection with Table 4.4.

Except for those who are about to die, the consumption coefficient on wealth in this setup is pretty small—a few percent per year for the middle-aged and near zero for the young. Such models correctly predicted that the paper losses of $1 or $2 trillion in the stock market crash of October 19, 1987, would not be large enough to cause a recession in 1988. In 2007–2009, by contrast, the wealth effect of the loss of value of residential capital *has* been substantial. As noted in Chapter 4, life cycle considerations also suggest that the real balance effect is of extremely limited significance for consumption. This observation is ignored by the mainstream.

Investment Demand

We turn now to investment demand. A theory stating that capital formation responds to capital asset prices was, as we have seen, introduced in variant forms by Kahn, Kaldor, Minsky, and Tobin. Tobin's version came to be justified by firm-level Ramsey optimal investment models featuring a *shadow price* of capital, that is, the capital stock valuation ratio q. Firms increase investment net of depreciation when q exceeds 1 and reduce it otherwise. Details appear below in the discussion of new classical macro.

Minsky ignored optimization, saying that a firm's required q is influenced by two forces also popularized by Kalecki: *lenders' risk* (the cost of capital rises as investment increases) and *borrower's risk* (the firm has to reduce internal liquidity and otherwise tighten ship when capital expenditures go up). The interaction of these forms of risk (or, better, Keynesian uncertainty) determines investment demand.

One or the other variant is central to much contemporary discussion of the determinants of investment.

Neoclassical Synthesis

Many of these ideas jelled into the neoclassical synthesis. Especially in the United States it dominated mainstream thinking until the 1970s. The root was Modigliani's 1944 exercise which built the Pigou effect into a complete macro model. The policy implication that he drew was that if the money wage could be made flexible in a downward direction, then full employment could be attained. As discussed in Chapter 4 and above in connection with the IS/LM diagram, a falling wage would reduce the price level, increase real balances, and cause effective demand to rise. A *nominal rigidity* was preventing the economy from performing as well as it could.

This mechanistic version vastly exaggerates the importance of the Pigou effect. It ignores Keynes's arguments about the ineffectiveness of wage-cutting in Chapter 19 and everything he said about fundamental uncertainty. But it took over the world. Paul Samuelson subsequently wrote, "Had Keynes begun his first few chapters with the simple statement that he found it realistic to assume that modern capitalist societies had money wage rates that were sticky and resistant to downward movements, most of his insights would have remained just as valid" (Samuelson, 1964, 332). This same narrow view was passed along by the postwar American Keynesians to their new Keynesian offspring, who also stressed nominal rigidities and in addition quietly forgot about the principle of effective demand.

Econometrics

By all reports, Keynes loved to bury himself in the numbers, searching for patterns and drawing inferences. As discussed in Chapter 4, he also put considerable effort into constructing macroeconomic accounting schemes. They supported a characteristic approach to macroeconomics. He started from structure as embodied in the numbers, accounts, and stylized facts, and then logically built up arguments to deal with the question at hand. With modest formal statistical backup, examples of this approach have been presented in Chapter 5.

In contrast, the mainstream and its Nobel prizewinners came to rely heavily on strictly *econometric* models for forecasting and policy analysis. They are constructed on the basis of parameters estimated statistically from NIPA and other data. Keynes was extremely critical of this approach, for example, in criticizing the work of the Dutch econometrician Jan Tinbergen (who shared the first economics Nobel with Ragnar Frisch), which he called statistical alchemy. One key point he raised is that to test reliably for trends, one needs long time series of data, but coefficients and behavioral relationships are likely to be stable only over short periods.

Another issue is that it is always possible to come up with an econometric approach that will "support" any given theory. *Falsification* of theories along the lines promoted by the philosopher Karl Popper rarely enters into discussion. As one cynical colleague once remarked, the Fundamental Theorem of Econometrics is that you can always find functional forms and estimation techniques that will get you the result you want. The observation applies to the large economy-wide models that began to be built in the 1940s. Through the 1970s they got bigger and more complicated but still adhered to the IS/LM causal scheme. Say's Law under rational expectations then took over at the design stage, with no apparent improvement or loss in the models' predictive powers. More on this shift in emphasis below.

Monetarism

Besides animating the neoclassical synthesis, the Pigou effect became the weapon of choice for attacking the *General Theory*. It was built into an influential book in 1956 by Don Patinkin which advanced the "rigidity" interpretation of the *General Theory* and attempted (unsuccessfully in the eyes of many) to marry general equilibrium theory with macroeconomics. The Pigou linkage also became the key to an inflation model proposed by Milton Friedman.

Friedman's Contributions

In the mainstream's Whig history of economics, Karl Marx at times is called a "minor post-Ricardian." (The label was coined by Paul Samuelson, who in my view was almost as good as Joan Robinson at insults.) With equal justice, Friedman might be labeled a minor post-Wicksellian. Yet he was the captain at the culmination of a forty-year orthodox reaction against the economics of John Maynard Keynes. He made three highly visible contributions.

One was the observation discussed in Chapter 3 that the Fed practiced restrictive monetary policy in the early 1930s and so deepened the Great Depression—a point made by contemporaries including Currie and Keynes, which Friedman later magicked into a complete and all-encompassing explanation for the collapse of real GDP. In 2009 this monetarist interpretation of the depression was the main plank for arguments against the Obama fiscal stimulus package.

Second came the permanent income hypothesis described in Chapter 2. Like the suggestions of Duesenberry and Modigliani, it was a response to the post–World War II stylized facts about consumption. Despite its artificial rational actor foundations, it became the most important "explanation" of aggregate consumer behavior. The hypothesis implied a small or zero propensity to consume from *transitory income* (swings up and down in one's income flow over time), meaning that the expenditure multiplier is close to 1. In other words, expansionary fiscal policy can't have much impact.

Friedman's third contribution was a model of inflation proposed in 1967 (independently formulated by the Columbia economist Edmund Phelps). It was a reprise of Wicksell's natural rate model, but focusing on the level of employment and saying that in the long run, attempts at expansionary policy will be ineffective. The narrative drew heavily on Pigou, Modigliani, and Patinkin.

Suppose that the economy initially is at its natural (un)employment equilibrium, usually called a *NAIRU*, or non-accelerating inflation rate of unemployment—an acronym only an economist could create. Following Friedman we can imagine that a helicopter drops an enormous sack of money. At the initial price level, extra cash in hand means that real money balances go up, stimulating demand through the Pigou effect. Let P and w

be the price and wage levels respectively. Both start to rise, but P increases more rapidly because it responds directly to the higher demand. According to the usual neoclassical reasoning, the consequent reduction in the real wage $\frac{w}{P}$ should induce business to hire more workers. As we know, Friedman's analysis does not conform to the empirical facts: real wages tend to go up, not down, in an economic upswing.

Meanwhile, workers are supposed to respond slowly to the price increase. They think in terms of an expected price level P^e, which responds sluggishly (under so-called *adaptive expectations*) to changes in P. Labor supply is assumed to depend positively on $\frac{w}{P^e}$ (this response is what Keynes called the *second classical postulate*), so with a rising w and stable value of P^e, it will increase as well. Sooner or later workers will wake up to the fact that their real income is falling, because the general price index is trending upward. They start bidding up money wages and reducing labor supply. As with Wicksell, negative feedback reactions take over. Firms cut back on employment because of more costly labor from the wage push, workers decrease labor supply, and everybody reduces consumption because real balances are eroded by rising prices à la Pigou. The system cycles back to the natural rate equilibrium, with higher levels of both nominal wages and prices but the real wage the same as before. Expansionary monetary policy cannot work in the long run.

More real government spending would be offset in a similar cycle, except that consumption would be crowded out by an amount equal to the real expenditure increase to hold output constant at its natural rate level. Along similar lines, an attempt by labor to raise national income by pushing up money wages and stimulating consumption would be doomed to fail.

The only way that a higher output growth rate can be attained in the Friedman-Phelps world is by ever more rapid expansion of the money supply, giving the model its *accelerationist* nickname. Prices will trend upward, supporting Friedman's slogan that "inflation is always and everywhere a monetary phenomenon." There is no mention of social conflict as a driving force behind inflation. For all its impact on politics and policy, there is no overt institutional content in the monetarist counterrevolution.

Empirical Support?

The Friedman-Phelps model "predicted" stagflation, or rising inflation with slowly growing output, in the 1970s as a response to the expansionary policy of the Johnson-Nixon years. But there are more plausible explanations such as the oil shocks, worldwide monetary disarray following the developing country debt crises, and social conflict. Moreover, Friedman's foresight was happenstance. During the reverse-stagflation (or *Goldilocks economy*) Clinton period, natural rate models notably failed. Expansionary monetary policy coincided with economic growth and falling inflation, the opposite of Friedman's predictions. Figure 6.3 summarizes the data on inflation and capacity utilization.

After the economy settled down following the war, there was a small spike in inflation in the mid-1950s, and then a fairly steady increase beginning a decade later during the Kennedy and Johnson administra-

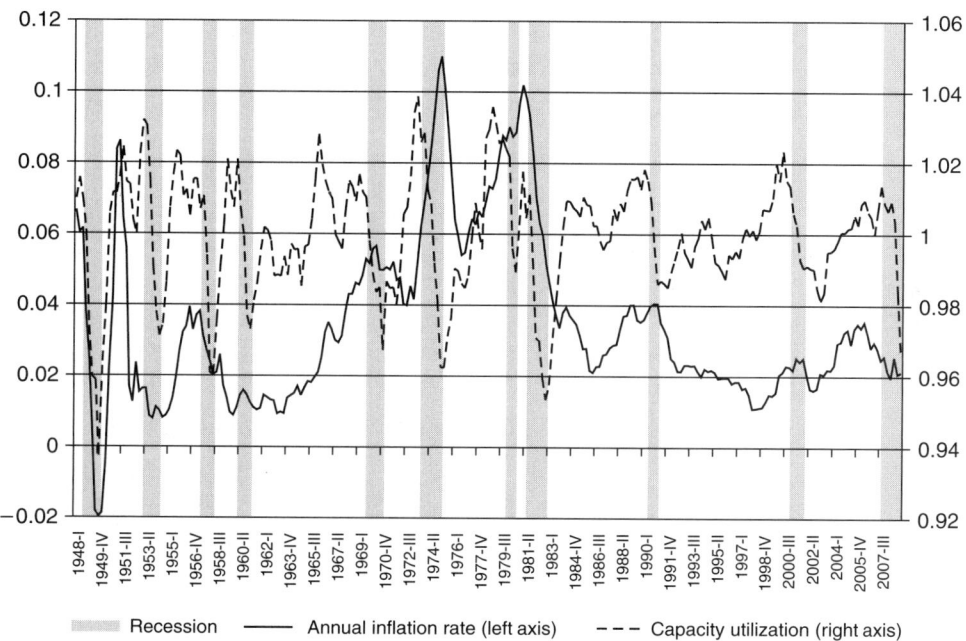

Figure 6.3 Annual inflation rate and rate of capacity utilization, with NBER recession periods

tions (Friedman's political target). The 1970s were the stagflation decade, marked by recessions and low levels of capacity utilization, which Friedman supposedly foresaw. Highly contractionary monetary policy then slowed inflation and provoked the double-dip recessions around 1980. By the mid-1980s inflation had fallen to the 2–4% range, where it has remained ever since. Interrupted by the recessions around 1990 and 2000, capacity utilization remained relatively stable.

One can scarcely accuse the Clinton administration of expansionary fiscal policy, but with Alan Greenspan in command, monetary policy became increasingly aggressive. As discussed in Chapter 7, the outcome was rapid growth in *asset* prices. Price inflation for goods and services did not happen. The Friedman-Phelps model was wrong.

Friedman in his day was the great rhetorician, as was Keynes in his. Powerfully restating its ancient fundamentals, he rode the crest of the reaction against the logic of the *General Theory*. Even so, he and his numerous collaborators did not fully succeed. To this day, mainstream macroeconomics remains conflicted about the reintroduction of Say's Law and the second classical postulate to counter the principle of effective demand. The mainstream believes in the natural rate as an article of faith but cannot deny that the macro system almost always follows the directions initially charted by Keynes.

Beyond Monetarism

There were two main shifts in thinking about the role of money after Friedman. One was a return to Wicksell's focus on the interest rate as opposed to the money supply. That change fed into the emergence of the idea of inflation targeting.

By way of history, Kaldor argued strongly against monetarism in the 1980s. As pointed out in Chapter 2, he followed the banking school in asserting that the central bank usually acts to ratify the ongoing pace of credit creation at some fixed interest rate. The inspiration may have come from Dennis Robertson, who observed in the 1920s that given the way the London discount market functioned, the Bank of England had no choice but to provide the reserves needed by commercial banks to hold the volume of debt the government wished to issue at current Bank rate.

Keynes and Friedman both reasoned in terms of a stable money demand function in which real balances were linked to output and the interest rate.

They mainly differed on which linkages to emphasize. In the 1970s, with a burst of inflation and the beginnings of financial market deregulation, econometric attempts to estimate a stable function began to fail. Ultimately that led to a proposal by the Stanford economist John Taylor that the Fed should seek not to control the money supply but rather to adjust the short-term interest rate up or down in response to deviations in inflation and/or the level of economic activity from preannounced or unstated targets. It could intervene in the Fed funds market (recall Chapter 4) to reach its goal.

Taylor of course was repeating Kaldor and Robertson and replicating Wicksell's proposal for banks to adjust the rate to achieve policy goals, but mainstream economists are oblivious to history. Inflation targeting became the preferred label for the "new" approach. If inflation is determined exclusively by demand, a Taylor rule is counter-cyclical. In a simplistic model, inflation would rise when unemployment falls below its NAIRU level and increase when it is above it. The rule would therefore tend to stabilize unemployment around the NAIRU. An "independent" central bank, basically meaning that the bank does not report directly to the Ministry of Finance, is supposed to lend credibility to the inflation target. Of course, with Congress periodically holding his feet to the fire, it is not clear in the United States just how politically independent the governor of the Fed really is.

The counter-cyclical effect may be absent if the source of rising inflation is not domestic demand but a supply shock, such as the sharp oil price hikes in 1973. A simple rule would be that the central bank should simply ignore these shocks as temporary. But if it fears that they will generate additional increases in wages and prices (the so called "second-round effects"), which risk transforming the price shock into permanent acceleration in inflation, it would try to counteract the price hikes by increasing the interest rate. The result is that the central bank would redirect the supply shock into a reduction of economic activity. In the U.S. economy that happened after 1973.

New Classical Macroeconomics

Friedman, to paraphrase Mary Wollstonecraft on women, was almost a reasonable creature. He operated within the principle of effective demand but sought to push it in peculiar directions. The same cannot be said of the new classical economists who brought forth the doctrine of *rational expectations*. The basic new classical ideas are presented here, with a couple of "digressions" in which the discussion gets a bit dense.

By way of introduction, new classical analysis can be interpreted as a friendly amendment to Friedman-Phelps. The political goal of that model was to show that interventionist policies would be ineffective in the long run. The mechanism was the adaptive expectations process whereby the expected price level P^e would catch up gradually to changes in the actual level P. With P^e converging toward P, the impact of any intervention would sooner or later diminish toward zero.

As already mentioned in Chapter 2, new classical economists short-circuited this lag by asserting that expected values of all macroeconomic variables of interest adjust "instantaneously" to observed values—the gist of *rational expectations*. Under these circumstances there is no way for policy to move the system, which is implicitly assumed to be in a Pareto optimal situation.

New classical economics was the wholly unexpected consequence of Harrod, Meade, Hicks, and Hansen's move to steer Keynes's economics in the Walrasian direction. For many economists the outcome forty years later was the complete replacement of effective demand by Say's Law. No halfway measures, as with Friedman.

Rational Expectations

A jumping-off point for understanding what the new classicals had in mind is their assumption of perfect foresight regarding future economic events. Their way to propagandize this idea was to set up models using optimal control theory—rocket science mathematics from the 1960s.

In formal terms, the course of economic evolution is assumed to be described by the solution to a Ramsey optimal saving model for a *representative agent*. Its actions are supposed to encapsulate the results of what all the individual agents in the economy do. The representative agent was invented as a typically fuzzy metaphor by Alfred Marshall, but the new classical economists made its existence into a concrete first article of faith.

The second article is that individual agents have *model-consistent* behavior. For example, households all set their saving and consumption levels according to the Ramsey-Keynes rule from the macro model. This behavioral assumption is at the heart of rational expectations. The details go as follows.

Strictly in *logical* time, the currently popular mainstream model incorporates an assumption that population and the labor force grow at rate n. Assume throughout the following discussion that the capital stock and consumption are expressed in per capita terms. The investment-saving balance becomes

Change in capital stock = Output − consumption − n × capital stock.

The term with the minus sign at the end of the equation shows up because population growth reduces the capital stock per capita.

The calculus of variations or optimal control procedure used to solve the model relies on an asset price (q again!) for capital. It obeys the equation

Growth rate of q = Pure rate of discount − marginal product of capital.

The absolute value of the growth rate of q can be interpreted as an own-rate of interest for capital which converges to zero at a steady state. The Ramsey-Keynes rule is derived from a further relationship stating that

Marginal utility of consumption = q.

These three equations set up a highly unstable system because of positive feedback between capital and its asset price. To trace it through, suppose that q increases. On the usual neoclassical assumptions, consumption must fall to raise marginal utility to be equal to the higher asset price. The resulting jump in saving will force the growth of capital to speed up, reducing the marginal product of capital and leading to a higher growth rate of q. Consumption will fall further . . . and so on.

Outside the model's fantasy world, a regulator could presumably intervene to retard the asset price growth. Or, as in Minsky's model and Maynard's Chapter 22, rising interest rates and debt burdens could break the positive feedback loop. New classical economists put their trust in the invisible hand to wave away the instability. For those masochists who may be interested in even more detail, the following digression gives a sketch.

Digression on a Saddlepath

The contortions the three equations force onto mainstream growth analysis are displayed in Figure 6.4. Nullclines for the capital stock and the asset price are labeled "Stable capital" and "Stable price" respectively. There is

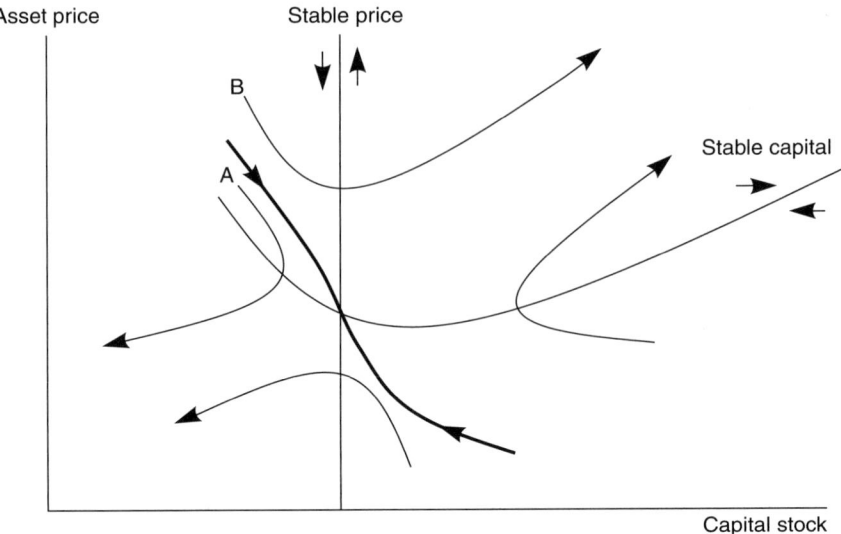

Figure 6.4 Dynamics of the capital stock and asset price in a Ramsey model

just one level of capital at which its marginal product equals the pure discount rate. This defines the "Stable price" nullcline as a vertical line.

The reasons why the capital stock nullcline has a U-shape are tricky. At a low level of capital stock, a reduction in the asset price would make consumption rise. To keep the growth of the stock at zero, more capital to raise production would be required, so toward the left of the diagram the "Stable capital" nullcline slopes downward. Toward the right the marginal product of capital is lower than n. An increase in capital reduces its growth rate. To hold growth constant, consumption would also have to fall, meaning that the asset price needs to rise.

The diagram shows that the dynamic model displays *saddlepoint* instability. (The image is that of a marble rolling on a saddle, which is bound to fall off unless it follows a single path along the middle between the pommel and the cantle. Eventually it will settle down on the lowest point along that path.) All capital and asset price trajectories except one fail to reach the steady state. Along the trajectory beginning at point A, for example, the asset price falls, while the capital stock increases until it hits the nullcline; at that point the asset price continues downward (so consumption rises to reduce its marginal utility), and the stock starts to decline. A trajectory from neighboring point B ends up with both the capital stock and the price going to infinity (so consumption tends toward zero with ever-rising marginal utility), and so on.

The one *saddlepath* trajectory (heavily shaded) goes to a steady state. At a point in time, for some initial level of capital stock (presumably inherited from the past), there is just *one* value of the asset price that will direct the economy toward a steady state.

Another Article of Faith

The sort of instability just described shows up in all optimal growth models. I have never understood why so many economists believe that the market is going to set an initially correct asset price to guide the trajectory of the capital stock precisely to the steady state while *every other* trajectory diverges from it. But let's go with the flow and let the invisible hand be infinitely precise in setting asset prices or be guided by perfect foresight forever. What about individual agents? They too have to make decisions as instructed by q.

In line with the definition used in Chapter 5, the growth rate of q is the *change* in its level over some short period of time, divided by the level at the beginning of the period. To know q's growth rate from the beginning, one has to have at least *myopic perfect foresight* about its value at the end of the period. If some unfortunate agent lacks such prescience and forecasts q according to its past trend or some other rule based on adaptive expectations, she will make an incorrect saving decision and suffer a loss in welfare. *With* rational expectations, she and her fellow agents will all get their forecasts right and the economy will be at a Pareto optimum.

Postulating model-consistent behavior means that all economic choices are made in this fashion. In a neat bit of circular reasoning involving four "nots," new classical economists argue that if choices are *not* model-consistent, then welfare will *not* be optimized, but we know that the invisible hand will *not* permit a loss in well-being to materialize. Because the loss can*not* occur, we all have rational expectations. The tautology is that model-consistent choices mean that we all have rational expectations.

So the third article of faith is that with agents (consumers and firms) behaving in this way, the economy will be at a stable Pareto optimum with full employment and will stay there regardless of whatever policies the government tries to implement. In contrast to Friedman's lagged responses, an attempt at expansionary monetary policy will be met by instantaneous jumps in prices and wages (rather like the scenario discussed in connection with own-rates of interest in Chapter 2), an increase in government spending will immediately crowd out household consumption by 100%, and so on.

Lucas's Contributions

Named after the Chicago economist Robert Lucas (another Nobel), a fourth article became the *Lucas critique* of macro policy. The idea sounds sensible, but Lucas's view of its practical implications does not fit common sense. The sensible bit is that policies based on observed past macro relationships may neglect consequent behavioral changes by economic agents, which, when added up, change the relationships themselves. In finance, for example, one of Minsky's fundamental points (further discussed in Chapter 7) is that continuing lender-of-last-resort interventions by the central bank will probably induce banks to behave in increasingly risky fashion because they believe that they will always be bailed out.

Lucas argued that this problem can be avoided by using models that explicitly describe decision making by each individual agent. On the other hand, Minsky would say that to offset the moral hazard problem just mentioned, the central bank might deploy policies such as imposing more aggressive counter-cyclical increases in required bank capital or simply shutting down banks with especially high leverage.

Lucas departed from a Keynesian world in thinking that each agent would have rational expectations and behave in model-consistent fashion. If so, then a policymaker could work out the probable implications of a policy change, as illustrated above in connection with the third article of new classical faith. But if the first through third articles do not apply, then the whole exercise collapses. Fundamentally, rational expectations models *assume* that the economy always obeys Say's Law and work out the consequences. If the assumption fails as in 2007–2009, then the models are useless.

Finally, rational expectations article of faith number five is that output responds very weakly to changes in prices. The implications can be illustrated in Figure 6.5, which plots capacity utilization measured as observed real output divided by its trend level versus inflation. The quarterly data for the United States run from 1948 through 2009, with inflation expressed

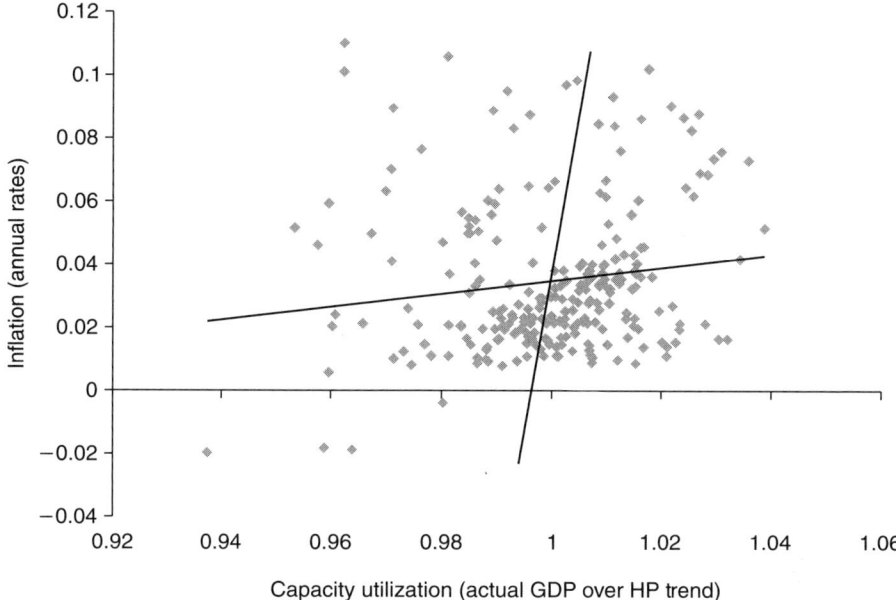

Figure 6.5 A price-inflation Phillips curve and a Lucas supply function for the United States, 1948–2008

at annual rates. There is a pretty dense cloud of points, inclining slightly from southwest to northeast in the diagram.

One interpretation is that higher capacity utilization stokes price inflation, but the relationship is neither strong nor statistically very tight. The nearly horizontal line has a slope of 0.205, which means that an increase in capacity utilization of one percentage point would increase the inflation rate by 0.2%: not very much. This sort of *Phillips curve* relationship (named after William Phillips, who first pointed it out in the late 1950s for wage inflation) shows up in the empirical Goodwin models discussed in Chapter 5. The slope of the curve in Figure 6.5 is consistent with econometric estimates for those models. From a Keynesian perspective the Phillips curve represents a natural way to look at the data. The implicit assumption is that inflation goes up when aggregate demand increases in response to tighter markets, supply bottlenecks, and so on.

The new classical alternative is to assume that faster inflation calls forth an increase in supply. In the diagram the line sloping steeply upward—like the one in the lower diagram of Figure 2.1—means that a jump in inflation of ten percentage points would be required to call forth an increase of one percentage point in output.

This version of the Phillips curve implies that capacity utilization stays close to a Say's Law full-employment level. The weak response of output to inflation comes from the *Lucas "surprise" supply function.* Output will depart from its Say's level only if inflation jumps unexpectedly from the rate consistent with full employment.

An emphasis on supply responses is built into a lot of new classical theorizing, which aims at applying the microeconomics underlying Figure 2.1 at the macro level. By way of contrast, Keynesians look toward determination of inflation from costs and market tightness, with output set by effective demand. The low inflation and plummeting output of the 2007–2009 period are consistent with this point of view.

Dynamics of Government Debt: Fiscal Hawks and Ricardian Equivalence

Robert Barro at Harvard (no Nobel as yet) starred in the next episode of the new classical chronicle. He kicked off an enormous debate about the *Ricardian equivalence* of tax and debt financing of government spending. (The label was not Barro's but came from James Buchanan, who argued that Ricardo toyed with the notion but ultimately rejected it.) Barro represented one side of a long-standing debate about the effects of fiscal policy; fiscal hawks tend toward the other extreme. Though they usually don't know it, politicians pronouncing about the national debt routinely repeat conclusions derived from two abstract and simplistic fiscal models.

The basic idea of Ricardian equivalence is that only government purchases and not the means by which they are financed—by taxation or borrowing—affect the real side of the economy. This message has resonated strongly with political conservatives since the 1980s—as Richard Cheney told Paul O'Neill, who was about to be fired as secretary of the treasury, in late 2002: "You know, Paul, Reagan proved deficits don't matter." Before we get to the details of the Barro-Cheney argument, I should say a bit more about the dynamics of fiscal debt (Evsey Domar first brought up the topic in the mid-1940s) and take a look at fiscal hawkery. It is simplest to think in terms of ratios of government debt and deficits to GDP.

The government's *primary deficit* is usually defined as its total spending net of interest minus tax revenues. Adding interest payments to the primary deficit gives the total deficit, or fiscal net borrowing as discussed in Chapter 5. Suppose for the moment that GDP is growing steadily at rate g, and that j is the real rate of interest. Following the discussion of a borrower's solvency condition in Chapter 5, one can show that

$$\text{Change in the Debt/GDP ratio} = \text{Primary deficit/GDP} + (j - g) \times \text{Debt/GDP}.$$

The interpretation is that both the current primary deficit and interest on debt contribute to an increase in the debt/GDP ratio, while it is reduced by growth of GDP in its denominator.

On the one hand, if the real interest rate exceeds the GDP growth rate so that the solvency condition is violated, then the debt ratio feeds positively into its own growth and the government is heading into a debt trap. On the other hand, if $j < g$, then the debt/GDP ratio will tend toward a stable steady state level (say, R). The steady state can be described by setting the change in the debt/GDP ratio in the equation above to zero. If we use algebraic notation to save space, R is given by

$$R = D/(g - j),$$

where D stands for the ratio of the primary deficit to GDP.

If we take 3% per year (productivity growth at 2% plus employment growth at 1%) as a rough-and-ready estimate of GDP growth, then a glance back at Figure 2.2 suggests that real interest rates *exceeded* the output growth rate from long periods in the late twentieth and early twenty-first centuries. The main exceptions were the stagflation years in the 1970s and the easy money period beginning in the 1990s. Nevertheless, to keep the discussion going, assume that the solvency condition is not violated. The accounting relationships just described support the ideas of fiscal hawks.

Fiscal Hawkery

If in fact there is a fiscal deficit, then in an economy closed to international transactions (definitely *not* the case for the United States), the government must be borrowing from the private sector. Fiscal deficit hawks pre- and post-Barro think in terms of a loanable funds model, illustrated in Figure 6.6. The basic idea is that private saving responds positively to the real interest rate along the lines of Hicks's extension of the *General Theory*'s model into IS/LM. Econometric support for this hypothesis is sparse, but it always crops up in the literature and policy discussion. Fiscal hawkery based on fear of rising interest rates was the main justification for the restrictive policy pursued by the Clinton administration. It can be rationalized in a model bearing a family resemblance to Joan Robinson's banana because it concentrates on one variable changing over logical time.

The equation for a stable debt ratio presented above can be written as

$$\dot{j} = g - \frac{D}{R},$$

which becomes the "Debt" schedule in Figure 6.6. Along this curve, the interest rate is zero when $R = D/g$, and rises asymptotically to the level g as the debt ratio R goes to infinity. The small arrows signal that the curve is a nullcline for R. If the current ratio lies below (to the left of) the nullcline, the ratio will be rising.

The schedule for "Saving" represents its alleged dependence on the in-

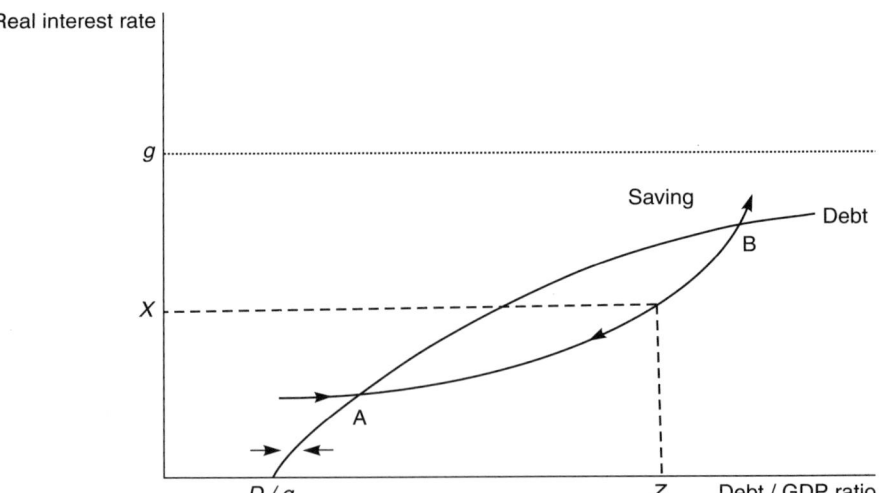

Figure 6.6 Debt dynamics in a fiscal hawk's model

terest rate. As drawn, it cuts the debt locus twice, with a stable equilibrium at A and an unstable one at B. The underlying assumption is that the government can always sell new bonds if the interest rate is high enough. For example, if the debt ratio takes the value at Z, then the interest rate will lie at point X. Saving will finance both investment and new loans to the government. If the output growth rate and the ratio of the primary deficit to GDP stay constant, the debt ratio will be falling, because we are still assuming that the growth rate exceeds the real interest rate.

Suppose that the economy is initially at A but that the government chooses "permanently" to increase its primary deficit. This policy shift will make D go up, moving the intercept of the "Debt" curve on the horizontal axis to the right and raising the steady state values of R and j. The debt ratio will have to increase to a new steady state level.

Basically, the increase in j will call forth more private saving to finance the government's bigger deficit and cut private consumption. In a Keynesian formulation as in Chapter 4, a higher interest rate would also reduce investment demand. If GDP growth dropped in response to reduced investment, the debt schedule would shift farther to the right, in a potentially destabilizing feedback.

If the government further pursues its profligate ways, the "Debt" schedule may drift far enough to the right not to intersect with the saving curve. The economy will fall into a true debt trap, with j and R both diverging toward infinity until someone on horseback canters in and straightens out the fiscal mess. The Clinton administration congratulated itself for avoiding disaster after Reagan. Note the reduction in government borrowing over the 1990s in Figure 5.8, which was violently reversed during the Cheney-Bush administration.

In the wake of the Obama stimulus package, it was not surprising to see fiscal hawks circling again. They have three prognoses, in increasing order of direness.

First, after the economy recovers, the primary deficit/GDP ratio could be cut by, say, 2%, mostly by higher income and capital gains taxes and/or a value-added tax.

Second, the government would do nothing, and a growing debt/GDP ratio would be financed, at the cost of steadily rising interest rates. The solvency condition would soon be violated, and the debt/GDP ratio would grow exponentially until there was some sort of crisis.

Finally, the crisis could occur in the not-too-distant future in the form of a run on the dollar, leading at first to massive devaluation and a spike in interest rates to be followed by fiscal correction as discussed just above. In other words, the bond market may shortly speak its mind.

Take your choice, or else hope that the fiscal hawks are wrong.

Ricardian Equivalance

Now quickly back to Barro. For practical purposes he assumes that the economy is described by a Ramsey model in steady state growth. Output and investment are thereby determined. If the government sets its consumption level as a matter of fiscal policy, private consumption must follow as a residual (because in a closed economy output equals the sum of investment, government consumption, and private consumption). Private income is the sum of output and current government interest payments. It is used to pay for consumption, taxes, and saving. With private income and consumption both constant, if the government cuts taxes, then private saving will have to go up. The steady state equilibrium is unaffected by how the government chooses to finance its spending—good news for Reagan, Cheney, and George W. Bush!

The non–steady state dynamics are all the more interesting because, as pointed out in Chapter 2, if Ramsey's state of Bliss is ruled out, then for the model to work, the pure discount or interest rate has to *exceed* the steady state growth rate. But we have just seen that the growth rate must exceed the interest rate to keep the debt/GDP ratio from blowing up to infinity. In other words, Barro is working with a highly unstable system—worse than Harrod's in that the debt ratio and (as discussed in connection with Figure 6.3) the Ramsey growth trajectory are *both* unstable.

In one presentation of his model Barro says that "individuals who optimize over an infinite horizon would not hold public debt that grows asymptotically at a rate as high as the interest rate. . . . This condition rules out Ponzi games or chain letters where the government issues debt and finances the payments of interest and principal by perpetual issues of new debt" (Barro, 1989, 203–204).

One interpretation is that the omnipotent invisible hand will force the government to keep its finances from blowing up by eventually running a primary surplus to pay the interest required to hold the debt/GDP ratio stable. If the government obeys this rule while the economy is on an optimal trajectory away from steady state, it must choose between "tax now" and "tax later." If it cuts taxes now, then to avoid Ponzi finance over infinite time, it will have to raise taxes at some point in the future. A private sector with perfect foresight will foresee this event and start saving now to pay the future higher taxes. So Ricardian equivalence is also supposed to happen away from steady states.

It is not clear how this sort of behavior can be "tested" in a finite span of time, but on the whole, econometric results seem to show that the private sector does not start saving more after tax reductions. After the financial crash, when their wealth was clobbered, in 2008 U.S. households did step up their saving at the same time that a fiscal stimulus was on the horizon. Keynes would have said that they did so from fear of the unknown implications of living out their lifetimes with greatly reduced wealth. Barro's potential fiscal Ponzi game was not foremost in their minds.

Supply-Side Nostrums

Keynes and his followers almost always trace business cycles to fluctuations in aggregate demand, emphasizing interconnections between phases within one cycle and across cycles; the severity and lengths of cycles; and co-movements of economic indicators and activities.

New classical economics is the foundation of more recent *real business cycle* or *RBC* models, emphasizing random as opposed to systematic behavior, ahistorical analysis in place of history-based discussion, and statistically independent sequencing of phases and cycles instead of their interconnections. Causes of output fluctuations come from the supply side.

Real Business Cycles and Dynamic Stochastic General Equilibrium

As we have seen, this idea of the real business cycle is not new. On the Left, the adverse cyclical effects of rising capital per worker—an increasing organic composition of capital—have long figured in Marxist discourse. On the Right, Wicksell, Hayek, and most Austrian economists saw recessions as retribution for excess investment and financial bubbles resulting from banks holding the market interest rate below its natural level. As Robert Heilbroner tells the story, a similar view underlay Schumpeter's contemporary description to credulous Harvard undergraduates of the Great Depression as an unavoidable capitalist "cold douche" (not that they knew what the French think a *douche* is, in any case). In a clear extension of the entrepreneur-driven technical change in his *Theory of Economic Development,* Schumpeter grounded his own massive work on cycles on waves of innovation, which could underlie output fluctuations ranging from periods of a few years to grand fifty-year *Kondratiev cycles.*

Minus the marvelous political economy of his *Capitalism, Socialism, and Democracy,* Schumpeter's temporally fluctuating technical progress has been picked up by the recent RBC school as the key factor underlying output fluctuations. The formal models assume that the level of output is determined by a neoclassical production function with shifts in total factor productivity as discussed in Chapter 5.

The basic RBC trick (which we will encounter again in Chapter 7 in the discussion of mainstream ideas about asset returns and volatility) is to assume that productivity "this period" depends strongly on its level "last period" plus a random shock. This random effect transforms the standard Ramsey model into a problem of dynamic optimization subject to a known probability distribution for the shocks. Such models are impossible to solve analytically in the general case, but with enough assumptions thrown in to guarantee a tractable solution, a Ramsey machine cranks out standard RBC results.

The first is that if there is a one-period lag between investment and completed capital formation, then the shock can generate a cyclical relationship with current output depending on its levels in the previous two periods. Over time this sort of dynamics usually generates a hump-shaped trajectory for the output: it goes up, and then it goes down.

Most of the cyclical action comes from the productivity growth forcing function. Unfortunately for the cause, big fluctuations in productivity are needed to get visible cycles in output. Failed attempts to explain the Great Depression in this fashion are a continuing RBC embarrassment.

What about real wages and employment? As in the full-employment Ramsey and Kaldor models at steady state, higher productivity automatically raises output per worker and the real wage. Although the results are built in by their assumptions, the ability of RBC models to generate procyclical productivity and real wage movements is usually taken as a major point in their favor.

Less enthusiastically received has been their presumption that employment fluctuations over the cycle are due to microeconomic substitution by households between "labor" (that is, working for money to buy goods) and "leisure" (not working) now and in the future, in response to wage and interest (= profit) rate changes. In detail, all the households making up the population are supposed to maximize a universally shared utility function based on consumption and leisure. Labor supply ends up depending on the current real wage and the interest rate expected next period. A high current rate wage or a high future interest rate makes working hard now to put the money in the bank more attractive than working hard next period.

Of course, RBC models have to replicate the stylized fact that employment correlates positively with output in the United States over the cycle. As we have seen in Chapter 5, the real wage and labor share also rise during a cyclical upswing. To fit the data, the models have to build in the assumption that labor supply responds strongly to wage and interest rate changes. Unfortunately for the theory, the econometric evidence disagrees.

There is also an implicit conflict between RBC models and the Lucas supply function. The latter resembles the steep supply curve in the lower diagram in Figure 2.1, while RBC models have a labor supply function with a shallow slope like the one in the upper diagram. In the neoclassical world the two positions can be reconciled if the labor demand curve is unresponsive to changes in the real wage induced by price increases. But that runs counter to the general new classical perception that market behavior tends to be price-responsive. I will leave it to the new classicals to sort the contradictions out.

A last criticism usually voiced by new Keynesians is that RBC models ignore monetary disturbances as a major determinant of aggregate demand. In making this assertion, RBC people are true to their mentors Friedman and Lucas in treating output as being determined from the supply side. But as discussed in connection with Table 2.2, they go one step further in assuming *reverse causality* in the equation of exchange: transactions demands scaled by velocity drive the *inside* (or commercial bank–generated component of) the money supply in RBC models, as credits and deposits rise to meet a higher volume of trade. This tendency toward heterodoxy goes only so far, however. RBC modelers ultimately need a nominal anchor to fix the price level. They are much happier to find it in a predetermined level of *outside* money or government debt held by the central bank than in a social process determining the money wage.

Over the years RBC models have evolved into *dynamic stochastic general equilibrium* or *DSGE* specifications. They basically add lagged responses of real variables and prices to behavioral equations from a Ramsey model to try to track the economy better. Whether the Ramsey optimizing agent living in the middle of the web of equations is content with its lot is never made clear. The modelers claim that their machines work better because they are partly based on optimizing foundations. Needless to say, they all failed to forecast the events of 2007–2009. The poor models had no way to generate such catastrophes.

Finally, the basic rational expectations/RBC model has been called into question because it appears to predict too high a value for a "riskless" interest rate, does not allow a rate of return to equity consistent with the data, and underpredicts the volatility of equity returns. We'll come back to these anomalies or "puzzles" in Chapter 7.

All in all, the high-tech new classical school attempted to reshape macroeconomics to make it as theoretically pure as it could possibly be. Josiah Willard Gibbs once remarked that if practical application is the goal of research, then a pure mathematician can proceed as she pleases, but an applied mathematician must be at least partially sane. The observation applies to pure and applied macroeconomists as well.

Supply-Side Economics

Supply-side economics appeals to the same crowd as Ricardian equivalence but is distinctly lower tech. It got its start at the University of Chicago in the form of a lifelong effort by Arnold Harberger there and later at UCLA to apply the little triangles of Figure 2.1 to concrete policy issues. Perhaps something was learned, but the effort was always bedeviled by the result that removing a distortion gave rise to a nugatory welfare gain. Jim Tobin once quipped, "It takes a heap of Harberger triangles to fill an Okun gap."

The response among a small group of advocates (Arthur Laffer, Jude Wanniski, and others) was to conjure into existence a large benefit from tax-cutting via the *Laffer curve* sketched in Figure 6.7.

The general idea is that a zero tax rate will generate no revenue. There would also be zero revenue at a 100% tax rate because nobody would pay it. The revenue curve between the two extremes is hypothetical but is meant to underline the observation that at very high tax rates there will be a lot of evasion. If the rate is on the right (or "wrong") side of the curve, a reduction will bring in more money.

There is no evidence to support the notion that the economy is on the bad side of the curve, but supply-siders found it easy to convince themselves and their political masters that the U.S. and UK economies (most

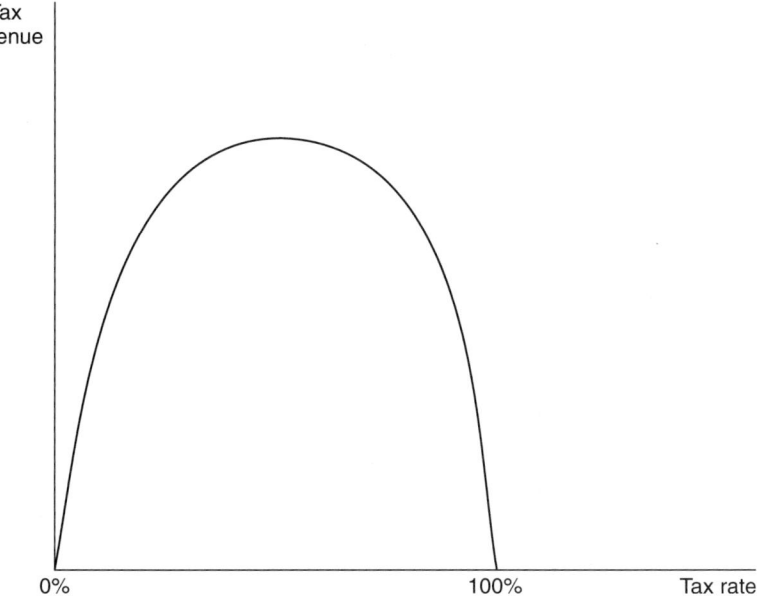

Figure 6.7 A Laffer curve

notably) were there. Hence cutting taxes would get rid of the fiscal deficit and by somehow greatly expanding Harberger triangles give a big boost to economic growth.

On fiscalist Keynesian grounds, tax-cutting should of course boost aggregate demand. But the revenue and efficiency gains claimed by the supply-siders were extreme. Nevertheless the doctrine lives on, at least among Republican politicians.

Macroeconomics after 1980

After around 1980 mainstream macroeconomics became pretty boring. Although they had been willing to fight tooth and nail with Joan Robinson and allies in the 1960s over whether J. B. Clark "parables" about production functions were valid, a decade or so later the lions of the neoclassical synthesis offered much less resistance to the new classical school.

There were several reasons, with the shift in the political climate to the right certainly one of them. The golden age had created a new class of financial stakeholders with vested interests in low inflation rates and continuing capital gains on the stock market, supported by high corporate profits and (beginning in the 1990s) low interest rates justified by stable prices. This new political economy stimulated the spread of Friedman's and Lucas's ideas far beyond the classrooms and professional journals to influential citizens and the media.

The new classicals threw around a lot of fairly recently invented applied mathematics; certainly not enough to frighten (for example) Paul Samuelson, but it still burnished their reputation. Perhaps their chief attraction was that they were unabashed Walrasians. By that time the American profession was so imbued with general equilibrium that its members could not raise the energy to combat the reenactment of Say's Law embellished with random shocks.

There had also been a changing of the guard. People like Samuelson, Solow, and Tobin came of age in the Great Depression, served in the war effort, and went into economics with a strong sense of social concern that found its voice in Keynesianism. By the 1970s baby boomer Ph.D.s coming into the profession had no such consciousness and had been immersed in mathematical models and tricks by their teachers. They were happy to settle down to apply (for the most part) Caltech or MIT sophomore and junior mathematics to well-defined toy problems in micro and macro. There was a great emphasis on "rigor," and scant attention paid to history and institutions.

So in macro there came a series of fads. You can almost see them in the order of chapters in the standard graduate textbook, *Advanced Macroeconomics* by David Romer. They began with nailing down the details of Ramsey models and a variant called *overlapping generations,* in which the age structure of the population (the most tedious form of class conflict) is considered.

New classical and real business cycle theories emerged, as did a "new" theory of *endogenous growth* which sought to provide rational actor foundations for technological progress. Academic reputations were made, but interest in the topic had fizzled by the 1990s. *New Keynesian* macro was in vogue for a while as a successor to the neoclassical synthesis, with its nominal rigidities. The approach was basically micro, built up around the fantasy framework of a Ramsey model or the flimsy scaffolding of AS/AD. The goal was to invent all kinds of justifications involving choices by rational actors for sticky price, wage, and output responses, under various forms of knowledge asymmetry. For the most part these obstacles are supposed to disappear in the long run so that the economy can get back to the NAIRU. People keep plugging away, but the key collection of papers appeared in 1993.

There was good empirical work on a range of topics—the Great Depression, open economy macro, labor market imperfections, and so on—but certainly no new vision of macroeconomics appeared. That is one reason why the profession was so unprepared for the events of 2007–2009. Before then, within the American wing a self-proclaimed division between *saltwater* (new Keynesian) and *freshwater* (new classical) economists had emerged. (The distinction was coined by Stanford's Robert Hall, an economist of distinctly freshwater inclination presumably illegally resident on the Left Coast.) The latter school took the Ramsey model as a self-evident truth; the former wanted wiggle room around the Figure 6.4 saddlepath. Both missed the possibility of crisis completely.

I taught in the economics department at MIT for around twenty years before moving to the New School. Once at some reception a vice provost asked me where I was working. When I told him, he said, "Ah, all those second-rate applied mathematicians." The vice provost wasn't quite being fair to his local economists, who even by the standards of the MIT faculty were and are pretty bright people. But he had a point. After the hue and cry over monetarism and new classical economics subsided, mainstream macroeconomics to a large extent did become second-rate applied mathematics aimed at problems with minimal social content. A pity.

Notes

Taylor (2004) gives the gory details of topics covered in this chapter and references to debates about consumption and investment demand functions and other parts of the neoclassical synthesis.

Hicks (1937) is the original statement of IS/LM. Hansen (1938) propounded secular stagnation. For Richard Kahn's views on Wynne Godley, see Kahn and Posner (1974). Duesenberry (1949) and Modigliani and Brumberg (1954) summarize their views on the consumption function. Tobin (1969) presents his q, and Minsky (1975) describes his investment theory. Samuelson (1964) provides the quotation in the text and other observations.

Friedman (1968) and Phelps (1969) lay out their accelerationist macro model. Kaldor (1982) fulminates vigorously against monetarism, and John Taylor (1993) pronounces his interest rate rule.

Robert Lucas (1972) and (1976) are representative statements of his take on the world. Domar (1944) first set out proper accounting for debt dynamics. For Dick Cheney's views on fiscal policy, see http://www.ontheissues.org/Dick_Cheney.htm. Barro (1974) is the initial statement of Ricardian equivalence; Buchanan (1976) attached the label. Real business cycle models got going with Kydland and Prescott (1982), and the technical literature has grown exponentially ever since. Gibbs's observation about mathematicians is paraphrased from Kline (2009, 341–342).

Harberger (1962) presents the first version of his triangles. The Laffer curve appeared in the late 1970s; there is a reminiscence in Laffer (2004). David Romer's (2001) *Advanced Macroeconomics* is the standard mainstream text.

Robert Gordon (1989) sketches the history of the distinction between Robert Hall's freshwater and saltwater economists.

— 7 —

Finance

This chapter is about how *finance theory* and *financial regulation* interact with macroeconomics. The theory analyzes financial decision making from a microeconomic point of view, ignoring all the fallacies of composition that Keynes emphasized. As the events of 2007–2009 demonstrated, escalating spillovers between financial markets and the macroeconomy can destroy the most finely honed micro calculations. Historically, regulation had never dealt with such possibilities. How well it can do so in the future remains to be seen.

Superficially the collapse of finance theory is surprising because its foundations look like pure common sense. One reason why it failed is shoddy construction; it is easy to raise serious objections to all the major models. Another problem is that common sense was left behind when theorists chose to concentrate on the instrumental rationality of a set of "agents" operating in highly structured artificial environments. The theory's inflexibility stood out in 2007–2009, when under novel conditions neither the agents embedded in financial computer programs nor most humans running the computers could think effectively in real time.

There are many examples in practice of how theorists went to extremes. The truism that both goods and securities sell for more or less the same prices within a single economy became a *no arbitrage* postulate which states that any price discrepancies in the past have already been traded away and new discrepancies will rapidly disappear. Assuming that all opportunities for arbitrage are swiftly removed by the financial markets comes close to saying that they generate a Pareto optimal allocation of resources as discussed in Chapter 2. The postulate is contrary to the facts, even in financial markets. *Bid-ask spreads* for securities can be wide, especially after mid-2007. Historically, closed-end mutual funds have traded at values differing from the worth of the shares they hold. Although they were issued by the same consolidated corporation, for many years Shell and Royal Dutch shares traded at different prices on the London and Amsterdam exchanges. Many other examples could be provided.

In combination with allegedly vanishing opportunities for arbitrage and consequent market optimality, the commonplace observation that very few people (at times not even Keynes) consistently earn more than the average returns available in financial markets became the *efficient market hypothesis* (or *EMH*). It was perhaps first proposed by a French mathematician, Louis Bachelier, around 1900 and again by the Chicago economist Eugene Fama in 1965. It implies that no one can ever beat the market. We all know that a few people do beat it, even with some regularity.

The fact that the price of an asset being purchased often doesn't depend on how the buyer raises the requisite finance became an all-encompassing *Modigliani-Miller theorem*. It draws on the logic of rational expectations to serve as a sort of Say's Law for financial markets, saying that a firm's real performance is not affected by its financial structure (notwithstanding Minsky's hedge/speculative/Ponzi classification described in Chapter 5 and below). In other words, leverage is irrelevant. At best, Modigliani-Miller works when a firm's profit flows can be reliably foreseen—certainly not always the case.

Similar assumptions apply to the *risks* (in this chapter the term means complete, objective probability distributions applied to a well-defined set of outcomes) built into models used to describe how people are supposed to behave in financial markets as well as to calculate prices of securities and associated derivatives. For the most part, fluctuations in asset prices are treated as the unique source of risk, with the likelihood of default entering into some discussions. If the metric for the risk associated with an asset price is the *standard deviation* or *sigma* (defined loosely below) of its fluctuations, then we get to a question posed by Harry Markowitz in 1952: How to choose a portfolio of assets that will maximize the expected utility from holding wealth subject to a known, well-behaved tradeoff between risk and return. *Expected value* here is calculated on the basis of probability distributions on asset price fluctuations. We are light-years away from Maynard Keynes's views about the financial world.

In extensions of Markowitz's analysis, computations of expected values and standard deviations have been combined with rational expectations to come up with recipes for pricing securities and derivatives. All of them can easily break down in practice.

In one major example, ancient wisdom about diversifying assets—not putting all of one's eggs in one basket or entrusting all of one's wealth to Bernie Madoff—became a *capital asset pricing model,* or *CAPM,* which for a variety of reasons fails to give good predictions for prices of shares. The model seems to suggest that one should diversify away from assets with correlated returns to avoid risk; but more risk has to be taken on if one seeks higher returns. The CAPM does not provide a mechanism apart from an arbitrarily specified utility function for choosing between these alternatives. For some preselected set of securities, all it does in practice (under an unrealistically strong set of assumptions) is provide a recipe for constructing a portfolio to minimize risk while offering a given return, or to maximize return subject to a given level of risk. Asset pricing, as will be seen below, comes in as an afterthought.

Faulty predictions also result from the famous *Black-Scholes-Merton* (or *BSM*) *formula* for pricing options, or contracts for forward sales and purchases of securities such as shares. "Common sense" here is the line of thought followed by Keynes in his description in the *Tract on Monetary Reform* of how arbitrage based on the differential between home and foreign spot exchange rates sets forward rates (details in Chapter 8). A forward exchange rate is not necessarily a good predictor of the value that the spot rate will take in the future. The standard formula for calculating option prices assumes that arbitrage will make the growth rate of the underlying asset price equal to the *risk-free* real interest rate, another assumption that does not fit the facts. As described in Chapter 4, the extensions of BSM analysis used to price CDOs and CDSs imploded when the price of residential housing, the underlying asset, departed from its long-term trend, as illustrated in Figures 1.2 and 1.3.

Finally, everybody knows that when a close marriage is ended by the death of one spouse, then the survivor runs a pretty high risk of dying within a short period of time. Statistical techniques have been devised to help insurance companies asses the relevant odds about death, which they can use in setting costs for policies and writing annuities. For use in pricing CDOs and CDSs the techniques were extended to calculate probabilities of default for sets of mortgage holders with many more members than two. These calculations fell apart beginning in the late 2000s as housing prices broke downward and mortgage default rates shot up.

The failures of finance theory in light of 2007–2009 are obvious to all, but that does not mean it will go away. *Behavioral finance,* a mainstream reversion toward Keynes, in part arose from the contradictions built into the standard EMH. The fact that very few people beat the market does not guarantee that all possibilities for arbitrage vanish and that there is a Pareto optimal allocation of financial resources. It is discussed briefly as a possible challenger to the finance theory built up from Markowitz's foundations laid long ago.

One area of great concern is a by-product of the mainstream's obsession with using a Ramsey model adorned with risk as the foundation for all macroeconomics. Various financial anomalies or "puzzles" appear when the model is confronted with data; a great deal of behavioral analysis has been devoted to explaining them away. Slightly further afield, new Keynesians have begun trying to bring ideas from the *General Theory* into an analytical framework based on methodological individualism exclusively (no significant socioeconomic interactions allowed). Examples of both approaches are provided.

After all this theory, the discussion turns to a review of major changes in the financial system during the period following World War II. Several developments have already been mentioned in previous chapters, and others will crop up in connection with financial theories, but a quick summary in one place makes sense as an input into the analysis of financial regulation. The focal point is Hyman Minsky's idea of *endogenous finance.*

Regulation has not historically been a part of macroeconomics. The events of 2007–2009, however, show that it has to become so. Economists are only now in the process of thinking through the issues. One key issue is how to deal with systemically important financial firms so that they don't build up excessive leverage and/or asset-liability mismatches. Questions immediately arise about how to set up a regulatory cordon around such firms (if the regulating government decides against breaking them up), what tools can be used in practice to guide their actions, how to respond if regulation fails, and which regulatory agency or agencies should be in charge.

As of early 2010 there was also a serious question as to whether an effective regulatory regime could be constructed in the United States. It is addressed briefly.

Efficient Market Hypothesis and Modigliani-Miller

To simplify, assume that returns and risks on holding an asset are calculated on the basis of its price. From Chapter 1 we have the idea that the return to holding a unit of an asset such as housing is the ratio of its rent to its value. For a share of stock the rule is

$$\text{Return} = (\text{Capital gain} + \text{dividend}) / \text{Price},$$

or for later reference

$$\text{Price} = (\text{Capital gain} + \text{dividend}) / \text{Return}.$$

Just to be clear on dimensions, a return is a rate per unit of time (such as 3% per year), and a capital gain or dividend is a value flow per unit of time which when divided by a price becomes equivalent to a rate.

In the discussion to follow, emphasis will be placed on the capital gain, and dividends will mostly be ignored. The capital gain is measured by the change in the share's price.

Efficient Markets

The basics of the EMH have already been sketched in Chapter 1. Here are two additional observations.

First, a weak form of the EMH states that it is impossible to construct trading rules based on observed prices which can generate better returns than market averages. A stronger form says that even if a trader uses all publicly available information, she still cannot beat the averages. Because price fluctuations are close to being random, most traders are operating on the basis of statistical noise about prices and cannot reap exceptional returns.

Now go back to Chapter 12 of the *General Theory*. On the one hand, Keynes's principal insight is that financial investment is a particular social process centering on each player's perceptions of what the others are doing (the beauty contest). On the other hand, in a long run in which some of us may not yet be dead, investors in enterprise may overcome speculation and generate socially useful investment returns.

For present purposes the key point about successful investing is that financial decisions take place in a social environment. All the EMH can say in that regard is that some investors may get access to insider information and profit thereby. The real world doesn't work so simply. Winning investors are more than just insiders. From Buffet and Soros on down to the local potentate in the little town in Maine where I live, successful investors suck in knowledge about their economic milieu and make money by using it. They certainly don't just look at correlations across time and markets of asset prices, but rather delve beneath the surface to understand causal relationships. Recall from Chapter 4 how Soros dissected the conglomerate and REIT booms.

The second point is that to make big money you have to make big bets. Recommendations from finance theory resemble those of Confucius and Aristotle: one should strive for some kind of economic golden mean balancing risk and return. Common sense comes in once again but fails to explain why 1 or 2% of the U.S. population have incomes exceeding $1 million per year (or financial and human capital wealth of more than $10 to $20 million). Inheritance, class connections more generally, and exceptional abilities in one direction or another can explain why many people are rich. But others got there by wagering on a big return from speculation or enterprise and happening to win.

Modigliani-Miller

Franco Modigliani's fingerprints are all over mainstream macroeconomics. One more specimen is the "theorem," or, better, the statement of principle about how corporate finance operates, which he announced together with Merton Miller in 1958. A decade or so *avant la lettre* Modigliani-Miller was an application of rational expectations to business accounting.

As usual in finance theory the argument begins with common sense. Suppose that you want to buy a new car costing $25,000 after the haggling over its sticker price, rebates, and all the rest has been resolved. Traditionally you would then have to make a down payment of a few thousand dollars (such obligations became much less pressing with financial deregulation after the 1980s but may still apply in some cases). On the one hand, if you could not come up with the cash, you would not be able to buy the car, so its price would effectively be infinite. On the other hand, if you were to lay 250 big bills on the dealer's desk, the price might well come down a bit. But between these extremes it would not change in response to the size of your down payment or equity in the car. The difference between $25,000 and the down payment would be made up by debt. With a down payment of $2,500, your leverage ratio would be $25,000 / $2,500 = 10, pretty high but not unusual for this kind of transaction. (In practice, of course, it would be a lot higher, maybe infinite, because the resale value of the car would plummet by a few thousand the moment those keys crossed into your hand.)

Modigliani and Miller carried this logic over to corporate finance. In so doing they created problems involving both accounting and the nature of foresight. They are discussed below, after a sketch of the basic argument.

Suppose that a firm has an *expected* profit flow P depending on its costs and revenues over some period in the immediate future. According to the rule discussed above, the firm's value V should be given by

$$V = \frac{P}{r}.$$

The rate of return r is supposed to be "appropriate" to the firm's "risk class" (loosely defined as a group of firms with highly correlated returns). As with buying the car, the firm's balance sheet will be

$$V = E + B,$$

with E as the market value of its equity and B (for "bonds") as debt. Both E and B are data points that can be observed on a computer screen.

Modigliani and Miller run through arbitrage arguments involving a pair of firms with the same expected profits P to show that traders will exchange stocks and bonds until the firms have the same value V regardless of their debt/equity ratio $\frac{B}{E}$ or leverage $\frac{V}{E}$. Moreover, let r_B be the real interest rate on bonds and r_E the return on equity (made up of dividends, capital gains, and share buybacks). Returns are paid out of profit flows according to the rule

$$P = r_B B + r_E E$$

so that all profits go into generating returns.

Together with the balance sheet, this equation implies that

$$r_E = r + (r - r_B)\left(B/E\right).$$

The firm's "required" return to equity r_E increases linearly with its debt/equity ratio B/E. Yet its total equity service obligation $r_E E$ goes down as its liabilities shift from equity toward debt. The overall profit flow P will be unaffected. Subject to caveats discussed below about how the numbers can be estimated, under "normal" circumstances the formula does not fit observed historical data badly.

Indeed, in untroubled times Modigliani-Miller is a pretty good first-order approximation to financial behavior. But it has at least two major problems. The first is that while the firm's value V can be calculated from the values of equity and debt on its balance sheet as stated above, it *cannot* be inferred from the relationship

$$V = \frac{P}{r}.$$

Applied historically to a firm's recorded V and P, all this formula can do is produce a number for its observed rate of return $r = \frac{P}{V}$.

The reason is that current and near future profit flows P will be affected by changes in quantities and prices which nobody can know in advance. We come back to Keynes's uncertainties regarding the future laid out in Chapter 4. One might try to estimate the level of P that will be observed over the current period from historical data (assuming that the future will be like the past, which we know from 2007–2009 is not always the case) or make a guess based on information gleaned from the market's social processes. But there is no way that future cash flows can be known with certainty. Modigliani and Miller did not even address the issue. In that way they invented rational expectations while Robert Lucas was still an undergraduate history major at the University of Chicago.

The second problem is that if one establishes a firm's value as the sum of its observable assets (value of tangible capital, cash on hand, and so on), then that number will always differ from the sum of its debt and market value of equity. The difference between such a measure of assets and "liabilities" including equity is the firm's net worth. Business net worth is an observable variable at both the micro and macro levels. (The latter appears regularly in the United States. FOF accounts and can be observed in Figure 5.17.) Modigliani and Miller's balance sheet relationship $V = E + B$ violates this sort of accounting. It becomes a sort of macroeconomic Say's Law because it does not allow for fluctuations in net worth which are crucial for the functioning of structuralist macro models—Hyman Minsky's, for example.

Similarly, a firm's profit flows do not all go into interest and dividends. It will typically have retained earnings. If the return to equity is computed as observed capital gains plus dividends and share buybacks, it will almost never be equal to profits minus interest payments and taxes. Again the Modigliani-Miller accounting does not fit the data.

Despite these drawbacks the "theorem" is a strong statement of the nineteenth-century and new classical belief that finance is a veil: a firm's performance just depends on expected profits P and will not be affected by the composition of its balance sheet. In particular, the magnitudes of its leverage and debt/equity ratios are irrelevant. After the leveraging and deleveraging adventures of the late twentieth and early twenty-first centuries, we have relearned that this assertion is not true. But it was the conventional financial wisdom for around fifty years.

Portfolio Choice and Security Pricing

The mathematics used in standard finance theory to describe how wealth holders arrange their portfolios and value securities and derivatives is not advanced; the MIT and Caltech undergraduates mentioned previously would be more than proficient after their junior year. But the manipulations are unfamiliar to most people, so only a sketch will be provided here. This section takes up two topics: how risk is quantified in standard finance models, and how agents (not real people as observed by Keynes) are supposed to behave when making risky choices.

Risk and Fat Tails

As noted above, for "small" changes of an asset's price, its return is usually expressed as the price's growth rate or capital gain. It is taken for granted that the only risk involved in holding the asset is due to fluctuations or volatility in its price. A risk-free asset with a constant interest rate is also supposed to exist. A Treasury bond is the standard example, on the questionable assumption that the central bank will not unexpectedly intervene with open market operations to shift its interest rate.

The price fluctuations of the risky asset are supposed to be random (basically meaning that they are impossible to predict) but subject to a known probability distribution which gives the odds on specific price movements.

An immediate question is: What is the shape of the distribution of asset returns?

The answer for most finance theory is that the distribution is *normal* or *Gaussian*, with the familiar bell curve mentioned in Chapter 4. It was utilized by several mathematicians in the eighteenth century, but the name of Carl Friedrich Gauss—perhaps the greatest mathematician ever—became attached to it for his work on celestial mechanics and geodesy around 1800.

In a bit more detail, any set of risks can be described by a *probability density function* (or *pdf*), which is a smoothed version of the standard *histogram*. A range of possible values for the growth rate of an asset price appears on the horizontal axis of the relevant diagram; the rate can be either positive or negative. As we read up the scale on the vertical axis, the height of the pdf curve above a point on the horizontal gives the probability that price growth rates within a small range of values around that point will occur. The total area under the pdf is equal to 1.0, which is the sum of the probabilities for all possible levels of asset price growth. Figure 7.1 provides an illustration.

The bell-shaped Gaussian distribution in the diagram in principle permits levels of asset price growth to range between minus infinity and plus infinity. In practice it limits the levels likely to be observed to a far more re-

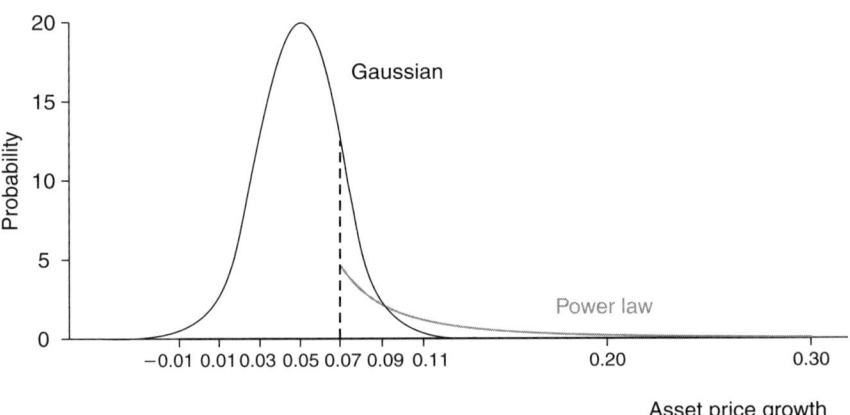

Figure 7.1 Gaussian and Pareto (power law) distributions for asset price growth rates, with thin and fat tails respectively.

stricted range. The distribution is fully described by two parameters: its *mean*, central, or expected value μ, and either its *standard deviation* σ or *variance* σ^2 (the square of σ). The *coefficient of variation* σ/μ is another commonly quoted metric for the "spread" of the distribution. In the diagram $\mu = 0.05$, so that the expected return to holding the asset is 5% over the relevant period of time. The standard deviation is $\sigma = 0.02$, so the coefficient of variation is 40%.

According to the Gaussian distribution there is a 20% chance that the return will lie within a small interval on the horizontal axis centered on 0.05. Around 68% of the possible returns are concentrated in the "one sigma" range of 0.03 to 0.07. The "three sigma" range of −0.01 to 0.11 includes 99.7% of all possible price growth rates.

This last observation implies that the normal distribution has *thin tails* in the sense that big positive or negative asset returns are extremely unlikely. In the early 1960s Benoit Mandelbrot, another highly creative mathematician, gathered evidence showing that empirical asset returns based on cotton and other commodity prices have a *Pareto* or *power law* distribution with *fat tails*. The underlying rule is as follows: the ratio of the probability of a 20% return to the probability of a 10% return is the same as the ratio of probabilities for 10% and 5% returns. Such self-similarity across scales of observation generates power laws and *fractal* phenomena more generally. Power laws describe an enormous range of empirical regularities—the inverse square law of Newtonian gravitation, the Gutenberg-Richter scale for the magnitude of earthquakes, Zipf's Law about the sizes of cities, Mandelbrot's fractals, and on and on.

Power law distributions are usually assumed to control probabilities above a certain level of the variable in question. Figure 7.1 shows a power law that takes over from the normal distribution at a price growth rate of 0.07 or the one sigma point. The ruling parameter for the power law distribution is called a *Pareto alpha*. The distribution demonstrates greater inequality or a fatter tail for a *lower* value of alpha. (A technical note about the diagram is that it shows a *discontinuity:* the height of the pdf jumps down along the dashed line when the pdf switches from Gaussian to power law at the one sigma point. Such a jump is hard to avoid when one switches between pdfs. The key point is that to the right of the switch point the areas under the two distributions are equal, meaning that the probability that asset price growth will exceed 0.07 is the same for both. The power law distribution's tail is fat precisely because its pdf lies well above that of the Gaussian for large values of asset price growth.)

As discussed by Nassim Nicholas Taleb and many others, alpha's estimated values across many phenomena range between 1.0 and 2.0; for the magnitude of earthquakes it may be around 2.8. For purposes of illustration the alpha for the pdf in Figure 7.1 is set to 2.0, and generates a moderately fat tail. For example, the probability of an asset price growth rate in the vicinity of 0.11 (three sigma) according to the power law distribution is about 1.17%. The Gaussian probability is 0.13%.

Estimating power law parameters is difficult because many data points are needed to get any degree of precision. For asset prices there are conflicting estimates, but most seem to be in the range of 3.0 and upwards, still low enough to generate significantly fatter tails than the Gaussian distribution. Of course, a tail can be fat in either direction. The "right-tailed" distribution in Figure 7.1 could just as easily run to the left for small positive and negative growth rates of asset returns.

As will be seen, standard finance theory models are built around Gaussian distributions on returns. They have been heavily criticized on those grounds. The critics, however, still seem to want to use quantitative (sometimes highly quantitative) calculations based on observed data on price variation over time to do financial analysis. That position falls well short of a halfway house between the standard theory and Keynes.

Portfolio Choice

The standard model about how agents are supposed to select assets to make up their portfolios, originally due to Markowitz, concentrates on risk and return. The shades of Say and Modigliani-Miller hover in the background. Each agent is insignificant, so that her decision about which assets to hold cannot influence returns. Each return is determined by an asset price growth rate or a firm's profit flow. Decisions about portfolio choice are supposed to depend only on the mean and variance of each return. When you work through the mathematics, this assumption turns out to be valid under just two sets of circumstances.

The first is that the probabilities of each return are fully described by its mean μ and standard deviation σ. The Gaussian distribution is the only one that satisfies this requirement. We've just seen how it does not fit the data.

Alternatively the agent's expected utility $U(W)$ from holding wealth W must be a quadratic function $U(W) = AW^2 + W$. From a microeconomic point of view this function has undesirable properties. Maybe the most important is that if A is negative, then at some level of W, utility from more wealth satiates as at Ramsey's Bliss. Neoclassical economists don't like this possibility, and there are other technical problems as well.

The conclusion is that the mean/variance portfolio choice model is stuck between an empirical rock and a theoretical hard place. Nevertheless it continues to be widely applied. The gist is illustrated in Figure 7.2.

A set of risky assets, each one labeled with a subscript i running up from the number 1, is assumed to be on hand. Asset i has a return μ_i and risk σ_i as measured by the standard deviation of its return. Putting together appropriate mixtures of the assets can generate an *efficient portfolio* characterized by combinations of an overall return μ and risk σ. It is illustrated in the diagram. At a low level of the overall return it is possible to construct

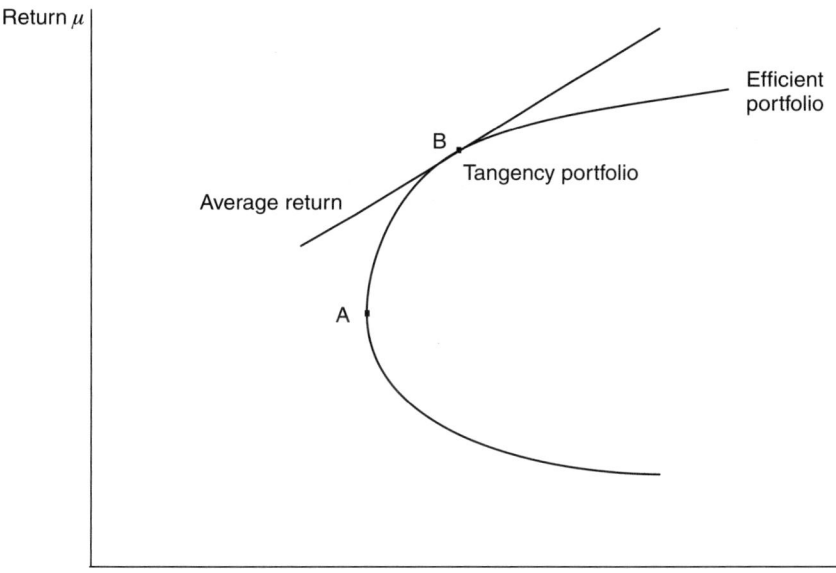

Figure 7.2 Efficient and tangency portfolios

portfolios which would have both a higher μ and a lower σ until *minimum risk* is reached at point A. Above that point an agent would have to accept more risk to get a higher return.

As mentioned above, also suppose that a risk-free asset with return R is available. The agent can combine that asset with the efficient risky portfolio to get an overall allocation of wealth, say, a fraction f of total wealth in the risk-free asset and $1 - f$ in the efficient portfolio. Presumably a young person far from retirement will choose a low value of f and a risk-averse retiree will pick a high one. Overall, the agent seeks a weighted average return $fR + (1 - f)\mu$ which is as high as possible.

Eyeballing the diagram suggests that the return is as high as it can be at the *tangency portfolio* point B. With a lower value of f, the line for the "Average return" will be less steep, so the younger agent will choose a tangency point having higher values of return and risk than her older counterpart (unless the latter has burned through her pension and so is forced to run risks to try to bring in money to keep going). Alternatively point B can be interpreted as providing the highest possible return for a given level of risk, or the lowest risk for a given return.

Despite its shaky foundations, the Markowitz model is a standard tool for portfolio analysis. Investment advisers zero in on risk versus return calculations even though the use of historical data to try to quantify future values of μ and σ is of dubious reliability. Portfolio choice analysis also led to the development of the capital asset pricing model, which has its own set of problems.

CAPM

Capital asset pricing rolled in among business school finance theorists in the early 1960s; not long after, it was picked up by mainstream macroeconomists. The CAPM is usually given a market-clearing interpretation along the lines of Irving Fisher's economy-wide model for interest rate determination discussed in Chapter 2. The adjusting variables in CAPM are a set of asset prices rather than Fisher's interest rate on loanable funds, but the logic of the model is much the same. It boils down to an elaboration of the portfolio choice model to compute how *covariances* or *correlations* among risks of assets can affect their valuations. (Like the variance as an indicator of the size of the risk dispersion of a single variable, the covariance of two variables measures the magnitude of the relationship between them. A correlation coefficient conveys much the same information but is scaled to vary between -1 and $+1$.) Because the CAPM is based on means and covariances of asset returns, it strictly applies only when their probability distributions are Gaussian or the agents in question have quadratic utility functions. These limitations have not prevented it from being very widely applied.

One reason why the model is so popular is that it provides a handy-dandy simple equation for the "required" return μ_i to risky asset number i,

$$\mu_i - R = \frac{\sigma_{ie}}{\sigma^2}(\mu - R) = \beta_i(\mu - R).$$

As before, R is the return to the "riskless" asset, and μ and σ are the return and standard deviation of the efficient portfolio. The equation says that the positive deviation of μ_i over R is proportional to the "average" deviation $\mu - R$.

The factor of proportionality β_i is computed using σ_{ie} or the covariance of the returns to asset i and the efficient portfolio. The conclusion usually drawn from CAPM is that competition will force an asset with a high beta to pay an extra-high return (even if its own-return has low variance) because its large positive correlation σ_{ie} with the efficient portfolio forces its owners to take additional steps to hedge against overall market fluctuations. If anything, the data suggest an opposite result. Portfolios with high betas typically yield lower returns than those with low values of the parameter.

The formula can be evaluated for an arbitrary collection of assets; all that one needs to know are the means, standard deviations, and covariances of their returns. CAPM basically aims to minimize variation of the overall return from the assets at hand. It can be interpreted as sending two somewhat contradictory messages.

On the one hand, selecting assets with returns having negative or low positive correlations with the efficient portfolio is a wise means to diversify. On the other hand, if you want to take a chance on a big return, then go long on an asset with a high beta and short on assets with low ones.

There is, however, no reason to assume that a stock exchange operates as a risk-minimizing CAPM computer. Identifying the efficient portfolio with "the market" confounds the CAPM and EMH notions of "efficiency" and is invalid. That does not prevent stock market analysts from doing it all the time.

Finally, finance theorists draw a distinction between systemic and diversifiable risk. CAPM may help reduce the latter but says nothing about the former. Maybe regulation, as discussed below, can be deployed to reduce market risks (or, better, Keynesian uncertainties).

Derivative Pricing and Option Pricing

Beginning in the 1970s rapid growth in trading of derivatives got under way. It was in part a response to the breakdown of the Bretton Woods system. Previously fixed exchange rates became highly flexible, with movements that needed to be hedged by futures or option contracts. After the recession in the early 1980s, there was relatively steady economic growth and low inflation (the political economy is discussed in Chapters 5 and 9), which stimulated the expansion of finance. Exponential increases in computer power allowed derivative prices to be calculated to an extent that had been inconceivable a few years previously.

Finance theory jumped on the bandwagon. Two examples—option pricing and evaluation of complex derivatives such as CDOs and CDSs—are sketched here in an effort to give some feel for how theory was applied and where it went astray. For options, the discussion is a bit more technical than heretofore—not intellectually deep but unavoidably messy.

Option pricing is the jewel in the crown of finance theory. The widely used BSM equation got a big boost in the early 1970s when it was (re)invented through the use of mathematics created a half-century previously and extended through the 1950s. The high-tech derivation added immensely to the prestige of the theory. How useful the formula is in practice is quite another matter.

An option is a contract guaranteeing the right to buy or sell objects such as traded shares and bonds, livestock, minerals, perishable goods, or illiquid securities at some future date. According to Aristotle's *Politics,* the philosopher-mathematician Thales of Miletus (ca. 624 BC–ca. 546 BC) anticipated a big olive harvest. Months in advance he put down money for the rights to use many olive presses when the crop came in. He exercised this option during the harvest and made a financial killing. The Romans and Phoenicians used option contracts, and they were available in Amsterdam in the 1600s. They started to be traded in the United States around 1850 and were deployed in bespoke transactions by Ivar Kreuger. Trading procedures were formalized at the Chicago Board Options Exchange in 1973, and in 2007 more than 2.8 billion contracts were cleared.

In contemporary usage, a *call option* on a share is the right to buy it at a pre-specified price (the *strike price*) at some future date. A *put option* is the right to sell at the strike price. The question is how to set a price now for such a right to make a transaction in the future. Because the mathematics is easier, only *European options* are discussed here. (The geography in the name is irrelevant.) They allow the contract to be exercised only at its expiration date. An *American option* allows the contract to be exercised on any date prior to the final one—a bit more complicated to evaluate, but the story is much the same as the one to follow.

Formulas for pricing options (then commonly traded in New York and London) began to appear around 1900. In 1973 Fisher Black and Myron Scholes, with Robert C. Merton lending a hand, proposed one such equation which, along with a few fudges, subsequently became widely utilized and earned its inventors a Nobel. (Black died in 1995, two years before the prize was awarded.) In fact the equation had been in use in the 1960s, but the Black-Scholes derivation had a big impact because it was a neat piece of applied math. (Recall the MIT vice provost's opinion of economists from Chapter 6.) We'll get to that later, but first a sketch of how a pit trader might approach the question of option pricing. As we will see, the pricing equation involves a combination of arbitrage as Keynes used it to discuss interest rate parity (see Chapter 8) and a Gaussian distribution on the returns to the underlying asset. As with CAPM, the resulting option pricing equations do not fit the data.

The notation is standard. The prices of a call and put are C and P respectively. The strike price is K. The current date is t, and the option contract can be exercised at time $T > t$ (say, a few months or quarters from now).

Discounting and exponential growth formulas are unavoidable in option pricing. It is simplest to bite the mathematical bullet and do the work with exponential functions of time expressed continuously (that is, not in the form of discrete periods). Compound growth and discounting formulas can be written as an "exponential" in the form $e^{a(T-t)}$, where a is a constant, $T - t$ is the relevant time lapse, and e is a crucial number in mathematics, like the familiar π used to describe properties of circles and a great deal else. It is roughly equal to 2.718. The great mathematician Leonhard

Euler discovered e in the eighteenth century; some say that he modestly named the number after himself.

The exponential function has many fascinating properties. I use just two. The product of $e^{a(T-t)}$ and $e^{b(T-t)}$ is $e^{(a+b)(T-t)}$ and $1/e^{a(T-t)} = e^{-a(T-t)}$. If an annual growth rate is 3% per year, and we are thinking about a period of two years, then $e^{(0.03)2} = 1.062$ and $e^{-(0.03)2} = 0.942$. For "small" rates and "short" time periods, exponential growth and discounting look like calculations with simple interest; compounding does not matter. Over a longer period, exponential growth does kick in: $e^{(0.03)20} = 1.822$. Over twenty years, 3% growth would raise the initial value of a variable by 82%, not 60%, which a computation based on twenty years of simple interest at 3% would imply.

The price of the share in play at any time t is $S(t)$. It is assumed to grow at rate μ while fluctuating along the growth path with standard deviation σ (more details below). Starting from an observed level $S(t)$, the expected value of the share at the expiration time T is $S(T) = S(t)e^{\mu(T-t)}$.

By and large, a trader will want to keep a balanced book of puts and calls. This decision gives rise to a *put-call parity (PCP)* relationship, which is crucial for option pricing. Suppose that at time t the trader buys a call option and offsets it by selling a put with the same strike price and time of expiration. His initial portfolio is $C(t) - P(t)$. Are his books really balanced after this transaction? We can check by writing out two valuation expressions for $C(t) - P(t)$ and asking under what conditions they will be equivalent. One is an actuarial formula given below. The other is constructed by simulating the portfolio $C - P$ with a combination of shares and riskless bonds. (This sort of simulation is a standard trick in financial engineering.) Table 7.1 summarizes the details at time T.

The table shows that two portfolios (one put plus one share and one call plus K bonds with a face value of $1) have the same value at time T. That will also be true at some earlier time $t < T$, because if one portfolio were cheaper, a trader could sell (or go short on) the more expensive one and buy (go long on) the other to make a riskless profit. Thus the values of the two portfolios will be driven back toward equality. The implicit assumption is that it is possible to trade any quantities of shares and bonds at their going prices. In a panic, of course, such trades would be impossible, and option valuation rules would fall apart. Rearranging the equation $C(T) +$

Table 7.1 Simulating put and call options

	Outcomes at time T	Put value	Share value	Portfolio value
Put + one Share	$S(T) \leq K$	$K - S(T)$	$S(T)$	K
	$S(T) \geq K$	0	$S(T)$	$S(T)$
	Outcomes at time T	Call value	Bond value	Portfolio value
Call + K bonds	$S(T) \leq K$	0	K	K
	$S(T) \geq K$	$S(T) - K$	K	$S(T)$

$K = P(T) + S(T)$ for time T and discounting the value of the bonds back from T to t at the riskless rate R, we get

$$C(t) - P(t) = S(t) - Ke^{-R(T-t)}.$$

Call this the financial engineering formula for $C(t) - P(t)$.

To get to the actuarial formula, note that at time t, the trader can calculate only the expected value of his position at T, because the share price S is subject to risk. As observed above, its expected value is $S(t)e^{\mu(T-t)}$. Either the put or the call will be in the money, so that the expected value of $C(T) - P(T)$ will be $S(t)e^{\mu(T-t)} - K$. Its present discounted value at the trader's own "appropriate" interest rate r becomes

$$C(t) - P(t) = e^{-r(T-t)}[S(t)e^{\mu(T-t)} - K].$$

The two expressions for $C(T) - P(T)$ look similar, but for PCP to be valid, they have to be the same. Using the rules for manipulating exponentials given above, one can see that they will be equivalent only if $r = \mu = R$. Both the appropriate discount rate and the expected growth rate of the share price must be equal to the interest rate on riskless bonds! If that is the case, the value of the portfolio $C(T) - P(T)$ is given by the financial engineering formula above. It is higher the higher the riskless rate of return R.

Presumably these equalities could result from very strong arbitrage of returns across asset classes. Comparing Figures 1.1, 1.4, and 2.2 shows that observed growth rates of the standard S&P share price index, interest rates, and corporate profit rates are highly dissimilar. The poor trader really can't calculate the value of his portfolio, except as an exercise in arbitrage pricing.

If we assume on the grounds of consistency that he should go ahead with a PCP calculation based on the riskless interest rate, he can write out the present value at time t of a call as

$$C(t) = e^{-R(T-t)}(E[S(T) - K]_+),$$

where E indicates that he must work with probabilistically expected values, and the + subscript means that he is interested in the probability that the share price is in the money with $S(T) > K$. This expression becomes the Black-Scholes valuation equation when the details of the Gaussian distribution for $S(T)$ are plugged in. (Other distributions could be used as well.) The final version is too complicated to be worth setting out here but is readily available in any finance theory textbook.

So we get to the Black-Scholes formula by assuming perfect market clearing for bonds and shares over the life of the option; strong arbitrage among the riskless interest rate, personal discount rates, and the growth of equity prices; and a Gaussian distribution on returns. In fact out-of-the-money options usually trade at a higher price than the formula predicts because it understates the probability of large price fluctuations due to fat tails. Insofar as traders use the equation to guess at option values (that is, when there is not an active market for the contracts in question), they try to arrive at realistic valuations by using kluges such as making the parameter σ a function of the strike price and similar maneuvers. Or else a value of σ consistent with a price of an option observed in the market could be inferred from the pricing formula and then used to value "similar" options. Messy, but maybe it works.

Einstein, Wiener, Itō, Black, and Scholes

Black and Scholes very successfully followed the neoclassical strategy of modifying an idea from mathematical physics to fit economists' preconceptions about how the market operates. They borrowed *Brownian motion* and its subsequent formalization into *stochastic differential equations.* Among others, Albert Einstein and Norbert Wiener were important contributors early in the twentieth century.

Looking through his microscope in 1827, the Scottish botanist Robert

Brown observed that pollen grains and dust particles floating in water were in constant jittery motion. Explanations based on collisions of the particles with water molecules began to appear around the turn of the century, from Bachelier, who also looked at fluctuating share prices, the Vienna physicist Marian Smoluchowski, and Einstein. In his anno mirabilis 1905 Einstein wrote out equations describing particle motions which were experimentally verified a few years later. This was one of the first confirmations of molecular theory: a dust particle is like a balloon being continually buffeted by the much smaller water molecules that surround it.

After taking freshman physics, our technological undergraduates could calculate that at room temperature each water molecule collides with its neighbors around 100 trillion times per second. After a tiny fraction of a second there is no way the molecule could remember the collisions it received before. Moreover, various *laws of large numbers*, including the *central limit theorem* from probability theory, show that whatever their distributions, a large number of small shocks will generate a Gaussian distribution of fluctuations for the molecule (at least in the vicinity of the mean value of the shocks).

Gaussians work well in statistical physics and quantum mechanics. In finance theory their use is often justified by invoking laws of large numbers. The smallest time unit in finance is one second. There are "only" about 31.5 million seconds in a year, and many financial shocks persist over days and weeks. Appealing to laws of large numbers to shoehorn the effects of the shocks into a Gaussian framework makes no sense.

Be that as it may, Black and Scholes based their analysis of asset returns on a Gaussian stochastic differential equation *(sde)* for asset price growth taken directly from statistical physics. With abuse of notation it can be written as

$$\text{Growth rate of asset price} = \mu + \sigma \times \text{Random shock}.$$

The "shock" is a *Wiener process,* introduced in an analysis of Brownian motion in 1923. *Itō's Lemma,* the analytical tool that finance theorists use to manipulate sdes, was discovered by Kiyoshi Itō in wartime Japan and became known to mathematicians in the West in the 1950s.

A Wiener process has a Gaussian distribution with a mean value of zero and variance proportional to an infinitesimal change in time. The equation can be interpreted as saying that on average the asset price grows at rate μ but continuously slows or speeds its growth in random fashion. In the jargon of statistical physics, this well-behaved process can occur only if the asset price (or pollen grain) is in *thermal equilibrium,* having the same temperature or magnitude of fluctuations as its surroundings. Why the μ or σ for the price should be unaffected by developments elsewhere in the economy is never explained.

The magnitude of the positive and negative shifts in the growth rate is greater for a higher value of σ. Without the shocks it would be easy to apply an exponential growth function to calculate how long the price would take to reach a certain level. In its random climb, however, the price will spend time sliding up and down, covering the same ground several times. Therefore it will take longer to reach a target value.

Similarly, its expected level after a given time period will be lower the stronger the effects of the shocks are as transmitted via σ. The expected return to holding the asset turns out to be

$$\text{Return} = \mu - \frac{\sigma^2}{2}.$$

For a higher value of σ, a call option on the asset will cost less.

In their 1973 paper Black and Scholes elegantly figured out a way to run an actuarial estimate of an option's value at the expiration time T backward in time to arrive at the valuation formula described above. It was the capstone of two decades of development of finance theory and helped put that discipline firmly on the academic map. Whether it had benefits beyond creating a cadre of highly paid professors and Wall Street "quants" or "rocket scientists" is another question.

Gaussian Copulas

Fluctuations in equity prices have the virtue of being visible. Even if one does not believe that their dynamics are described by a Gaussian sde, it is easy to take on board the main message from the expected return formula quoted above: returns are reduced by price volatility. The same observation does not apply to debt. To revert to Keynesian language, the uncertainties underlying any debt contract become manifest only if and when the borrower defaults.

The response of financial analysts was to try to turn uncertainties into quantifiable risks of default. Their chosen vehicle was the use of correlations. To see the details, we can go back to the example mentioned above of a marriage dissolved by death. The basic data would be *marginal* probability distributions on the survival times of the two spouses. A statistical tool called a *copula* (from the Latin for "link" or "tie") can be used to combine the two one-variable distributions into a two-dimensional pdf with a particular structure of dependence between survival times. If both variables are assumed to be Gaussian, the relevant parameter would be a correlation coefficient between survival probabilities. With that information one could assess the likelihood that the surviving spouse will die within a given period. The statistical philosophy differs, but the analysis resembles Bayesian probability calculations discussed in Chapter 4.

Gaussian copulas were widely used in pricing CDOs. (One might add that to compute a joint pdf if all probabilities are assumed to be Gaussian, one doesn't need to use the copula methodology at all. Copulas were basically part of the propaganda for the technique.) Marginal probability distributions on the default of each tranche of a CDO were put together through the use of prices of CDSs relevant to the tranches. The joint distribution was simulated with mysterious "base correlations" across tranches. How they were derived was not made clear. With the joint distribution computed, pricing calculations akin to CAPM and Black-Scholes could be used to put prices on the tranches. Although the exercises were presumably run in earnest, it is hard to avoid the feeling that they embodied an element of charade. When the crash got under way, rising prices on CDSs and falling valuations of CDOs generated one more destabilizing positive feedback loop.

Summing Up

Counterfactual history is a snare and a delusion. Nevertheless it is intriguing to wonder if the events of 2007–2009 would have been substantially different if finance theory had never been invented. Four quick observations follow.

For one, there were clearly first-order effects of domestic distributive shifts (Chapter 5) and of changes in the global macroeconomic configuration (Chapter 8) on the pattern of U.S. debt expansion that led into the crisis, especially for the household sector.

Second, deregulation of financial markets beginning around 1980 contributed another first-order effect by permitting debt securitization and the originate-and-distribute model of finance to become well established. Decisions to deregulate were taken at the political level and were certainly ideologically driven, but they were intellectually supported by rational expectations, the efficient market hypothesis, and Modigliani-Miller. As discussed below, they also arose from pressures toward deregulation emerging from market processes themselves.

Third, financial pricing models supported deregulation by adding the patina of "scientifically based" valuation to CDOs/CDSs and other derivatives—perhaps a first-order contribution to the boom and bust. The *shadow banking system* that emerged in the 2000s was built on complicated and opaque custom-made financial products. Many were never traded, but the financial firms which put them together received massive fees and bonuses. The only way the products could be valued was by using models. They provided an essential public relations (not to mention ideological) cover-up for what was really going on.

Finally, in somewhat more academic terms, finance theory supported a "complicitous silence" (a phrase due to the French sociologist Pierre Bourdieu) that allowed bankers to engage in destabilizing transactions without any criticism being raised. It helped maintain the convention that the market was doing perfectly well. The regulators shared the same mentality. Small wonder that there was a crash.

Behavioral Finance

As we have seen, finance theory is based on rational actor microeconomics. Keynes was highly proficient at this sort of analysis, for example, his invention of interest rate parity as detailed in Chapter 8 (an idea that by itself would have made a lesser economist's reputation), the Keynes-Ellsberg paradox in decision theory, use of own-rates of interest to analyze the investment decision, justification of liquidity preference from the mechanics of bond pricing, and the Ramsey-Keynes rule. The *General Theory*'s core financial analysis, however, rested on three entirely different pillars:

> The presence of fundamental, unavoidable uncertainty with regard to the future. One implication is that financial actors will have a bias toward holding seemingly safe, liquid assets, especially in troubled times.
> The impact on asset price determination and investment decisions of social processes such as the beauty contest and Wittgensteinian formation of knowledge from social conventions more generally.
> Decision making which relies not on instrumental rationality but

rather on intuition and caprice, with animal spirits being the most prominent example.

Behavioral finance comes from the Keynesian antipodes. It basically seeks to relax some of the more extreme assumptions of rational expectations and the EMH. It allows no role for fundamental uncertainty, however, and focuses on the individual psychology of economic actors while mostly ignoring social processes. There is some interface with macroeconomics, but to a large extent the emphasis is still on the actions of individual agents. So far the field is very academic, like the work of the new classical macroeconomists in the 1960s and 1970s, but practitioners have high hopes for the future. At least two lines of work may push thinking in a truly Keynesian direction. Before getting to that, I consider some ideas from behavioral finance relevant for later discussion.

Asset Price Arbitrage and Efficient Investment

In practice, asset price arbitrage can be conspicuous by its absence. Several examples were noted at the beginning of this chapter. Maintaining the hypothesis that asset price movements are basically random noise, a body of theory tries to explain lack of arbitrage by *transactions costs* or the presence of *noise traders* who prevent prices from arriving at their fundamental values. Regrettably, the reasoning rests on shifting sands because it postulates that market fundamentals exist. On that assumption, if noise trading abounds, then arbitrageurs may fail to drive asset prices to their fundamental values because they deplete their capital and/or cannot borrow enough to carry out their job. On the real side, lack of collateral may force firms to forgo socially productive investment projects (a line of thought associated with Ben Bernanke in his academic incarnation).

These and similar ideas certainly capture a piece of reality. What they miss is social forces. Market fundamentals are conventional social constructs which can rapidly change. Investment is driven by animal spirits tempered by inherited financial positions and the cost of capital, not an asset price q as cranked out by the Ramsey model in Figure 6.4.

Expected Utility Maximization

The Markowitz model is based on maximization of (objective) expected utility, as introduced axiomatically by John von Neumann and Oscar Morgenstern in their pioneering presentation of game theory in 1944. Much effort in experimental economics has been devoted to showing that the von Neumann–Morgenstern axioms do not apply to how people actually make decisions. The Keynes-Ellsberg paradox and similar complications imply that the same conclusion extends to the Ramsey–de Finetti–Savage axioms describing decisions made on the basis of subjective expected utility.

Financial "Puzzles"

A lot of behavioral finance has concentrated on "puzzles" about observed market behavior. A better label might be "pitfalls" of the financial economists' own devising. Macro-level data violate predictions from extensions of the Ramsey model in which growth of consumption or output is subject to random shocks (as in real business cycle models). The details become quite technical but are sketched here as a good illustration of the main obsession of mainstream macroeconomists for the last twenty or thirty years or so: keeping the leaking rational expectations boat afloat. Here are three typical puzzles.

The *equity premium puzzle* follows from a version of CAPM set up in terms of utility derived from consumption. Modifying the CAPM equation presented above, it says that the excess of the return to equity over the riskless rate should be given by the product of a utility function parameter γ (which can be interpreted as an indicator of risk aversion) and the covariance of the return to equity with the growth rate of consumption.

In the United States, the *long-run* observed premium of the real return to equity over the riskless rate is about 0.06, based on both dividends and capital gains. For capital gains the "run" is long indeed. A glance at Figure 1.1 shows that the real S&P share price index moved "sideways" between around 1970 and the mid-1980s. The index in the late 2000s was below its level a decade before. Moreover, the 6% premium applies to the United States. There is a fairly wide range of long-run returns to equity in different countries with well-established stock markets—from less than 3% in Germany to 4% in Japan and more than 7% in Australia. Behavioral finance people have not paid a lot of attention to these differences.

The correlation of the U.S. real return with consumption growth is 0.4 and the covariance is 0.0024. An *extremely* high value of γ (25 with the numbers just quoted) would be required to "explain" the equity premium. The consensus value for γ is around 2.

The *risk-free rate puzzle* arises from the Keynes-Ramsey rule. Extended from Chapter 2 to deal with risk, it says that

Marginal product of capital = Pure discount rate
+ γ × Expected consumption growth − γ^2
× Variance of consumption growth,

with γ showing up again as a key parameter. The use of the variance of consumption growth in the last term is explained below. It plays the same role as the correction for volatility in the equation for the return to equity presented above.

The pure discount rate is usually assigned a value of 0.02, which is also the growth rate of per capita consumption in the United States. If we use the consensus value for γ of 2 and take into account the final term, the right-hand side takes a value of about 0.059. This is an *under*estimate of the business profit rate (see Figure 2.2), but that has not been a source of concern. Rather, attention has focused on the fact that the real long-run riskless interest rate in the United States is around 1%. If one wants to link finance with the real side of the economy, that is the relevant left-hand-side variable in the Keynes-Ramsey rule, because riskless bonds and physical capital should be close substitutes. So the question is, why are people willing to accept such a low return on an asset mostly held to reduce their fear of the unknown? They could do better by investing directly in tangible capital.

Finally, the standard deviation of consumption growth is about 0.02, which presumably should serve as a reference point for the macroeconomy's overall fluctuations. The standard deviation of the return to equity is 0.17. This *equity volatility puzzle* is inconsistent with the golden mean behavior built into standard finance theory. It looks more like the result of jittery investors jumping in and out of the market in response to rapidly shifting expectations about what is happening on the real side of the economy.

These observations are certainly consistent with a Keynesian perspective. Investors operating in a world subject to fundamental uncertainty are likely to accept a very low return on a safe asset. The rationale is the fear of the unknown that underlies liquidity preference. Requiring a high return on risky assets and inducing price volatility by moving in and out of the stock market represent the other side of the coin. But for new classical macro, the puzzles are a continuing embarrassment. There have been numerous attempts to resolve them. A 2007 paper by the Harvard economist

Martin Weitzman can be interpreted as trying to add a Keynesian epicycle to preserve the standard model—not a clear break from orthodoxy but at least a recognition that there *is* a problem. The analysis relies on high-tech mathematics, but the highlights are interesting enough to take a look at here.

The formal Ramsey-style macro model as usually applied to an economy with a financial sector has an "agent" optimizing discounted utility subject to a production or consumption growth path determined by a Gaussian sde. The model's predicted value for the risk-free rate follows from the Ramsey rule above. There is no market for equity per se, so it is treated as a claim on future consumption flows. The CAPM "risk" term becomes γ^2 times the variance of consumption growth (replacing the covariance of market-based equity returns with consumption growth discussed above). With a standard deviation of consumption growth of 0.02, the equity premium and equity volatility puzzles remain intact.

The key unknown parameters are the mean and (especially) the variance of consumption growth. As discussed in Chapter 6, the simplest rational expectations position is that the representative agent and its sub-agents *know* the values of these parameters. A more relaxed point of view is that the parameters can be estimated rapidly and precisely from time series information about the economy.

To borrow yet another idea from nineteenth-century statistical physics, the estimation will be theoretically justified if the economy is *ergodic*. The meaning emerges when one imagines that the history of the economy unfolds many times, on each occasion with a different set of random shocks. (We ourselves are presumably living out our economic lives along one of these paths. The others are "out there" somewhere. Historically, to justify parameter estimation from time series data, the notion of ergodicity was introduced by the Swedish theoretical econometrician Herman Wold in the 1930s. Paul Samuelson picked it up in the late 1960s. Soon after, the post-Keynesian Paul Davidson launched a campaign in favor of non-ergodic macroeconomics, with no visible impact on the mainstream to date.)

If an *ensemble average* of the parameter values across the many time series is the same as a *time average* generated by one of them (for example, the one describing economic history as we observe it), the system is ergodic. One example is the state of a floating pollen grain in Brownian motion thermal equilibrium with the water around it. Its movements across both time and space are random. In another metaphor, the mean height of the wet sand along a straight beach being washed by small waves is an ensemble average. A time average can be calculated at any point along the beach over some period. A really big wave washing up at that point will make time and ensemble averages differ. The Great Crash/Depression and 2007–2009 waves that hit capitalism suggest that the ergodic hypothesis does not apply.

But let's assume that the economy is ergodic and soldier on with Weitzman a step or two further. Suppose that one parameter—say, the variance of the growth rate—shifts randomly over time subject to a Gaussian distribution. Then the rational agent will have to be updating its estimate of the Gaussian pdf of the variance in Bayesian fashion. Weitzman shows that one plausible estimation procedure will lead the agent to think that the distribution of the variance is *not* Gaussian but rather has a fat tail to the left, meaning that the probability of an adverse shock will appear to be relatively high. The agent will behave defensively in such a way as to generate the puzzles, even in a basically ergodic system in which rational expectations logic should apply.

On my interpretation of Occam's razor, the parsimonious description of macro finance is that the observed distribution of asset price movements over time displays fat tails (especially to the left). We simply live in an unstable economic environment. The ergodic metaphor misses the point. Saying that the system is ergodic but that a standard Bayesian estimation procedure has a built-in non-ergodic bias toward estimating fat tails is a valiant attempt to salvage a worldview that is irrelevant to the world. As noted above, we are back to the pre-Copernican astronomers' epicycles. But at least Weitzman's paper may switch mainstream economists' attention toward a more sensible approach to their puzzles. If they wish to continue to concentrate on asset price changes as the key to financial behavior, they will have to ditch the extended Ramsey model and study how firms and people behave in the world in which they live—with black swans, fat tails, and fundamental uncertainty.

Market Psychology

Behavioral finance borrows heavily from psychology. It imports many models to try to rationalize the absence of arbitrage and explain away the puzzles. Most of the effort has a micro focus and is not relevant here. There is, however, a recent book on finance and macroeconomics more generally called *Animal Spirits* by George Akerlof and Robert Shiller which follows Keynes in considering macro psychology explicitly. I wish it had gone a lot further.

The authors use "animal spirits" in a broad sense to include several motivations for economic action. The list includes confidence, fairness, corruption and bad faith, money illusion, and "stories," or widely accepted narratives about the economy and the places of different groups within it. Confidence, which resembles Keynes's own concept of animal spirits, gets top billing.

The various forms of spirit are used to discuss in historical terms many aspects of the economy. They include the S&L crisis, Enron, the LTCM hedge fund, and subprime mortgages; housing price cycles; and Bryan and the silver panic of 1893. Introducing history is well meaning and informative. But there is also ample recycling of orthodox new Keynesian macroeconomics, such as twenty-five-year-old models of wage-setting based on asymmetric knowledge.

The organizing principle which the book does not address is that the economy is a social-political entity. With some exceptions such as wage rigidity resulting from gift exchange, political economy is absent. In this regard *Animal Spirits* hews to the course laid out by the original neoclassical economists a century and a half ago, with an interesting dose of psychologizing thrown in.

To borrow a phrase from the macro debate in early 2009 about whether or not the world economy was recovering, an optimistic view is that Weitzman, Akerlof, and Shiller are "green shoots" of a return to relevance by academic economics. One can always hope.

Endogenous Finance

Finance theory did not just appear out of the clear blue sky. The neoclassical mind loves new toys like stochastic differential equations. It enjoyed them greatly when they came into view from statistical physics in the 1960s. But the theory also responded to a felt need in the finance industry for quantitative tools to deal with all the new products it was inventing. As a transition toward discussing financial regulation, it makes sense to undertake a quick historical sketch of the institutional changes that have occurred.

A good place to begin is with Hyman Minsky's emphasis on how inherited positions influence the choices available to financial actors. Recall his distinctions from Chapter 5 among "hedge," "speculative," and "Ponzi" units. With this classification at the back of the mind, we can assess the evolution of the American financial system, beginning before the Great Depression.

Shifts in Financial Structure

As discussed in Chapter 3, business cycles prior to the Depression involved significant price decreases and, implicitly, rising real interest rates in the downswing. This pro-cyclical feature later weakened as markup pricing and labor's ability to defend the money wage became more widespread. During a recession, debtors such as middle western farmers found their obligations mounting in real terms and were pushed toward speculative and Ponzi positions. Waves of debt repudiation followed. Along with a collapse in effective demand on the part of the debtors, the entire financial system could be drastically simplified, requiring years to rebuild, as may well be the case after the 2007–2009 crisis. Irving Fisher's debt-deflation chronicle (Chapter 2) is the classic description of such a process. A trend in that direction in late 2009 was increasing recourse by corporate borrowers toward traditional bond finance.

In the United States, debt deflation became less important after the 1930s, as the Federal Reserve and Treasury began to engage in counter-cyclical policy aimed at moderating real/financial cycles. Deposit insurance from the Federal Deposit Insurance Corporation (FDIC) helped rule out bank runs. *Automatic stabilizers* such as unemployment insurance were created beginning with the New Deal. Interacting with the responses of the financial system itself, these bits of economic engineering had unexpected consequences. One was that an inflationary bias was added to the system by the presence of demand supports. Broadly in line with Fisher arbitrage, interest rates trended upward, creating pressures for financial deregulation as described below.

Another unanticipated outcome was a move of corporations toward speculative and Ponzi positions, leading them to seek higher short-term profitability to try to keep their financial houses "in order." Absent fears of price and sales downswings, high-risk/high-return projects became more attractive. Such a shift was notable in increased short-termism of investment activities and the push toward merger and acquisition (M&A) activity in the 1970s and 1980s, when corporate q was less than 1.

Finally, the intermediaries financing such initiatives gained more explicit protection against risky actions by their borrowers through lender of last resort interventions on the part of the Fed and savings and loan (S&L) regulators. The resulting moral hazard induced both banks and firms to seek more risky placements of resources. Financial institutions in particular pursued innovations that changed the system's structures in ways that Minsky, who died in 1996, did not live to savor.

Much of his (and Keynes's) analysis addressed finance built around banks. But as discussed in connection with Figure 5.17, the relative importance of the banking system per se diminished notably beginning in the 1980s. Off–balance sheet vehicles proliferated, and the originate-and-distribute model of securitization expanded enormously. Banks metamorphosed from simple creatures accepting deposits and making loans into chimeras using their deposit bases to fund all manner of exotic and ill-understood trading activities that would have been better left to hedge funds.

In particular, a breakdown of restrictions on the activities of banks inherited from the New Deal (examples presented below) led to an increased emphasis on their equity capital as the sole object of regulatory scrutiny. At the same time, potentially destabilizing interactions between asset prices and leverage emerged, as discussed in Chapter 4, and provoked the crisis. Minsky (not to mention Keynes) never had the opportunity to analyze these developments. It would have been good if he had.

New Inventions and Regulatory Retreat

In 1933 the Glass-Steagall Act banned positive interest rates on demand deposits (checking accounts) and imposed interest rate ceilings on time deposits in a rule called *Regulation Q*. In the 1970s, banks seeking deposits (especially the newly invented negotiable *certificates of deposit*) began to find ways to circumvent the ceilings because they spawned the emergence of money market funds and the commercial paper market as competitors on the deposit and lending sides respectively. In the late 1970s with the jump in interest rates (Figure 1.4), banks lost deposits and were forced to call loans. They protested, and in 1980 Regulation Q was abolished.

Also in the 1960s unregulated Eurodollar and then Eurocurrency markets started to thrive. A Eurodollar deposit is just a liability denominated in dollars issued by a bank outside the political jurisdiction of the United States. British and American authorities winked and nodded at such placements at the outset because they seemed like a sensible way for commercial banks to make use of their excess reserves. A major contributing factor to growth in Eurocurrency markets was the American *interest equalization tax* of 1964–1973, enacted in an attempt to defend the capital controls in force at the time. Basically, the tax raised costs for banks to lend offshore from their domestic branches. The resulting higher external rates led dollar depositors such as foreign corporations to switch their funds from onshore U.S. institutions to Eurobanks.

Eurocurrency transactions rapidly taught market players that they could shift their deposits, loans, and investments from one currency or jurisdiction to another in response to actual or anticipated changes in interest and exchange rates. These moves were early warnings of a pervasive regulatory problem that dominates the world economy today: any nation's financial controls seem to be made for the sole purpose of being evaded. Even the ability of central banks to regulate the supply of money and credit was undermined by commercial banks' borrowing and lending offshore (a problem later exacerbated by non-bank investors engaging in *carry trade*, as discussed in Chapter 8, and similar activities). All national authorities were forced to scrap long-established interest rate ceilings such as Regulation Q, lending limits, portfolio restrictions, reserve and liquidity requirements, and other regulatory paraphernalia.

Another outcome of higher deposit rates was the savings and loan crisis. S&L institutions were originally set up in the United States to encourage homeownership by offering relatively low interest rates on mortgage loans. In the 1970s they began to have severe mismatch problems because inflation pushed up rates on deposits via Fisher arbitrage while at the same time rates on S&L loans remained fixed. One response was to change the rules so that S&Ls could have a wider loan portfolio like that of banks, but without the banking system's regulation.

The *Garn–St. Germain Act* of 1982 allowed depositors to hold any number of fully insured $100,000 deposits with any S&L. (Utah Republican senator Jake Garn was extremely conservative and possibly not the sharpest tack in the box; Rhode Island Democratic congressman Fernand St. Germain was close to the S&L industry. On signing the legislation, President Reagan said: "This bill is the most important legislation for financial institutions in the last 50 years. It provides a long-term solution for troubled thrift institutions. . . . All in all, I think we hit the jackpot.")

There certainly was a jackpot. With their prudential responsibilities to depositors removed by the act, S&L managers were freed to engage in high-uncertainty/high-return lending as they saw fit. Loan failures set off a crisis during the years around 1990, which ultimately cost $150 billion or so to clean up—small potatoes by late 2000s standards but still significant.

Perhaps more important for the future, S&Ls invested heavily in high-yield *junk bonds* issued by Michael Milken and others to finance lightning-fast hostile takeovers of firms during the M&A frenzy. The firms were left with heavy debt burdens, while the takeover artists and S&L executives were amply rewarded by options on their shares. Milken was ultimately convicted of securities fraud, but he left a long-lasting legacy of financial maneuvering (such as executives taking their firms private through *leveraged buyouts*) associated with escalating executive pay. The junk bond explosion is one reason why the S&L crisis is usually taken as the leading example of moral hazard created by misdirected regulation. Along with the abolition of Regulation Q, it signaled the beginning of the push toward liberalizing financial markets that led to 2007–2009.

As discussed in Chapter 4, a further step was the formation of investment funds and (later) off–balance sheet special purpose vehicles, in the first instance for asset securitization, expanding on the activities of Freddie Mac and Fannie Mae. Banks sold packages of assets to trusts or SPVs, which in turn issued shares or bonds, with payouts passing the interest receipts to their creditors. High fees were involved in all these transactions. In many cases the primary assets were high-uncertainty (credit cards, car loans), but packaging them permitted reduction of perceived risk through diversification.

Novel packages were put together for investors who inhabit that segment of the market. Innovations took the form of derivatives like CDOs and CDSs. *Hedge funds* appeared to trade in derivatives, typically financing their operations with heavy borrowing on the margin (with liabilities reaching tens of times the value of their equity).

All these maneuvers set the stage for the crisis. There was also a continuing breakdown in financial regulation, which leads us to the problem of the present. How can regulation be reinvented to reduce the likelihood of another catastrophe in the near future? If a few centuries of history are any guide, in the more or less distant future there will almost certainly be another major crash. That's the sort of capitalist world that we live in. At most, all that reconstructed regulation can do is make the future crash more distant.

Financial Regulation

By way of introduction two observations are worth making. First, the Yale political scientist Charles Lindblom in a classic 1977 book called *Politics and Markets* pointed out that the state retains the power of coercion or *authority* over markets. It can always take them over if it so wishes (as and when the political process permits, one might add). Often, however, the state can only apply coercion without precision: it is "all thumbs." The market, by contrast, has "nimble fingers," but there is no guarantee that it will use them to further social ends. The financial market's fingers certainly were nimble in the 2000s, but they created a disaster. The goal of financial regulation as exercised by the state is to use authority to restrain financial excess—not an easy task!

Second, a fairly effective regulatory system was set up by the New Deal. It provoked the wrath of Wall Street, but FDR frankly did not care. As just recounted, the New Deal regulatory apparatus began to break down in the 1980s as conservatives settled into power, but enough remnants survived to keep the system functional until the late 1990s, when they were abolished.

The following discussion summarizes the main points that Keynesian economists have raised about proper regulatory structures for the future in light of institutional changes over the past few decades. Possibilities for revitalizing regulation are also considered. There is no sense in getting into the political machinations, which in any case will have their own dynamics. But as of spring 2010 prospects for a new and effective system of regulation were not heartening.

Macro and Micro Regulation

The emphasis here is on *macro*economic financial regulation, a topic that has not been widely explored in the past. Most regulators are concerned with *micro* intervention aimed at insuring the stability of a financial firm and its customers. They try to enforce laws against insider trading, fraud, market manipulation, and so on, and prosecute violations. Regulators license providers of financial services and often have powers to shut them down.

One key example of coercive power in the United States is the ability of the FDIC to take over and restructure banks. A common trigger is for the bank's leverage, measured as its assets/common equity ratio to approach a limit of, say, 20. The reason to impose a minimum capital requirement of 5% (in this case) is to ensure that the ability of the FDIC to insure banks' deposits is preserved.

The process can involve a number of interventions. Management usually gets sacked. The liability side of the balance sheet is rebuilt, with liquidation or dilution of existing equity and transformation of at least some debt into new equity, perhaps beautified with a haircut. Nonperforming assets may be spun off and performing assets incorporated into a new or merged bank which can engage in ordinary business activities.

The practical limitation on such interventions in the United States is that it is restricted to mere banks and not the *bank holding companies* (regulated by the *Comptroller of the Currency*) that control the major firms. There is no legally sanctioned resolution process for very large institutions. Lehman Brothers was one such example. In public, U.S. officials claimed that they had no legal authority to impose an orderly failure procedure on the investment bank (although they did intervene dramatically for AIG a day later). In private, they may have thought that letting Lehman fail would deliver a stern warning to other institutions about moral hazard. There are dark hints about other motivations, but in any case as of early 2010 legal provision for orderly resolution was not on the books.

Short of such major interventions, micro regulation differs according to the nature of financial firms. Insurance companies and pension funds are (or should be) closely supervised. AIG was the glaring exception. Hedge funds which deal almost exclusively with rich, presumably well-informed investors, are lightly regulated. Securities broker-dealers such as the firm run by Bernard Madoff are supervised by the Securities and Exchange Commission (SEC), which failed to observe his fraud and manipulation.

The 2007–2009 crisis shows that simple prudential regulation of individual firms is not enough. There were interconnections among financial firms, especially banks, which proved strong enough to upset the entire system. Here is a quick summary of macroeconomically important linkages.

Banks maintain large-scale transactions with one another and other segments of the broad financial market, creating *counterparty risk*. The growing extent of that risk shows up clearly in Figure 5.17, with its big increases in total assets and liabilities of the financial sector. If one institution with connections to many others collapses, there can be systemic repercussions. As noted in Chapter 4, the failure of Lehman Brothers immediately destabilized the commercial paper and money markets and precipitated the punitive government takeover of AIG (associated with large payments ultimately channeled to counterparties such as Goldman Sachs).

When a bank fails, very often the customers to whom it has been lending have no other sources of credit and must curtail their operations. This problem has been well known since the Great Depression. Surviving banks may not want to lend. As Keynes pointed out in Chapter 12 of the *General Theory,* when a poor state of credit from lenders combines with an adverse state of confidence on the part of potential borrowers, a prolonged slump in output is likely to ensue.

When conventions in the market are stable, as Keynes also observed, then it can continue seemingly unperturbed for a considerable time, even in the midst of a bubble. The conventions are supported by homogeneous behavior, for example, the use by most players of the same models (extensions of those discussed above) manipulating the same data to price derivatives in the 2000s upswing. When all the models simultaneously collapsed, panic was inevitable. Keynes's observations in Chapter 12 on the contagion of ignorance were right on target.

Finally, and most important, during the run-up to the crash, the importance of pro-cyclical financial behavior increased tremendously. Leverage ratios went up; maturity mismatches worsened; simply unsustainable positions such as AIG's CDSs proliferated. The clear lesson is that macro-level regulation has to be counter-cyclical, especially in an upswing, if it is to have any chance of success.

Several questions immediately arise:

What sorts of financial firms should be subject to regulation beyond standard micro-level supervision?
How should regulation be done?
What should be the backup if regulation fails?
What sorts of regulators should take responsibility?

The Boundary Problem

In addressing the first question, we need to recognize that there will always be a *boundary problem*. Not all financial firms can or should be closely regulated at the macro and micro levels. Special attention must be paid to those most likely to generate systemic instabilities. The firms within the regulatory boundary will have less opportunity to take profits than those outside. They will fight against being more tightly regulated and seek to circumvent regulation once it is imposed. Examples of boundary violations abound in financial history: I have already noted the abrogation of Regulation Q, the S&L crisis, and—most important—the weakened powers of regulators to control their local markets in a world in which restrictions on international capital movements have vanished.

One recent major case involved the Glass-Steagall Act. It had imposed *firewalls* between activities of financial institutions. That is, a firm could not act as both an investment bank dealing in securities and a commercial bank relying on deposits and loans, nor could it operate as both a bank and an insurance company. The financial industry began to push against these limitations in the 1980s, and in 1999 it succeeded. The *Gramm-Leach-Bliley Act* abolished the restrictions. The emergence of Citigroup and other financial conglomerates which played a central role in setting off the 2007–2009 crisis was an immediate consequence. (The sponsoring senator, Phil Gramm from Texas, was closely tied to Enron and was the political messiah for financial deregulation in the 1990s. In the executive branch, abolishing Glass-Steagall was heavily supported by the reigning financial triumvirate of Robert Rubin, Alan Greenspan, and Lawrence Summers. In 1999, after Rubin had resigned as secretary of the treasury, he joined the top management of Citigroup. As the conglomerate's share price headed rapidly downward in late 2008, he virtually disappeared from public view. Presumably he lost a lot of money.)

Another important example was the *Commodity Futures Modernization Act* of 2000, which explicitly ruled out any attempt at regulation of the market for credit default swaps. (In a presidential working group, Greenspan, Rubin, and former SEC chairman Arthur Levitt outvoted the feminist lawyer Brooksley Born, who headed the *Commodity Futures Trading Commission,* in a decision not to regulate CDS transactions.)

All the cases in which regulations were relaxed point to two conclusions.

One is that financial regulatory rules have to be carefully designed to avoid unanticipated (in a Keynesian sense!) consequences. The other is that if they have any bite, they will be resisted. With these observations in mind, what can be said about selecting systemically important firms that should be subject to macro-level regulation? Here are four possible categories.

First, there are individual firms such the major commercial and investment banks which are so large and have so many counterparties that each one is systemically significant. They are usually recognizable and require both macro and micro regulation. "Everyone" knows the names of the few dozen such companies around the world, but there can always be surprises.

A fair question is whether these creatures should be permitted to exist. *Universal banks* have long been commonplace in Europe, where they are part of the furniture, but they emerged in the United States only with the abolition of Glass-Steagall. They have been accused of blurring risk (or, in Keynesian terms, raising fundamental uncertainty), adding complexity, and eating up capital. Certainly the U.S., German, Swiss, or British government could use coercive authority to break up its nation's universal banks. In the United States, part of the "Volcker rule" (named after former Fed governor Paul Volcker) advanced by President Obama in January 2010 would put a cap on the liabilities of any single bank, relative to total liabilities of the system. As of April, prospects for the proposal in Congress were unclear.

Even if it did pass it was not obvious what difference the rule would make. In early 2010 the six largest banks had assets exceeding 60% of GDP, up from 55% in 2006 and 15% in 1995. (Numbers consistent with data for the entire financial sector are shown in Figure 5.17.) The Obama administration was *not* proposing to break up these banks, but rather was proposing just to keep them from growing more. If they are already "too big to fail," then keeping them that way would not be much of an improvement.

Another option would be selective nationalization and state management, which has been pursued with some success in developing economies, including the now fashionable BRIC group (Brazil, Russia, India, China). In 2008–9 such moves were under active discussion in Europe. Largely for ideological reasons they have stayed in the background of the U.S. regulation debate since Bear Stearns collapsed in March 2008. Who knows if they will come to the forefront?

Second, some institutions—hedge funds or private equity investors—

could be systemically important as a group if they engage in herding behavior. Macro regulation for the group could be important, combined with light-touch micro surveillance.

Third, uncertainty absorbers such as insurance companies and pension funds require serious micro regulation. If a firm like AIG migrates to the first group, it would also require macro regulation.

Finally, tiny entities don't require macro regulation unless, like the S&Ls in the 1980s, they engage in herding behavior. They are of course capable of failing if they are engulfed in a macro crisis—back to the FDIC.

Tools for Macro Regulation

Tools are available to regulate the first two groups of firms, especially the large individuals. The topic is complicated and fraught with controversy among experts. There are, however, several points that stand out.

The first one is that regulation must be counter-cyclical, focusing on leverage, mismatches, and proper accountability. The obvious example of how not to do it was a unanimous decision by the SEC commissioners in April 2004 to allow the five large New York investment banks, two of which survived in 2009, to increase their debt/equity ratios to 30:1 from their historically fixed levels of 12:1. They were also given enhanced self-regulatory powers based on their own risk modeling. (Henry Paulson, later George W. Bush's beleaguered secretary of the treasury, was then the CEO of Goldman Sachs. He pushed aggressively for relaxation of restrictions on leverage.)

At the same time, Democrats in Congress supported more relaxed regulation of Fannie Mae and Freddie Mac. The outcomes are well known. The investment banks pushed their leverage up toward and above their new limits, and Fannie and Freddie followed suit. A crash became virtually inevitable.

What the SEC *should* have done is increase capital requirements at a time when the firms it was regulating were lobbying for their relaxation. An alternative which in fact has been put into practice in Spain is to require increased *provisioning* of reserves against possible loan losses. As discussed in Chapters 4 and 5, in a boom rising asset prices have the initial impact of reducing leverage, creating incentives for firms to raise their ratios back up. Lowering ceilings on ratios of assets or debt to common equity can counter that trend by forcing firms to build up equity to offset expanding balance sheets. A rule-based *laddered response* to balance sheet expansion should be a basic regulatory tool.

Maturity mismatches can also worsen. The obvious task for a regulator is to monitor the maturity structure of funding for recognizable pools of assets. If funding quality deteriorates, capital requirements should again be raised. Such a *mark-to-funding* approach would concentrate on ensuring that firms have sufficient liquidity to offset unexpected reductions in the value of their assets such as the super senior tranches of CDSs which wreaked such havoc in 2007. If it is not prohibited, then proprietary trading activity by banks (highly profitable in volatile markets throughout 2009) should be funded by their capital, not deposits or advances from the Treasury and Fed. On the one hand, such restrictions (consistent with the spirit of Obama's Volcker rule proposals) would serve as a partial replacement for Glass-Steagall. They were conspicuously absent in 2009 as banks used funds received from the *Troubled Asset Relief Program* or *TARP* to support trading as opposed to lending activities. On the other hand, it is also true that in "normal" times, revenue from such trading in most banks is less than 5% of the total (and only 10% for Goldman Sachs).

More generally, regulatory policy in 2009-2010 was geared toward creating high earnings for Wall Street. There was a steep yield curve on bonds anchored by a Fed funds rate of 0.25%; the lending that occurred became highly profitable. The low short-term rate also supported a massive carry trade based on borrowing in the United States for investments in areas such as commodities and equity in emerging market economies. The regulatory goal was to enable banks to build up high-quality or *tier one* capital in the form of common equity *and* retained earnings.

In practice they did not behave the way they were supposed to. A large share of income flows went not to retained earnings but to bonuses for traders; the ghost of Chuck Prince thrived on ample liquidity underwritten by the state. At year's end and into 2010 huge bonuses became a hot political issue, and another example of how difficult it is to push financial firms in the direction in which regulators want them to go.

One key reason is that accountability during the boom and thereafter was vested in firms via self-regulation. Even worse, it was backed by the credit rating agencies. That approach obviously failed. The agencies supply a *public good* in the form of assessments of uncertainties associated with different financial instruments. (Again, on Keynesian grounds, they *cannot* credibly provide probabilistic risk estimates, although they pretend to do so.) They are inevitably subject to conflicts of interest, depending on which interested parties pay for the assessments. In 2007–2009 they allegedly shared their rating models with banks, allowing them to reverse-engineer the computer code to create derivatives that would be assessed to be safe. Unsurprisingly, e-mail traffic released in 2010 by the Senate Permanent Subcommittee on Investigations suggests that the banks also played the agencies off against one another to make sure their products got favorable ratings.

The conclusion must be that the agencies' views should not be key components of the regulatory process. Rather, regulators should investigate the approaches to uncertainty assessment that firms themselves are using to try to avoid a herding mentality. It would be desirable if both firms and agencies could devise separate ratings schedules for primary securities such as equity and bonds on the one hand and derivatives including commodity futures on the other.

Beyond dealing with leverage, mismatches, and accountability, several other regulatory changes would make sense.

There are several areas in which transactions costs can be regulated counter-cyclically. One is margin requirements for purchasing equity. After his "irrational exuberance" speech, Alan Greenspan notably did not move to raise required margins. He should have.

Guidelines on remunerations could be tied to capital requirements and limits on proportions of income flows that can be diverted away from retained earnings. That is, "excessive" remunerations would raise capital and reinvestment requirements. High leverage, however, could trigger reductions in bonuses and/or dividends to shareholders. *Not* paying bonuses and fees up front on contracts that will run over several years is also widely suggested. Restrictions on compensation packages for proprietary traders within banks would tend to push such activity toward hedge funds, which is where it should be.

On the consumer side, limitations on loan-to-value *(LTV)* ratios for mortgages on housing would make sense, taking into account *all* obligations including home equity loans and second mortgages. LTV restrictions could be adjusted counter-cyclically. They could be complemented by simplification and transparency of lending criteria, and better policing of potential borrowers' economic situations.

In early 2010 possible taxes on banks became a contentious issue. In late 2009 the UK tried to impose one-off excess profits taxes on bonuses paid during that year. Banks in response increased bonus pools, thereby reducing growth of tier one capital. One implication is that high *permanent* tax rates on capital gains and related bonuses and fees could be required to slow trading and speculation.

Such interventions were being discussed internationally in 2010. In April the International Monetary Fund recommended a package of three separate taxes: a flat tax on total liabilities and levies (at equal rates) on pay and profits in the form of a neatly named financial activities tax or FAT, comparable to a value-added tax or VAT on the nonfinancial sector. The idea was that the taxes would be imposed in coordinated fashion by federal authorities. According to the initial numbers floating around, the IMF proposal could be seen as a mild application of the old saying about a mishap in the china shop, "If you break it, you own it." The banks would seem to own the damage under a deferred payment plan.

In the United States the fiscal cost of the bank bailouts after the crisis was on the order of $500 billion. For banks at the end of 2009, total liabilities minus tier-one capital and insured deposits were around $2,200 billion, so that a 1% levy would yield $22 billion. Annual operating revenues were around $500 billion, so that a 6% tax would yield $30 billion. It would require ten years of taxes at such rates for the banks to pay only what they owe the government for the china they broke. Thereafter the receipts could be applied to building up a resolution fund for future crises.

Keynes's suggestion that there should be a tax on financial transactions should not be forgotten. Brazil, for example, has had one since the 1990s. By throwing "sand in the wheels," a tax can hold down the volume of transactions, which never hurts in a bubble. It can bring in revenue: roughly 2% of GDP from a 0.4% tax rate in Brazil. In addition, the tax apparatus provides regulators with information about every trade by every client of a bank or brokerage, identified by a registered account number. With such a system in place, a Madoff-style fraud scheme would be impossible. It would become easier for regulators to recognize if there are too many participants on one side of a market with positions that in a crunch could not be readily funded.

Along similar lines, if a firm issues a CDS, it assumes uncertainty which the buyer of the instrument sheds. Leverage restrictions could be tightened in a rules-based fashion for the seller and relaxed slightly for the buyer. Even if the buyer does not respond to this incentive to report the transaction (perhaps because it is engaged in a bear raid), the fact that the transaction would have to be recorded to be taxed could provide useful information to regulators.

On the down side, transactions taxes do not directly target funding mismatches and excessive leverage, the root causes of financial upheavals. They can only be complements to the sorts of measures discussed above.

Brazil, of course, has a small financial market which is rather isolated from the rest of the world. A turnover tax in a major market like the United States or Euroland would divert transactions to other financial centers unless they imposed taxes as well. (Recall the fate of the U.S. interest rate equalization tax in the 1960s.) During 2009 and 2010 there was initial discussion of the idea of an internationally coordinated *Tobin tax* on (at least) cross-border transactions.

As noted several times previously, following the crisis banks cut back on lending and held high reserves. Between mid-2008 and late 2009 Fed base money increased from around $900 billion to $2 trillion, while commercial bank deposits with the Fed increased by about $1 trillion. A tax such as a negative interest rate on reserves might at the margin push banks toward higher lending.

There are also possibilities for expanding non-cost-based regulations.

Transparency in the form of standardized contracts and clearinghouses for derivatives is a broadly supported goal (except by inside players, of course).
Banning or very tightly regulating some derivatives such as CDSs is also widely recommended.
Creditors engaging in originate-and-distribute activities should be required to keep *skin in the game* by holding some fraction, say, 10% or 20%, of the loans that they make and securitize, to ensure that they practice prudent lending.

As noted above, in past banking crises, enforced *debt-to-equity* conversions (at times with haircuts on bond face values) have been imposed to recapitalize banks. This option should be available to regulators if a bad situation gets worse.

If Regulation Fails

No regulatory scheme is perfect, and all deteriorate over time. Franklin Roosevelt appointed the renowned speculator Joseph Kennedy (who cashed in his holdings before the Great Crash) as his first chairman of the SEC, saying, "It takes a thief to catch one" or something similar. Ferdinand Pecora, who spearheaded the 1932–1934 Senate hearings into financial abuses, was another commissioner. Kennedy, Pecora, and their immediate successors were effective regulators, especially in comparison to the commission's pathetic performance seventy years later. So it makes sense to ask who should pick up the pieces by acting as a lender or *market-maker of last resort* if macro regulation in fact fails. There are four possibilities.

First, banks or financial institutions themselves could organize a rescue, as did J. P. Morgan and colleagues around the turn of the twentieth century. In the late 1990s the Long-Term Capital Management (*LTCM*) hedge fund was hit by a bear raid after its strategy of highly leveraged bond transactions based on reversion of interest rate differentials to historical levels broke down. The Fed prevented system-wide repercussions by subsidizing the private sector to carve up the dead elephant (the cost was $3.5 billion). But these efforts have been dwarfed by the 2007–2009 crisis. The private sector simply lacks the wherewithal to rescue the contemporary financial system.

Second, there could be private insurance against a big crash. Again, there is not likely to be sufficient funding, as AIG amply demonstrated.

Third, the central bank could enter vigorously to support the market, as did the Fed, European Central Bank, and Bank of England in 2007–2009 by massively expanding their balance sheets. There were, however, huge shocks along the way, such as the Lehman Brothers–AIG crisis.

Fourth, national treasuries can always recapitalize central banks if that is required. That has occurred in the United States as Federal Reserve assets rose from $850 billion in 2006 to over $2 trillion in 2009, largely because of the Fed's acquisition of private-sector liabilities. Monetary policy per se began to be based in part on bonds issued by a Treasury Department Supplementary Financing Program. In effect the Fed and Treasury began to share responsibility for monetary interventions.

Responsibility for Macro Regulation

The obvious conclusion is that the central bank backed up by the Treasury should carry ultimate regulatory responsibility. How that might come to pass in the United States with its alphabet soup of federal and state regulators each supervised by a legislative committee seeking to defend its turf is an open question.

One wonders if the people running the Fed and Treasury can even carry out the task. Just to recall, Maynard Keynes was a creature of the City of London, perhaps more so than the financial authorities of the 2000s were creatures of Wall Street. After all, he organized hedge funds (described in Chapter 8) and made serious money, in contrast to the academics and bureaucrats prominent under Obama. At the same time, he was bound to Cambridge and somewhat above the financial fray. As Bertrand Russell put it: "He went about the world carrying with him everywhere a feeling of the bishop *in partibus*. True salvation was elsewhere, among the faithful in Cambridge." This independent position and true intellectual distinction were important factors contributing to Keynes's success as a policymaker.

Lacking Maynard's genius, Alan Greenspan was bound only to Wall Street and the Republican Party. (In 2005, then Senate minority leader Harry Reid said that Greenspan was "one of the biggest political hacks we have here in Washington.") To please both constituencies, he orchestrated the *Greenspan put,* via which interest rates were cut after every market wobble. (The list includes the 1987 stock market crash, the Gulf War, the Mexican crisis, the Asian crisis, the LTCM collapse, the Y2K scare, the end of the Internet bubble, and 9/11.) Ben Bernanke and Obama's secretary of the treasury Tim Geithner were active collaborators. Combined with other contributing forces such as the carry trade, the result was an interest rate regime highly conducive to a bubble. How other figures such as Lawrence Summers contributed to deregulation has already been mentioned.

Given their market-friendly orientation, whether such people will advance re-regulation seriously remains to be seen as of this writing. Their academic peers commenting on the issue praise the benefits of financial innovation and warn ominously about the dangers of going back toward an "overly regulated" system like the one that was created by the New Deal.

With the benefit of hindsight, in 2010 Bill Clinton regretted not having tried to rein in derivatives: "On derivatives, yeah I think they [Rubin and Summers] were wrong and I think I was wrong to take [their advice] because the argument on derivatives was that these things are expensive and sophisticated and only a handful of investors will buy them and they don't need any extra protection, and any extra transparency. The money they're putting up guarantees them transparency. And the flaw in that argument was that first of all sometimes people with a lot of money make stupid decisions and make it without transparency. . . . I wish I should have been caught trying [to regulate]. I mean, that was a mistake I made."

Prospects?

It is impossible to say how the regulatory debate will play out. As the IMF proposal discussed above demonstrates, outside the United States there appeared to be a growing consensus on the need to impose taxes on balance sheets, remunerations, and profits in the financial sector. Whether the United States would go along was by no means clear.

In the domestic debate, recall that setting up the New Deal package took up most of Roosevelt's first term. The process was aided immensely by the Pecora investigation. Through early 2010 the activities of the Financial Crisis Inquiry Commission were a pale imitation. The performance of the Senate Permanent Subcommittee on Investigations was somewhat better.

Change will not come any faster in the political system of the 2010s than in the 1930s. It may not come at all, given the clout of the financial industry. Here is a quick rundown of topics at hand in early 2010.

Setting up a high-powered council of regulators was under discussion. People like those discussed just above would presumably make up the membership. Cheerleaders for a boom are not likely to foresee a looming crisis.

Some form of consumer protection may be enacted. Unless the intervention also restricts destabilizing household behavior by imposing loan-to-value limits and similar provisions, it will not add to the effective regulation of finance. Any form of consumer protection was being fiercely opposed by Wall Street.

Restrictions on financial pay packages seem likely in the United States as well as abroad. The real question is whether they can somehow be tied to counter-cyclical restrictions on leverage and mismatches. A tax aimed at short-term borrowing (at least) by financial firms would be a complementary move.

Maybe the Fed will be enthroned as a system-wide regulatory authority. Maybe not.

The Lehman Brothers–AIG catastrophe demonstrates that there should be well-defined mechanisms in place to deal with the failure of a systemically important institution. There was strong opposition by Republicans in early 2010.

In 2009–10 trade in derivatives remained virtually unregulated, and new inventions in securitization were coming off Wall Street's drawing boards. Whether such innovations can be reined in remains to be seen. Interventions under discussion included requiring derivatives to be traded in transparent exchanges. Little was being said about banning CDSs and other highly destabilizing financial instruments. Again, banks were united in opposition to almost all such regulation.

Serious regulatory initiatives such as laddered tightening of restrictions on balance sheet expansion (as opposed to simply increasing fixed capital ratios) and mark-to-funding barriers to mismatches did not appear to be under active discussion at the political level. At most, minimal requirements for keeping skin in the game on the part of originate-and-distribute creditors were being discussed.

Financial transactions taxes have been mooted (as the British like to say) in Europe but not in policymaking circles in Washington or New York.

The social problem thrust into the spotlight by 2007–2009 is that the benefits from financial innovation largely ended up with the rich, while the middle class and the poor were damaged in the process and in 2009 started paying for the cleanup. Government outlays from the TARP package appeared likely to be repaid, but low interest rates continued to serve as a conduit for the transfer of hundreds of billions of dollars from savers to banks. Prior to the 1980s the New Deal's system did support fairly solid performance on the real side of the economy, while the money to be made on Wall Street was no greater than in other sectors. Beginning in the Milken era, the distributive balance shifted.

We have a pretty clear case of class conflict here, with financiers fighting to maintain their position and the government and its regulators in the middle. Given political realities, it is not obvious that Wall Street will lose the battle. And then . . .

Notes

The discussion of finance theory draws heavily on McCauley (2004) and also Eichberger and Harper (1997). Fama (1965) is the initial statement of the efficient market hypothesis, and Modigliani and Miller (1962) presents their "theorem." Mandelbrot (1997) puts together much of his work beginning in the 1960s on fat-tailed distributions in pricing and other areas.

Markowitz (1952) on portfolio selection is the cornerstone for all subsequent finance theory. Black and Scholes (1973) and Merton (1973) set out derivations of the BSM option pricing equation based on statistical physics. The discussion of option pricing in the text takes off from Derman and

Taleb (2005). Samuelson (1968) and Davidson (2003) talk past each other about ergodicity.

Barberis and Thaler (2003) surveys behavioral finance through the early 2000s; the main ideas were well in place by then. Weitzman (2007) and Akerlof and Shiller (2009) are the pieces discussed in the text. On the side of anthropology, Ho (2009) provides a fascinating ethnography of Wall Street.

President Ronald Reagan's remarks in the signing ceremony for the Garn–St. Germain Act are available at http://www.reagan.utexas.edu/archives/speeches/1982/101582b.htm. For a retrospective view of the 2004 SEC decision regarding the New York investment banks, see Stephen Labaton, "Agency's '04 Rule Let Banks Pile Up New Debt," *New York Times*, October 2, 2008. The Harry Reid quotation is from the *Washington Post*, March 4, 2005. The Bill Clinton quotation is from http://blogs.abcnews.com/politicalpunch/2010/04/clinton-rubin-and-summers-gave-me-wrong- advice-on-derivatives-and-i-was-wrong-to-take-it.html.

Reports with partially overlapping authorship by Alexander et al. (2008) and Brunnermeier et al. (2009) provide essential background on regulation. The discussion here draws on them. Soros (2009) is helpful as well. Lindblom (1977) is a thoughtful analysis of how the state and business interact.

— 8 —

The International Dimension

Historically, *open economy macroeconomics* was developed to analyze the behavior of a single economy open to trade with the capital account lurking in the background. The models were later extended in haphazard fashion to deal explicitly with capital movements and the interactions of separate economies in *global macroeconomics*. The latter shows that the whole system behaves differently from the sum of its parts—no surprise for anyone who has read Keynes. This chapter addresses this material, with an eye toward the current global macro situation. Another book would be required to cover the field in depth. Only a few highpoints can be brought up here.

In an economy closed to all international transactions—for the most part the sort of economy analyzed in the *General Theory* and the preceding chapters—key questions center on the direction of macro-level causality. Does Say's Law or the principle of effective demand generally apply? Regarding distribution, does labor or capital have the upper hand in the strife of the two souls? In finance, how far has a tendency toward fragility and instability as discussed in Chapter 7 advanced?

For a single economy these questions are not easy to answer. In international macro with two or more national systems, additional difficulties immediately arise. Each country acquires at least three souls, for there is potential distributive conflict among its own recipients of labor and capital income as well as with the rest of the world. Some economies may be largely supply-constrained (often for poor countries by acute shortages of foreign exchange), while output in others is determined by effective demand. Cross-border financial flows interact with macro causal linkages on the real side and make the regulatory issues discussed in Chapter 7 more tangled.

Patterns of macro causality not only are interwoven across economies but also shift over time, in many cases for institutional reasons. How the capital and current accounts of the balance of payments, which must sum to zero, affect each other is the most important example. It already came up in Chapter 3 and reappears below in a quick historical and institutional summary of how the international system and the position of the United States within it evolved after World War II.

The next topic is an expanded presentation of the international economic accounting already outlined in Chapters 1 and 3. Determination of the exchange rate—the central price in an open system—is then analyzed from various angles. Nominal and real exchange rates emerge as key prices regulating output and employment levels across economies, and so influence the behavior of the global system. Tomorrow morning when you pick up the *Wall Street Journal* or *Financial Times*, you will likely find one or another of two dozen theories of the exchange rate and its impacts being ardently advanced. *Caveat lector* regarding how the rate is determined and what it affects!

One group of theories includes long-term effects of real-side developments on the real exchange rate, purchasing power parity, interest rate parity, and impacts of speculative capital movements. They can help explain how the rate behaves, with spillovers to the rest of the economy. The parity theories are also of interest because they are closely connected with Keynes.

A second group of models grew out of IS/LM in an attempt to incorporate capital and current accounts within a coherent frame. They include elasticities and absorption approaches to analyzing the trade account, the Mundell-Fleming and portfolio balance models of current and capital accounts, and full accounting along lines set out by Wynne Godley, which embeds open economies into the global system. These theories focus on current account adjustment associated with exchange rate changes and movements in the capital account. Quick presentations of other orthodox approaches round out the discussion.

With all this theory in hand, an effort is made to sort out causal linkages in the global macroeconomy going into the 2010s. The chapter ends with a summary of the key policy questions at hand.

Global Economic Governance

The post–Bretton Woods deregulation of international capital flows as sketched in Chapter 7 was but one aspect of a general thrust toward liberalization of all economic relationships that came to dominate policy formulation after the 1940s. The history of global economic governance of trade and monetary arrangements serves as background for changes in balance-of-payments positions that have been observed.

Governance of Trade

During the early 1940s Keynes wrestled with ideas for remaking the world economy after the war. Full employment and avoidance of debt deflation were his top priorities. Along with many others he wanted to prevent the reemergence of the beggar-my-neighbor policies that were rife in the 1930s. International economic cooperation organized around recognized institutions could further these goals. Liberalizing trade and international finance was certainly not his principal concern.

We have already seen in Chapter 1 how two of a trio of institutions that he proposed—the International Monetary Fund and the World Bank—had their missions diverted toward liberalization, especially after the conservative uprising in the 1970s. His third proposed institution—an International Trade Organization or ITO—was stillborn even though a charter was negotiated at a conference in Havana in 1947, the year after Keynes died. The reason it failed was that the U.S. Congress balked at the ITO's powers of intervention into internal economic affairs. Something called the *General Agreement on Tariffs and Trade* (the *GATT* for short) that had also been adopted in Havana *was* accepted by Congress. It served as a forum for negotiation over trade conflicts until it was succeeded by the *World Trade Organization (WTO)*, set up in 1995.

The ideological rationale for GATT/WTO actions and deliberations is the doctrine of free trade established by Ricardo and partially repudiated by Keynes. If you have never seen a coven of free traders in one room, go to a WTO meeting in Geneva! The practicality of their negotiations, however, is unabashedly mercantilist. It involves horse trading and logrolling among blocs of countries, each with its own special interests, over reductions in tariffs and other trade barriers such as quotas on imports. Substantial reductions in protection for manufactured products over successive "rounds" of negotiation were attained. In 2008 a *Doha Round* bogged down over disagreements between rich and poor countries about protection for agriculture, industry, services, and intellectual property rights. Meanwhile the United States and the EU were squabbling over the relative demerits of their particular systems for subsidizing agriculture.

The thrust toward trade liberalization paid off in the sense that the ratio of all the world's imports to its GDP (in real terms) more than doubled from 13% to 29% between 1970 and the mid-2000s. This increase in trade represented rising export injections of demand for all economies. Both mainstream economists and structuralists such as Kaldor (recall Figure 5.2) emphasize that expanding exports can serve as an engine of growth. Time series data at the country level indicate that correlation between export and output growth is often (though not always) observed.

The GATT/WTO apparatus also provides quasi-judicial mechanisms for countries to launch complaints against one another about "excessive" protectionism (or lack of protection for intellectual property). One example has been an ongoing attempt by Brazil and other developing countries to persuade the WTO to impose sanctions on the United States for its subsidies to domestic cotton growers. Late in 2009 Brazil's right to impose sanctions was approved by the WTO; whether the United States would change its practices remained to be seen.

Monetary Arrangements

Although much ink has been spilled about their differences, Harry Dexter White and John Maynard Keynes came to the Bretton Woods conference with complementary plans for post–World War II international monetary arrangements. Keynes wanted to set up an *International Clearing Union* or *ICU* in which countries with current account surpluses would have to deposit funds and from which countries with deficits could borrow or run up overdrafts. Transactions were to be denominated in a new unit of account, which Keynes called *bancor*. White saw the dollar as the unit of account but thought that an ICU should intervene more actively in the system, accepting deposits of securities and advancing repos counter-cyclically to economies undertaking foreign net borrowing.

As already discussed in Chapter 1, both proposals fell by the wayside, replaced by the IMF's conditionality-laden pro-cyclical interventions to attack current account deficits. Be that as it may, the Bretton Woods system as it emerged—with closed capital accounts and fixed exchange rates—did provide part of the international framework that supported the golden age. Moreover, as the financial crises around both the developed and developing world beginning in the 1970s demonstrate, capital market liberalization after the Bretton Woods system broke down did not lead to improved real economic performance. It did generate enormous international capital movements and the proliferation of derivatives. With that genie out of the bottle, global economic policymaking has become much more difficult than it was in the financially stodgy Bretton Woods period—for better or for worse.

The Position of the United States

The U.S. position in the global economy has shifted markedly over the decades. Emerging from the war, the United States was clearly the international hegemon (in a favorite label from Charlie Kindleberger), but its potency deteriorated over time. Following Hyman Minsky's schematic from Table 3.1, Table 8.1 illustrates world payments flows in the early postwar period (late 1940s and early 1950s).

At the time, developing countries had no significant debt after a period of high export prices for raw materials; debt service obligations among the rich countries were ill-defined. As a consequence, international payments of interest and dividends were minimal. The United States had a strong trade surplus, so its overall current account $(+A)$ was positive. On capital account there were large flows from the United States to the rest of the world of long-term investment $(-B)$ and transfers $(-C)$ supporting postwar reconstruction.

These flows exceeded the current account surplus and had to be offset by movements of short-term capital and/or changes in reserves. On the U.S. side the capital inflow $(+D)$ took the form of increasing foreign deposits in money center banks and sales of Treasury bonds abroad. These dollar "exports" added liquidity and propelled credit expansion by banking systems in the rest of the world.

The structure of international payments outlined in Table 8.1 was a foundation for historically rapid and stable output growth worldwide during the golden age in the 1950s and 1960s. Other supporting factors were the stable Bretton Woods system of exchange rates and the reconstruction boom. Perhaps unsurprisingly the long bonanza carried the seeds of its

Table 8.1 Schematic balance-of-payments flows around 1950

	USA	Rest of world
1. Interest and dividends	0	0
2. Trade and services	$+A$	$-A$
1 + 2	$+A$	$-A$
3. Long-term investments	$-B$	$+B$
4. Unilateral transfers	$-C$	$+C$
1 + 2 + 3 + 4	$-D$	$+D$
5. Short-term capital, changes in reserves	$+D$	$-D$
1 + 2 + 3 + 4 + 5	0	0

own destruction in the form of dynamics of stocks and flows over time (a point neglected by Keynes but emphasized by Minsky and Godley).

The problem was that the long-term capital movements from the United States exceeded its short-term capital inflows. The resulting increase in net foreign assets meant that interest and dividend income rose from approximately zero in Table 8.1. With both major components of the current account positive, on capital account there would have to be ever-rising U.S. foreign investment and transfers $[-(B + C)]$, or reduced short-term inflows $(+D)$.

While these capital movements went on, the United States also maintained a strong exchange rate. The result was increasing net export penetration from abroad, which ultimately pushed the United States to emulate Great Britain under the high gold standard by "going negative" on the trade and service account. (Recall the discussion in Chapter 3.) For reasons detailed below, the international payments system has very few means to adjust, or *degrees of freedom*. Recognizing this fact, Robert Triffin invented a *dilemma* to describe the situation. So long as the United States undertook positive long-term investment abroad, it would need to run a trade and services deficit to permit short-term capital inflows to generate liquidity for the rest of the world. Deficits began to show up sporadically in the 1970s. The other horn of the dilemma was that the United States presumably could not sustain deficits indefinitely (another stock flow argument).

Dollar devaluation might ultimately be needed to reduce the U.S. current account gap.

Triffin's proposed remedy was to create an international reserve currency to take the burden off the United States; that is, he wanted to revive the ideas of Keynes and White leading into Bretton Woods. The institutional response that actually occurred was to give the IMF power to issue *special drawing rights (SDR)* to serve as an international reserve asset. SDRs in practice never got anywhere. There was no felt need for them because, beginning with Eurodollars and expanding exponentially thereafter, the world financial system could produce international liquidity without limit.

Numbers for the United States and Partners

In any case the overall U.S. current account (the sum of lines 1 and 2 in Table 8.1) turned permanently negative in the early 1980s. We have already seen in Chapter 5 how private consumption became the engine of growth. Whether the consumption surge propelled the trade deficit or vice versa remains controversial, as discussed below. As illustrated by the evolution of foreign net borrowing in Figures 5.8 and 5.9, the process took time. For the period after 1980 it is possible to insert numbers into the format of Table 8.1. Table 8.2 takes up the story for selected years through 2008, presenting payments flows as shares of world GDP. There are entries for the United States and the rest of the world. The changing positions of several key countries (as data for them become available) are summarized in the columns to the right. Several points stand out.

By 1980, U.S. interest and dividend income from abroad had risen to 0.26% of world GDP. The overall current account was still positive but small (0.1%), and short-term capital movements were negligible. Already in 1983 the configuration of flows had begun to shift markedly. Driven by a deteriorating trade balance, the current account became visibly negative (−0.18%). With continuing net foreign investment and transfers (mostly the latter in 1983), short-term capital movements toward the United States reappeared at 0.34%. But now the United States was issuing short-term liabilities to finance foreign investment and transfers *plus* a current account deficit, not investment and transfers *minus* a current surplus as during the golden age. Its hegemonic role was beginning to erode.

The situation deteriorated further after 1983. As a share of world GDP, dividend and interest income hovered at or below 0.1% until 2008, and the trade and services account steadily worsened until the crisis hit in that

Table 8.2 Balance-of-payments flows—selected years 1980–2008 (percentage shares of world GDP)

	Total transactions		Of which			
	USA	RofW	Japan	Germany	China	OPEC
1980						
Interest and dividends	0.26	−0.26	0.01			
Trade and services	−0.16	0.16	−0.08			
Long-term investment	−0.02	0.02	0.01			
Unilateral transfers	−0.07	0.07	0.00			
Short-term capital	0.00	0.00	-0.01			
Total	0.00	0.00	-0.08			
1983						
Interest and dividends	0.30	−0.30	−0.01			
Trade and services	−0.48	0.48	−0.17			
Long-term investment	−0.02	0.02	0.00			
Unilateral transfers	−0.14	0.14	0.00			
Short-term capital	0.34	−0.34	0.03			
Total	0.00	0.00	−0.14			
1986						
Interest and dividends	0.10	−0.10	−0.03	−0.01		
Trade and services	−0.91	0.91	−0.35	−0.13		
Long-term investment	0.07	−0.07	0.04	0.01		
Unilateral transfers	−0.16	0.16	0.00	0.00		
Short-term capital	0.89	−0.89	0.12	0.02		
Total	0.00	0.00	−0.21	−0.11		
1992						
Interest and dividends	0.10	−0.10	−0.01	0.01		
Trade and services	−0.16	0.16	−0.15	−0.04		
Long-term investment	−0.12	0.12	0.01	0.00		
Unilateral transfers	−0.15	0.15	0.00	0.01		
Short-term capital	0.33	−0.33	0.14	0.06		
Total	0.00	0.00	−0.01	0.04		
1994						
Interest and dividends	0.06	−0.06	−0.03	0.00		
Trade and services	−0.37	0.37	−0.19	−0.05		
Long-term investment	−0.13	0.13	0.01	0.01		

Table 8.2 (continued)

	Total transactions		Of which			
	USA	RofW	Japan	Germany	China	OPEC
Unilateral transfers	−0.15	0.15	0.00	0.00		
Short-term capital	0.58	−0.58	0.10	0.03		
Total	0.00	0.00	−0.11	0.00		
1999						
Interest and dividends	0.04	−0.04	−0.06	−0.01	−0.01	0.00
Trade and services	−0.85	0.85	−0.19	−0.09	−0.22	−0.04
Long-term investment	0.21	−0.21	0.00	0.06	−0.01	0.00
Unilateral transfers	−0.16	0.16	0.00	0.00	0.00	0.00
Short-term capital	0.76	−0.76	−0.05	−0.01	0.05	0.03
Total	0.00	0.00	−0.31	−0.04	−0.19	−0.01
2002						
Interest and dividends	0.08	−0.08	−0.06	0.03	−0.02	0.00
Trade and services	−1.27	1.27	−0.18	−0.12	−0.31	−0.09
Long-term investment	−0.21	0.21	−0.01	0.00	0.00	−0.01
Unilateral transfers	−0.20	0.20	0.00	0.00	0.00	0.00
Short-term capital	1.59	−1.59	0.14	0.09	0.23	−0.01
Total	0.00	0.00	−0.11	−0.01	−0.10	−0.12
2006						
Interest and dividends	0.10	−0.10	−0.08	−0.01	−0.05	0.00
Trade and services	−1.55	1.55	−0.15	−0.12	−0.47	−0.20
Long-term investment	0.00	0.00	0.03	0.08	−0.01	−0.01
Unilateral transfers	−0.19	0.19	0.00	0.00	0.00	−0.03
Short-term capital	1.64	−1.64	−0.02	0.13	0.49	0.08
Total	0.00	0.00	−0.22	0.08	−0.04	−0.16
2008						
Interest and dividends	0.19	−0.19	−0.05	0.01	−0.07	0.00
Trade and services	−1.14	1.14	−0.10	−0.08	−0.43	−0.28
Long-term investment	−0.02	0.02	0.06	0.00	−0.03	−0.01
Unilateral transfers	−0.21	0.21	0.00	0.00	0.00	−0.02
Short-term capital	1.18	−1.18	−0.01	−0.04	0.77	0.14
Total	0.00	0.00	−0.09	−0.11	0.24	−0.16

Sources: BEA—U.S. International Transactions Accounts Data, September 16, 2009; and IMF—World Economic Outlook Database, October 2009, for World GDP in current U.S. dollars.

year. (The early 1990s were an exception, when recession, exports of military services for the Gulf War against Iraq, and the dollar devaluation orchestrated at the September 1985 *Plaza Accord* among leading economies permitted some relief.) In most years long-term investment and transfers continued to be negative items, but their importance diminished in comparison to the trade deficit. By the mid-2000s short-term capital inflows were 1.6% of world GDP—a macroeconomically important movement of funds.

The U.S. deficit on trade and services of course had to be met by surpluses in the rest of the world. Japan made a significant though declining contribution after a peak of 0.35% in 1986. (It was a major player in the Plaza agreement.) Germany also had a structural surplus. After 1999, when data become available, it is clear that surpluses on the part of China and OPEC contributed strongly to the U.S. deficit. All four were also sources of significant short-term capital inflows. The balancing items for the countries concerned, especially China, took the form of large increases in international reserves. (Remember from Chapter 1 that reserve increases equal the difference between the current account and the private capital account surpluses.)

The reserve growth outside the United States can be interpreted as being defensive in part, to build up a hedge against replays of the Latin American crises in the 1980s and the Asian crises a decade later. But it was also the counterpart of the consumption-led U.S. trade deficit. The gap had to be financed by rising capital inflows, which to a large extent took the form of acquisition of U.S. Treasury and government-sponsored agency bonds (issued by Fannie Mae and Freddie Mac) by foreign central banks. Diversification of these holdings into *sovereign wealth funds* and other vehicles got under way in the 2000s, but as a share of world GDP it has not advanced very far.

As shown in Figures 5.8 and 5.9 and the entries for 2008 in Table 8.2, the U.S. payments situation began to change with the onset of crisis; there was at least a modest reduction in net short-term lending from the rest of the world. Whether the economy can switch back toward external current balance or even a surplus is an open question.

The Dance of the Dollar

The stream of short-term capital toward the United States that began in the 1950s during the period of *dollar shortage* led ultimately to a *dollar glut* in the 1970s. It helped support generally expansionary macro policy during the golden age. As Triffin observed, there were also increasing pressures for dollar devaluation. A series of crises began in 1960 involving runs against gold and the dollar. The first wave prompted the interest equalization tax and the birth of Eurocurrency markets noted in Chapter 7. There was a second crisis in 1967, forcing the Fed to raise interest rates. When it relaxed its stance, funds moved back toward Europe, setting off the next crisis in 1969.

The dam finally broke in 1971, when President Nixon closed the window to trade in gold and subsequently devalued the dollar against the metal, imposed a 10% tariff surcharge on Japanese imports, and negotiated appreciations of other currencies. A final crisis in 1973 involved another run against the dollar and led to the establishment of a global system of floating exchange rates, more or less manipulated by central banks.

Since that time the United States has on the whole pursued a policy of benign neglect of its exchange rate. (The main exception was the 1985 Plaza agreement mentioned above.) Figure 8.1 shows how the dollar fared against other major currencies.

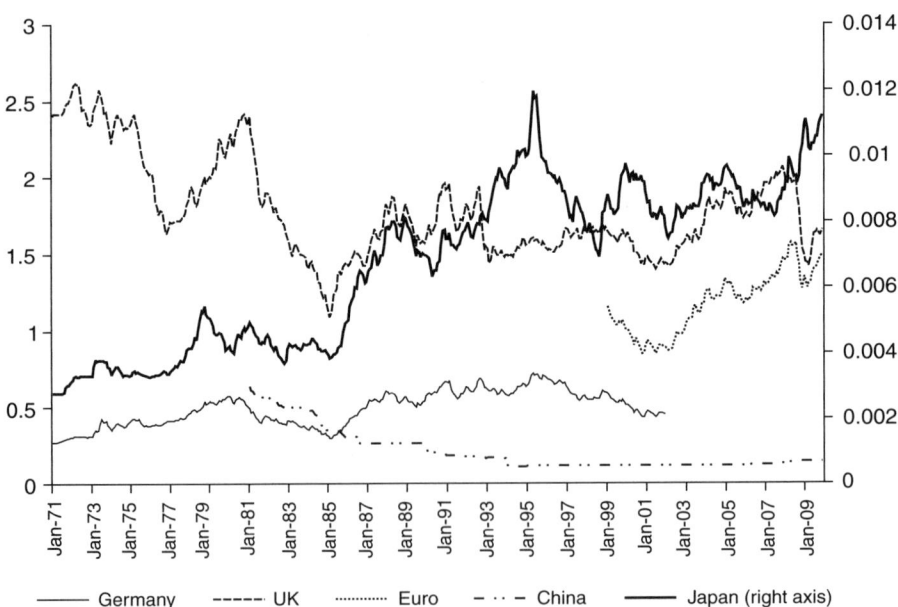

Figure 8.1 U.S. bilateral exchange rates (U.S. dollars per unit of foreign currency, monthly data)

Until the mid-1990s there was fairly steady depreciation against the yen boosted by the Plaza arrangement. Reasons involving relative interest rates for the subsequent fluctuations are discussed below. There was minor depreciation against the Deutschmark through the 1990s, followed by a more steady weakening of the dollar against its successor currency, the euro. The pound sterling also benefited from this trend until crisis hit. Beginning in the 1980s the dollar tended to appreciate against the renminbi, which was aggressively managed by the Chinese authorities. Currency devaluation contributed significantly to China's rising surplus on trade and services as a share of world GDP which stands out in Table 8.2.

Balance-of-Payments Accounting

With this sketch of global economic relationships and macroeconomic balances in hand, we can try to delve deeper in open economy macro analysis. Much policy discussion suffers from a lack of understanding about balance-of-payments adjustment mechanisms. The descriptions to follow are an attempt to sort them out. The time frame in which various flows adjust turns out to be a central issue. Some components of an economy's external balances change more rapidly than others. In each case the exchange rate plays a different role. That's why arguments about it are often so confusing.

Restating the accounting described in Chapter 1 and used in Tables 8.1 and 8.2, Table 8.3 gives a schematic description of the balance of payments between a home country with the dollar ($) as its unit of account and a foreign country using the euro (€). The two-country case is a template for thinking about a global economy encompassing many countries. I mostly do not go beyond two in the models summarized here.

The accounting rule built into the table is that total inflows should equal total outflows, or the sums of the entries in the left-hand and right-hand columns should be equal. To make the equality possible, all entries must be stated in dollars. The *nominal spot exchange rate e* is the scaling factor between euros and dollars, multiplying the entries in brackets which are valued in euros. The rate is defined in units of dollars to one euro. (In practice it took a value of around 1.35 in spring 2010.) Factor payments and the trade account in the table sum to the current account as usually stated. As in Chapter 1, each country's current account and capital account (including changes in reserves) must sum to zero.

In the time units relevant to most policy questions in macroeconomics

Table 8.3 Components of the balance of payments (in $ or "home currency")

Inflows (sources)		Outflows (uses)
	Factor payments	
e[Interest and dividends to home private sector (€)]		Interest and dividends to foreign private sector ($)
e[Interest on home reserves (€)]		Interest on foreign reserves ($)
	Trade account	
Exports ($)		e[Imports (€)]
	Capital account	
Increase in home liabilities to foreign private sector ($)		e[Increase in foreign liabilities to home private sector (€)]
Increase in foreign reserves ($)		e[Increase in home reserves (€)]

—ranging from weeks to a few years—adjustment in the capital account at the bottom of the table can be blindingly fast. The details involve the home economy's *net foreign assets* or *NFA,* which, following the discussion in Chapter 1, can be written as

NFA = e[Net foreign liabilities to home private sector (€)]
 + e[Home reserves (€)] − Net home liabilities to
 foreign private sector ($) − Foreign reserves ($).

As the currency symbols indicate, the home private sector's net holdings of euro-denominated liabilities plus the home central bank's reserves (typically liabilities of the foreign government) are the economy's gross foreign assets. Its gross dollar-denominated liabilities are held by the foreign private sector and central bank.

NFA can change in two ways. *If* net foreign liabilities to the home economy are positive, an increase in the exchange rate would generate a capital gain, because depreciation makes euro liabilities held at home more valuable in terms of dollars. (The other side of the coin is that the Chinese authorities are not keen to have the renminbi-dollar exchange rate go down or appreciate, creating a capital loss on their dollar-denominated reserves.)

The caveat is that the private sector, or an important segment of it, may be a net debtor in foreign currency terms. That is,

[Net foreign liabilities to home private sector (€)] = [Euro liabilities held by home (€)] − [Home liabilities in euros held abroad (€)].

This accounting is relevant because, in just one example, in the 2000s Polish households took mortgages in Swiss francs, but their incomes and assets were priced in zlotys. Devaluation of the zloty affected both their income flows and balance sheets adversely. There have been many similar instances in developing countries worldwide. In such circumstances, through income and wealth effects, devaluation is likely to have a contractionary effect on domestic output. In the academic literature the inability of many counties to borrow in terms of their own currency is called *original sin*, with a theological justification that I have never been able to fathom.

The other way that the NFA can shift is through national saving (or negative net foreign borrowing as discussed in connection with Figures 5.8 and 5.9). These flows take place over weeks and months. By contrast, an exchange trader in the foreign country can buy home liabilities, say U.S. Treasury bonds, with a point and a click (or, increasingly the case, her preprogrammed computer can make the transaction in milliseconds). This operation creates a *capital inflow* into the home country.

When the purchase is transacted, NFA must stay basically constant because trade and factor payments take much longer to complete. But the euros the trader spends for home's liabilities must go somewhere. The most likely destination is an increase in euro-denominated home reserves (because the seller of the home liabilities will probably turn the euros over to the banking system). Monetary expansions in developing countries provoked by reserve increases were an important factor leading into their financial collapses from the 1970s through the 1990s. The crises occurred when capital inflow manias in those countries switched into Kindleberger-Soros crashes. They are an important reason why China and other countries built up massive foreign exchange reserves in the 2000s. Those countries wanted to protect themselves against external crises set off by sudden stops in external lending and massive capital flight.

An additional implication of NFA accounting is that an uncontrolled (or partially controlled) nominal exchange rate has to be determined somehow in capital markets. Various mechanisms are set out below. Trade and factor payments flows occur too slowly to have much effect on the rate when capital markets are liberalized, an institutional transition that began with the breakdown of the Bretton Woods system—which featured fixed exchange rates and strong controls on capital movements—in the early 1970s. Among rich economies, financial capital movements are now virtually instantaneous and unregulated.

"Fundamentals," Portfolio Balance, and the Exchange Rate

As emphasized above, there are many theories about the exchange rate. We are back to the blind men and the elephant. Yet along with the wage and interest rate, it is a crucial macroeconomic price. The goal (or hope!) of the following presentation is to put the theories, or descriptions of the elephant, into some sort of coherent frame. One overriding theme is "fundamentals" for the rate, or the lack of same. There are many candidates, meaning that it is impossible to produce a generally applicable theory. The exchange rate thrives in a badly overdetermined environment.

Nominal and Real Exchange Rate

The spot rate e appearing in Table 8.3 is a *nominal* variable. In practice a *real* exchange rate can be defined in at least two ways:

$$\text{Definition 1: Real rate} = e \times \text{Traded goods price index / Home price index}$$

and

$$\text{Definition 2: Real rate} = \text{Price index of traded goods / Price index of non-tradeds.}$$

In definition 1, the traded (or "tradable") goods price index is often approximated by a weighted average of the GDP deflators of the home country's trading partners. In the denominator the index could be home's own GDP deflator.

In definition 2, services are typical *non-traded goods*. Most people do not import haircuts, takeout Chinese, or the plumber's ministrations (though financial and business service payments certainly do cross borders, for example, service exports from India after the outsourcing boom got under way). The home consumer price index is often used as a proxy for prices of non-tradeds in the numerator of the ratio and the wholesale price index in the denominator. We obviously are not talking about precise estimates; crude approximations would be a better description.

Because the *level* of an index is arbitrary, in practice we can investigate only how a real rate changes in response to changes in the ratios on the right-hand sides of the definitions. In definition 1, if the nominal rate e is constant and home inflation is faster than foreign inflation, then the real rate will decrease or appreciate. Keynes was not immune to the effects of differential rates of inflation, as discussed below.

Long-Run Exchange Rate

Despite the fact that financial markets adjust much more rapidly than trade flows, it is still true that the level of the real exchange rate responds to forces coming from the price/quantity side of the economy. In the macro policy context two linkages are important.

One is that in some "long run" in an economy with sustained per capita income growth supported by rising productivity, the real exchange rate according to both definitions should get stronger, or appreciate. As we have seen, in a closed economy productivity increases are fully passed through into higher real wages in steady state growth. In an economy open to trade, real appreciation is a means to this end because it boosts the real wage through cheaper imports of goods and services, not excluding foreign travel. Policymakers may resist this trend, however, because they want a weak currency to stimulate employment creation through export-led growth. The Chinese authorities wrestle with this dilemma, along with the complication noted above that renminbi appreciation would impose big capital losses on their hoard of dollar reserves. Chances are that over time, Chinese consumers' desires for cheap foreign products will carry the day—but it may take a while.

The real rate can also respond to the economy's long-run position with regard to foreign trade, as influenced from the supply side by developments in the real economy. For example, the Canadian loonie was roughly at par with the U.S. dollar in the mid-1970s, fell to around sixty-five U.S. cents in the early 2000s, and then recovered to par value with the opening up of oil shale extraction.

Purchasing Power Parity

The nominal spot exchange rate can interact with the real rate in complicated ways. Suppose that the real rate from definition 1 is stable and conveniently scaled to equal 1. Then we get back to *purchasing power parity* or *PPP*, an old idea already mentioned in Chapter 2. It is based on arbitrage among commodity prices, saying that exchange rates should adjust so that prices for "similar" goods in two countries will be close. PPP is a hardy fundamental, without much empirical bite.

Roughly speaking, the relationship

$$\text{Home price index} = e \times \text{Foreign price index}$$

should apply. If the level of *border prices* on the right side is smaller than a home price index, then traded goods are relatively cheap or the real exchange rate is strong. It should presumably generate a trade deficit. Along Hume's lines (Chapter 2), the situation may become unsustainable, to be resolved by a devaluation.

PPP price convergence at the micro level is never observed, but big violations can imply exchange rate misalignment. Converted at the ruling nominal rate between the two countries, the bolivar price of ice cream in Venezuela should be about the same as the peso price in Chile plus transport costs. The fact that Venezuela often imports ice cream from its distant neighbor to the south suggests that the bolivar is overvalued (although I might add that *chirimoya alegre* ice cream from Chile is *very* good).

Following definition 2, the rationale is that, as in many resource-exporting economies with ample access to foreign exchange (as in Canada, with its newly exploitable oil shale), a price index in Venezuela of traded goods such as ice cream is often low relative to an index for non-traded goods. Incentives are biased in favor of non-traded goods production, so that the local ice cream supply is zero or very small. In the academic literature Venezuela's problem is labeled the *Dutch disease* in honor of the exchange appreciation and degree of deindustrialization which followed natural gas discoveries in the Netherlands in the 1960s. (In fact the phenomenon was first noted after gold discoveries in Australia a century before.) The traded/non-traded goods price ratio is one more fundamental against which the exchange rate is often judged. As will be seen below, Dutch disease considerations figure strongly in contemporary mainstream views about global macroeconomics.

Maynard and PPP

As noted above, looking at comparative inflation rates in two countries provides perspective on PPP. If inflation is faster in the home country than abroad, then to keep the real exchange rate constant, its nominal rate of devaluation should follow the rule

Rate of devaluation = Home inflation rate − Foreign inflation rate.

Thereby hangs a tale.

Oswald "Foxy" Falk was a London money man who became a close friend of Keynes in the 1910s. He imparted much of the business lore which Keynes later wrote into Chapter 12 of the *General Theory*. In 1919 Foxy and Maynard set up a "Syndicate" (these days it would be called a hedge fund) to speculate in currencies. They borrowed heavily in early 1920 to sell several European currencies short and buy dollars and Indian rupees. Their decisions were guided by the PPP relationship just sketched as well as interest rate parity as discussed below.

During the spring of 1920 the European currencies rose against sterling and the dollar and rupee fell. (You can see some of the evidence in charts in the *Tract on Monetary Reform*.) Keynes had made exactly the wrong bets, and the Syndicate was wiped out. He did recover his position using loans from friends, family, and an obliging capitalist to set up a new syndicate which made the right currency wagers; he later went on to make a great deal of money. Although its dealings were supposedly based on sound theory, the Syndicate was Maynard's major speculative blunder. You never really know which way an exchange rate is going to move.

Interest Rate Parity

Interest rate parity (*IRP*, also called *UIP* for "uncovered" or unhedged IRP) can be interpreted as either a theory of interest rate determination or an explanation of the rate of growth of the exchange rate. It can also underlie pro-cyclical interactions between national economies and the international capital market.

Keynes presented the idea in the *Tract on Monetary Reform*, treating it as a theory of the exchange rate. We will come back to that, but as a lead-in about interest rates, a standard interpretation of IRP says that

Home interest rate = Foreign interest rate + Expected growth rate of the exchange rate.

(The reason to use the proportional or percentage growth of the exchange rate is to give it the same time dimension as interest—a rate per unit of time.) If I take a loan from abroad, the local cost of paying it back in the future will be the interest on it plus a capital loss on the foreign debt due to depreciation. Arbitrage between borrowing at home and abroad should make the cost of the foreign loan equal to the home interest rate.

This form of arbitrage is never complete, but an interest rate linkage can be expected when capital markets have been liberalized. In developing countries it can be highly destabilizing. Historically they have had to pay a *premium* over international rates which reflects (among other factors) expected depreciation of the local currency. If capital inflows into a country speed up and its foreign reserves begin to rise, foreign investors often anticipate exchange rate appreciation (or at least less rapid depreciation) for reasons discussed below in connection with the portfolio balance model. Consequently they reduce the premium. The implication from IRP is that local interest rate will fall, at a time when the central bank should be tightening policy in advance of a boom.

This pro-cyclicality can get worse after a capital inflow bubble bursts. External investors will anticipate devaluation and increase the relevant interest rate premium, pushing up the local rate just when the central bank should be pursuing expansionary policy.

IRP and Forward Exchange Rates

The equation above can be restated to make IRP into a theory of the exchange rate,

Expected growth rate of the exchange rate =
Home interest rate − foreign interest rate,

so that for a country with a high local interest rate one should expect devaluation.

Suppose that along the lines of rational expectations analysis as discussed in Chapter 7 investors have short-term perfect foresight (at least). Then the theory would say that the

Observed growth rate of the exchange rate =
Home interest rate − foreign interest rate.

Inventing the intertemporal arbitrage-based reasoning used in Chapter 7 to discuss option pricing, Keynes interpreted the "observed" growth rate as the difference between spot and forward exchange rates quoted in the market. From the *Tract* we learn that "[i]f by lending dollars in New York for one month the lender could earn interest at 5½% per annum, whereas by lending sterling in London for one month he could earn interest at 4%[,] then . . . forward quotations for the purchase of the currency of dearer money market tend to be cheaper . . . [by] the excess of the interest which can be earned in a month in the dearer market over what can be earned in the cheaper" (4:103–104).

That is, to equalize the returns on the two loans, the one-month forward price of the dollar against sterling will be discounted against spot in response to the interest rate discrepancy. In "thick" markets in which contracts can be easily hedged (say, the markets among dollars, euros, sterling, and yen), IRP holds, at least in normal times. But times are not always normal.

Speculative Capital Movements and Carry Trade

As discussed by Keynes, IRP is an arbitrage condition that will be enforced by agile traders in the market for forward exchange rates. We saw in Chapter 7 how such relationships may (or may not) apply in other financial markets. Despite the fact that it is an arbitrage relationship, the IRP formula looks paradoxical. Insofar as the forward dollar/sterling rate is a good predictor of the spot rate one month hence, IRP seems to imply that in a country with a low interest rate, the currency will appreciate over time. One can read from Figure 8.1 that such a trend in fact applied between Japan and the United States after the mid-1990s. (That is, the way the figure is drawn, the dollar/yen rate rose or depreciated.) The dollar, however, fell by only around 1% per year, while the interest rate spread between Japan and the United States was far wider.

Already in 1983 Hyman Minsky was asking why speculators shouldn't be moving funds out of the low interest rate country to get higher returns abroad (on the implicit expectation that the return differential would persist, at least for a time). That sort of move is called a *carry trade* because an asset such as a foreign bond with a high interest rate generates a "carry," or return, if one just holds on to it.

The portfolio balance model discussed just below suggests that the currency in the low interest rate country should weaken in response to the financial outflow. Simply put, there is a shift in portfolio preferences against liabilities issued at home so that their international price—the exchange rate—should depreciate.

Instead of the IRP equation for exchange rate growth, we should have

Observed growth rate of the home exchange rate =
$A \times$ (Foreign interest rate − home interest rate),

with A as an "adjustment parameter."

Carry trade transactions became important beginning in the 1990s, when *Mrs. Watanabe,* the personification of Japanese asset holders, began to shift money out of her country into better-paying precincts abroad. (She was later joined by many non-Japanese borrowing enthusiastically in yen to acquire third-country liabilities worldwide.) Iceland was one example, with the krona appreciating strongly against the yen. There were also carry trade flows toward the United States—hundreds of billions of dollars per year—but as just noted, the yen still appreciated slowly against the dollar. One interpretation is that portfolio balance and interest rate parity effects were pulling in opposite directions, and gradual dollar depreciation was the outcome.

In addition, strongly pro-cyclical financial market responses were provoked. The mechanisms differed, but the outcomes resembled the developing country cycles discussed above. Note in Figure 5.15 how the U.S. interest rate began to swing up in response to a move by the Fed toward restrictive policy in 2004–5. The financial economist Jane d'Arista observes that the rate increase spurred carry trade purchases of dollar liabilities. Most of the capital inflow, which was twice as big as the current account deficit, went to financial institutions. Some of the foreign money supported their speculative investments at home—offsetting the Fed's attempt at monetary restraint—and some went back abroad as the United States assumed an entrepôt function for global markets. Foreign country central banks often sterilized the reverse flows to hold their exchange rates stable and redirected the money back toward the United States, frustrating attempts to impose restrictive monetary policy worldwide in a pro-cyclical financial round robin.

The carry trade thus helped exacerbate the increase in U.S. financial system leverage discussed in Chapter 4. The flows began to reverse in 2007, feeding into the deleveraging process then getting under way. The carry trade was one more factor stimulating the bubble and crash.

Portfolio Balance

The *portfolio balance* model provides another way to think about floating exchange rates. It was set up in the 1960s (in part under James Tobin's inspiration) to argue that the exchange rate helps clear capital markets. The idea was that in a two-country LM-style world there will be four financial markets—for domestically created money supplies and bonds from both countries. As the model was originally proposed, the money supplies were set by the authorities in both countries using open market operations with both bonds. Then presumably two interest rates and the exchange rate would adjust to clear three markets with the final one coming into equilibrium by Walras's Law from Chapter 2.

Appealing to a complete set of balance sheet accounts (including the NFA restriction described above), one can show that in fact all four markets will clear if the interest rates adjust to bring demands and supplies for the two flavors of bonds into balance. When that happens, money demands will automatically become equal to money supplies. This result is directly analogous to the simultaneous clearing of bond and money markets solely by interest rate adjustments in the closed economy LM setup discussed in Chapter 6. The exchange rate has no market-clearing role to play, in the sense that capital markets will tend toward equilibrium through interest rate adjustments regardless of its level.

In a more modern interpretation the two central banks would use open market operations to determine the two interest rates (not money supplies). A floating exchange rate then can assume an equilibrating role if the authorities maintain fixed interest rates and *also* aim for target levels of reserves. For example, the foreign authorities operating behind Table 8.3 could sell euro securities to buy dollar securities in the market. The goals would be to build up reserves and simultaneously weaken their exchange rate by creating an excess supply of euro-denominated liabilities. The rate becomes the market equilibrating price. With fixed interest rates there is no other possibility.

As discussed in Chapter 3, such competitive devaluation policies were rife in the 1930s. In 2009 several central banks (in Switzerland, Sweden, Australia, and probably elsewhere) were holding down interest rates and selling local currencies against dollars and euros to devalue their exchange rates in support of commodity exports.

To get back to the carry trade, suppose that there is a capital inflow toward the home economy, or a switch of foreign preferences toward home bonds. The spot rate e will then appreciate. The intuition is as follows: The exchange rate and fixed interest rates determine the level of money demand. After the inflow, the central bank's holdings of home bonds have to go up to help sterilize the resulting increase in reserves. Both private sectors' holdings of home bonds have to go down, and/or their demand for home money has to drop. Appreciation of home's exchange rate makes holding its liabilities more expensive and should have just these effects. We are presuming stable microeconomic adjustment processes here, but they usually seem to apply. Devaluation at times follows a capital inflow, but such events are rare.

Current Account Adjustment

The exchange theories just recounted—long-term effects of real side developments, PPP, IRP, implications of the carry trade, and portfolio balance—focus on specific factors that may influence the rate. The next question is how it influences macroeconomic adjustment at the country level. Depending on historical and institutional circumstances, different answers can arise. Postwar Keynesians worked hard at setting up open economy macroeconomics as an extended version of IS/LM. Contemporary debate is framed around their main ideas.

Exchange appreciation or depreciation can have impacts all across the economy. To trace them through, trade and payments flows have to be analyzed in a complete, consistent set of accounts for both stocks and flows which has no "black holes." The basic ideas have been laid out by Wynne Godley. The details are too complicated to set out here (see the readings mentioned at the end of this chapter), but even when combined with other theories, complete accounting leaves the exchange rate as the least understood object in macroeconomics. One fundamental reason is that different explanations for exchange rate behavior involve mutually contradictory assumptions about how the open economy operates. Be alert to changing patterns of causality in the following discussion!

The Keynesian Open Economy

Changes in the exchange rate presumably will not strongly influence the volumes of factor payments flows at the top of Table 8.3. The same is not true for imports and exports of goods and services. The key question is whether foreign trade flows largely determine or are determined by the exchange rate. The answer depends on the assumptions one makes about directions of causality in global macroeconomics, as well as technological and institutional arrangements which evolve over time.

The general Keynesian perception is that at the macro level output is not limited from the supply side, for instance, by Say's Law. There are two main exceptions. One is that there may be binding capacity constraints in specific industries. For example, the number of automobiles and light trucks sold in the United States during the 2000s prior to the crisis averaged around 17 million units per year (with a spike or two up to 20 million). The production level was around 12 million. In a closed economy, presumably more production capacity would have been created, or car prices would have risen sharply to limit demand. In an open economy the shortfall could readily be covered by imports, but the volume would be affected to a certain extent by the exchange rate. Devaluation (or a higher level of protection) would presumably stimulate some additional domestic production and cut back on demand for imported vehicles.

As already observed, the other exception has occurred many times in developing countries. There simply may not be enough hard currency available to pay for essential imports of intermediate goods (automobiles bundled into "kits" which are imported and then assembled and sold domestically are a classic example), so that output has to be cut back. The main mechanisms are familiar: inflation-induced forced saving, the inflation tax, and the well-honed recession-running skills of the IMF when it gets called in after a crisis (once again the case worldwide after 2007–2009).

Ease of international (financial) capital movements is an important institutional factor. If financial flows across borders are restricted, then together with the level of economic activity the exchange rate may have time to adjust to clear markets for imports and exports. In the 1930s models of the trade balance under two polar assumptions about the spot exchange rate e began to appear: it was taken as alternatively *floating* or *fixed.*

For the moment, suppose that the rate is pegged by the monetary authorities, as during the gold standard and Bretton Woods eras. By the 1950s discussions about the balance of trade began to focus on a simple IS-type model of the home and foreign countries, each with an exogenously fixed level of investment (leaving out government for simplicity). Output levels in the model are assumed to vary according to the principle of effective demand. Home exports are foreign country imports and vice versa. In each country import demand depends on output and the exchange rate. Dollar and euro price systems are anchored by fixed money wages, along with the exchange rate if imports are treated as intermediate inputs into production by the business sector.

A useful way to think about the system is in terms of *injections* and *leakages* as introduced in Chapter 4. The main injections in an economy open to trade are investment *and* the trade surplus. Domestic saving is the leakage. The macro balance condition becomes

$$\text{Investment} + \text{Trade Surplus} - \text{Saving} = 0.$$

According to the principle of effective demand, an increase in the trade surplus will boost the level of economic activity. Mercantilism gets reborn in Keynesian open economy macroeconomics, with the policy goal being not so much accumulation of international reserves (though that happens) but job creation. Soon after World War II, Germany and the East Asian export powerhouses learned about the advantages of running a trade surplus. Under the Bretton Woods system, with its fixed exchange rates and a strong dollar, they were able to do so. Table 8.2 shows that they continued this course into the late 2000s.

In a reprise of the transfer problem introduced in Chapter 3, if the foreign country is running a current account surplus, then, like the United States in the early postwar period, it must direct financial flows abroad. If the foreign private sector is the key actor, it sends an amount [Transfer(€)] in euros to the home private sector on capital account (via long-term investment or short-term capital outflows). In the home economy there has to be a dollar current account deficit equal to e[Transfer(€)]. The macro balance equation becomes

$$\text{Investment} - \text{Trade deficit} - \text{Saving} = 0.$$

In the United States, for example, after around 1980 a rising trade deficit supplemented falling saving to permit macro balance to be attained at a tolerably high level of economic activity. Without the deficit, as mentioned above, more productive capacity for traded goods would presumably have been brought on-line, or else there could have been inflation to limit demand by boosting the rate of saving. Of course we will never know which counterfactual history would have unrolled.

Elasticities and Absorption

In another scenario, assume that the exchange rate is still fixed but that investment demand rises in the home country. On Keynesian principles the demand stimulus should spill over into higher levels of activity in both countries. (In the jargon, a *foreign trade multiplier* is in action.) The trade balance between the countries will shift, meaning that the transfer is now being determined endogenously. Presumably short-term capital flows permit the transfer to be effected.

This way of analyzing transfers and shifts in aggregate demand in a two-country world came to be known as the *absorption approach*. It remains relevant to contemporary discussion because as emphasized above, the exchange rate is nowadays determined in capital markets which operate far more rapidly than markets for imports and exports.

Nevertheless, models in which the exchange rate interacts with trade flows are worth considering. They surfaced 250 years ago in Hume's price-specie flow model described in Chapter 2 and remain relevant today in poor developing countries with restricted access to international capital markets. If levels of imports and exports are assumed to respond to the exchange rate, then it can vary along with output levels to ensure that a given level of the transfer can be achieved. Changes in the rate will also influence effective demand; for example, appreciation of the dollar/euro rate raises real spending power at home and reduces it abroad. This mechanism amounts to forced saving operating across national boundaries.

Imports in both countries have to respond "strongly enough" to the exchange rate change for these processes to go through. In formal terms a *Marshall-Lerner condition* on the parameters of the import demand functions for the two countries has to be satisfied. This way of analyzing trade balance adjustment is called the *elasticities approach,* after the form in which the import demand parameters are usually parameterized.

One way to summarize the foregoing discussion goes as follows: Let imports of the two regions be [Home imports(€)] and [Foreign imports($)]. For global trade balance it will have to be true that

$$e[\text{Home imports}(€)] - [\text{Foreign imports}(\$)] = e[\text{Transfer}(€)].$$

In the absorption approach, with the exchange rate fixed, each country's activity level is driven by effective demand, and the transfer is determined from this equation. Causality, so to speak, runs from left to right.

If the transfer is set exogenously (presumably from capital markets under contemporary institutional arrangements), then along with output levels the exchange rate has to float to allow the equation to hold. This is the elasticities approach in action.

Mundell-Fleming

With elasticities and absorption as contending variants of a two-country IS model, the next step in the 1960s was to try to bring in LM. That happened via the Mundell-Fleming (a Nobel for Robert Mundell in 1999 after Marcus Fleming's death) and portfolio balance models.

Old-fashioned LM curves will determine interest rates in both countries if their money supplies are fixed by their central banks. The contemporary approach, discussed above in connection with portfolio balance, is to assume that the rates are set by the banks which conduct open market operations in domestic bonds. Money supplies adjust endogenously to allow interest rate targets to be met.

If the exchange rate is fixed, then applying complete Godley-style accounting (including all payments flows in a Keynesian income = expenditure framework) shows that in the two-country IS/LM system the home country current account balance, including trade, service, and factor service payments, will be equal to the dollar value of financial capital and reserve movements. Regardless of the value of the pegged exchange rate, the balance of payments accounting in Table 8.3 will be satisfied or "clear" because markets for all its components clear in flow macroeconomic equilibrium.

Mundell and Fleming independently introduced a model for one country which allegedly has three markets: for money via an LM curve which clears via the interest rate or an endogenous money supply, output which is determined from an IS curve for goods and services, *and* a balance of payments or BP. The external accounts are supposedly brought into balance by a changing exchange rate, but as we have seen, in a demand-driven absorption model they will already clear for any level at which the rate is pegged. In effect the "balance of payments" is an artifact of working with a model for only one open economy.

Because the Mundell-Fleming model did not impose fully consistent macro accounting, it was thought to have a degree of freedom available to set the exchange rate in a "market for foreign exchange." At the macro level, that market does not exist. The exchange rate can follow its own rules. For example, it could be determined by forces from the capital market as described above or be fixed by the authorities. In the latter case one or another fundamental (a list appears below) might appear to be violated, which could trigger capital movements that the central bank might feel obliged to counter. But there is no reason to be sure that a floating rate will make these tremors go away.

When it was invented, the Mundell-Fleming model met practical policy concerns, but it is not relevant today because it is built around responses of trade to exchange rate changes. Rich country exchange rates in the twenty-first century are not *directly* affected by sluggish movements in international markets for goods and services, although as noted above their levels in the long run can be affected by forces from the real side of the economy. In the short run they can be manipulated in capital account transactions with the goal of influencing imports and exports.

A provisional summary of the discussion about macroeconomic adjustment is that a two-country absorption model with the exchange rate fixed outside that system can illustrate the real side of global macroeconomics. Under certain assumptions portfolio balance relationships might determine the exchange rate, which would get stronger in response to a capital inflow. There are, however, many other mainstream theories about the exchange rate floating around. For the sake of completeness we turn to some of them next.

Other Orthodox Theories

One theory is open economy monetarism, which dates back to Hume's model from Chapter 2. With Say's Law in force, an attempt at monetary expansion will just spill over into a current account deficit, leading to nominal devaluation and a return to the economy's initial situation but with higher prices. We get an international version of Friedman-Phelps from Chapter 6.

Various fundamentals have been proposed to explain the exchange rate. Examples mentioned so far include PPP, the relative prices of traded and non-traded goods, and IRP. Such indicators can supposedly signal when the exchange rate is out of line and due for a correction. One could add three others to the list.

First, a persistent current account deficit should be a trigger for devaluation. This may be true in some countries but certainly not for the United States since the early 1980s. This immunity to external pressure is at times called an *exorbitant privilege,* the opposite of developing economies' original sin.

Second, twin deficit theory, already criticized in Chapters 2 and 5, suggests that a big fiscal deficit will create an external gap and then the economy will be in trouble. The difficulty is that in time series data for most countries, government net borrowing and foreign net lending are rarely twins.

Finally, there is a *trilemma* based on the Mundell-Fleming model which states that central bank interventions cannot simultaneously combine (1) full capital mobility, (2) a controlled exchange rate, and (3) independent monetary policy. Supposedly only two of these policy lines can be consistently maintained. This theorem appears in all the textbooks, but as discussed in connection with portfolio balance and Mundell-Fleming, the authorities can in fact intervene to influence the interest rate regardless of what is happening with the exchange rate. They can even manipulate the exchange rate if they pursue competitive devaluation through monetary policy. As in China, capital controls can make it easier to pursue these strategies, but they are in principle available even when capital movements are not restricted.

The trilemma misses these points, although it is not completely irrelevant if the market reacts against "overly aggressive" policies by one country. Especially in developing economies, capital movements provoked by national policies can be highly destabilizing.

Global Macro Balance

Can all this theory tell us anything useful about dealing with the global imbalances apparent in Table 8.2? Policy discussion through early 2010 centered on three ways of looking at the issue. Their credibility or lack of same depends crucially on how one views patterns of causality in the global macro system.

Global Savings Glut

The best-known high-tech mainstream approach was already sketched in Chapter 2. It amounts to a diagnosis of Dutch disease in the United States, except that the source of ample foreign exchange is not a natural resource bonanza but rather massive capital inflows which are supposed to release forces (notably real exchange appreciation) that create a deficit on current account.

In formal terms a Ramsey model can be set up for two economies with both producing the same traded good as well as a local non-traded good. It emphasizes how different rates of time preference can "explain" why one country (say, the United States, with a high rate like Robinson Crusoe's) runs a trade deficit and another (say, China, with a low rate like Friday's) has a surplus. On capital account there will be a transfer from China to the United States (China will acquire U.S. liabilities) to finance the latter's current account deficit.

Within each country the relative price between traded and non-traded goods will govern resource allocation along the lines of definition 2 of the real exchange set out above. Given ample access to foreign resources, the United States will suffer from a version of Dutch disease: it will have high relative non-traded goods prices accompanied by deindustrialization.

This analysis fits well with a pre-crisis *global savings glut* hypothesis popularized by Federal Reserve governor Ben Bernanke. In a speech in 2005 he said that it "helps to explain both the increase in the U.S. current account deficit and the relatively low level of long-term real interest rates in the world today." If one believes the Ramsey models, then payments imbalances are an optimal result of different intertemporal preferences. Individuals in Asia want to save more, individuals in the United States want to consume more, and the whole exchange is the best possible because otherwise nobody would do it. Deep financial markets are (or before 2007 were assumed to be) the efficient means to achieve such consumption smoothing. This narrative fit perfectly into pre-crisis financial orthodoxy. Whether it will have much traction in the 2010s remains to be seen.

Bretton Woods II

An almost polar view, at times called Bretton Woods II, suggests that a quasi-stable system based on partially fixed exchange rates has emerged. It amounts to a revival of the Triffin paradox. International payments are still mostly denominated in dollars, and as noted above, most countries' central bank reserves are U.S. "official" liabilities. In such an environment, China and the other export-led economies have a vested interest in a strong dollar to help sustain their trade surpluses. At the same time, as emphasized above, Chinese monetary authorities fret over capital losses in the value of their dollar reserves which would result from possible dollar devaluation.

They would feel safer with an international reserve asset with a stable value such as the SDR and in 2009 pushed the issue back onto the international agenda.

Meanwhile, as depicted in Figure 8.1, the renminbi has been fairly closely linked to the dollar since the mid-1990s; subject to the vagaries of IRP and the carry trade, the same is true for the yen. From this perspective China becomes the key player. If it can devise policies to reduce its high saving rate and thereby divert traded goods production toward satisfying higher levels of domestic consumption, the rest of the world would presumably breathe a sigh of relief. But if it maintains a weak real exchange rate and continues to direct massive transfers abroad, the question is which countries will run current account deficits to absorb China's financial outflow.

These observations suggest that macro causal linkages in the global system are unclear. Recall the external balance condition,

$$e[\text{Home imports}(\text{€})] - [\text{Foreign imports}(\$)] = e[\text{Transfer}(\text{€})],$$

from the two-country IS model discussed above. Each country determines its own levels of demand injections and leakages. There is only one degree of freedom in this equation. If the exchange rate e is determined from the capital market, then the transfer must vary endogenously on the real side and would have to be financed by short-term capital movements. If the transfer is somehow fixed, the exchange rate would have to adjust.

In a three-country model (say, the dollar area implicitly including the UK, export-oriented economies led by China and the Gulf oil exporters with trade surpluses, and Euroland), there are two degrees of freedom. Also note that if two of the three bilateral exchange rates are fixed, then capital market arbitrage will determine the third rate. Table 8.2 gives a feel for the associated payments flows, and Figure 8.1 illustrates the relevant exchange rates.

An exaggerated version of Bretton Woods II would say that the exporter bloc pegs its bilateral exchange rate to the dollar by using capital market interventions. That exhausts one degree of freedom. Suppose that the bloc can take charge of the second degree of freedom by adjusting domestic demand, volumes of exports (by subsidies), and imports (by tariffs and quotas) to control its overall current account surplus. The United States consumes a large share of the exporting bloc's products at the pegged rate. Euroland is left as the buffer. Its bilateral (euro/renminbi) rate with the bloc varies to allow it to absorb the remaining surplus. The dollar/euro exchange rate must adjust to be consistent with the other two bilateral rates. Throughout most of the 2000s the dollar depreciated against the euro and was nearly stable against the renminbi. The euro had to rise against the renminbi as well.

U.S. Net Borrowing

The implication is that the United States in economic terms is a "pitiful helpless giant," in Richard Nixon's famously sardonic phrase regarding his nation's role in Vietnam. An alternative narrative is that because of the economy's inherent distributive conflicts discussed in Chapter 5, rising household borrowing beginning in the 1980s spilled over into foreign borrowing in a *demand glut*. Again with Euroland serving as a buffer, all that the export powerhouses did was respond to demand pressure. The United States collectively chose to borrow to support consumption, then invented the financial vehicles that enabled it to do so, and the rest of world was willing to play along.

Global Overdetermination

We are basically back with Freud in his *Interpretation of Dreams* trying to sort out an overdetermined situation in which there are too many explanations for a single reality. He thought that the content of dreams was shaped by factors ranging from recent events in the dreamer's life ("the residue of the day") to repressed traumas and unconscious desires.

The theories just discussed try to explain global macro imbalances by diverse forces—national time preferences plus the invisible hand, or positions of power in international trade and capital markets, or external debt accumulation as a means to sidestep the two souls conflict in the United States.

From a Keynesian perspective, trying to explain open economy economics with a Ramsey model is an exercise in futility. The other two broad explanations have some content but can scarcely serve as sound bases for prediction or policy formation because they leave too many questions unanswered. On the one hand, from Chapter 5, for example, it is clear that the disequilibrium nature of the U.S. economy since around 1980 cannot persist indefinitely, but how it will terminate is difficult to foresee. On the other hand, there are likely to be increasing contradictions in the Chinese (and German) export-led growth models.

The global macroeconomy is always overdetermined because it has too few degrees of freedom for adjustment. Under such circumstances, the observed patterns of trade and financial flows can change rapidly and unexpectedly. That could well be the situation in the 2010s. Throughout 2007–2010 there were incessant policy pronouncements that the Chinese should consume more and the Americans less while somehow retooling their productive apparatuses to produce less and more traded goods respectively. The recommendations went on: Exchange rates should be realigned. Governments should avoid international debt traps. Destabilizing international capital movements should be avoided. There should be effective international cooperation by countries at the level of the G20 (twenty presidents plus innumerable other potentates and appendages in the same room!).

The aspirations were high, but the mechanisms needed to attain them had yet to be spelled out. The 1944 Bretton Woods agreements set up institutions which lasted for a generation and then broke down fairly gracefully. Nothing similar is in sight.

Notes

Williamson and Milner (1991) is a bit out of date but still provides a historically aware introduction to open economy macro. Eatwell and Taylor (2000) concentrates on developments in capital markets. Robert Triffin (1960) poses his dilemma.

Jane d'Arista (2009a) discusses the evolution of the international monetary system, and D'Arista (2009b) describes the carry trade and other issues. Godley and Lavoie (2007) presents the first author's open economy accounting (illustrated with computer simulations) over several chapters. Taylor (2008) is more succinct but heavily infected with accounting matrixes for international payments flows and balance sheets.

Bernanke (2005) lays out his ideas about the global saving glut. The Bretton Woods II versus the saving glut discussion draws on Rudi von Arnim (2009), based on his New School thesis.

— 9 —

Keynesianism and the Crisis

This chapter presents a Keynesian analysis of the crisis of 2007–2009 and its possible aftermath. With a little help from the rest of the book (passages from the other chapters, tables, and diagrams), it is largely self-contained.

The macroeconomics created by Keynes and his closest followers provides the only plausible path toward understanding the huge changes that engulfed the world economy in the latter part of the twentieth century. The neoliberal political economy that led into the crisis took shape in the 1970s and 1980s. Reasons why it broke down can be read from the data, with major shifts in behavior on the real and financial sides of the U.S. and global economies playing crucial roles. Redistribution of income and wealth among socioeconomic groups was especially important. In George Soros's terminology introduced in Chapter 1, economic actors' imperfect cognitive perceptions about the economic system combined with their limited ability to manipulate it to produce the near collapse of the neoliberal system.

Toward the future, cognition and manipulation will mutate in ways that are impossible to foresee. The political economy that emerges in the 2010s will differ markedly from the one in place during the late twentieth and early twenty-first centuries. At the level of mere macroeconomics, Keynesian principles are the only tools available to help guide the system through a fraught transition to a new regime whose nature is hidden by what Maynard called "the dark forces of time and ignorance which envelop our future" (7:155).

Turning to the broad contours of history, the first part of the chapter is about long-term shifts from a political economic perspective. I then review the major macroeconomic changes that took place after around 1980. With this material as background, there is an analysis of how key forces acted together to create the crisis, leading into observations about developments that may be in store and how policies may be designed to help cope with them.

Long Swings in Political Economy

The share in income (including realized capital gains subject to the income tax) of the richest 1% of the U.S. population in 1929 was around 22.5%. It fell to about 9% in 1979, and then rose again to 22.5% in 2006. An index of the share of wages in GDP discussed below fell from cyclical peak levels of about 105 during the 1960s and 1970s to around 97 when the business cycle peaked in the mid-2000s. The average real wage has dropped steadily since 1980, with the implication that all real income growth (plus a bit more) accrued to profits. As documented in previous chapters and summarized below, the swing toward greater income inequality in the United States after the 1970s was associated with notable changes in the way the macroeconomy worked.

Great political economists have emphasized that there are long waves in the way economies function, going well beyond the tedious trudge of formal growth models toward a state in which all relevant ratios of macroeconomic variables stay constant. In his *Great Transformation*, Karl Polanyi saw a *double movement* in nineteenth-century Europe, first toward a liberalized market system largely created by state intervention. It was followed by regulation aimed at reducing the worst aspects of capitalism, such as child labor, a long workweek, and unemployment. A counterreaction to regulation and the trauma of World War I helped set the stage for rising inequality and fascism in the first third of the twentieth century.

In a famous article called "Political Aspects of Full Employment" Michal Kalecki (1943) described a political business cycle in which capitalists can at times persuade the state to hold economic activity below the full-employment level, to cut into the power of workers. The contemporary Cambridge economist Gabriel Palma describes how the two adversary classes operate. "Both seek to change the balance of power between income groups: [workers advocate] Keynesianism in order to prevent the disruptive effects of crisis-ridden capitalism, [capitalists advance] neo-liberalism in order to return power and control to their 'rightful owners'—capital" (Palma, 2009, 837).

A similar cycle between public and private domination of the economy was pointed out by Albert Hirschman. Characteristically he adopted a dialectic built around a *rebound effect* between social preferences for public and private control. After general frustration with the ruling situation crosses a threshold, the rebound kicks in.

Broadly speaking, such theories are consistent with a long-term political economy cycle in the twentieth century. As discussed in Chapter 3, the early-twentieth-century liberal phase (in the European sense of the word) ended with the Great Crash and Great Depression. The rebound continued through the New Deal and World War II into the "golden age" of unprecedented worldwide output growth in the 1950s and 1960s. Building the welfare state (a development not anticipated by Keynes) was a major contributing factor to the sustained and historically unprecedented output boom. This long cycle broke down during the stagflation of the 1970s and was succeeded by a new liberal resurgence beginning around 1980.

One problem with these theories is that they are unclear about *agency*: how do actors (individual or collective) proceed to alter the situation at hand, and why do they do it? Palma quotes an adviser to Mrs. Thatcher who apparently had read his Kalecki on the benefits of recessions for capital, but such observations are unusual. Nor is it clear whether the latest liberal cycle really ended in 2009. Even if in some sense it did, the extended transitions between Polanyi's nineteenth- and twentieth-century cycles suggest that macroeconomic changes during the decade of the 2010s are unpredictable, and may be dramatically unstable.

The best way to think about these issues is to use the economic theory devised by Keynes and his close followers including Kalecki, Josef Steindl, Nicholas Kaldor, Joan Robinson, Richard Goodwin, Hyman Minsky, Charles Kindleberger, and Wynne Godley. Summaries could be presented here, but to avoid repetition, see the reviews of Keynes's central ideas in Chapter 1 and more compactly at the end of Chapter 4. A quick review of the contributions of later Keynesians appears at the end of Chapter 5.

The only point to be added relates to the interest rate. Keynesians have always been in favor of easy money; a low cost of funds stimulates investment and supports aggregate demand. Although the possibility that a low real interest rate could support a boom in asset prices with an associated run-up in debt can be read into Keynes's 1930 *Treatise on Money* and is explicit with Kindleberger and Minsky, it was not a central theme. Rather the thought comes more from Austrian economists including Keynes's friend and rival Friedrich von Hayek. It will figure importantly below.

Keynesian Theory and the Data for the United States

Keynesian analysis sheds light on how the decisions of different social groups shaped post–World War II developments in the U.S. and world economies, especially during the long-term liberal cycle that settled in after 1980. Much of the material has been covered in previous chapters. Now I pull it together, beginning with changes over time in the United States. The discussion begins on the real side of the economy, switches to the financial side, and then brings in international complications. A synthesis is proposed after the details have been set out.

To interpret the data, it is crucial to follow Joan Robinson in drawing a key distinction between *history and equilibrium,* or between thinking in historical and logical time. Growth and cycle theories operate in the latter domain and do occupy space in this chapter. But the theory is useless unless it can also shed light on observed historical changes and future prospects. Using theory and data together in such a fashion is precisely the goal.

Labor Productivity and the Goodwin Cycle

A good place to begin is with relationships between income distribution and economic activity. For macroeconomics it is most convenient to measure distribution in terms of claims on different payments flows—wages versus profits—rather than the overall distribution by size of household incomes. The latter contains more information, for example, increasing dispersion of wage incomes over the past several decades, but the former is much easier to work with. Fortunately for present purposes, as mentioned above, the two measures of inequality have moved together.

Figure 5.4 illustrates cyclical behavior of labor productivity or the output/labor ratio. The data are presented in the form of quarterly logarithmic deviations (basically growth rates) of productivity from its trend. The shaded areas represent recessions as defined by the National Bureau of Economic Research. The general picture fits the stylized description of the

Goodwin model from Chapter 5, with productivity rising as the economy moves out of a recession trough, and then leveling off or growing more slowly than the trend. (The big spike in 2009 reflects the economy's high rate of unemployment.) In most industrialized economies trend productivity growth itself has historically been on the order of 2% per year, and may respond to output growth along lines proposed by Kaldor.

Together with rising real wages near the top of the cycle, this pattern of productivity change generated the fluctuations in the index of the labor share of income. It can be expressed as the ratio of the real wage to productivity and is shown as the solid curve in Figure 5.5. It continued to fall throughout 2009.

Economic activity also appears in the diagram, represented by "capacity utilization," or output divided by its trend (the dashed curve). Typically, utilization jumped up rapidly in a "V" shape as the economy emerged from recession. In 2007 utilization moved down sharply. Its uptick in mid-2009 suggests that the fall will not be as great as the one between 1979 and 1983 (of course the possibility that there will be a double-dip recession like the one around 1980 remains).

Prior to 1980, periods between recessions were relatively brief. This tendency began to weaken in the 1960s but reappeared in the following decade of stagflation. Between the early 1980s and late 2000s there were only three recessions. The change is usually attributed to the ability of households and firms to smooth their spending flows by using new sources of finance.

Throughout the period, the labor share followed the Goodwin cycle, moving downward as the economy emerged from recession and then rising later in the upswing. The pattern persisted after 1980, but it was superimposed on a clear downward trend. Notably, the share continued to fall throughout 2009.

Net Borrowing

Any individual or collective economic actor's net borrowing is its expenditure minus income (or investment minus saving). The sum of net borrowing flows for all actors in the economy must be zero, because a net borrower has to receive net loans from some of the others. In a diagram proposed by Godley and Steindl, Figure 5.8 summarizes U.S. data on net borrowing flows by households, the rest of the private sector ("Business"), government, and the rest of the world ("Foreign"). Household borrowing is approximated by the difference between residential investment and gross saving. The flows are presented as shares of GDP. The shaded areas again signal periods of recession. Several changes over time stand out.

After the pattern break in the early 1980s there was a steady downward movement in foreign net borrowing (or foreign net lending *to* the United States went up). The trend was interrupted by a brief recovery around 1990, mostly due to capital inflows which financed military services rendered during the Gulf War. The external deficit fell during 2007–2009 in response to the sharp reduction in economic activity illustrated in Figure 5.5.

After around 1980 the pattern for household net borrowing was almost a mirror image of foreign borrowing, with the sign reversed. The question about which movement "caused" the other is under intense debate, as discussed below.

During the golden age and stagflation, household borrowing was negative (or the sector's lending was positive). The foreign gap as a share of GDP was around zero, implying that households financed deficits of business and the government, a pattern built into traditional Keynesian models. As discussed below, the change in the household borrowing pattern was the result of an increasing consumption share in disposable income and a corresponding fall in saving. These trends reversed abruptly in the mid-2000s, accompanied by a big drop in residential investment, setting off the subsequent recession—a clear violation of Say's Law, Keynes's chief theoretical target, which says that the economy has strong tendencies toward full employment.

Two points about the business cycle should be mentioned. First, throughout the period, household net borrowing led the cycle in capacity utilization, swinging upward as the economy emerged from recession. Rising residential investment was the driving force. Whether or not this pattern reappears will play a big role in determining the strength of recovery after 2010.

Second, government net borrowing is counter-cyclical because of changes in tax receipts and pro-cyclical spending driven by "automatic stabilizers" such as unemployment insurance along with conscious shifts in fiscal policy. The Obama stimulus package shows up clearly at the right side of the diagram. It persisted throughout 2009.

Asset Prices

With these developments on the real side as background, we can bring asset prices into the discussion. Two key points are relevant to macroeconomics post-1980.

Figure 1.1 shows how a prolonged upswing in the stock market got under way around 1980. It peaked in the late 1990s, followed by a sharp decline and then recovery. Using the GDP deflator for prices of goods and services (the broadest index available) to restate the S&P 500 index in real terms shows that equity prices did not recover their late 1990s level after the upswing in the mid-2000s.

Prior to the mid-1990s, housing price indexes shown in Figure 1.3 tracked the GDP deflator rather closely. Thereafter their growth accelerated, with the move upward lasting for roughly a decade. From the data shown in the diagram, it is difficult to avoid calling the housing price excursion a bubble.

Interest and Profit Rates

The business cycle theory due to Keynes and Minsky sketched in Chapters 4 and 5 suggests that interest and profit rates do not move together. Along with a falling labor share, low interest rates as the economy emerges from a trough stimulate rising profitability, which gets cut back at the peak. Standard (Irving) Fisher arbitrage arguments from mainstream theory suggest that the profit and real interest rates should tend toward equality, but this tendency is not observed in the data.

This cyclical pattern can be seen in Figure 2.2, which adds the interesting twist of opposing movements of the two rates over the Keynesian and liberal long cycles after World War II. (Profit rates are computed from national accounts and flows of funds data, but similar movements show up in other estimates.)

Real interest rates prior to the 1970s were low but positive. They went negative during the stagflation period, shot up with the Fed's monetary shock at the end of the decade, and then drifted downward. The decrease after the mid-1990s reflects the "Greenspan put" in Fed policy, which took the form of cutting interest rates after each financial tremor. An attempt at monetary tightening in the mid-2000s had some impact in real terms but was limited in part by factors such as capital inflows from the "carry trade."

The profit rate gradually fell during the Keynesian golden age, hit a trough after the interest rate shock, and rose strongly thereafter. The increase since the 1980s is the counterpart of the decrease in the labor share noted above. (At the macro level, the profit share is the profit rate times the output/capital ratio.) It also was a response to steadily falling interest rates.

Institutional Changes in Finance

Minsky's insights into financial evolution played out in detail, beginning in 1980 with the abolition of the Fed's Regulation Q, putting a ceiling on deposit rates. This step was followed by a long sequence of moves relaxing financial sector controls, all pushed politically by the financial industry. Deregulation continued through the Garn–St. Germain Act, which was supposed to rescue the savings and loan system but in fact provoked a crisis, went on to hands-off policy regarding derivative transactions in the 1990s and the abolition of the Glass-Steagall Act in 1999, and then to relaxation of leverage restrictions on big investment banks in 2004. During the same period, policies (backed by both political parties) aggressively promoted homeownership. They fed into the subprime mortgage boom and subsequent crash.

All these changes encouraged financial firms to engage in high-uncertainty/high-return trading operations, which took the form of running up debt to acquire assets with prices that in effect were assumed to be rising along exponential growth paths (subject to mild shocks) that would go on forever. When prices inevitably fell, leverage, or the ratio of assets to equity, shot up, forcing firms to try to dispose of their assets in an imploding market.

Derivative transactions, off–balance sheet vehicles, and the expansion of the originate-and-distribute model of asset securitization through the shadow banking system made financial fragility that much worse.

A final contributing factor was the emergence of academic finance theory beginning in the 1950s. It added a luster of "scientifically based" valuations to collaterized debt obligations, credit default swaps, and any number of other forms of derivatives. Along the lines argued by the French sociologist Pierre Bourdieu, finance theory, with its key assumption of fully efficient, completely deregulated markets, dominated the discourse about financial practices. It supported a "complicitous silence" that allowed bankers to engage in destabilizing transactions without any criticism being raised. Their regulators shared the same mentality. Small wonder there was a crash.

Housing Prices, Household Debt, and Interest Rates

In retrospect, the major channel by which asset price movements and institutional changes in the financial sector affected the real side of the economy ran through shifts in household consumption and borrowing. Distributive changes were at the heart of the matter, as illustrated in Figure 5.14.

The diagram shows that the post-1980 decline in the wage share of total income noted above was accompanied by a steady increase in an index of the consumption share of households' disposable income. Much of the consumption increase was due to rising spending on health care. The household saving rate fell sharply over the period.

How did households sustain rising consumption at the same time that the wage share declined and real income was stagnant or falling across most deciles of the size distribution of income? The answer, of course, is steadily rising indebtedness, with the debt/income ratio more than doubling between the early 1980s and the mid-2000s. Potential distributive conflict, as Hirschman has suggested, was diverted into increasing debt. George W. Bush's cheerleading about an emerging "ownership society" was a rationalization of this change.

Associated trends show up in Figure 5.15. The decline in the real medium-term interest rate has already been noted. By bidding up the ratio of returns to holding housing (including capital gains) to the cost of finance, it fed into the growth of the real housing price index. That increase, in turn, was accompanied by growth in real debt. Toward the end of the period, the debt expansion continued for a year or two after the break in price growth, overshooting its source of nourishment. There is some inconsistency in the literature about whether or not expansion of liabilities typically continues after a boom in asset prices ends. Kindleberger suggests that credit expansion ends with the crash, while Soros gives examples of overshooting.

Be that as it may, Figure 5.16 adds another viewpoint on households' behavior. Prior to the stock market crash in the late 1990s, the ratio of their spending to net worth (with equity and mutual fund valuations and the value of housing as major components) declined steadily after the late 1970s. They could be seen as rationally converting part of their income from capital gains into current spending power, presumably on the implicit assumption that the gains would continue to roll in.

The equity crash set off a jump in the expenditure/net worth ratio because the denominator went down. It subsequently fell back and then shot up again after housing prices dropped. Meanwhile the debt/net worth ratio was quite stable until its denominator went down and its numerator rose after the mid-1990s. Unlike the financial sector, households did not engage in active leverage games until falling asset prices boosted their debt/net worth ratio in the 2000s.

Cognitive misperceptions and inappropriate actions worked together at many levels to produce this most recent Kindlebergian mania, panic, and crash. Its unfolding can be understood as encompassing distinct groups of social actors with imperfect knowledge. There was effectively an alliance between mostly non-affluent households, finance, and politicians in power (backing the expansion of Fannie Mae and Freddie Mac, for example) in support of more debt. Even if each group could be seen as pursuing its own self-interest, macroeconomically they created an unstable situation. A Keynesian fallacy of composition came into play with a vengeance.

A mainstream economist might well ask how macroeconomic output determination by effective demand, combined with a shifting income distribution, could translate into incentives for millions of households to go into debt, aided and abetted by financial innovation. But it happened. Capital gains on equity and housing spilled over into behavior on the real side which overwhelmed presumptions of perfect foresight and the applicability of Say's Law.

No Steady State

There is a strong presumption in economic growth theory that the economy will tend toward or cycle around a steady state position at which all ratios of stocks and flows are stable. During the long reign of liberalism in the late twentieth and early twenty-first centuries, no such pattern emerged. The Goodwin distribution-demand cycle appears to persist, but the level of the labor share at its focus fell after 1980. As we have seen, household and foreign net borrowing flows were strongly trended until 2007–2009.

The only stable ratio on the real side appears to be between GDP and "primary wealth," or the value of the capital stock plus government debt. Since around 1950 this ratio has been close to one-quarter. Because government debt is a fraction of the value of capital, this observation means that the U.S. capital/output ratio fluctuates around a level of 4, consistent with the range of variation in capacity utilization shown in Figure 5.5.

On the financial side, the structure of the economy has changed dramatically—especially since 1980. The FIRE (finance, insurance, and real estate) sector had visible productivity gains (Figures 5.11 and 5.12), but to a large extent they represent money illusion. Spiraling asset prices and purely speculative transactions generated profits and fees which became part of value added. In the future the sector's labor payments and profits, deflated by a price index for goods and services, might be expected to go down. If so, the resulting negative productivity growth will be as "real"—or fictional—as the positive growth observed after 1980.

There were similar shifts in balance sheets. The changes show up clearly in Figure 5.17, which presents ratios of financial positions to U.S. primary wealth for households, the rest of the world, the financial sector, and nonfinancial business.

The most striking change is the growth of total assets and liabilities of the financial sector from around 40% of primary wealth in 1980 to over 100% in the late 2000s. Much of the shift can be explained by the expansion of mutual and retirement funds. But it also reflected the explosion of securitization. There was a major reallocation of sources of the nonfinancial sector's debt from the balance sheets of banks (mortgages, credit cards, and so on) to securities markets (corporate bonds, commercial paper, asset-backed securities). The banks' share fell from over 45% to 30%, and the securities markets' participation rose correspondingly.

The asset and liability positions of the rest of the world rose by around 20% of total wealth. More important, the share in total wealth of the sector's net worth rose by more than five percentage points, building up with the string of current account deficits that began after 1980.

The share of net worth of households fluctuated parallel to the value of their financial assets. The value of tangible assets rose in line with the price of residential capital, and as already illustrated in Figure 5.15, debt rose a bit faster. The nonfinancial business borrowing binge during the 1990s shown in Figure 5.8 (the dot-com episode) was reflected in a rising share of debt before 2000.

These financial movements provide another angle to view the economy after 1980. Divergent trends emerged, with contradictions that became apparent during 2007–2009. How they will move in the 2010s remains to be seen.

International Complications

The U.S. position in the global economy has shifted markedly over the decades. Emerging from the war, it was clearly the international hegemon (Kindleberger's label again), but its potency deteriorated steadily over time. Following a schematic proposed by Minsky, Table 8.1 illustrates world payments flows in the early postwar period (late 1940s and early 1950s).

At that time, developing countries had no significant debt after a period of high export prices for raw materials; debt service obligations among the rich countries were ill-defined. As a consequence, international payments of interest and dividends were minimal. The United States had a strong trade surplus, so its overall current account *(+A)* was positive. On capital account there were large flows from the United States to the rest of the world of long-term investment *(-B)* and transfers *(-C)* supporting postwar reconstruction.

These flows exceeded the current account surplus and had to be offset by movements of short-term capital toward the United States and/or changes in reserves. On the U.S. side the capital inflow took the form of increasing foreign deposits in money center banks and sales of Treasury bonds abroad. These dollar "exports" added liquidity and propelled credit expansion by banking systems in the rest of the world. Meanwhile the trade surplus propped up profits and employment in the United States.

The structure of international payments outlined in Table 8.1 was the foundation for historically rapid and stable output growth worldwide during the golden age in the 1950s and 1960s. Perhaps unsurprisingly the long bonanza carried the seeds of its own destruction in the form of dynamics of stocks and flows over time (a point neglected by Keynes but emphasized by Minsky and Godley).

The problem was that the long-term capital movements from the United States exceeded its short-term capital inflows. The resulting increase in net foreign assets meant that interest and dividend income rose from near zero in Table 8.1. With both major components of the current account positive, on capital account there would have to be ever-rising U.S. foreign investment and transfers, or reduced short-term inflows.

The response of the United States was to "go negative" on its trade and service account, absorbing rising net exports from the rest of the world. Recognizing that the international payments system lacks degrees of freedom, in 1960 the Yale economist Robert Triffin invented a *dilemma* to describe the situation. One horn was that a trade and services deficit was required of the United States to permit short-term capital inflows to generate liquidity for the rest of the world. The other horn was that the United States presumably could not sustain the deficit indefinitely (another stock flow argument). Dollar devaluation might ultimately be needed to reduce the U.S. current account deficit.

Triffin's proposed remedy was to create an international reserve currency to take the burden off the United States. The institutional response that actually occurred was to give the IMF power to issue *special drawing rights (SDR)* to serve as an international reserve asset. SDRs in practice never got anywhere. There was no felt need because, beginning with Eurodollars and expanding exponentially thereafter, the world financial system could produce international liquidity without limit. In any case the overall U.S. current account turned negative in the early 1980s.

For the period after 1980 it is possible to insert numbers into the format of Table 8.1. Table 8.2 takes up the story for selected years through 2006, presenting payments flows as shares of world GDP. Several points stand out.

By 1980 U.S. interest and dividend income from abroad had risen to 0.26% of world GDP. The overall current account was still positive but small (0.1%), and short-term capital movements were negligible. Already in 1983 the configuration of flows had begun to shift markedly. The current account became visibly negative (-0.18%). With continuing net foreign investment and transfers (mostly the latter in 1983), short-term capital movements toward the United States reappeared at 0.34%. But now the United States was issuing short-term liabilities to finance foreign investment and transfers *plus* a current account deficit, not investment and transfers *minus* a current surplus, as during the golden age. Its hegemonic role was beginning to erode.

The situation deteriorated further after 1983. As a share of world GDP, dividend and interest income declined, and the trade and services account steadily worsened. Long-term investment and transfers continued to be negative items, but their importance diminished in comparison to the trade deficit. By the mid-2000s short-term capital inflows were around 1.6% of world GDP—a macroeconomically important movement of funds.

The U.S. deficit on trade and services of course had to be met by surpluses in the rest of the world. China (following Japan) became a key player, with its surplus rising from 0.23% in 1999 to 0.47% in 2006. In that year China, OPEC, and Japan (in that order) transferred almost 1% of world GDP to the United States in the form of short-term financial capital.

China also received large inflows of net foreign investment and transfers, although the magnitude was smaller than the current account surplus. The balancing item in Chinese accounts took the form of large increases in international reserves, that is, acquisition of short-term liabilities from the United States. China's reserve growth can be interpreted as being defensive in part, to build up a hedge against a replay of the Asian crises of the late 1990s. But it was also the counterpart of the consumption-led U.S. trade deficit, which had to be financed by rising capital inflows, which to a large extent took the form of acquisition of U.S. Treasury and government-sponsored agency (Fannie Mae and Freddie Mac) bonds by the Chinese and other foreign central banks.

As shown in Figures 5.8 and 5.9, the U.S. payments situation began to change with the onset of crisis. There was at least a modest reduction in net lending from the rest of the world. Whether the economy can switch back toward external current balance or even a surplus is an open question.

Deciphering the Past

One way to summarize the discussion so far is to list the forces that led into the 2007–2009 crisis.

Factors Contributing to the Crisis

Nine factors can be distinguished as helping to precipitate the crisis.

1. There was a major shift in the political economic environment. The liberal rebound gathered strength beginning in the 1960s and triumphed

in the United States with the election of Ronald Reagan. The practical effects of (neo)liberalism included the dismantling of financial regulation, successful attacks on labor's bargaining power, and an ideological shift in support of God and capitalism. It remains to be seen if this wave will recede.

2. The American business cycle continued, with changes over time in the real interest rate, the labor share and profit rate, and household net borrowing, helping to drive fluctuations in output. But all four variables began to trend after 1980, weakening their cyclical role but generating effects that spilled over into asset prices and the balance of payments. Specifically, the interest rate declined while the profit share went up; the labor share and household borrowing respectively fell and increased. At the same time, inequality in the size distribution of income went up markedly.

3. Numerically, the ratio of annual household net borrowing to GDP rose by around ten percentage points between the early 1980s and the mid-2000s. The household debt-to-income ratio roughly doubled over the same period

4. The real S&P 500 index of equity prices grew more than fivefold between the early 1980s and late 1990s. Thereafter it fell and rose but did not attain its previous peak. Real housing prices roughly doubled over twenty-five years. Growth in indexes of nominal housing prices outpaced the inflation rate for goods and services after the mid-1990s.

5. Real interest rates fell steadily from high single-digit levels to near zero between the early 1980s and mid-2000s. Standard arguments suggest that falling rates probably stimulated (and certainly did not retard) the booms in equity and housing prices.

6. Much of the higher household borrowing was collateralized by rising prices of equity and (especially) housing. The ratios of household debt and expenditure to net worth respectively were stable and fell until the late 1990s, when both shot up as the dot-com and housing crashes cut into net worth. The obvious interpretation of all these trends is that households with incomes below the top percentiles of the size distribution took advantage of the opportunity that capital gains on equity and housing provided to run up debt to maintain their living standards in the face of stagnating or falling real incomes.

7. As a share of GDP, foreign net borrowing decreased (or net lending by the rest of the world to the United States increased) by around seven percentage points, roughly "twinned" to rising household net borrow-

ing. By the mid-2000s the U.S. deficit for foreign trade and services was around 1.5% of world GDP, offset by short-term capital inflows of roughly the same magnitude. Meanwhile, China's current account surplus grew to around 0.4% of world GDP. One might argue on functionalist lines that the U.S. deficit was driven by a strong exchange rate, which in turn both allowed cheap imports to help offset overall stagnation of real wages and supported capital inflows.

8. The ratios of assets and liabilities of the financial sector to total wealth rose from around 0.4 to 1.15 between 1980 and 2005. This increase in financial depth was accompanied by a steady relaxation of regulatory controls over finance imposed during the New Deal. In most instances, regulation was eased in response to innovations in the market. The possibilities they created to make paper profits generated political pressure on regulators to relax existing controls. A "light touch" regulatory regime was put into place, on the assumption that firms would effectively police themselves to avoid financial breakdowns.

9. Beyond the changes in ideology mentioned above, the intellectual rationale for much of the shift in regulation came from the abolition of Keynesian concepts in macroeconomic theory and the orogeny of finance theory beginning in the 1950s. Wall Street applauded both developments because they veiled extreme speculation with intellectual respectability.

Weighing the Contributions

All nine factors acted together to cause the crisis. Nevertheless, there may be room to ponder the relative significance of each. Factors 5, 8, and 9 would probably have supported a financial mania, followed by panic and crash, regardless of what happened on the real side of the economy. After the long ascent of equity prices mentioned in point 4, the system was ripe for a shakeout, while deregulation set the stage for a major crisis. The key question is how it was transmitted to the real side.

The shift in household behavior noted in points 3 and 6 provided the crucial link. Households were pushed in the direction of running up debt to maintain living standards in the face of their deteriorating earned income position (point 2). The booms in asset prices provided collateral to enable them to borrow domestically. With the U.S. economy as a whole becoming a positive net borrower, it needed short-term capital inflows. The rest of the world was willing to provide the finance (point 7), with China and the oil exporters directing short-term capital flows to the United States. The strong dollar exchange rate vis-à-vis the renminbi (especially) greased the net import skids.

In global macroeconomic terms all these economic factors acted together, as of course they had to. The shift in political economy (factor 1) made the whole process possible. That environment will have to change if a relapse into economic crisis is to be avoided. In fall 2009 irrational enthusiasms supported by extremely cheap money provided by the Fed reemerged in the financial sector—not a good omen.

Pondering the Future

Donald Rumsfeld is probably not a close student of Keynes. But he does know how military planners think, no doubt including the early-nineteenth-century Prussian theorist Carl von Clausewitz, who wrote about the "fog of war." Maynard himself would probably have approved of Rumsfeld's 2002 observation (with its own version of fundamental uncertainty) that "[t]here are known knowns. These are things we know that we know. There are known unknowns. That is to say, there are things that we now know we don't know. But there are also unknown unknowns. These are things we do not know we don't know." Rumsfeld's formulation was on target for the future of U.S. and global macroeconomics. Even more than usual, it undoubtedly holds unknowns that we cannot possibly know.

As we consider the prospects, it makes sense to begin by thinking about known knowns. Among them are the facts that U.S. net borrowing flows must sum to zero, and that there are very few degrees of freedom in an aggregated global macro model comprising the United States, "China" broadly construed to include countries with structural trade surpluses, Euroland, oil exporters, and the rest.

Net Borrowing

It is not hard to put together unpleasant scenarios. A more interesting question is what a favorable one might look like. One component could be a return of household net borrowing to its circa 1980 levels in the range of −7% of GDP at the trough of a recession. (That is, households would be lending +7% of GDP to the rest of the system.) By the end of 2009 it had fallen below −3%. Where it will bottom out depends on how strongly fear of the future will drive households toward increased saving. The relevant historical parallel is the Great Depression. U.S. consumers practiced conservative finance for more than a generation thereafter.

If residential investment recovers on the upswing, a return to the range of net borrowing prior to and immediately after 1980 in Figure 5.8 is a possibility. Say that households borrow −3% of GDP (or lend +3%) near the top of the cycle.

There will have to be fiscal contraction in the wake of the Obama stimulus package. If government net borrowing drops to the +3% range, then government and household borrowing flows would be offsetting, with foreign and business net borrowing becoming "twins."

International Implications

If these changes play out, the peak U.S. current account deficit could fall to the range of 0.5% of world GDP, or roughly 2% of local output. How would the global economy adjust? On capital account, it probably would have no problem in providing short-term capital flows to "finance" a U.S. deficit of that magnitude. On trade account, the non-oil economies with structural export surpluses such as Germany and China would have to go through a large readjustment; to a lesser extent oil exporters would be in trouble as well.

One relevant question is whether the United States retains enough hegemonic power to force such an adjustment. Contemporary theories discussed in Chapter 8, such as the global savings glut or Bretton Woods II, assign a passive role to the United States. In an update of the Triffin dilemma it reacts to whatever the rest of the world chooses to do. Controlling national net borrowing is not easy, but there are highly imperfect policies discussed below that might allow it to be done. A related question is whether the United States still has the industrial capacity to increase exports and/or substitute imports to the tune of 1% of world GDP or 4% of local GDP at the top of the cycle.

Income Distribution

Another known unknown involves future shifts in the income distribution, with the labor share and the interest rate as the key variables. Exiting from the stimulus will require interest rate increases, which would dampen asset price excursions and presumably discourage household borrowing. Whether there will be a recovery in households' earnings big enough to let them pay for desired consumption without running up new liabilities is a key known unknown.

The standard explanation of income inequalities from the economic mainstream is that they are inevitable. The economy is operating perfectly efficiently, so that there is no slack that could be utilized for income redistribution. The simple truth is that factors such as globalization and financial innovation have shifted incomes in favor of affluent agents. A more fundamental cause was systematic repression of labor's bargaining power beginning with the Reagan administration.

From a broader perspective, the sociopolitical question is why such income concentration has been permitted to occur. Surely changes in the nature of the social contract must be involved. Consider the head of Norway's Norsk Hydro. A few years ago he was getting around $1 million per year in salary plus rather less in realized stock options, levels that his board's compensation committee allowed him. This was less than 10% of what CEOs at smaller American competitors were paid. His relative penury was in part a consequence of the Nordic socioeconomic model, which has rested for decades on income equalization. The United States was never anywhere near as egalitarian as Norway, but it is striking how its societal tolerance for enormous payments to people at the top has grown over the past two or three decades.

Finance

The main question is *not* about formulating policies to help the financial sector restrain its own excesses, although that would certainly be desirable. On that front the prospects are not promising. After all, over a period of twenty years the sector staged the 1987 stock market crash, the Mexican crisis, the Asian crisis, Enron, the LTCM collapse, the end of the Internet bubble, and 2007–2009. An almost known known is that finance has some new catastrophe hiding up its sleeve.

Policy Options

The real policy challenge in this area is to build a firewall between finance and the real economy so as to shield the rest of us from the bankers' excesses. A revived version of Glass-Steagall on the financial side would be helpful (as was being promoted by Paul Volcker in early 2010), along with breaking up or imposing high capital requirements on large institutions. Restrictions on households such as ceilings on loan-to-value ratios for residential mortgages along with protection against fraud would be helpful.

Long before James Tobin, in the *General Theory* Keynes recommended a transfer tax on financial transactions. Restrictions or taxes on short-term borrowing by financial firms could help avoid maturity mismatches between assets and liabilities. The IMF recommendation for a capital levy and a FAT tax on banks' financial activities may enter into discussion. Such policies might prove politically feasible if congressional hearings into finance that got under way in early 2010 follow the path blazed by the Pecora hearings after the Great Crash.

The state can be all thumbs when it attempts intervention to reduce income inequality. Nevertheless, tools do exist. Progressive taxes on income and capital gains which could be used to hold back growth of high incomes, steps to strengthen union recruiting and bargaining power, aggressive congressional or judicial investigations of Wall Street, salutary jail sentences for financial insiders besides Bernie Madoff, and the taxes just mentioned to recoup part of the cost of the bailout all spring to mind. One reason why the Norsk Hydro chief mentioned above was so "poor" is that the government as part owner of the company intervened to hold his remuneration down.

The trade balance does respond to the exchange rate in the United States, meaning that there is room for intervention by the Fed to devalue the dollar. Selective capital controls might ease the task. (Wall Street would resist furiously but would not necessarily be 100% successful.) Export subsidies and import restrictions, disguised or not, might also have a role to play. So would conscious industrial policy, expanding on the ones included in the Obama stimulus package. The point is not so much beggar-my-neighbor but rather rebalancing the external position of the U.S. economy so that it does not have to operate in self-destructive fashion.

All these and similar policies will not be applied unless the world and national economies go through a double movement, toward a more egalitarian and antiliberal sociopolitical regime. That happened late in the nineteenth century and in the wake of the Great Depression. This possibility is the most important known unknown. It is not obvious that it will come to pass. The unknown unknowns will seal its fate.

Notes

The discussion of long political economy cycles is based on Palma (2009). He reviews the ideas of Kalecki, Polanyi (1944), and Hirschman (1982). All three are well worth reading.

Piketty and Saez (2003) is the standard source on the U.S. size distribution of income, based on income tax data. Kindleberger and Aliber (2005) and Soros (2009) provide helpful empirical background on combined expansions of asset prices and leverage, followed by a crash. In his *Treatise on Money* (1930) Keynes outlines a similar cycle involving bulls and bear speculators.

Barbosa-Filho et al. (2008) gives more detail on net borrowing and household consumption patterns.

References

Adrian, Tobias, and Hyun Song Shin (2008). "Liquidity and Leverage." New York: Federal Reserve Bank of New York. http://www.princeton.edu/~hsshin/www/LiquidityLeverage.pdf.

Akerlof, George A., and Robert J. Shiller (2009). *Animal Spirits: How Human Psychology Drives the Economy and Why It Matters for Global Capitalism*. Princeton, NJ: Princeton University Press.

Alexander, Kern, John Eatwell, Avinash Persaud, and Robert Reoch (2008). *Financial Supervision and Crisis Management in the EU*. Strasbourg: European Parliament.

Amadeo, Edward J. (1989). *Keynes's Principle of Effective Demand*. Brookfield, VT: Gower.

Arnim, Rudiger von (2009). "Recession and Rebalancing: How the Housing and Credit Crises Will Impact U.S. Real Activity." *Journal of Policy Modeling*, 31: 309–324.

Backhouse, Roger E., and Bradley W. Bateman, eds. (2006). *The Cambridge Companion to Keynes*. New York: Cambridge University Press.

Barberis, Nicholas C., and Richard H. Thaler (2003). "A Survey of Behavioral Finance." In George Constantinides et al., eds., *Handbook of the Economics of Finance: Financial Markets and Asset Pricing*, 1053–1124. Amsterdam: Elsevier.

Barbosa-Filho, Nelson H., and Lance Taylor (2006). "Distributive and Demand Cycles in the U.S. Economy—A Structuralist Goodwin Model." *Metroeconomica*, 57: 389–411.

Barbosa-Filho, Nelson H., Codrina Rada, Lance Taylor, and Luca Zamparelli (2008). "Cycles and Trend in U.S. Net Borrowing Flows." *Journal of Post-Keynesian Economics*, 30: 623–647.

Barro, Robert J. (1974). "Are Government Bonds Net Worth?" *Journal of Political Economy*, 82: 1095–1117.

——— (1989). "The Neoclassical Approach to Fiscal Policy." In Robert J. Barro, ed., *Modern Business Cycle Theory*, 178–235. Cambridge, MA: Harvard University Press.

Bernanke, Ben (2005). "The Global Savings Glut and the U.S. Current Account Deficit." http://www.federalreserve.gov/boarddocs/speeches/2005/200503102/.

Black, Fischer, and Myron Scholes (1973). "The Pricing of Options and Corporate Liabilities." *Journal of Political Economy,* 81: 637–654.

Blaug, Mark (1997). *Economic Theory in Retrospect.* 5th edition. New York: Cambridge University Press.

Brunnermeier, Markus, Andrew Crockett, Charles Goodhart, Avinash D. Presaud, and Hyun Shin (2009). "The Fundamental Principles of Financial Regulation." Geneva: International Center for Monetary and Banking Studies. Available at http://wyplosz.eu/fichier/Geneva11_ebook.pdf.

Buchanan, James M. (1976). "Barro on the Ricardian Equivalence Theorem." *Journal of Political Economy,* 84: 337–342.

Cassidy, John (2009). *How Markets Fail: The Logic of Economic Calamities.* New York: Farrar, Straus and Giroux.

Clark, John Bates (1908, 2008). Reprint. *The Distribution of Wealth: A Theory of Wages, Interest, and Profits.* Gloucester, UK: Dodo Press.

Copeland, Morris A. (1952). *A Study of Money-flows in the United States.* New York: National Bureau of Economic Research.

Crotty, James (1999). "Was Keynes a Corporatist? Keynes's Radical Views on Industrial Policy and Macro Policy in the 1920s." *Journal of Economic Issues,* 33: 555–577.

D'Arista, Jane (2009a). "The Evolving International Monetary System." *Cambridge Journal of Economics,* 33: 633–652.

——— (2009b). "Setting an Agenda for Monetary Reform." Working Paper no. 190. Amherst, MA: Political Economy Research Institute.

Davidson, Paul (2003). "The Terminology of Uncertainty in Economics and the Philosophy of an Active Role for Government Policies." In Runde and Mizuhara (2003), 229–238.

Derman, Emanuel, and Nassim Nicholas Taleb (2005). "The Illusions of Dynamic Replication." *Quantitative Finance,* 5: 323–326.

Diamond, Jared (1997). *Guns, Germs, and Steel: The Fates of Human Societies.* New York: W. W. Norton.

Dobb, Maurice (1973). *Theories of Value and Distribution since Adam Smith: Ideology and Economic Theory.* Cambridge: Cambridge University Press.

Domar, Evsey (1944). "The 'Burden of Debt' and the National Income. *American Economic Review,* 34: 798–827.

——— (1946). "Capital Expansion, Rate of Growth, and Employment." *Econometrica,* 14: 137–147.

Dooley, Michael P., David-Folkerts-Landau, and Peter M. Garber (2003). "An Essay on the Revived Bretton Woods System." NBER Working Paper no. W9971. http://papers.ssrn.com/sol3/papers.cfm?abstract_id=447259.

Duesenberry, James S. (1949). *Income, Saving, and the Theory of Consumer Behavior.* Cambridge, MA: Harvard University Press.

Dutt, Amitava Krishna (1984). "Stagnation, Income Distribution, and Monopoly Power." *Cambridge Journal of Economics,* 8: 25–40.

——— (2002). "Aggregate Demand–Aggregate Supply Analysis: A History." *History of Political Economy,* 34: 321–363.

Eatwell, John, and Lance Taylor (2000). *Global Finance at Risk: The Case for International Regulation.* New York: New Press.

Eichberger, Jürgen, and Ian R. Harper (1997). *Financial Economics.* New York: Oxford University Press.

Eichengreen, Barry J. (1996). *Golden Fetters: The Gold Standard and the Great Depression, 1919–1939* New York: Oxford University Press.

Ellsberg, Daniel (2001). *Risk, Ambiguity, and Decision.* New York: Garland.

Fama, Eugene F. (1965). "The Behavior of Stock Market Prices." *Journal of Business,* 38 (January): 34–105.

Feduzi, Alberto (2005). "On the Relationship between Keynes's Conception of Evidential Weight and the Ellsberg Paradox." *Journal of Economic Psychology,* 28: 545–565.

Fisher, Irving (1930, 1967). Reprint. *The Theory of Interest: As Determined by Impatience to Spend Income and Opportunity to Invest It.* New York: Augustus M. Kelly.

——— (1933). "The Debt-Deflation Theory of Great Depressions." *Econometrica,* 1: 337–357.

Flaschel, Peter (2009). *The Macrodynamics of Capitalism: Elements for a Synthesis of Marx, Keynes, and Schumpeter.* Berlin: Springer-Verlag.

Foley, Duncan K. (1986). *Understanding Capital: Marx's Economic Theory.* Cambridge, MA: Harvard University Press.

——— (2006). *Adam's Fallacy: A Guide to Economic Theology.* Cambridge, MA: Harvard University Press.

Foley, Duncan K., and Thomas R. Michl (1999). *Growth and Distribution.* Cambridge, MA: Harvard University Press.

Friedman, Milton (1957). *A Theory of the Consumption Function.* Princeton, NJ: Princeton University Press.

——— (1968). "The Role of Monetary Policy." *American Economic Review,* 58: 1–17.

Friedman, Milton, and Anna Jacobson Schwartz (1963). *A Monetary History of the United States, 1867–1960.* Princeton, NJ: Princeton University Press.

Galbraith, John Kenneth (1954). *The Great Crash, 1929.* Boston: Houghton Mifflin.

Godley, Wynne, and Francis Cripps (1983). *Macroeconomics.* London: Fontana.

Godley, Wynne, and Marc Lavoie (2007). *Monetary Economics: An Integrated Ap-*

proach to Credit, Money, Income, Production, and Wealth. London: Palgrave/Macmillan.

Goodwin, Richard M. (1967). "A Growth Cycle." In C. H. Feinstein, ed., *Socialism, Capitalism, and Growth,* 54–58. Cambridge: Cambridge University Press.

Gordon, Robert J. (1989). "Fresh Water, Salt Water, and Other Macroeconomic Elixirs." *The Economic Record,* 65: 177–184.

Hansen, Alvin (1938). *Full Recovery or Stagnation?* New York: Norton.

Harberger, Arnold C. (1962). "The Incidence of the Corporate Income Tax." *Journal of Political Economy,* 70: 215–240.

Harcourt, G. C. (2006). *The Structure of Post-Keynesian Economics: The Core Contributions of the Pioneers.* Cambridge: Cambridge University Press.

Harrod, Roy F. (1939). "An Essay in Dynamic Theory." *Economic Journal,* 49: 14–33.

——— (1951). *The Life of John Maynard Keynes.* London: Macmillan.

Heilbroner, Robert (1999). *The Worldly Philosophers.* 7th revised edition. New York: Simon and Schuster.

Hicks, John R. (1937). "Mr Keynes and the 'Classics': A Suggested Interpretation." *Econometrica,* 5: 147–159.

Hirschman, Albert O. (1981). "The Social and Political Matrix of Inflation: Elaborations on the Latin American Experience." In *Essays in Trespassing: Economics to Politics and Beyond,* 177–207. New York: Cambridge University Press.

——— (1982). *Shifting Involvements: Private Interest and Public Action.* Princeton, NJ: Princeton University Press.

Ho, Karen Z. (2009). *Liquidated: An Ethnography of Wall Street.* Durham, NC: Duke University Press.

Hobsbawm, Eric (1962). *The Age of Revolution: Europe, 1789–1848.* New York: Viking.

——— (1975). *The Age of Capital.* New York: Viking.

——— (1987). *The Age of Empire.* New York: Viking.

——— (1994). *The Age of Extremes: The Short Twentieth Century, 1914–1991.* New York: Viking.

Ingrao, Bruna, and Giorgio Israel (1990). *The Invisible Hand: Economic Equilibrium in the History of Science.* Cambridge, MA: MIT Press.

Kahn, Richard F., and Michael V. Posner (1974). "Cambridge Economics and the Balance of Payments." *London and Cambridge Economic Bulletin,* 85: 19–32.

Kaldor, Nicholas (1961). "Capital Accumulation and Economic Growth." In F. A. Lutz and D. C. Hague, eds., *The Theory of Capital Accumulation,* 177–222. London: Macmillan.

——— (1978). "Causes of the Slow Rate of Growth of the United Kingdom." In *Further Essays on Economic Theory,* 100–138. London: Duckworth..

——— (1982). *The Scourge of Monetarism.* Oxford: Oxford University Press.

Kalecki, Michal (1943). "Political Aspects of Full Employment," *Political Quarterly, 14*: 204-223.

――― (1971). *Selected Essays on the Dynamics of the Capitalist Economy: 1933–1940.* Cambridge: Cambridge University Press.

Kaplan, Daniel, and Leon Glass (1995). *Understanding Nonlinear Dynamics.* New York: Springer-Verlag.

Keynes, John Maynard (1971–1989). *The Collected Writings of John Maynard Keynes.* 30 volumes. London: Macmillan/Cambridge University Press for the Royal Economic Society. Volumes referred to herein are:
  2. *The Economic Consequences of the Peace* (1919, 1971)
  4. *A Tract on Monetary Reform* (1923, 1971)
  5. *A Treatise on Money, 1: The Pure Theory of Money* (1930, 1971)
  7. *The General Theory of Employment, Interest, and Money* (1936, 1973)
  8. *A Treatise on Probability* (1921, 1973)
  9. *Essays in Persuasion* (1931, 1972)
  10. *Essays in Biography* (1933, 1972)
  14. *The General Theory and After, 2: Defense and Development* (1973)
  21. *Activities, 1931–9: World Crises and Policies in Britain and America* (1982)

Kindleberger, Charles P. (1985). *Keynesianism vs. Monetarism and Other Essays in Financial History.* London: George Allen and Unwin.

――― (1986). *The World in Depression: 1929–1939.* 2nd edition. Berkeley: University of California Press.

――― (1993). *A Financial History of Western Europe.* 2nd edition. New York: Oxford University Press.

Kindleberger, Charles P., and Robert Z. Aliber (2005). *Manias, Panics, and Crises: A History of Financial Crises.* 5th edition. Hoboken, NJ: John Wiley and Sons.

Kline, Morris (1980, 2009). Reprint. *Mathematics: The Loss of Certainty.* New York: Barnes and Noble.

Knight, Frank (1921). *Risk, Uncertainty, and Profit.* Boston: Houghton Mifflin.

Kydland, Finn E., and Edward C. Prescott (1982). "Time to Build and Aggregate Fluctuations." *Econometrica,* 50: 1345–70.

Laffer, Arthur B. (2004). "The Laffer Curve: Past, Present, and Future." http://www.heritage.org/research/taxes/bg1765.cfm.

Leontief, Wassily W. (1986). *Input-Output Economics.* 2nd edition. New York: Oxford University Press.

Lindblom, Charles (1977). *Politics and Markets: The World's Political-Economic Systems.* New York: Basic Books.

Lucas, Robert E., Jr. (1972). "Expectations and the Neutrality of Money." *Journal of Economic Theory,* 4: 103–124.

——— (1976). "Econometric Policy Evaluation: A Critique." *Carnegie-Rochester Conference Series on Public Policy,* 1: 19–46.

Mandelbrot, Benoit B. (1997). *Fractals and Scaling in Finance: Discontinuities, Concentration, Risk.* New York: Springer.

Marglin, Stephen A. (1984). *Growth, Distribution, and Prices.* Cambridge, MA: Harvard University Press.

Markowitz, Harry (1952). "Portfolio Selection." *Journal of Finance,* 7: 77–91.

McCauley, Joseph L. (2004). *Dynamics of Markets: Econophysics and Finance.* New York: Cambridge University Press.

Merton, Robert C. (1973). "Theory of Rational Option Pricing." *Bell Journal of Economics and Management Science,* 4: 141–183.

Minsky, Hyman P. (1975, 2008). Reprint. *John Maynard Keynes.* New York: McGraw-Hill.

——— (1983). "Monetary Policies and the International Financial Environment." Mimeo. Department of Economics, Washington University St. Louis.

Mirowski, Philip (1989). *More Heat than Light: Economics as Social Physics, Physics as Nature's Economics.* Cambridge: Cambridge University Press.

Mitra-Kahn, Benjamin H. (2009). "What Is an Economy? From the Emergence of an Economic Sphere to Modern GDP." Ph.D. dissertation, City University, London, chaps. 8 and 9. www.mitrakahn.com.

Modigliani, Franco (1944). "Liquidity Preference and the Theory of Interest and Money." *Econometrica,* 12: 45–88.

Modigliani, Franco, and Richard E. Brumberg (1954). "Utility Analysis and the Consumption Function: An Interpretation of Cross-Section Data." In Kenneth K. Kurihara, ed., *Post-Keynesian Economics,* 388–436. New Brunswick, NJ: Rutgers University Press.

Modigliani, Franco, and Merton H. Miller (1962). "The Cost of Capital, Corporate Finance, and the Theory of Investment. *American Economic Review,* 48: 262–297.

Ocampo, José Antonio, Codrina Rada, and Lance Taylor (2009). *Growth and Policy in Developing Countries: A Structural Approach.* New York: Columbia University Press.

Okun, Arthur M. (1962, 1983). "'Potential GNP': Its Measurement and Significance." Reprinted in Joseph Pechman, ed., *Economics for Policy-Making: Selected Essays of Arthur M. Okun,* 145–158. Cambridge, MA: MIT Press.

Palma, José Gabriel (2009). "The Revenge of the Market on the Rentiers: Why Neo-Liberal Reports of the End of History Turned Out to Be Premature." *Cambridge Journal of Economics,* 33: 829–869.

Partnoy, Frank (2009). *The Match King: Ivar Kreuger, the Financial Genius behind a Century of Wall Street Scandals.* New York: Public Affairs.

Pasinetti, Luigi L. (1974). *Growth and Income Distribution*. Cambridge: Cambridge University Press.

——— (1981). *Structural Change and Economic Growth*. Cambridge: Cambridge University Press.

Patinkin, Don (1966). *Money, Interest, and Prices*. New York: Harper and Row.

Phelps, Edmund S. (1969). "The New Microeconomics in Employment and Inflation Theory." *American Economic Review (Papers and Proceedings)*, 59: 147–160.

Pigou, A. C. (1929). *Industrial Fluctuations*. London: Macmillan.

——— (1943). "The Classical Stationary State." *Economic Journal*, 53: 343–351.

Piketty, Thomas, and Emmanuel Saez (2003). "Income Inequality in the United States, 1913–1998." *Quarterly Journal of Economics*, 118: 1–39. Data update available at http://elsa.berkeley.edu/~saez/.

Polanyi, Karl (1944). *The Great Transformation*. New York: Rinehart.

Rada, Codrina, and Lance Taylor (2006). "Empty Sources of Growth Accounting, and Empirical Replacements à la Goodwin and Kaldor with Some Beef." *Structural Change and Economic Dynamics*, 17: 486–500.

Ramsey, Frank P. (1928). "A Mathematical Theory of Saving." *Economic Journal*, 38: 543–559.

Rauchway, Eric (2008). *The Great Depression and the New Deal*. New York: Oxford University Press.

Robertson, D. H. (1922). *Money*. Cambridge Economic Handbook. London: Bisbet and Co.

——— (1933). "Saving and Hoarding." *Economic Journal*, 43: 399–413.

Robinson, Joan (1962). *Essays in the Theory of Economic Growth*. London: Macmillan.

——— (1969). *The Accumulation of Capital*. 3rd edition. London: Macmillan.

——— (1974). *History versus Equilibrium*. London: Thames Papers in Economics, Thames Polytechnic.

Romer, Christina D. (1992). "What Ended the Great Depression." *Journal of Economic History*, 52: 757–784.

Romer, David (2001). *Advanced Macroeconomics*. 2nd edition. New York: McGraw-Hill.

Rowthorn, Robert E. (1982). "Demand, Real Wages, and Economic Growth." *Studi Economici*, 18: 2–53.

Runde, Jochen, and Sohei Mizuhara (2003). *The Philosophy of Keynes's Economics: Probability, Uncertainty, and Convention*. London: Routledge.

Russell, Bertrand (1967). *The Autobiography of Bertrand Russell: 1872–1914*. Boston: Little Brown.

Samuelson, Paul A. (1939). "Interactions between the Multiplier Analysis and the Principle of Acceleration." *Review of Economics and Statistics,* 21: 75–78.

——— (1964). "A Brief Survey of Post-Keynesian Developments." In Robert Lekachman, ed., *Keynes's General Theory: A Report of Three Decades.* New York: St. Martin's.

——— (1968). "What Classical and Neo-Classical Monetary Theory Really Was." *Canadian Journal of Economics,* 1: 1–15.

Schumpeter, Joseph (1934). *The Theory of Economic Development.* Cambridge, MA: Harvard University Press.

——— (1947). *Capitalism, Socialism, and Democracy.* Revised edition. New York: Harper and Brothers.

——— (1954). *History of Economic Analysis.* New York: Oxford University Press.

Skidelsky, Robert (1983, 1992, 2001). *John Maynard Keynes.* 3 volumes. London: Macmillan.

——— (2009). *Keynes: The Return of the Master.* New York: PublicAffairs.

Skott, Peter (2008). "Theoretical and Empirical Shortcomings of the Kaleckian Investment Function." http://www.umass.edu/economics/publications/2008-11.pdf.

Smith, Adam (1776, 1994). Reprint. *The Wealth of Nations,* edited by Edwin Cannan. New York: Modern Library.

Solow, Robert M. (1956). "A Contribution to the Theory of Economic Growth." *Quarterly Journal of Economics,* 70: 65–94.

——— (1957). "Technical Change and the Aggregate Production Function." *Review of Economics and Statistics,* 39: 312–320.

Soros, George (2009). *The Crash of 2008 and What It Means.* New York: PublicAffairs.

Steindl, Josef (1990). "Saving and Debt" and "The Control of the Economy." In *Economic Papers, 1941–88,* 208–229. London: Macmillan

Sunkel, Osvaldo (1960). "Inflation in Chile: An Unorthodox Approach." *International Economic Papers,* 10: 107–131.

Syrquin, Moshe (1984). "Resource Reallocation and Productivity Growth." In Moshe Syrquin, Lance Taylor, and Larry E. Westphal, , *Economic Structure and Performance: Essays in Honor of Hollis B. Chenery,* 75–101. Orlando: Academic Press.

Taleb, Nassim Nicholas (2007). *The Black Swan: The Impact of the Highly Improbable.* New York: Random House.

Taylor, John B. (1993). "Discretion versus Policy Rules in Practice." *Carnegie-Rochester Series on Public Policy,* 39: 195–214.

Taylor, Lance (2004). *Reconstructing Macroeconomics: Structuralist Proposals and Critiques of the Mainstream.* Cambridge, MA: Harvard University Press.

——— (2008). "A Foxy Hedgehog: Wynne Godley and Macroeconomic Modeling." *Cambridge Journal of Economics*, 32: 639–663.

——— (2010). "Growth, Cycles, Asset Prices, and Finance," *Metroeconomica*, forthcoming.

Taylor, Lance, and Rudiger von Arnim (2006). "Modeling the Impact of Trade Liberalization: A Critique of Computable General Equilibrium Models." Oxford: Oxfam International.

Tett, Gillian (2009). *Fool's Gold: How the Bold Dream of a Small Tribe at J. P. Morgan Was Corrupted by Wall Street Greed and Unleashed a Catastrophe.* New York: Free Press.

Tobin, James (1969). "A General Equilibrium Approach to Monetary Theory." *Journal of Money, Credit, and Banking,* 1: 15–29.

Triffin, Robert (1960). *Gold and the Dollar Crisis.* New Haven, CT: Yale University Press.

——— (1964). *The Evolution of the International Monetary System: Historical Reappraisal and Future Perspectives.* Princeton, NJ: Princeton Studies in International Finance no. 12.

Veblen, Thorstein (1899, 1994). Reprint. *The Theory of the Leisure Class.* New York: Dover.

——— (1904, 2006). Reprint. *The Theory of Business Enterprise.* Whitefish, MT: Kessinger Publishing.

Weitzman, Martin L. (2007). "Adaptive Expectations and Asset-Return Puzzles." *American Economic Review,* 97: 1102–30.

Wiener, Norbert (1961). *Cybernetics: Or Control and Communication in the Animal and the Machine.* 2nd edition. Cambridge, MA: MIT Press.

Williamson, John, and Chris Milner (1991). *The World Economy.* New York: New York University Press.

Index

Italicized page numbers with a *t* or an *f* indicate a table or a figure respectively.

absorption approach, 305, 326–331
accountability, 295–296
AFDC (Aid to Families with Dependent Children), 112
aggregate demand/aggregate supply (AD/AS) model. *See* AS/AD (aggregate supply/aggregate demand) model
AIG, 126, 138, 290–291, 294, 299, 301
animal spirits, 119, 121; Cambridge equation and, 182–183, *183f*; finance theory and, 279, 284; growth models and, 163, 165, 168, 169, 173–174
anti-neoclassical economics, 67–68
arbitrage: asset price and, 279; finance theory and, 255–256; IRP and, 322; neoclassical economics and, 46; real interest rate determination theory and, 57–58, *58f*, 61–62; *Tract on Monetary Reform* (Keynes) and, 257. *See also* exchange rates
AS/AD (aggregate supply/aggregate demand) model: aggregate demand described, 3–6, 53–56; aggregate production function and, 63; forced saving and, 82; GDP and, 4; interest rates and, 169; macroeconomics and, 159–161, *160f*, 223, 225; microeconomics and, 159; new classical economics and, 223; output and profit income flows responses and, 169
Asian crisis of 1998, 22, 30, 106, 313, 350
asset prices: business cycles and, 24; deficits and, 16–17; depression during gold standard era and, 88, 96; entropy versus reversibility and, 57; finance theory and, 234, 279; financial crises and, 73; financial cycles and, 124, 140–142, *143t*, 144–145, 168; GDP and, 9–12, *9f*; global financial crisis of 2007–2009 and, *10f*, *11f*, 126–127, 198, 257–258, 343; Great Crash and, 98; Great Depression and, 55, 106; Keynesian economics and, 9–12, *9f*, *10f*; liquidity and, 131, 133, 134–136; liquidity preference and, 129; liquidity trap effects and, 12; macroeconomics and, 169, 170; own-rate of interest and, 60; permanent income hypothesis, and falling, 48; probability theories and, 117, 120; real side of economy and, 146–147; risk and, 256–257, 264–266; trade cycle dynamics and, 163; wealth effects and, 51
asymmetric knowledge, 33–35

balance-of-payments flows, 89–92, *91t*, *309t*, 310, *311t*–*312t*, 313, 315–318, *316t*
bank holding companies, 290
Banking Act of 1935, 112. *See also* Federal Reserve (Fed)
banking school, and endogenous money, 73, *74t*, 75–76, 78–81, 109, 234, 284–289, 329–330
banking systems: credit, and assets of, 73–75, *74t*, 76–82; finance theory and, *214f*, 286, 290; interdependent and, 104; nationalization of banks and, 293; shadow, 103, 134–135, 228–229, 278, 344

369

Barro, Robert, 242–243, 246–247
Bayes's Law/Bayesian analysis, 114, 117–118, 121–127, 162, 193, 277, 283
beggar-my-neighbor policies, 22
behavioral finance, 122, 167, 258, 278–284
Bernanke, Ben, 2, 18, 120, 279, 300, 333
bimetalism, 88, 89
Black, Fisher, 257, 270, 271, 274–277, 302
Black-Scholes-Merton (BSM) formula, 257, 270, 302
Black-Scholes valuation, 271, 274–277
Böhm-Bawerk, Eugen von, 54, 65–66
boom/bust model: finance theory and, 114–115, 218; financial cycles and, 114–115, 139–140, 142, 144–145, 168; Kindleberger and, 114–115, 167, 218, 317, 340; Minsky's cycle/crisis model and, 135, *141f*, 174, 192–198, *196f*, 218; Minsky's hedge/speculative Ponzi classification finance and, 144, 193–194, 197, 256; Soros and, 140, 142
boundary problem (firewalls), 111, 292–294, 355–356
Bretton Woods system, 22, 26, 29, 108, 170, 270, 307–308, 327–328
Bretton Woods II, *309t*, *311t–312t*, 333–336, 354
Brown, Robert, 274–275, 282–283
Brownian motion thermal equilibrium (stochastic differential equations), 274–275, 282–283, 284
Bryan, William Jennings, 88, 90, 97, 159, 284
BSM (Black-Scholes-Merton) formula, 257, 270, 302
bubbles, financial. *See* boom/bust model
business cycle model: asset price effects in, 147; Keynesian economics and, 24, 173–174, 181, 183, 196–198, 202–206; positive feedback effect and, 173–174, 181, 183, 196–198; pro-cyclical behavior and, 174, 202–206; real interest rate determination theory and, 56–58, *58f*, 61–62
business cycles: capital formation and, 59–61, 130; Fisher arbitrage and, 57–58, *58f*, 61–62; global financial crisis of 2007–2009 and, 342–343, 351; liquidity preference and, 24; political, 338; RBC models and, 202–203, 247–250, 252, 280;

real business cycle school and, 45, 54–55, 67, *74t*, 80–81; residential investment decisions and, 127

call option, 271–274, *273f*, 276, 279
Cambridge equation, 23, 180, 182–183, *183f*, 216, 221, 244
capital: capital formation and, 59–61, 127, 130, 173; CAPM, 257, 268; LTCM, 284, 299, 300, 355; marginal efficiency of, 58, 127, 149–150, 162–163, 181, 208; Marxist capitalism and, 25, 44–45; speculative capital movements and, 305, 323–324
capital asset price model (CAPM), 257, 268
carry trade, 287, 300, 323–326, 334
CDOs. *See* collateralized debt obligations (CDOs)
CDSs. *See* credit default swaps (CDSs)
Churchill, Winston, 97, 105, 164
Clark, John Bates, 56, 62–65, 84–85, 176–178, 251
classical economics: collective actors and, 13, 16, 29–31, 62, 83; industrial economic policy and, 33, 41, 42, 83; macroeconomics history and, 25–26, 30, 231. *See also* economic thought in 19th century; neoclassical economics; *specific classical economists*
collateralized debt obligations (CDOs), 100, 133, 134–139, 211, 257, 270, 277–278, 288
collective actors: behavioral finance and, 122, 167, 258, 278–284; classical economics and, 13, 16, 29–31, 62, 83; income distribution and, 167–168; Keynesian economics and, 3, 16, 62, 83, 167–169, 215; national income accounts and, 167–168; rationality and, 167; real side of economy and, 167; Soros on, 1–2
Commodity Futures Modernization Act, 292
commodity prices, 13, 39, 57, 95–96, 145–147, 166–167, 219, 265, 320. *See also* prices of goods and services
Commons, John R., 67
competition, 33, 46
consumption: conspicuous, 23, 67, 210; consumption function, *158t*, 226–228,

227f; life cycle consumption model, 227–228; long-run and, 226–228, 227f
counter-cyclicality, stabilization/destabilization, 91–92, 169, 285
counter-party positions (interdependent banking system), 104
credit: banking system assets and, 73–75, 74t, 76–82; CDSs and, 8, 10f, 11f, 35, 101, 136–139, 257–258, 292, 344; finance theory and, 126–127; forced saving adjustment process and, 74t, 77–79, 81, 165; global financial crisis of 2007–2009 and, 126–127; Kindleberger on expansion of, 345; macro money/credit discussion and, 73–74, 74t; money/credit effects, 3, 73–74, 74t
credit default swaps (CDSs), 8, 10f, 11f, 35, 101, 136–139, 257–258, 292, 344
Crusoe and Friday, and loanable funds, 61–62, 333
currency school, 74t, 76–77, 79
Currie, Lauchlin, 108–110, 231

Davidson, Paul, 282, 303
debt deflation, 59, 87–88, 97, 108, 285
debt/GDP ratio, 16, 226, 242–246
debt movement, 168, 209, 213f, 214f
debt-to-income ratios, 2, 209f, 211, 298, 351
deficits: asset prices and, 16–17; devaluations, and reduction of, 349; Keynesian economics and, 15–19, 18f; liability finance and, 16–17, 35, 91–92; twin deficit theory and, 71–72, 201, 331–332, 354
"degrees of freedom"/variables in international trade and financial flows, 92, 217–218, 309, 334, 336, 353
demand-driven growth: Cambridge equation and, 23, 180, 182–183, 183f, 216, 221, 244; current account adjustments and, 330; cyclical growth and, 186, 188–189, 188t; distributive cycles and, 216–217; Domar and, 180–182, 221; financial cycles and, 194; global financial crisis of 2007–2009 and, 171, 208; Harrod and, 180–182, 221; Kaldor and, 179–180, 184, 185f, 215–216, 221; macroeconomics and, 215–216; positive feedback and, 33; productivity growth and, 180; wage- or profit-led, 174. See also growth models
derivatives, 8–9, 270, 300, 301
destabilization/stabilization. See stabilization/destabilization
devaluations: balance-of-payments accounting and, 317; Bretton Woods II and, 333; deficit reduction and, 349; exchange rate and, 22, 59, 320–322; government debt and, 246; monetarism and, 331; net borrowing and, 199; New Deal and, 106–108, 162, 325–327; reparations and, 92, 95; trilemma and, 332; U.S. economic policy and, 310, 313–315
distributive cycles, 216–217, 256–257
diversifiable risk, 2, 270, 288
dollar: dollar glut and, 313–315, 314f; gold exchange standard and, 97, 107–108; silver standard and, 88–90, 105, 107, 284. See also exchange rates
Domar, Evsey, 173–175, 180–182, 188, 221
Duesenberry, James S., 210, 227–228, 231
"Dutch disease" (overly strong exchange rate), 320, 332, 333
dynamic stochastic general equilibrium (DSGE), 247, 249

econometrics, 229–230
Economic Consequences of the Peace (Keynes), 94
economic dynamics, 41–43
economic growth models. See growth models
economic thought in 19th century: cost-based/structuralist inflation theories and, 13, 53, 83, 147–148, 149f, 169; credit/banking system assets and, 73–75, 74t, 76–82; currency school and, 74t, 76–77, 79; economies of scale and, 31–33, 50, 63; financial systems and, 68–71, 69t; forced saving adjustment process and, 74t, 77–79, 81, 165; growth models and, 23, 64–67; income distribution and, 62–64; inflation tax and, 7, 81–83, 108, 163–165; open economy monetarism and, 80, 320, 331; own-rates of interest and, 59–61; price species flow model and, 74t, 75–76,

economic thought in 19th century (*continued*)
  86, 90, 329; quantity theory and, 72, 73–74, *74t*, 76; summary, 28–29, 83–84. *See also* classical economics; gold standard; neoclassical economics; Say's Law; *specific classical economists*
effective demand, 92, 167, 169
efficient market hypothesis (EMH), 12, 256, 258, 259–260, 270, 279
Einstein, Albert, 147, 274–275
elasticities approach, 305, 329–330
Ellsberg, Daniel, 121
employment: growth of, 173, 203–208, *204t, 205f, 206f, 207f,* 215–216; macroeconomic supply function criticism and, 25, 53, 240–242, *241f,* 249, 252; NAIRU and, 231, 235, 253
endogenous money, 73, *74t,* 75–76, 78–81, 109, 234, 284–289, 329–330
Enron Corporation, 57, 133, 194, 284, 292
ensemble average (time average), 282–283
entrepreneurship, 46, 54–56
entropy, 56–57
equation of exchange, 71–72, 84, 108, 160, 249
equilibrium: Brownian motion thermal, 274–275, 282–283, 284; DSGE, 247, 249; economic disequilibrium and, 25; general, 49–53, *52f,* 54; history/equilibrium distinction, 173, 340; NAIRU and, 231, 235, 253
equity premium puzzle, 280, 282
equity volatility puzzle, 281–282
ergodic, 282–283, 303
Eurocurrency transactions, 286–287, 314
exchange rates: balance-of-payments flows and, 310, *311t–312t,* 313; Bretton Woods system and, 22, 26, 29, 108, 170, 270, 307–308; Bretton Woods II and, *309t, 311t–312t,* 333–336, 354; devaluations and, 22, 59, 320–322; "Dutch disease" and, 320, 332, 333; foreign trade flows under fixed, *316t,* 326–328; forward, 322–323; global economic governance and, 21, 307–308; nominal, *316t,* 318–319; real, 318–319. *See also* arbitrage
exogeny, and macroeconomics, 176–177, 185, 327, 329

expectations: economic perceptions and, 122–124, 167; rational, 222, 236–237, 239–242, *241f*

Fair Labor Standards Act, 112
fallacy of composition, 4–5, 12, 135, 136, 212, 346
Fannie Mae (Federal National Mortgage Association), 111, 133, 288, 294, 313, 346, 350
"fat tails" (Pareto or power law distribution), 51, 120,125, 263, 274, 283
FDIC (Federal Deposit Insurance Corporation), 111, 285, 290, 294. *See also* Glass-Steagall Act
Federal Reserve (Fed): asset prices and, 18; Bernanke and, 2, 18, 120, 279, 300, 333; counter-cyclicality and, 285; Fed funds rate and, 130; financial crash, and role of, 109; Great Crash and, 97, 99–101; Greenspan as governor of, 2, 18, 55–56, 99, 234, 292, 296, 300, 343; history of, 88, 97–98, 112, 333; macro regulation responsibility and, 300; monetarism and, 6; monetary interventions and, 299; New Deal monetary policies and, 108, 109
Federal Reserve Act, 89
finance, insurance, and real estate (FIRE), 174, 203–208, 347
finance theory: animal spirits and, 279, 284; arbitrage and, 255–256, 279; asset prices and, 234, 279; automatic stabilizers and, 203, 285, 342; bank holding companies and, 290; banking system and, *214f,* 286, 290; behavioral finance and, 122, 258, 278–284; Black-Scholes valuation and, 271, 274–277; boom/bust model and, 114–115, 218; Brownian motion and, 274–275, 282–283; BSM formula and, 257, 270, 302; call option and, 271–274, *273f,* 276, 279; CAPM and, 257, 268; cost-based/structuralist inflation and, 13, 53, 83, 147–148, *149f,* 169; credit and, 126–127; debt deflation and, 285; diversifiable risk and, 2, 270, 288; Einstein and, 147, 274–275; EMH and, 12, 256, 258, 259–260, 270, 279; endogenous finance and, 284–289; equity premium puzzle and, 280, 282; equity

volatility puzzle and, 281–282; Eurocurrency transactions and, 286–287, 314; finance structure shifts and, 285–286; financial regulations, and interaction with, 255, 258; financial risk and, 125; Garn–St. Germain Act and, 287–288, 344; Gaussian copulas and, 276–277; Gaussian distribution and, 120, 264–267, 269, 271, 274–277, 282–283; growth models and, 234; hedge finance and, 193, 197, 288; Itō's Lemma and, 275; junk bonds and, 288; lender of last resort and, 77, 286; liabilities and leverage destabilization and, 131–136, *132t*, 286; long-run observed premium and, 280–281; market psychology and, 283–284; maximization of (objective) expected utility and, 279–280; microeconomics and, 255, 267, 278; Modigliani-Miller theorem and, 256, 259–263, 266, 278; off–balance sheet vehicles and, 17, 114, 134–135, 137, 211, 286, 288, 344; option pricing and, 12, 270–274, 302–303, 322; pitfalls/puzzles from extensions of Ramsey model and, 258, 280–283; Ponzi games and, 101–103, 285–286; portfolio choice and, 266–268, *267f*; positive feedback effect and, 277; private capital formation and, 127; probabilities of default and, 257–258; pro-cyclical behavior and, 285; put option and, 161, 271–272, *273f*; quantifiable risk and, 263–266, *264f*; Regulation Q and, 286–288, 292, 344; risk defined and, 256–257; risk-free asset and, 263, 268; risk-free rate and, *58f*, 257, 281, 282; risk/return balance and, 260; SPVs and, 133, 288; Stock Exchange revaluations and, 126, 269–270; strike price and, 271–272, 274; summary of, 277–278; systemic risk and, 136, 270; time average and, 282–283; Weiner and, 139, 274, 275–276. *See also* financial regulations

financial crises: asset prices and, 73; financial instability and, 15–19, *18f*, 72–73; Great Depression and, 103–106; interest rate cuts and, 219; Kindleberger and, 88, 193, 198; state position for economy and, *200f, 214f,* 289, 346–348; stimulus packages and, 169, 219, 225, 231, 245, 342, 356; trade cycle dynamics and, 218–219. *See also* global financial crisis of 2007–2009

financial cycles: animal spirits and, 127; asset prices and, 140–142, *143t,* 144–145, 168; boom/bust model and, 114–115, 139–140, 142, 144–145, 168; Kindleberger and, 114–115, 144–145, 163, 167, 174, 193; macroeconomics and, 56–58, *58f,* 61–62, 169; Minsky and, 135, 144, 147, 162, 221; positive feedback effect and, 5, 134, 139–140, 143, 152, 163; Soros and, 124–127, 140–142, *141f,* 143–144, 167, 174, 193; speculation and, 124–126; *Treatise on Money* (Keynes) and, 140, 142, 143–147, *143t, 144f*

financial fragility, 193, 218, 304, 344

financial instability: financial crises and, 15–19, *18f,* 72–73; GDP and, 338; global financial crisis of 2007–2009 and, *10f, 18f, 58f, 199f,* 208–213, *209f, 210f, 214f,* 215, 338–340; liability finance and, 16–17, 35, 91–92; potential, 174; pro-cyclical, 151–152, 169

financial markets: commercial paper market and, 130; financial system accounting and, 127, *128t,* 129; loanable funds theory, and structure of, 127, 244; market psychology and, 283–284; probability theories and, 46; pro-cyclical behavior and, 114, 133, 134, 136, 156, 164

financial regulations: accountability and, 295–296; breakdowns in, 286–289; debt-to-equity conversions and, 298; finance theory, and interaction with, 255, 258; firewalls and, 111, 292–294, 355–356; fundamental uncertainty and, 293; future prospects for, 301–302; hedge finance and, 293–294; income distribution and, 356; Keynesian economics and, 289; LTV ratio limits and, 296; macroeconomics and, 258, 289–291, 293–300; market-maker of last resort and, 298–299; mark-to-funding and, 295, 302; nationalization of banks and, 293; New Deal and, 88, 97–98, 106–112, 289; S&L regulators and, 284, 286, 287–288, 292, 294; TARP and, financial regulations *(continued)* 295, 302; taxes on financial transactions and, 296–298, 356; universal banks and, 293; U.S. authority over markets and, 289; Volcker rule and, 293, 295, 356. *See also* finance theory

financial systems, structure of 19th-century, 68–71, *69t*

FIRE (finance, insurance, and real estate), 174, 203–208, 347

firewalls (boundary problem), 111, 292–294, 355–356

Fisher, Irving: currency school and, *74t, 77t;* debt deflation and, 59, 285; entropy and, 56; own-rates of interest and, 59–61; quantity theory and, 6; real interest rate determination theory and, 56–58, *58f,* 61–62

Flaschel, Peter, 38, 63, 83, 85, 148, 177–178, 210, 335

forced saving adjustment process, *74f,* 77–79, 81–83, 108, 165

Freddie Mac (Federal Home Loan Mortgage Corporation), 133, 288, 294, 313, 346, 350

Friedman, Milton: depression and, 109, 231; Friedman-Phelps model of inflation, 232–234, 236, 331; interest rates and, 234; monetarism and, 222, 231–232, 235; "natural rate of unemployment" and, 7, 25; permanent income hypothesis and, 25, 48, 64, 153, 231; quantity theory and, 6–7

fundamental uncertainty: Bayesian analysis and, 114, 117–118, 121–127, 162, 193, 277, 283; CDSs and, *10f, 11f,* 136–138, 257; description of, 3, 119, 215; financial regulations and, 293; Keynesian economics and, 3; liquidity and, 135–136; macroeconomics and, 147–148, 166, 168–169; output and profit income flows framework and, 168–169; philosophy and, 115–116; probability theories and, 114, 116–118, 122–127, 193; risk versus, 125–126, 168; systemic uncertainty and, 136, 270

Galbraith, John Kenneth, 98, 100, 101
Garn–St. Germain Act, 287–288, 344

GATT (General Agreement on Tariffs and Trade), 306–307

Gaussian (normal) distribution: finance theory and, 120, 264–267, 269, 271, 274–277, 282–283; Gaussian copulas and, 276–277; probability theories and, 117

GDP (gross domestic product): aggregate demand and, 4; asset prices and, 9–12, *9f;* boundaries and, 293; debt/GDP ratio and, 16, 226, 242–246; financial instability and, 338; GDP deflator and, 9–11, *9f, 10f,* 55, 63, 318, 343; global financial crisis of 2007–2009 and, 347, 349–354; government budget constraints and, 225–226; Great Depression and, 103; growth rates and, 153, 163, 175, 199, *200f,* 201–203, *201f, 202f;* labor productivity, and growth of, 33; macro financial regulation and, 297; at market prices and, 62–64; net borrowing and, 342; New Deal and, 108, 110; real, 231, *241f;* reparations, and world and, 94, 96; wealth/GDP ratio and, 213; world and, 94, 96, 101–102, 307, 310, *311t–312t,* 313, 315

General Agreement on Tariffs and Trade (GATT), 306–307

General Theory (Keynes), 1, 7, 147

Gibbs, Josiah Willard, 56–57, 140, 250

Glass-Steagall Act, 110, 126, 135, 286, 288, 292–293, 295, 344, 356. *See also* FDIC (Federal Deposit Insurance Corporation)

global economic governance: aggressive exports and, 31, 74–76, *74t,* 308, *316t,* 325–329, 334; balance-of-payments flows and, 310, *312t–313t,* 313; Bretton Woods system and, 22, 26, 29, 108, 170, 270, 307–308, 327–328; Bretton Woods II and, *309t, 311t–312t,* 333–336, 354; "degrees of freedom"/variables in international trade and financial flows and, 92, 217–218, 309, 334, 336, 353; description of, 21–23, 170; dollar glut and, 313–315, *314f;* history of, 306–308; industrial economic policy and, 23; international exchange rate and, 21, 307–308; macro adjustments and, 86–87; net borrowing and, 335; pro-cyclical behavior and, 321,

324; trade and, 306–307, 356; U.S. position and, *91f,* 308–315, *309t. See also* open economy macroeconomics

global financial crisis of 2007–2009: asset prices and, *10f, 11f,* 126–127, 198, 257–258, 343; boom/bust model and, 218; business cycles and, 342–343, 351; causation and description of, 2–3, 8, 34, 211, 346, 350–353; CDOs and, 100, 133, 134–139, 211, 257, 270, 277–278, 288; counter-cyclicality as destabilizing during and, 92; counter-party positions and, 104; credit and, 126–127; debt movement and, 168, 209, *213f, 214f;* Fed funds rate and, 130; financial developments and, 212–213, *213f, 214f,* 215, 355; financial instability and, *10f, 18f, 58f, 199f,* 208–213, *209f, 210f, 214f,* 215, 338–340; forced saving adjustment process and, 82–83; future prospects after and, 353–355; GDP and, 347, 349–354; Goodwin cyclical growth and, 341, 346; household debt and, 2, 16–18, *18f,* 201, *209f,* 211–212, *213f,* 345; housing prices and, 2, 10–11, *10f, 18f, 166–167,* 201, *209f, 210f,* 211, 213, 345, 346, 351; income distribution and, *10f, 18f, 58f, 199f,* 208–213, *209f, 210f, 214f,* 215, 354–355; institutional changes in finance and, 344–345; interest rates and, *58f,* 219, 343–344; international complications and, *200f,* 211, 340, 348–350; international implications of, 354; invisible hand and, 335; Keynesian economics, and analysis of, 5–7, 337, 340–348; labor productivity and, *190f,* 340–341; "liberal" orientation transformation of political economy and, 339–340, 346; net borrowing and, *190f,* 341–342, 353–354; policy options after and, 355–356; private capital formation and, 127; pro-cyclical behavior and, 342; profit rates and, *58f,* 343–344; regressive tax cuts and, 109–110; risks and, 104, 125–126; U.S. projected position after and, *200f, 214f,* 346–348; wage- and profit-led demand and, 104. *See also* financial crises

Godley, Wynne, 174, 198–199, 201, 217, 305, 326, 330, 339

Goldman, Sachs, and Company (Goldman Sachs), 100–101, 138, 172, 291, 294–295

gold standard: balance-of-payments flows, 89–92, *91t;* counter-cyclicality, and stabilization, 91–92; debt deflation, and depression, 87–88; financial panics, 88–89; German hyperinflation, 14, 87, 96; gold exchange standard, 96–97; Great Crash, 97–103; Great Depression, 103–106; industrial policy, 103; international financial system, 86–87, 105–106; leverage and speculation, 98–100; national balance sheet mismatches, 106; New Deal, 88, 97–98, 106–112, 289; Ponzi games, 101–103; pro-cyclical behavior, 92; reparations, 89–90, 92–96, *93t,* 111; Roosevelt and, 101, 105, 108–112, 162, 170, 298–299, 301; run for gold, 76–77, 105–106; stabilization, 91–92, 105–106. *See also* economic thought in 19th century

Goodwin, Richard: cyclical growth and, *58f,* 188, 191–192, *191f,* 209, *209f,* 216, 221, 341, 346; income distribution effects on growth cycle and, 174, 186–187, *187f*

government, state: budget constraint and, 225–226; debt dynamics and, 242–247, *244f;* government budget constraints and, 225–226; Ricardian equivalence of tax and debt financing of spending and, 242–243, 246–247

government spending boost ("increase G"), 4, 7, 106, 152–153, 155, 169–170, 224, 226, 242

Gramm-Leach-Bliley Act, 292

Great Depression, 103–106

Greenspan, Alan, 2, 18, 55–56, 99, 234, 292, 296, 300, 343

gross domestic product (GDP). *See* GDP (gross domestic product)

growth models: animal spirits and, 163, 165, 168, 169, 173–174; conspicuous consumption and, 23, 67, 210; empirical analysis and, 67, 355; finance theory and, 234; Goodwin-style dynamics and, *58f,* 188, 191–192, *191f,* 209, *209f;* growth accounting models and, 175–179; interest rates and, 174; investment decisions and, 173; Keynesian economics and, 23–24;

growth models *(continued)*
  Keynes-Ramsey rule and, 65–66, 176, 281; loanable funds theory and, 64; macroeconomics and, 215–218; net borrowing trends and, 198–203, *200f, 201f, 202f;* Nordic socioeconomic model and, 67, 355; positive feedback effect and, 173–174, 181, 183, 196–198; pro-cyclical behavior and, 174, 188–189, *188t, 190f,* 198, 201–206; productivity dynamics and, 188–189, *188t, 190f;* productivity/employment growth and, 173, 203–208, *204t, 205f, 206f, 207f;* profit squeeze and, 44, 87, 188–189, 191–192, 217; real income per capita and, 175–180; real wage dynamics and, 188–189, *188t, 190f;* Say's Law and, 23–24; Solow-Swan rule and, 176–177; stylized facts and, 46, 131, 177, 179. *See also* demand-driven growth

Hansen, Alvin, 223, 225, 236
Harberger, Arnold, 250–251
Harrod, Roy: demand-driven growth and, 180–182, 221; growth model and, 23, 174; Harrod-Domar equation and, 175–176; Keynes biography and, 26–27; Keynesian economics in terms of mathematics and, *149f,* 222–223; positive feedback and, 163, 221; potential financial instability and, 174; wage- or profit-led growth and, 174
Harrod-Domar equation, 175–176
Hayek, Friedrich von, 37, 55, 59–60, 147, 247, 340
hedge finance, 193, 197, 288, 293–294, 321–322
Hicks, John, 223–224, 236, 244
Hirschman, Albert O., 14, 94–95, 168, 211, 339, 345
Hoover, Herbert, 98, 107, 109, 110
household debt, 2, 16–18, *18f,* 201, *209f,* 211–212, *213f,* 345
housing prices, 2, 10–11, *10f,* 18–19, *18f, 166–167,* 201, *209f, 210f,* 211, 213, 345, 346, 351
How to Pay for the War (Keynes), 164, 165–166
Hume, David, 45, *74t,* 75–76, 80, 86, 90, 320, 329, 331
hyperinflation, 14, 87, 96, 168

ICU (International Clearing Union), 21, 307
income distribution: collective actors and, 167–168; financial regulations and, 356; global financial crisis of 2007–2009 and, *10f, 18f, 58f, 199f,* 208–213, *209f, 210f, 214f,* 215, 354–355; growth cycle, and effects of, 174, 186–187, *187f;* Kaldor and, 174, 216; Kalecki and, 13–14, 38; Keynesian economics and, 13–15, 38; neoclassical economics and, 62–64; 19th-century economic thought and, 62–64; permanent income hypothesis and, 47–48; production and, 62–64; real income per capita and, 175–180; *Treatise on Money* (Keynes) and, 13; wealth effects and, 51, 227; wealth/GDP ratio and, 213
income inequity. *See* income distribution
"increase G" (government spending boost), 4, 7, 106, 152–153, 155, 169–170, 224, 226, 242
industrial policy: classical economics and, 33, 41, 42, 83; global economic governance and, 23; gold standard era and, 103; laissez-faire and, 19; macroeconomics and, 15, 67, 170; monetarism and, 72, 76; New Deal and, 106–107
inflation: analysis of, 13, 95–96, 107–108, 144–145, 165, 285; capacity utilization and, 232–234, *233f;* cost-based/structuralist inflation theories and, 13, 53, 83, 147–148, *149f,* 169; Friedman-Phelps model and, 232–234, 236, 331; hyperinflation and, 14, 87, 96, 168; inflation targeting and, 25, 234–235; inflation tax and, 7, 24, 81–83, 95, 108, 163–165; long-run rate of, 10
interdependent banking system (counter-party positions), 104
interest rate parity (IRP), 321–323
interest rates: entropy and, 56–57; financial crises and, *58f,* 219, 343–344; global financial crisis of 2007–2009 and, *58f,* 219, 343–344; growth models and, 174; liquidity and, 7–8, 84, 124–125, 129–130, 131; liquidity preference, and setting, 127, *128t,* 129–130; loanable funds theory, and determination of, 54, 57, 84; money supply versus, 234–235; own-

rates of interest and, 59–61, 130–131, 169; real interest rate determination theory and, 54, 56–58, *58f*, 61–62, 84; real side of economy and, 124–125, 127, *128t*, 129–130, 131, 145, 148–149, 157–158, 161–164, 168–169, 170
International Clearing Union (ICU), 21, 307
international economic policy. *See* global economic governance; open economy macroeconomics
international system. *See* global economic governance
International Trade Organization (ITO), 306–307
investment: demand for, 228–229; residential, 127; saving, and coordination with, 5, 29–30, 77, 173, 176
invisible hand, 31–33, 49–51, 67, 237–239, *238f*, 246, 335
IRP (interest rate parity), 321–323
IS/LM diagram, *128t*, 223–224, *223f*
ITO (International Trade Organization), 306–307
Itō's Lemma, 274

Jevons, William Stanley, 47–49, 53
junk bonds, 288

Kaldor, Nicholas: aggregate production function and, 63; on cyclical growth with productivity and real wage dynamics, 189; demand-driven growth and, 179–180, 184, *185f*, 215–216, 221; employment growth and, 203, 205–206, 215–216; growth models and, 23, 31, 33, 39, 45, 84, 174, 177, 179–180, 216; income distribution and, 174, 216; money as endogenous and, *74t*, 80; productive growth and, 184–186, *185f*, 203, 205–206, 215–216; real business cycle school and, 80
Kalecki, Michal: economic disequilibrium and, 25; growth model and, 173, 174, 216, 221; income distribution and, 13–14, 38; political business cycle and, 338; on principle of effective demand and associated relationships, 28; real side of economy and, 3, 149; wage- and profit-led demand and, 38, 64

Keynes, John Maynard: active monetary policy and, *74t*, 77, 81, 109; biographical information about, 26, 108, 164; on debt deflation, 97, 108; on devaluation, 108; *Economic Consequences of the Peace*, 94; *General Theory*, 1, 7, 147; *How to Pay for the War*, 164, 165–166; on reparations, 93–95; scholarship on, 26–27; on spending cuts, 110; *Treatise on Money*, 194; *Treatise on Probability*, 26, 114, 116, 118–123. See also *Tract on Monetary Reform* (Keynes); *Treatise on Money* (Keynes)
Keynes-Ellsberg paradox, 121, 278, 280
Keynesian economics: asset prices and, 9–12, *9f, 10f*; business cycle model and, 24, 173–174, 181, 183, 196–198, 202–206; collective actors and, 3, 16, 62, 83, 167–169, 215; decreasing costs and, 32–33; deficits and, 15–19, *18f*; described, 215; economic growth and, 23–24; fallacy of composition and, 4–5, 12; financial regulations and, 289; first classical postulate and, 64, 149, 154, 157, 160; fundamental uncertainty and, 3; global financial crisis of 2007–2009 analysis and, 5–7, 337, 340–348; income distribution and, 13–15; invisible hand and, 5; laissez-faire demise and, 19–20, 64; loanable funds and, 6–8; loanable funds theory and, 6–8; long run and, 15; macro money and, 3; marginal efficiency of capital and, 127, 149–150, 162–163, 181, 208; mathematical terms and, *149f*, 222–223; military, 110, 225; neoclassical synthesis and, 222, 251; paradox of thrift and, 3–5, 7; placement/displacement history of, 1–2; probability and financial markets and, 46; quantifiable risk and, 3; quantity theory and, 6, 15, 81, 145, 166; saving and investment decisions and, 5, 29–30, 77, 173, 176; Say's Law absence and, 5–7, 13, 28–30, 36, 38, 83; second classical postulate and, 148, 232, 234. *See also* Keynesian economics criticism; macroeconomics; *specific Keynesian economists*
Keynesian economics criticism: description of, 24–25; Friedman-Phelps model of inflation and, 232–234, 236, 331;

Keynesian economics criticism *(continued)* nominal rigidity of wage and, 24–25; permanent income hypothesis and, 25, 48, 64, 153, 231; supply function critique and, 25, 53, 240–242, *241f,* 249, 252; unemployment and, 7, 24–25. *See also* Keynesian economics

Keynes-Ramsey rule, 65–66, 176, 236–237, 278, 281

Kindleberger, Charles: asset prices and, 218; boom/bust model and, 114–115, 167, 218, 317, 340; on credit expansion, 345; financial crisis/panics and, 88, 193, 198; financial cycle and, 114–115, 144–145, 163, 167, 174, 193; international hegemon label and, 308, 348; on liability finance, 17, 91–92; Minsky-cycle/crisis model and, *141f,* 193, *196f,* 198; on tariffs, 107

Knight, Frank, 119, 125

Kreuger, Ivar, 101–102, 114, 271

Kuznets, Simon, 68, 226

labor productivity growth, 23, 32–33, 170–171, 173, *190f,* 340–341

labor theory of value, 36–37, 39–40, 55

Laffer curve, 250–251, *251f*

laissez-faire, 19–20, 64

Law, John, 73, *74t,* 75

Lehman Brothers, 130, 138, 290–291, 299, 301

lender of last resort, 77, 286

liabilities, and leverage destabilization, 131–136, *132t,* 286

"liberal" orientation transformation of political economy, 339–340, 346

life cycle consumption model, 227–228

liquidity: animal spirits and, 135; asset prices and, 131, 133, 134–136; financial assets and, 71–73; fundamental uncertainty and, 135–136; interest rates and, 7–8, 84, 124–125, 129–130, 131; IS/LM diagram and, *128t,* 223–224, *223f;* liabilities and leverage as, 131–136, *132t*

liquidity preference: asset prices and, 129; business cycles and, 24; description of, 60; interest rate, and setting with, 127, *128t,* 129–130; liquidity trap effects and, 161; macroeconomics and, 147–148; probability and, 121; trade cycle dynamics and, 163

liquidity trap effects, 12, 161–162, 170

little triangles *(triangulitos),* 52–53, *52f,* 222, 250

loanable funds theory: CAPM and, 268; codification of doctrine of, 77; financial market structure and, 127, 244; growth models and, 64; inflation tax and, 81; interest rate determination and, 54, 57, 84; IS/LM diagram and, 224; liquidity trap effects and, 162; monetarism and, 6–8; rate of time preference/Crusoe and Friday and, 33, 61–62

loan-to-value (LTV) ratio limits, 296

long-run: consumption function and, 226–228, *227f;* economic policy and, 15, 84, 122, 171, 174, 280–281

long-run equity premium, 280–281

long-run exchange rate, 319

long-run inflation rate, 10

LTCM (Long-Term Capital Management), 284, 299, 300, 355

LTV (loan-to-value) ratio limits, 296

Lucas, Robert, Jr., 25, 53, 240–242, *241f,* 249, 252

Luddite movement, 38, 180, 186, 212

macroeconomics: AS/AD model and, 159–161, *160f,* 223, 225; asset prices and, 169, 170; country-level macro adjustments in, 4, 83, 86–87, 326–331; demand-driven growth and, 215–216; endogenous growth and, 3, 192–193, 252, 258, 284, 334; exogeny and, 176–177, 185, 327, 329; financial cycles and, 56–58, *58f,* 61–62, 169; financial regulations and, 258, 289–291, 293–300; fundamental uncertainty and, 147–148, 166, 168–169; growth models and, 215–218; history of, 25–26, 30, 231, 251–253; industrial economic policy and, 15, 67, 170; liquidity preference and, 147; Marx and, 44–45; money/credit discussion and, 3, 73–74, *74t;* new Keynesian, 34, 222, 229, 252–253, 284; real side of economy and, 147–151, *149f;* supply function critique

and, 25, 53, 240–242, *241f,* 249, 252. *See also* Keynesian economics; open economy macroeconomics
Madoff, Bernard, 101–103, 111, 257, 290, 297, 356
Malthus, Thomas Robert: classical economics and, 25; general gluts in trade cycle dynamics and, 30; growth models and, 171; money as endogenous and, *74t,* 76; productivity growth and, 171; real wage theory and, 36–37, 42–44
Mandelbrot, Benoit, 265, 302
marginalism: marginal efficiency of capital, 58, 127, 149–150, 162–163, 181, 208; neoclassical economics and, 45–47, 53–54, 79
Marglin, Stephen, 227–228
market-maker of last resort, 298–299
market prices, and GDP, 62–64
markets. *See* financial markets
Markowitz, Harry, 256, 258, 266, 268, 279
mark-to-funding, 295, 302
Marshall, Alfred, 49, 75, 77, 236, 329
Marshall-Lerner condition, 75, 329
Marx, Karl: capitalism and, 25, 44–45; classical economics and, 25, 30, 231; distributive cycles and, 216; economic dynamics and, 42; entrepreneur and, 54; excess competition and, 33; labor theory value and, 36–37, 39–40, 55; macroeconomics and, 44–45; money as endogenous and, *74t,* 80–81; real business cycle school and, 45, 54–55, 67, *74t,* 80–81
maximization of (objective) expected utility, 279–280
Meade, James, 68, 147, 166, 167–168, 199, 222–223, 236
Menger, Carl, 53–54
mercantilism (aggressive exports), 74–76, *74t,* 308, *316t,* 325–329, 334
Merton, Robert C., 257, 270, 271, 302
microeconomics: finance theory and, 255, 267, 278; little triangles and, 53; neoclassical economics and, 25–26, 47–48, 51, *52f,* 53; new Keynesian macroeconomics and, 34, 222, 229, 252–253, 284; open economy

macroeconomics and, 326; RBC and, 248; risk management and, 136
military Keynesianism, 110, 225
Milken, Michael, 288, 302
Mill, John Stuart, *74t, 77t*
Miller, Merton, 256, 259–263, 266, 278
Minsky, Hyman: asset price effects and, 147; capital formation and, 60; cycle/crisis model and, 135, *141f,* 174, 192–198, *196f,* 218; financial cycles and, 135, 144, 147, 162, 221; financial fragility and, 218; hedge/speculative/Ponzi classification finance and, 144, 193–194, 197, 256; on liability finance, 16–17, 35, 91–92; money as endogenous and, *74t,* 80, 284–289
Mitchell, Charles, 100–101
Mitchell, Wesley Clair, 67–68
Modigliani, Franco, 24–25, 227, 256, 259–263, 266, 278
Modigliani-Miller theorem, 256, 259–263, 266, 278
monetarism: currency school and, *74t,* 76–77, 79; devaluations and, 331; equation of exchange, and policy analysis, 71–72; industrial economic policy and, 72, 76; loanable funds theory and, 6–8; money as endogenous and, *74t,* 80; new classical economics and, 6–9, 230–235; open economy, 80, 320, 331; Say's Law and, 13; Soros and, 9; unemployment and, 7, 24–25; Wicksell-Keynes framework and, 222
monetary policies, *74t,* 77, 81, 108, 109
money: endogenous, 73, *74t,* 75–76, 78–81, 109, 234, 284–289, 329–330; exogenous supply of, 73, 77; interest rate versus supply of, 234–235; macroeconomics and, 3; money/credit effects and, 3, 73–74, *74t*
Morgan, J. P., 89–90, 299
Morgenstern, Oscar, 279–280
multiplier, and real side of economy, 152–153
Mundell-Fleming model, 305, 330–331, 332

NAIRU ("non-accelerating inflation rate of unemployment"), 231, 235, 253

National Bureau of Economic Research (NBER), 68f, 189, 199, 200f, 201f, 202f, 209–210, 209f, 210f, 233f
national health insurance program, 112, 153
national income accounts: collective actors and, 167–168; devaluation and, 95; macro adjustment mechanisms and, 165–166, 167–168; NBER and, 68; NIPA system and, 4, 23, 31, 57–58, 165–166, 175, 177, 198–199, 230
national income and product accounts (NIPA) system, 4, 23, 31, 57–58, 165–166, 175, 177, 198–199, 230
National Labor Relations Board (NLRB), 111
natural (un)employment equilibrium (NAIRU), 231, 235, 253
NBER (National Bureau of Economic Research), 68f, 189, 199, 200f, 201f, 202f, 209–210, 209f, 210f, 233f
neoclassical economics: accounting for market interactions and, 46; anti-neoclassical economics and, 67–68; arbitrage and, 46; competition and, 46; entrepreneurship and, 46, 54–56; entropy and, 56–57; general equilibrium and, 49–53, 52f; income distribution and, 62–64; invisible hand and, 237–239, 238f; loanable funds and, 54, 57, 61–62; macroeconomics history and, 25–26; marginalism and, 45–47, 53–54, 79; microeconomics and, 25–26, 47–48, 51, 52f, 53; models and, 43; permanent income hypothesis and, 47–48. See also classical economics; economic thought in 19th century; new classical economics; *specific economists*
neoclassical synthesis, 25, 221–222, 229, 230, 251–252
net borrowing: devaluations and, 199; GDP and, 342; global economic governance and, 335; global financial crisis of 2007–2009 and, 190f, 341–342, 353–354; growth models and, 198–203, 200f, 201f, 202f
new classical economics: AS/AD diagram and, 223; consumption function and, 158t, 226–228, 227f; econometrics and, 229–230; Friedman-Phelps model of inflation and, 232–234, 236, 331; government budget constraint and, 225–226; government debt dynamics and, 242–247, 244f; inflation targeting and, 225, 234–235; interest rate versus money supply and, 234–235; investment demand and, 228–229; IS/LM diagram and, 128t, 223–224, 223f; Modigliani-Miller theorem and, 256, 259–263, 266, 278; monetarism and, 6–9, 230–235; neoclassical synthesis and, 25, 221–222, 229, 230, 251–252; positive feedback effect and, 237; rational expectations and, 222, 236–237, 239–242, 241f; RBC and, 247–250; Ricardian equivalence and, 242–243, 246–247; Say's Law reintroduction and, 222, 234; secular stagnation and, 225; supply-side economics and, 247, 250–251, 251f. See also classical economics; neoclassical economics; *specific new classical economists*
New Deal, 88, 97–98, 106–112, 162, 289, 325–327
new Keynesian macroeconomics, 34, 222, 229, 252–253, 284
NIPA (national income and product accounts) system, 175, 177, 198–199
NLRB (National Labor Relations Board), 111
Nordic socioeconomic model, 67, 355
normal (Gaussian) distribution. *See* Gaussian (normal) distribution

Obama stimulus package of 2009, 169, 225, 231, 245, 342, 356
off–balance sheet vehicles, 17, 114, 134–135, 137, 211, 286, 288, 344
Okun, Arthur, 184
Okun gap, 184, 250
open economy macroeconomics: absorption approach and, 305, 326–331; aggressive exports and, 74–76, 74t, 308, 316t, 325–329, 334; balance-of-payments flows and, 309t, 311t–312t, 315–318, 316t; carry trade and, 287, 300, 323–326, 334; elasticities approach and, 305, 329–330; exchange rate and, 305, 318; foreign

trade flows under fixed exchange rates and, *316t*, 326–328; forward exchange rates and, 322–323; global macro balance and, 305, 332–336; global savings glut and, 332–333; IRP and, 321–323; IS/LM diagram and, 224; long-run exchange rate and, 319; macro adjustments and, 326–331; microeconomics and, 326; Mundell-Fleming model and, 305, 330–331, 332; nominal exchange rates and, *316t*, 318–319; portfolio balance model and, 324–326; PPP and, 76, 320–321, 326, 331; real exchange rate and, 318–319; speculative capital movements and, 305, 323–324; trilemma model and, 332; twin deficit theory and, 71–72, 201, 331–332, 354. *See also* global economic governance; macroeconomics
open economy monetarism, 80, 320, 331
open market operations (quantitative easing), 72, 129–130, 149, 263, 325, 330
optimal control theory, 25, 47–48, 64, 153, 231
option pricing, 12, 270–274, 302–303, 322
output and profit income flows framework, 3–7, 14–16, 23–24, 168–169, 217
overlapping generations model, 14, 168, 252
own-rates of interest, 59–61, 130–131, 169

Palma, Gabriel, 338–339
paradox of cost, 38
paradox of thrift, 3–5, 7, 43, 158
Pareto, Vilfredo, 50–51, 54–55, 236, 239–240, 255, 258, *264f*, 265
Pareto (power law) distribution, *264f*, 265
Pasinetti, Luigi, 148, 171, 173
Patinkin, Don, 23, 230–231
Pecora investigation, 101–102, 114, 271, 299, 301, 356
permanent income hypothesis, 25, 47–48, 64, 153, 231
Phelps, Edmund, 25, 231, 232–234, 236, 331
philosophy, 115–116
Pigou, A. C., 24–25, 157
Pigou effect, 157–159, *158t*, 229–232
Polanyi, Karl, 67, 338–339
Ponzi games: finance theory and, 101–103, 285–286; Great Crash and, 101; Kreuger and, 101–102, 114, 271; Madoff and, 101–103, 111, 257, 290, 297, 356; Minsky and, 144, 193–194, 197
portfolio balance model, 324–326
portfolio choice, 266–268, *267f*
positive feedback effect: business cycle model and, 173–174, 181, 183, 196–198; decreasing costs and, 33; demand-driven growth and, 33; finance theory and, 277; financial cycles and, 5, 134, 139–140, 143, 152, 163; global financial crisis of 2007–2009 and, 342; growth models and, 173–174, 181, 183, 196–198; Harrod on, 163, 221; new classical economics and, 237. *See also* pro-cyclical behavior
post-Keynesian (structuralist) economists, 13, 53, 83, 147–148, *149f*, 169, 221–222, 282, 307
prices of goods and services: asset prices and, 166–167; commodity prices and, 13, 39, 57, 95–96, 145–147, 166–167, 219, 265, 320; real side of economy and, 148, *149f*, 155, *156f*
price specie flow model, *74t*, 75–76, 86, 90, 329
Prince, Chuck, 102, 295
principle of effective demand, 92, 167, 169
private capital formation, 127
probability theories: animal spirits and, 119; asset prices and, 117, 120; default and, 257–258; description of, 116–118; expected value and, 122, 193, 256–257, 265, 273–274; financial markets and, 46; fundamental uncertainty and, 114, 116–118, 122–127, 193; Gaussian distribution and, 117; Keynes-Ellsberg paradox and, 121, 278, 280; liquidity preference and, 121; probabilities of default and, 257–258; Ramsey and, 23, 118–119, 121; risk and, 256–257; *Treatise* on, 118–122
pro-cyclical behavior: business cycle model and, 174, 202–206; finance theory and, 285; financial instability and, 151–152, 169; financial markets and, 114, 133, 134, 136, 156, 164; global economic governance and, 321, 324; global financial crisis of 2007–2009 and, 342; gold standard era and, 92; in growth models, 174, 198–199, 201; IRP and, 322; Keynesian economics and, 5;

pro-cyclical behavior *(continued)*
productivity dynamics and, *58f*, 188–189, *188t*, *190f*, 191–192, *191f*, 209, *209f*; real wage dynamics and, *58f*, 154–155, 188–189, *188t*, *190f*, 191–192, *191f*, 209, *209f*. *See also* positive feedback effect
product accounts, 4, 164, 167–168
productivity: employment growth and, 173, 203–208, *204t*, *205f*, *206f*, *207f*; long-run implications of growth in, 171; productivity dynamics and, 188–189, *188t*, *190f*
profit rates, *58f*, 343–344
profit squeeze, 44, 188–189, 191–192, 217
purchasing power parity (PPP), 76, 320–321, 326, 331
put option (put warrant), 161, 271–272, *273f*

quantifiable risk, 3, 263–266, *264f*
quantitative easing (open market operations), 72, 129–130, 149, 263, 325, 330
quantity theory: description of, 6; equation of exchange and, 72; Fisher and, 6; Friedman and, 6–7; Keynesian economics and, 6, 15, 81, 145, 166; money supply and, 73–74, *74t*, 76, 169; 19th-century economic thought and, 72, 73–74, *74t*, 76

Ramsey, Frank: asset price and, 237–239, *238f*; growth models and, 23, 64–67, 84, 170–171, 258, 332–333; Keynes-Ramsey rule and, 65–66, 176, 236–237, 278, 281; probability theories and, 23, 118–119, 121
ratchet effect, 210, 226
real business cycle (RBC) models, 202–203, 247–250, 252, 280
real business cycle school, 45, 54–55, 67, *74t*, 80–81
real estate investment trusts (REITs), 140, 142, 260
real interest rate determination theory, 54, 56–58, *58f*, 61–62, 84
real side of economy: asset prices and, 146–147; collective actors and, 167; counter-cyclical stabilization and, 169; economic perceptions/expectations and, 122–124, 167; implications of, 151; interest rates and, 124–125, 127, *128t*, 129–130, 131, 145, 149, 157–158, 161–164, 168–169, 170; Kalecki and, 3, 149; Keynes effect and, 155, 157; liquidity and, 124–125, 131; liquidity preference and, 127, *128t*, 129–130; liquidity trap effects and, 161–162, 170; macroeconomics of, 147–151, *149f*; Minsky-cycle/crisis model and, 195–197, *196f*; money wage cuts and, 153–154; multiplier and, 152–153; output and profit income flows framework and, 3–7, 14–16, 23–24, 168–169, 217; own-rates of interest and, 130–131, 169; Pigou effect and, 157–159, *158t*; prices and, 148, *149f*, 155, *156f*; pro-cyclical financial instability and, 151–152, 169; pro-cyclical real wage dynamics and, 154–155, 188–189; trade cycle dynamics and, 162–164, 174; *Treatise on Money* (Keynes) and, 146–147, 152–153; wages and, 148, *149f*, 155, *156f*
real wage theory, 36–39, 42–43
reflux, law of, 80
Regulation Q, 286–288, 292, 344. *See also* Glass-Steagall Act
reparations and gold standard era, 89–90, 92–96, *93t*, 111
Ricardo, David: currency school and, *74t*, 76–77; economic dynamics and, 41–43; free trade and, 40–41, 61; labor theory of value and, 39–40; macroeconomics and, 25; productivity growth and, 171; real wage theory and, 36–38, 42–43; Ricardian equivalence and, 242–243, 246–247; wage- and profit-led demand and, 38–39
risks: defined, 256–257; fundamental uncertainty versus, 168; global financial crisis of 2007–2009 and, 104, 125–126; microeconomics and, 136; quantifiable and, 3, 263–266, *264f*; return balance and, 260; risk-free asset and, 263, 268; risk-free rate and, *58f*, 257, 281, 282; standard deviation and, 256–257, 265–267, 269, 272, 281–282
Robertson, D. H. (Dennis), 82, 147, 161, 234–235

Robinson, Joan: aggregate production function and, 63; beggar-my-neighbor policies and, 22; Cambridge equation/demand-driven growth and, 23, 180, 182–183, *183f*, 216, 221, 244; history/equilibrium distinction and, 173, 340; on neoclassical synthesis, 222, 251

Roosevelt, Franklin Delano, 101, 105, 108–112, 162, 170, 298–299, 301

Rothbarth, Erwin, 68, 165

Rubin, Robert, 102, 135, 235

Rumsfeld, Donald, 353

Samuelson, Paul, 63, 221, 229, 231, 252, 282, 303

S&L (savings and loan) regulators, 284, 286, 287–288, 292, 294

savings, 167, 169, 332–333

Say's Law: description of, 5–7; distributive cycles and, 216; effective demand principle and, 92, 167, 169; forced saving adjustment process and, 79, 147; full employment level and, 242; full employment level assumption and, 167, 176; gold standard era and, 87; Goodwin cycle and, 187; growth models and, 23–24; housing prices and, 346; income/expenditure imbalances and, 87; inflation tax and, 7; invisible hand and, 31–32; Kaldor's growth model and, 179; Keynesian economics, and absence of, 5–7, 13, 28–30, 36, 38, 68, 83; Modigliani-Miller theorem and, 256, 262; monetarism and, 13, 72; net borrowing and, 342; new classical economics, and reintroduction of, 212, 222, 234, 252; open economy monetarism and, 331; open global economy and, 75, 82–83, 327; profit squeeze and, 87; rational expectations assumptions and, 230, 240; real-side macro and, 146; real wage theory and, 37–38, 39; supply-side economics and, 53; wartime and, 164

Scholes, Myron, 257, 270, 271, 274–277, 302

Schumpeter, Joseph, 43, 44, 49, 54–56, *74t*, 77–79

Schwartz, Anna, 109

secular stagnation, 225

Securities and Exchange Commission (SEC), 102, 111, 138, 292–294

services, prices of goods and. *See* commodity prices; prices of goods and services

shadow banking system, 103, 134–135, 228–229, 278, 344

sigma (standard deviation), 256–257, 265–267, 269, 272, 281–282

silver standard, 88–90, 105, 107, 284

Skidelsky, Robert, 161, 221–222

Smith, Adam, 5, 25, 31–36, 144

Smoot-Hawley Tariff Act, 107, 109

Social Security Act, *93t*, 111–112

Solow, Robert, 63, 176–177, 252

Solow-Swan rule, 176–177

Soros, George: boom/bust model and, 124, 140, 142, 167; on "cognitive" and "manipulative" activities of economists, 1–2; on collective actors, 1–2; financial cycles and, 124–127, 140–142, *141f*, 143–144, 167, 174, 193; Minsky-cycle/crisis model and, *141f*, 193, *196f*, 197–198; monetarism and, 9; on probability and financial markets, 46

special purpose vehicles (SPVs), 133, 288

speculation, 91, 98–100, 124–126, 193–194, 197, 305, 323–324

Sraffa, Piero, 59–60, 116, 147

stabilization/destabilization: automatic stabilizers and, 203, 285, 342; counter-cyclicality and, 91–92, 169; gold standard era and, 91–92, 105–106; leverage destabilization and, 131–136, *132t*, 286; liabilities and, 131–136, *132t*, 286

stagflation, 112, 168, 206, 233–234, 243, 339, 341–343

standard deviation (sigma), 256–257, 265–267, 269, 272, 281–282

state government. *See* government, state

Steindl, Josef, 38, 45, 85, 169, 173–174, 199, *200f*, 216–217, 341

stimulus packages, 169, 219, 225, 231, 245, 342, 356

stochastic differential equations, 274–275, 282–283, 284

Stock Exchange revaluations, 126, 269–270

Stone, Richard, 68, 164, 166, 167–168

strike price, 271–272, 274
structuralist (post-Keynesian) economists, 13, 53, 83, 147–148, *149f*, 169, 221–222, 282, 307
stylized facts, 46, 131, 177, 179, 191, 227, 230–231, 249, 340–341
supply-side economics, 52–53, *52f*, 222, 247, 250–251, *251f*
Swan, Trevor, 176–177
systemic risk (systemic uncertainty), 136, 270

Taleb, Nassim Nicholas, 120, 171, 266, 303
tariffs, 21, 51, 106–107, 306–307, 314
taxes, 109–110, 296–298, 356
Taylor, John, 235
Temporary Assistance to Needy Families (TANF), 112
Thornton, Henry, *74t, 77t*, 81
time average (ensemble average), 282–283
Tobin, James, 11, 60, 126, 147, 194, 198, 228–229, 250, 252, 298
Tooke, Thomas, 79–80
Tract on Monetary Reform (Keynes): arbitrage and, 257; exchange rate theory and, 321; inflationary dynamics in terms of class conflict and, 13, 95, 97, 145; IRP and, 321–323; quantity theory and, 6, 15, 81, 145, 166
trade: carry, 287, 300, 323–326, 334; "degrees of freedom," and variables in international, 92, 217–218, 309, 334, 336, 353; free, 40–41, 61; trade cycle dynamics, 30, 162–164, 174, 218–219, 306–307, 356
Treatise on Money (Keynes): approach to ideas in, 114–115; criticism of, 118; financial cycles and, 140, 142, *143t*, 144–147, 194; forced saving adjustment process and, 177; income distribution and, 13; labor productivity growth and, 340–341; national income accounts and, 165; natural rate and, 7; real side of economy and, 146–147, 152–153; wage-squeeze/wage-led dynamics and, 189
Treatise on Probability (Keynes), 26, 114, 116, 118–123
triangulitos (little triangles), 52–53, *52f*, 222, 250

Triffin, Robert, 91, 105, 309–310, 314, 333, 349, 354
trilemma model, 332
Troubled Asset Relief Program (TARP), 295, 302
twin deficit theory, 71–72, 201, 331–332, 354
two souls problem/wage-profit relationship, 38, 63, 83, 85, 148, 177–178, 210, 335

unbalanced budgets, 22, 164, 165, 170
uncovered/unhedged IRP (UIP), 321–322
unemployment, 7, 24–25, 171
United States: authority over markets and, 289; devaluations and, 310, 313–315; economy after 1980 in, *10f, 18f, 58f, 199f,* 208–213, *209f, 210f, 214f,* 215; financial crises, and position for economy in, *200f, 214f,* 289, 346–348; global economic governance, and historic position of, *91f,* 308–315, *309t;* global financial crisis of 2007–2009, and projected position of, *200f, 214f,* 346–348; Great Depression and, 103–106; institutional changes in finance and, 344–345; international hegemon label and, 308, 348; New Deal and, 88, 97–98, 106–112, 289; spending cuts and, 110. *See also* global financial crisis of 2007–2009; gold standard
universal banks, 293

value-at-risk (VaR), 135–136, 142, 197
values: expected, 122, 193, 256–257, 265, 273–274; labor theory value, 36–37, 39–40, 55; LTV ratio limits and, 296; VaR and, 135–136, 142, 197
VaR (value-at-risk), 135–136, 142, 197
Veblen, Thorstein, 23, 28, 66–68, 210, 226
Volcker rule, 293, 295, 356
Von Neumann, John, 279–280
Von Neumann–Morgenstern axioms, 279–280

wage- and profit-led demand, 38–39, 64, 104, 164, 174, 188, *188t*, 217
wage-cutting effects, 13, 115, 158
wage-profit relationship, 38, 63, 83, 85, 148–149, 177–178, 210, 335

wages: money wage cuts and, 153–154; nominal rigidity of, 24–25; prices and, 148, *149f*, 155, *156f*; real wage theory and, 36–39, 42–43
Wagner Act, 111
Walras, Léon, 46, 49–53, 55–56, 78–80, 222–223, 236, 252, 325
wealth effects, 51, 227
Weiner, Norbert, 139, 274, 275–276
Weitzman, Martin, 282, 283
White, Harry Dexter, 22, 307, 310

Wicksell, Knut: forced saving adjustment process and, *74f*, 77–79, 81, 108, 165; general equilibrium and, 54; inflation tax synthesis and, 7, 81–83, 108, 163; Wicksell-Keynes framework, 222
Wittgenstein, Ludwig, 46, 64, 116, 120–121, 124, 278–279
World Trade Organization (WTO), 306–307